797,885 Books

are available to read at

www.ForgottenBooks.com

Forgotten Books' App
Available for mobile, tablet & eReader

ISBN 978-1-331-86799-9
PIBN 10244401

This book is a reproduction of an important historical work. Forgotten Books uses state-of-the-art technology to digitally reconstruct the work, preserving the original format whilst repairing imperfections present in the aged copy. In rare cases, an imperfection in the original, such as a blemish or missing page, may be replicated in our edition. We do, however, repair the vast majority of imperfections successfully; any imperfections that remain are intentionally left to preserve the state of such historical works.

Forgotten Books is a registered trademark of FB &c Ltd.
Copyright © 2015 FB &c Ltd.
FB &c Ltd, Dalton House, 60 Windsor Avenue, London, SW19 2RR.
Company number 08720141. Registered in England and Wales.

For support please visit www.forgottenbooks.com

1 MONTH OF
FREE
READING

at
www.ForgottenBooks.com

By purchasing this book you are eligible for one month membership to ForgottenBooks.com, giving you unlimited access to our entire collection of over 700,000 titles via our web site and mobile apps.

To claim your free month visit:

www.forgottenbooks.com/free244401

* Offer is valid for 45 days from date of purchase. Terms and conditions apply.

English
Français
Deutsche
Italiano
Español
Português

www.forgottenbooks.com

Mythology Photography **Fiction**
Fishing Christianity **Art** Cooking
Essays Buddhism Freemasonry
Medicine **Biology** Music **Ancient
Egypt** Evolution Carpentry Physics
Dance Geology **Mathematics** Fitness
Shakespeare **Folklore** Yoga Marketing
Confidence Immortality Biographies
Poetry **Psychology** Witchcraft
Electronics Chemistry History **Law**
Accounting **Philosophy** Anthropology
Alchemy Drama Quantum Mechanics
Atheism Sexual Health **Ancient History**
Entrepreneurship Languages Sport
Paleontology Needlework Islam
Metaphysics Investment Archaeology
Parenting Statistics Criminology
Motivational

MEMORABILIA DOMESTICA;

OR

PARISH LIFE IN THE NORTH OF SCOTLAND.

BY THE
LATE REV. DONALD SAGE, A.M.,
MINISTER OF RESOLIS.

EDITED BY HIS SON.

SECOND EDITION.

WICK:
WILLIAM RAE.
EDINBURGH: JOHN MENZIES & CO.
1899.

· PRINTED AT THE
NORTHERN ENSIGN OFFICE,
WICK.

EDITOR'S PREFACE.

*T*HIS volume is issued in response to numerous enquiries regarding manuscripts of reminiscences which it was known the late Mr. Sage, minister of Resolis in Ross-shire, had left, complete but unpublished. The author's modest and retiring character had made him shrink, as is seen in his own preface, from bringing his "Memorabilia" before the public eye. Repeated requests for its perusal, and the knowledge that the information here recorded was derived from original and authentic sources, are the editor's apology for its present appearance in print. What has weighed with him also is, that these pages delineate Christian life and social manners, as they existed in northern Scotland, during a period of which hitherto little has been known except by tradition.

The graphic sketches of prominent people, and of manners and customs prevailing in various localities, are drawn from personal observation which the author had the best opportunities of exercising. The many-sided characters of persons of all ranks and professions are here vividly portrayed; picturesque districts of country, hitherto comparatively unvisited and unknown, are minutely described; changes, which have altered the face of the Highlands, are pointed out and traced to their original causes; the state of religion and morals, as connected with the persons who mainly influenced the people for good or evil, is brought under review; and all these are woven into a connected narrative, held together by the continuous thread of the author's autobiography.

While thus portraying what passed around him, the author at the same time supplies sufficient material to enable thoughtful readers to form a correct estimate of his personal character and

2017664

ministerial qualifications. Warm-hearted and lovable; endowed with a well-furnished and cultivated mind; keenly interested in the public events of his time; and having great conversational powers, he was regarded by his friends as a most fascinating and instructive companion. His theological attainments were extensive, accurate, and profound. As a preacher he displayed a personality peculiarly his own; all classes of hearers felt and acknowledged his originality in exposition and illustration; while the more distinguished and discerning Christians agreed that he was worthy of a place in their regard alongside of his many eminent contemporaries in the north. His taste for literature continued with him through life, and many of his leisure hours were devoted to study and research. During the sittings of the first Disruption Assembly he passed much of the time at home alone in prayer. Followed by his large and attached congregation, he joined the Free Church of Scotland, in connection with which he continued to labour with the same zeal, ability, and success for which he had been always distinguished. For a few years, however, before his death, owing to bodily infirmity, he was unable to preach. On the 31st of March, 1869, in the 80th year of his age and 53rd of his ministry, he "fell asleep," longing to be with Christ, that he might "see his face." He left a widow, who has since passed away, and a large family of sons and daughters, to mourn his loss.

The MSS., in their original proportions, were too voluminous to be printed in full. The work of the editor has been to eliminate repetitions and irrelevant matter, and here and there to condense the narrative. He hopes that, by the division into chapters, and the addition of notes derived from various authorities, most of them acknowledged, and by a table of contents, he has contributed what will facilitate the use of the book· for reference, and make it more interesting for general reading.

DONALD FRASER SAGE.

FREE MANSE OF KEISS, CAITHNESS,
July 1889.

AUTHOR'S PREFACE.

WHEN a man sits down to write his own life with the view of giving it to the public, however well known to the public he may be, or however highly recommended by rank, or station, or mental abilities, he can after all scarcely, we think, escape from the rather ugly charges of egotism or self-conceit. Hume and Gibbon were unquestionably great men. So the "learned of this world" pronounced them to be. But "The Author's Memoirs of Himself" by the one, and "My Own Life" by the other, evince, particularly the former, a degree of self-complacency and arrogance which all the literary merit of their works can scarcely, if at all, redeem. How much more then, and heavily, does the charge fasten upon one who, to the public, is nothing, and who has notwithstanding taken up the doughty resolution of filling this volume with *memorabilia* of his grandfather, his father, and himself. Ajax had to present in battle against the sword's point of his adversary a shield of seven folds. Against the charge above-mentioned the writer of these memoirs has to present a shield only of two folds, which he thinks will be fully sufficient to defend him. The first is, that he writes, not with the most distant intention to publish these memoirs himself, or not with the slightest desire or expectation that they should be published when the hand that now writes them shall be stiff in death—when the mind that indites them shall be a disembodied spirit in eternity. Then another fold in his shield is, that he records these family reminiscences, not to tell the public what he or his were, but to tell it to himself. There is something peculiarly solemn and edifying—something which betters a man's spirit—in the truly believing consciousness, not only that *we* ourselves are but " pilgrims on earth," but that we are so " even as all our fathers also have been." Their race is run ; their course—involving the every-day duties, occurrences, crosses, businesses, joys, and sorrows, in short, all the "lights and shadows" of an earthly existence—is finished, never again to be begun. They are gone—never to return—and where am I ? Unceasingly following them ; like them, now conscious of things earthly ; like them, at last to know eternity ! To look back on the years they spent on earth, to recount the incidents of their humble, but I trust in some measure useful, lives, to connect them with my own, and to view the whole in the spirit and temper of a pilgrim, are to me sufficiently good reasons why I should write these memoirs.

DOND. SAGE.

MANSE OF RESOLIS,
    25th May, 1840.

CONTENTS.

—◇◇◇—

CHAPTER I.

THE MINISTER OF LOCHCARRON AND HIS TIMES.

CHAPTER II.

THE MINISTER OF LOCHCARRON—*continued.*

CHAPTER III.

ALEXANDER SAGE; HIS EARLY DAYS. THE REAY COUNTRY.

CHAPTER IV.

CHAPTER V.

CHAPTER VI.

CHAPTER X.

HOME AND COLLEGE LIFE.

CHAPTER XI.

ABERDEEN PROFESSORS. NORTHERN NOTABILITIES.

CHAPTER XII.

ABERDEEN AND EDINBURGH; DIVINITY HALLS.

CHAPTER XVI.
THE SUTHERLAND CLEARANCE OF 1819.

CHAPTER XVII.
MINISTRY AND CONTEMPORARIES IN ABERDEEN.

CHAPTER XVIII.
THE GENERAL ASSEMBLY OF 1820.

CHAPTER XIX.
MINISTERIAL PROSPECTS—MARRIAGE.

CHAPTER XXIII.

EVANGELISTIC JOURNEYS.

CHAPTER XXIV.

SECOND MARRIAGE. PERSONAL FRIENDSHIPS.

CHAPTER XXV.

CHANGES IN THE NATIONAL CHURCH.

Memorabilia Domestica;

OR,

PARISH LIFE IN THE NORTH OF SCOTLAND.

CHAPTER I.

THE MINISTER OF LOCHCARRON AND HIS TIMES.

1725-1734.

MY grandfather, Eneas Sage, was born on the 12th of March, 1694, at Chapelton, a small farm on the estate of Redcastle, parish of Killearnan, Ross-shire. His father, Murdoch Sage, occupied the farm, and held office as a messenger-at-arms, an office which in those turbulent times was very arduous, and connected with much personal danger. My great-grandfather was bred a Scottish Episcopalian. He was a subject of the "last Stuarts" who had thrust Episcopacy on their Scottish subjects by the sacrifice of everything that might have contributed either to the stability of their throne or to the peace and prosperity of their people. He lived at the close of the reign of Charles II., and during that of James II., and he was privileged to witness the glorious and memorable Revolution of 1688. Previous to that period, and long before the abolition of Episcopacy, he became a Presbyterian. Some years after the Revolution, he came by a sudden and violent death. Employed to arrest a man of rank, but of loose habits and violent temper, he went to his house to apprehend him. But the reckless object of his pursuit, becoming aware of his intentions, fired at him from a loophole in a small turret which commanded the entrance, and mortally wounded him. He was carried homewards, and soon after expired. His ancestors for two generations had been settled in the Highlands of Ross and Inverness, but came originally from the south. He married Miss MacDonnell of Ardnafuarain, a near relative of Glengarry. His eldest son, Eneas Sage, about the year 1715, entered King's College, Aberdeen. On the 18th of August, 1725, and at the age of thirty-one, he was licensed to preach by the Presbytery of Tain. He was soon afterwards appointed to a charge in the mountainous district of Ross-shire, comprehending the extensive parishes of Lochcarron, Applecross, and Gairloch. In this wild district he for some years laboured as a

A

missionary, preaching alternately at certain stations, and going about from house to house catechising or instructing the people in the principles of religion. His appointment arose from the peculiar circumstances of the Church as a national establishment. It was then in its infancy, particularly in the north of Scotland, and presbyteries often comprehended an entire county. The extension of the Church, too, although the plantation of kirks was enforced by law, could not ultimately be carried into effect until after a determined and almost sanguinary struggle with the adherents of Episcopacy. Parishes in the north, and in Ross-shire particularly, were for many years kept vacant solely by the influence of Episcopacy. For example, the eminent James Fraser of Alness was inducted by the Presbytery of Chanonry and Dingwall, but the service was conducted in the churchyard, as the doors of the church were barricaded by the heritors, rigid Episcopalians, seconded by their tenantry, who abhorred the settlement among them of a "Whig minister," as they reproachfully termed the Presbyterian clergy. The churches of Avoch and of Kilmuir Wester were for many years in circumstances even more unfavourable. Sir Kenneth Mackenzie of Scatwell, an ardent Episcopalian, contrived, even after the Presbytery had duly inducted the ministers of these parishes, to exercise his feudal authority so as to prevent them from officiating in their pulpits; and the early Records contain minutes in which these ministers are stated to have reported to that effect.

My grandfather officiated in the district for some years. Some curious incidents will afterwards be related of his adventures when he came more immediately into contact with the Episcopalian inhabitants of the district in the discharge of his pastoral duties. On the 10th February, 1726, he was ordained minister of Lochcarron, a parish comprehending about a third of the territory in which he had officiated as missionary. He found the people sunk in ignorance, with modes of worship allied to Paganism. Before the close of his long and efficient ministry the moral aspects of the people were entirely changed. It is not, I think, too much for me to say of so near a relative that he was undoubtedly one of the Fathers of that Church which has proved herself to be a real and lasting benefit to Scotland—a national church —which, by her constitution, and her rational, scriptural, and efficient form of government, has embalmed herself in the hearts of her true children. In the purity of her doctrines and in the fidelity and devotedness of her first ministers, her true members found and felt that she was "the house of God and the gate of Heaven;" whilst the mighty moral influence which she at the same time exerted on the masses of the people, formed their national character, and placed them in the front of other nations as regards moral excellence.

In bodily stature Eneas Sage approached the gigantic. He was six feet two inches in height, with dark eyes and hair, and with more than ordinary strength. His zeal as a minister, the rough subjects he had to deal with, and the rude age he lived in, rendered this last quality of no ordinary service to him. It has already been remarked that he was a licentiate of the Presbytery of Tain. He resided in Easter-Ross during his attendance at the divinity hall; and on the minutes of the presbytery there is an entry to the effect that he was schoolmaster of Logie Easter in 1719, when he entered to be teacher at Cromarty. Thus it would appear he was parochial teacher of these parishes previous to his being licensed in 1725. During his attendance at college, a curious, and from the heated temperature of the times, a rather dangerous incident befel him in connection with the first rebellion. The battle of Sheriffmuir was fought on Sabbath, the 13th of November, 1715, and the Chevalier St. George debarked at Peterhead on the 22nd of December following. From thence, with five attendants, he passed through Aberdeen on his way to the headquarters of his army, and arrived at Fetteresso Castle, the principal residence of the Earl Marischal. Detained by an ague, his rank was soon discovered, and the non-jurant clergy of Aberdeenshire presented him with addresses. My grandfather, then about twenty-one, was curious to see this royal personage, and so prompted, he, in company with some of his fellow-students, proceeded to Fetteresso. There he saw the Prince, and often did he afterwards, in graphic terms, describe this feeble descendant of ancient royalty. His countenance, he said, was considerably above the common cast of faces, and was even royal, but it had a pale, sickly hue, expressive of weakness. His fierce and mailed followers, the Earls of Mar and Marischal, Cameron of Lochiel, General Hamilton, and others, stood around him with heads uncovered, and to these men of bold and vigorous spirit he yielded himself much as would a child to its nurse. This adventure, while it gratified their curiosity, had well nigh proved serious in its consequences to my grandfather and his companions. No sooner did they arrive at their lodgings in Aberdeen than a Government official visited them, and gave them to understand that, from various circumstances connected with their late expedition to Stonehaven, they had fallen under suspicion, and must appear before a magistrate. They did appear, and the circumstances were strong against them. For nearly two days they had been absent from their classes; they had gone to Fetteresso to see the Prince; they had done so at the very time that malcontents had resorted thither; and being Highland students, they came from a quarter where the Pretender's adherents were especially numerous. These facts, not one of which could be contravened, bore hard upon them, and they were in imminent risk of being sent to prison, and tried for high treason. But the professors of King's College interposed, matters were explained, and it was found that curiosity alone had induced the young men to act as they had done. My grandfather owed his escape to a circumstance which happened in the month of October previous, and which was duly presented in evidence on his behalf. It was as follows:—The Earl of Seaforth had warmly abetted the Jacobite cause. About two months before the battle of Sheriffmuir, Inverness had been captured by Mackintosh of Borlum, at the head of five hundred men, and the Pretender was proclaimed. When Borlum went south to unite his troops to those of the insurgents under Mar at Perth, Seaforth sent a detachment under Sir John Mackenzie of Coul to take possession of Inverness. In these rebellious proceedings, Seaforth was opposed by Colonel Munro, son of Sir Robert Munro of Foulis, who had been appointed commander of Inverness Castle. Colonel Munro had sent two hundred men to protect the lands of Culloden against the depredations of the Mackenzies. He also formed a camp at the Bridge of Alness, consisting of nearly 600 men of the clans of Munro and Ross, and soon after he was joined by John, Earl of Sutherland; his son, the Lord Strathnaver; and George, Lord Reay, at the head of a body of their clansmen, the Sutherlands and Mackays, their united forces numbering about 1800 men. Their object was to protect the lives and properties of the Royalists against Seaforth, and to prevent his joining the Earl of Mar at Perth. Seaforth was able to defeat this object. He had a camp at Brahan Castle, his principal residence, where he also collected a body of 1800 men. But his numbers were increased to nearly 3000 by the accession to his army of the Macdonalds, Mackinnons, Macraes, the Chisholms of Strathglass, and other clans, and with this superior force he bore down upon Sutherland's camp at Alness. The issue was that the Royalists, under Lords Sutherland and Mackay, were compelled rapidly to retreat across the hill to Bonar. My grandfather, as a well-wisher to the cause, was in the Royalist camp; and while the men were in full retreat up the hill, he ventured to accost Lord Reay, saying, " It is a pity, my lord, that such a brave body of men, and they Highlanders, should be seen turning their backs upon their enemies when they have right on their side." What you say, young man, may be true," replied the sagacious nobleman; "but is it not better to make a wise retreat than a foolish engagement?" The retreat and Seaforth's success formed the subject of a highly satirical Gaelic song, reflecting severely on the Lords Sutherland and Reay, under the title of " Caberfeidh." This song was composed by Norman Macleod, a native of Lochbroom, in revenge against the Munroes. His son, Eneas Macleod, was minister of Rogart, in Sutherland. I never met him, but with his widow and family I was acquainted intimately.

On the evening previous to his settlement at Lochcarron, my grandfather had no better lodging than a barn. This barn, too, was of peculiar construction. The walls were principally of wicker work interwoven between pillars of turf and stone. The moisture of the climate, particularly in harvest, rendered this peculiar mode of construction necessary to dry the corn, which, when cut, was housed, and not stacked in the yard, as in more genial districts. Such was the anchorite's cell in which the first Presbyterian minister of Lochcarron was lodged on the evening previous to his settlement; no better was offered, and, perhaps, no better could be found. In this hovel, where he took up his quarters for the time, some of his friends lodged with him; but during the night the barn was set on fire. The smoke and flames roused them from their slumbers; and while his friends busied themselves in securing the safety of the dwelling and extinguishing the fire, the future minister of Lochcarron took that opportunity of cultivating his first acquaintance with a parishioner. Rushing out half dressed, he saw the incendiary throwing away the torch, and making good his retreat. My grandfather pursued, and, continuing the chase for some time, at last got up with him, and just as the fellow neared his own door, planted an irresistible grip on his collar. The culprit was dragged back to the minister's lodgings, expecting nothing else than a beating, even to the breaking of his bones. Than this, however, nothing was further from my grandfather's intentions. No violence was used. The culprit was placed in the middle of the floor, and asked whether he set the house on fire, and, if so, what were his motives? The man frankly confessed what he had done, and assigned as his reason that it was to rid the parish of a Whig minister; "but I am now in your power," he added, "and take your revenge." "We shall do so," said my grandfather, "but mark well how we do it." He ordered meat and drink to be set before him, asked the divine blessing, and invited him to proceed. The fellow was hungry, and made a hearty meal. My grandfather then said to him, "You came here with no less evil an intention than to deprive me of my life. I have returned good for evil. Go and tell your neighbours how the Whig ministers avenge their wrongs." The poor fellow poured out his thanks, and failed not to report to his fellow-parishioners both the generosity and the strength of the new minister. Of the particulars of the settlement, I can give no authentic account. But of the members of presbytery by whom he was inducted, I have, by accident, fallen in with official and accurate information. My library contains, among many books belonging to my grandfather, a fine, old copy of Turretine, which was gifted to me by his eminent successor, the Rev. Lachlan Mackenzie. Opening this book one evening, I discovered, between the leaves of the second volume, a slip of paper in my grandfather's hand-writing, containing these words :—

"At Lochbroom, 16th March, 1726. — The presbytery met, and after prayer—*sederunt*, Mr. Æneas Sage, moderator; Mr. Murdo Macleod and Mr. Archibald Ballantyne, minrs. ; and John Paip, schoolmaster of Gairloch, ruling elder ; Mr. James Smith, minister, absent.

The presbytery being called to this place for a visitation of the parish of Lochbroom, by petition from the Rev. Mr. Archibald Ballantyne, minr. of Lochbroom, at their last diet at Keanlochow ; and their clerk having served out warrants to cite masons, wrights, and land metters, one or more, for designing glebe and grass, and for valuing manse, office, houses, and garden ; as also appointing the said Mr. Archibald Ballantyne to give an edictal citation from the pulpit to heritors, wadsetters, life-renters of the parish of Lochbroom, fifteen days before this date, to compear before the presbytery to join and concur with them, to have glebe, grass, manse, and garden provided for their minister. The said masons, wrights, and land-melsters being solemnly sworn, purged of malice and partial counsel, gave in the following reports, viz."

The venerable document ends thus abruptly, and without a signature. Like all presbyterian minutes, the sederunt mentions the names of the ministers who constituted the meeting, but not the parishes of which they were the ministers. Mr. Murdo Macleod was minister of Glenelg. He was settled in that parish in 1707, and was one of those ministers of the Presbytery of Gairloch (now Lochcarron) who were mobbed at Lochalsh on the 16th of Sepr., 1724, by the people, who were then in a state of ignorance and ferocity little or nothing removed above savage life.[*] Mr Ballantyne was the first Presbyterian minister of Lochbroom, and was settled in the same year as my grandfather.[†] Mr James Smith, the absent minister referred to in the minute, was minister of Gairloch.[‡]

About two years previous to my grandfather's settlement at Loch-carron, the presbytery having met at Lochalsh to hold a parish visitation there, were so rudely assailed by the mob that they were obliged to hold their meeting next time at Kilmorack, considering themselves in danger of their lives in meeting within their own bounds. The records of the Presbytery of Lochcarron, or of Gairloch, as it was then called, commence in 1724. The presbytery was then formed by the General Assembly. The parish of Applecross is coëval with the parish of Lochcarron as a Presbyterian establishment. Its first minister was Mr. Aneas Macaulay, who was ordained in 1731.[§] Mr. Ballantyne, Lochbroom, was succeeded in 1731 by Mr. Donald Ross, who in 1742 was translated to Fearn in Easter-Ross.[*] Mr. Ross, previous to his translation, had employed, as an assistant, Mr. James Robertson, a native of Athole, a young man of more than ordinary ability, both corporeal and mental. After Mr. Donald Ross' transla-tion, Mr. Robertson was strongly recommended by the Duke of Athole to the patron, the Earl of Cromartie, as Mr. Ross' successor. The Earl of Cromartie was, however, so much occupied in preparations for the Rebellion of '45, in which he was so deeply implicated on the rebel side, that he neglected the issuing of the presentation within the prescribed term. The presbytery, availing themselves of the *jus devolutum*, presented Mr Roderick Mackenzie. But the influence of Cromartie and Athole was paramount. Mr Mackenzie was ejected, and Mr Robertson, the Earl's presentee, settled as minister. He was primitive and truly apostolic, and the almost preternatural exertion of bodily strength by which he saved the lives of Mr. Ross and of many of his parishioners at the church of Fearn, procured for him ever afterwards the appellative of "am ministeir laidir," or the strong minister.[†]

[*] Mr. Murdoch Macleod, minister of Glenelg, demitted his charge, 29th May, 1735; he died 23rd August, 1760, at about the age of 85 years —ED.

[†] Mr. Archibald Ballantyne, minister of Lochbroom, was, on the 17th July, 1728, translated to Ardchattan, and from thence was, on 6th August, 1731, translated to Dores in Inverness-shire. On the anniversary of the King's birth 30th October, 1745, his fuel was seized by the rebels, who made a bonfire of it in honour of the Pretender. Mr. Ballantyne died on the 20th June, 1752.—*Ibid.*

[‡] Mr. James Smith was a licentiate of the Presbytery of Haddington. He was ordained at Dingwall to the ministerial charge of Gairloch, on the 11th May, 1721. There he died on the 17th November, 1758, in his 75th year.—*Ibid.*

[§] Aneas Macaulay was son of Mr. Daniel Macaulay, minister of Braeadale; he died minister of Applecross, on the 15th January, 1760.—*Ibid.*

[*] A licentiate of the Presbytery of St. Andrews, Donald Ross was ordained minister of Lochbroom on the 11th August, 1731. Translated to Fearn in 1742, he was seri-ously injured by the falling of the roof of the Abbey church on Sabbath the 10th October following, when thirty-six persons were killed. He died 2nd September, 1775, in his 83rd year.—*Ibid.*

[†] Mr. James Robertson received his designation of "Am ministeir laidir," or the strong minister, consequent on an act of strength and heroism. Present at service in the church of Fearn, when the stone roof gave way and was in course of pressing

During my grandfather's incumbency, Mr. Bethune was on the 16th June, 1739, ordained in the parish of Glenshiel, as its first Presbyterian minister. Though possessed of much energy and zeal, his bodily frame was slender. The Highlanders called him " ministeir na tunu," as he employed the arguments of meat and drink to effect the same good ends towards which the ministers of Lochcarron and Lochbroom would have used the hand or baton. His son, Dr. John Bethune, first minister of Harris, and afterwards of Dornoch, was for many years my father's co-presbyter. His eldest son, Angus Bethune, died minister of Alness in 1801. He was succeeded by his son, Hector Bethune, minister of Dingwall, who died in 1849.

On the 29th of August, 1728, my grandfather was united in marriage to Miss Elizabeth Mackay, eldest daughter of Mr. John Mackay, first Presbyterian minister of Lairg, in Sutherlandshire. Mr. Mackay was of the family of Scoury, one of the oldest branches of the noble family of Farr or Reay. Third son of Captain William Mackay of Borley, he was born in the parish of Durness, in the Reay Country, in 1677, and, after prosecuting his studies, first at Edinburgh and afterwards at Utrecht, he was licensed to preach in 1706, and on the 16th March, 1707, was settled at Durness, which included the wide alpine district of the Reay Country. In that extensive field, my great-grandfather, for seven years, laboured most zealously. Strong in mind and in body, and, above all, "strong in faith," he not only preached every Sabbath at different and central stations in the district, but also catechised annually *all* the families of that immense tract of country, and, while so occupied, would necessarily be absent from home for three months together.

In the year 1714 he was translated to the parish of Lairg, and inducted as its first Presbyterian minister. The moral condition of that parish was such as to demand the services of a faithful and able minister of the New Testament, for the inhabitants were plunged in ignorance and superstition, owing to the want of a stated pastorate for a course of years. The earls of Sutherland were hereditary sheriffs of that county, and patrons of the several parishes; and John, 15th earl, one of the Scottish Commissioners for the Union, warmly espoused and promoted the best interests of Presbytery. With the Earl, Lord Reay was on the most friendly terms, and, by his chief, my great-grandfather was strongly recommended to the Earl as suitable for the vacant charge. At the time of his settlement in Lairg, the churchyard, even on the Sabbath, often exhibited scenes of violence and of bloodshed. Aware of these disorders, Earl John, in his capacity of sheriff, invested my great-grandfather with power to inflict corporal punishment. Thus

out the walls, he rushed to the door, and then, placing his shoulder under the lintel, supported it until the majority of the people passed out. He next extricated the minister. He was ordained minister of Lochbroom, 8th May, 1745. He was reputed for checking with his fists his offending parishioners. While nearly his whole flock espoused the cause of Prince Charles Edward, he remained firm in his attachment to the reigning family. When some of the people were arraigned criminally for taking part in the Rebellion, he made a journey to London on their behalf. By his successful exertions on behalf of the accused he earned the gratitude and admiration of his parishioners.—*Ibid.*

furnished, he entered upon his ministry, and while with the obstinate and refractory he was compelled to use strong measures, yet making these subservient to a strain of preaching at once pure, powerful, and profound, he became eminently instrumental in reforming the habits of his people, and in winning many souls to Christ. He married in August, 1700, and had a family of two sons and five daughters. His wife, my great-grandmother Catherine Mackay, was eldest daughter of John Mackay, of Kirtomy, descended from Lady Jean Gordon, daughter of Alexander, 11th Earl of Sutherland. Lady Jean, who was married to Hugh Mackay, of Farr, had two sons, Donald, first Lord Reay, and John, first Laird of Dirlot and Strathy. John of Strathy married, in 1619, Agnes, daughter of Sir James Sinclair of Murkle, second son of the Earl of Caithness, by his wife, Lady Elizabeth Stewart, daughter of the Earl of Orkney. He had three sons, Hugh, John, and James, the last, in 1670, obtained the lands of Kirtomy, and married Jane, daughter of the Honble. Sir James Fraser of Brae, third son of Simon, Lord Lovat. James had two sons, John of Kirtomy and James of Borgy. John married Elizabeth, daughter of James Sinclair of Lybster, by whom he had three sons and six daughters. The eldest of the daughters was Catherine, my great-grandmother, a woman of decided and ardent piety, the worthy " helpmeet " of a pious husband. My great-grandfather's eldest son, Thomas Mackay, succeeded him as minister of Lairg. He was a man of deep piety, but of peculiar temper. He had imbibed, when he became a preacher, certain opinions of a very exclusive character, and on one occasion carried them to such extremity as to secede from his father's ministry. The father and son were afterwards reconciled, and that reconciliation my grandfather, the minister of Lochcarron, was chiefly instrumental in effecting. My great-grandfather had another son, John, but he died young. Elizabeth, his eldest daughter, was married to my grandfather. They met in Ross-shire, in the house of Mr. Gordon of Ardoch. Mr. Gordon was one of the heritors of the parish of Kirkmichael, as well as of Lairg, and was remarkable for the incidents of his life. His wife, a sister of Sir Robert Munro of Foulis, who was killed at Falkirk, was a woman of remarkable piety. During the greater part of his wife's lifetime, Mr. Gordon was a man of unsettled opinions and of an irreligious life. He was a fond husband, but his affection for the best of wives could not reconcile him to her piety. One evening, on coming home, he found her seated in the parlour with a number of devout persons who were engaging in spiritual exercises. Suddenly he rushed out of the house, and attempted to kill himself. But in an instant the words occurred to him, " Do thyself no harm," and from that moment he became a new man. His remaining life was consecrated to the cause of godliness. His wife died after a long and painful illness patiently borne. Her remains are interred at Kirkmichael, in the parish of Resolis, and around them her nephew, Sir Harry Munro of Foulis, erected a square enclosure, filled up with lime and stone, in order to prevent any future interment at the spot. In the house of Mr. and Mrs. Gordon, my grandfather became acquainted with his future wife, and at Ardoch they were married. A copy of their marriage contract, drawn out by the Rev. John Balfour, minister of Logie Easter, has been handed down to me. It thus proceeds:—

" At Ardoch, the nineteenth day of July, one thousand seven hundred and twenty-eight years. It is matrimonially contracted, agreed, and finally ended, betwixt Mr. Eneas Sage, minister of the gospel at Lochcarron, and Elizabeth Mackay, eldest lawful daughter of Mr. John Mackay, minister of the gospel at Lairg, and the said Mr. John Mackay, as undertaker for his said daughter, as follows: that is to say, the said Mr. Eneas Sage and Elizabeth Mackay, with the special advice and consent of the said Mr. John Mackay, her father, do hereby promise faithfully to each other that they shall, twixt and the first day of September next to come, solemnize the lawful bond of marriage together. In contemplation of which marriage, the said Mr. Eneas Sage binds and obligdes him for the soume of three thousand merks Scots money, unto the children of the forsaid marriage, in ffie, and in liferent for the interest thereof to the said Elizabeth Mackay his (of date) spouse in case she shall happen to survive him. And in case of no children of the said marriage, and that she shall survive him, the said Mr. Eneas Sage provides his said (of date) spouse to the one half of his moveables at the time of his decease ; and in case there shall be children existent of the marriage, to the third share of his said moveables which shall be redeemable by him or his heirs for the soume of two hundred merks Scots money, payable at the next term of Whitsunday or Martinmas after his decease. In consideration of all which, the said Mr. John Mackay has instantly advanced and paid to the said Mr. Eneas Sage, in name of tocher (good) with the said Elizabeth Mackay, his daughter, all and haill, the soume of one thousand merks Scots, of which soume the said Mr. Eneas Sage acknowledges him to be fully satisfied, renouncing the exception of not numerate money, and all other objections to the contrary. And likewise, the said Mr. Eneas Sage and Elizabeth Mackay do hereby discharge the said Mr. John Mackay of all bairn's part of gair or any other demand whatsoever, excepting goodwill allenarly ; and both parties bind other under the failzie of three hundred merks Scots money, to be paid by the party ffailer to the party performer. And both parties consent to the registration hereof in the books of Council and Session, or any other books competent, that letters of horning and all other executorials may pass hereupon in fform as effeirs, and to that effect constitute,

their Prors.

" In witness whereof (written by Mr. John Balfour, minister of the gospel at Logie Easter, on stamp paper conform to law) they have subscribed these presents, place, date, and year of God abovewritten before these two witnesses; Mr. Alexander Gordon of Ardoch and Mr. John Balfour foresaid, writer hereof.

" Eneas Sage.
" Alexander Gordon, *Witns.*   " Elizabeth Mackay.
" John Balfour, *Witness.*"

Mr. Balfour, who wrote and witnessed the marriage, was a minister of eminence. In 1729 he was translated to Nigg. where, among a people sunk in the grossest ignorance, his ministry became eminently successful. Two interesting anecdotes of him have been handed down. When he came to Nigg, he found the people addicted to the deliberate profanation of the Lord's day. That was the day of all others on which the parishioners assembled to exercise themselves in athletic games.

They had a leader, a strong, bold man, to whom all looked up. Mr. Balfour watched his opportunity. He was elected one of the presbytery's commissioners to the General Assembly; and previous to his departure for Edinburgh, he sent for this ringleader of Sunday sports, and told him that, as his duty called him from home, he left the east end of the parish in his charge, and would hold him responsible that the people spent the Sabbath not in games and rioting, but in prayer and in reading and hearing the word. " You are surely aware, sir," said the man, "that of these games I myself am the leader, and the first to begin; how then can you ask me to stop them?" " I charge you before God to do so," said the minister; "let all the guilt of a refusal lie upon your conscience." " Well, sir, if it must be so," replied the man, " I'll try what I can do." He was as good as his word; the Sunday games were discontinued, and the ringleader himself became a devoted Christian. Mr. Balfour was a preacher of the very first order. His discourses were profound, searching, scriptural, and experimental. A Sabbath seldom passed without saving impressions being produced upon the minds of many of his hearers. He lived too as he preached. A woman under deep conviction came to consult him. She found him at the side of a burn. Her case she endeavoured to lay before him. It was in her view a hopeless one. He set forth to her the hopes and consolations of the gospel, so that she felt relieved and comforted. As she proceeded to leave, Mr. Balfour took up a stone and threw it into the stream, and as the stone sunk to the bottom, he exclaimed, " So will John Balfour to hell; after preaching to others, he himself will be a castaway!" Hearing his exclamation, the woman came back in deep distress. " Alas, sir," said she, " how can I receive the consolation you refuse to take yourself?" " Take it notwithstanding," he replied, " my temptations I expressed not to you, but to Him who alone can deliver us both. I could know but little of gospel comfort either for myself or others, if my heart did not know its own bitterness."*

The manse of Lochcarron to which my grandfather conducted his young wife was a humble fabric. It stood upon a little eminence removed about sixty yards from the north shore of an inlet of the sea or loch, which was also the estuary of the Carron, a stream from which the parish derives its name. The manse was constructed after the fashion of all Highland houses about the end of the seventeenth century. About 100 feet long, the walls were built of stone for about three feet in height above the foundation, and around the roots of the couples, which were previously fixed in the ground; over this were several layers of turf or fail, so as to bring the wall to the height of 10 feet. The whole was then thatched with heather. This long building was divided into several apartments : the first was called the chamber, where there was a chimney at one end, a small glazed window looking to the south, and a tent bed inserted into the partition which divided it from the next room. In this apartment the heads of the family sat and took their meals. The bed in it was usually appropriated for

* Mr. John Balfour, minister of Nigg, died on the 6th February, 1752. Under his ministry was experienced, in 1744, a remarkable awakening, which continued during the following years. The effect was alike salutary and permanent.—ED.

guests ; the next apartment contained tent beds for the junior branches, with an entry door by which access to the principal apartment was provided for the heads of the family as well as for their guests. This second apartment opened into a third, where the heads of the family slept. Next came what was called the " cearn "* (or servants' hall). This compartment of the Highland house, or "tigh slathait," was larger or longer than the others. It had cross lights, namely, a small boarded window on each side. The fire-place was usually an old mill-stone placed in the centre of the apartment, on which the peat-fire was kindled, with no other substitute for a chimney than a hole in the roof, fenced with a basket of wicker work open at both ends. Around the fire sat the servants, and in the farmers' houses, the heads of the family, along with their children. Divided from the " cearn," and often by a very slender partition, and as the last division of the tenement, was the cow-house (or byre) occupying at least 50 feet of the entire length.

The church was a low, ill - lighted, irregularly - seated building thatched with a heather roof. The local scenery was grand and impos-ing, for Nature had done everything—Art nothing. The mountains rose up on every side, and presented their scathed and rocky summits to the clouds. Beneath was an oblong level, about ten miles in length and two in breadth, all of which could be taken in at a glance.

The lower part was occupied by an arm of the sea, which washed the bases of the mountains on the one side, and, on the other, flowed upon a shelving shore. The upper part presented a dark, heathy surface rising into detached eminences. The Carron, issuing from a lake at the upper extremity, divided the valley, and, after executing a few windings, emptied itself into the sea. On the north side of the sea-inlet, and in the background, Sguir a' Chaorachan and Glasbheinn presented their rugged and rocky fronts, forming an indented line on the horizon ; and at their bases stood the humble dwelling of the minister and his hermitage-like church towards the east, and the ruins of the Castle of Strome to the west, surmounted by the mountains of Lochalsh and Skye. On the south side of the loch appeared an almost

* Rob Donn, in his song on the pleasures of a country life, says :—

Cha'n eil' seòmar aig' Righ Bhreatainn
'S taitneich' leam na'n *Cearn*,
Oir tha uaignidheach do ghruagaich,
'S ni e fuaim 'n uair is àill' ;
Feur 'us coille, blath 'us duille !
'S iad fo iomadh neul,
'Us is', 'us *echo*, mar na teudan,
Seirm gach téis a 's fearr.

TRANSLATION.

No room the King of Britain has
More pleasant than the *Cearn*,
To maidens, whiles, it private is,
And social, too, in turn ;
Grass and trees, bloom and leaves !
With various hues they spring,
While *echo*, and the maiden's lays,
In strains responsive, sing.

unbroken chain of eminences. Exactly opposite the manse, one opening between the mountains met the eye to the south, and looked into the romantic and beautifully-situated valley of Attadale.

On the 26th of October, 1729, my grandmother gave birth to her first child, a daughter, who was named Catherine. She was married about the age of twenty to Charles Gordon of Pulrossie, Sutherland-shire, by whom she had a numerous family. The early years of my grandfather's ministry were to him very disheartening. The parish-ioners, with the exception of one or two families, refused to attend his ministry; and not content with this negative opposition, the more desperate characters among them attacked him violently. After his settlement, to show their dislike, the people assembled every Lord's day in a plat of ground about twenty yards from the church door for the practice of athletic games. This unbecoming behaviour my grand-father had, during the early years of his ministry, to witness weekly. Of such impiety, however, he was not an uninterested spectator. He watched his opportunity, and sought to gain the offenders, even using Paul's "craftiness" in his endeavours. He put himself in the way of some as they retired. With one he made a bargain that, if every Lord's day he came with his family to church, he would give him at the close of the service a pound of snuff. The agreement was made, and for the space of nearly a year was most scrupulously acted on by the minister and his parishioner. The minister regularly preached, the parishioner as regularly heard, and afterwards duly received his modicum of snuff. The poor man's hour came at last. My grandfather had preached a sermon from these words, "What shall it profit a man if he should," etc. When he thereafter went up to his pensioned hearer and reached out to him his usual allowance, the poor fellow turned away and burst into tears. "No, sir," said he, "I receive that no longer. Too long have I been hearing God's word for hire, to-day I have heard it to my condemnation." My grandfather exhorted and encouraged him, and he ultimately became one of the best fruits of his ministry. It was to this very individual, when he became an aged and experienced Christian, that my grandfather, at a diet of catechising. put the question, "Where was God before he created the heavens and the earth?" "You have, sir," he solemnly replied, "put a question to me hard indeed to answer, and far above my comprehension; but where could God be before the heaven and the earth were, but wrapped up in his own eternal and uncreated glory." The second anecdote is not quite so pleasing. On one of the Christmas holidays, which the Highlanders observed by assembling to play at club and shinty, he observed a body of young fellows approaching his dwelling. The road they took passed close by the manse, and led to a plain east of the church. The minister's domestics regarded with some suspicion the first part of them as they passed the manse. They looked at the roof and then at each other and passed on, some of them saying, loud enough to be heard, that, on their return, they would set the roof in a blaze, either to burn the Whig minister in his bed, or smoke him out in his shirt. The intelligence was communicated to my grandfather, and he acted with due precaution. Towards evening, when the gamesters were about to close their sport, he went among them. "Well," said he, "lads, you have worked pretty hard for a dram." "And who would be such a good fellow," said one of them, "as to give us one." "You pass my house," said my grandfather, "as you go home; wait at the door, and I will give each of you bread and cheese, and a glass of whisky." The fellows said nothing, but, conscious of their evil intentions, exchanged with each other a look of self-reproach. Appearing at the manse door, each received his promised refreshment. They felt grateful, and the safety of the dwelling was secured. About the year 1731 matters got worse, insomuch that, despairing of being of any service in the parish, he, in the year just stated, petitioned the Presbytery of Gairloch for a translation. His petition gives a very gloomy view of the moral aspect of the parish. His life, he set forth, was in constant danger, and one family constituted his sole audience. His petition, however, was not granted. It was presented in a moment of despondency, which time and ministerial fidelity, under the divine blessing, subsequently cleared away.

On the 6th of February, 1734, Mary, his second daughter, was born. She married a respectable tenant at Kishorn, now a part of Applecross, but then in the parish of Lochcarron. When they were first married, her husband, Donald Kennedy, took the charge of a small farm which my grandfather then occupied, now the site of the large and populous village of Jeantown. This farm he managed till the death of his father. Towards the close of a wet, cold, and protracted harvest, Donald Kennedy toiled from morning to night in securing his father-in-law's crop. In the evening my grandfather, after being closeted all day in his study, walked out to witness operations. He saw his son-in-law hard at work, and almost exhausted. "Well, Donald," he said, "you have been toiling hard all day, and you perhaps think that to promote the welfare of my family, you are sacrificing both yourself and your children; but be not discouraged; while you were working for me I was praying for you, and it is borne in upon me that neither you nor yours shall ever want all that is necessary for this life, nor a name and an inheritance in the church and in the country."[*]

---

[*] Their eldest son, Mr. Angus Kennedy, minister of Dornoch, to whom reference is afterwards made, married Isabella, daughter of Mr. George Rainy, minister of Creich. He was succeeded at Dornoch by his son, Mr. George Rainy Kennedy, who, in 1887, completed fifty years of a most useful and honoured ministry in that parish.—ED.

THE vexatious opposition which my grandfather met with from his parishioners, and which at first so heavily pressed upon him, gradually gave way. He had, it is true, to fight every inch of his way. The whole course of his ministry was one continued contest with ignorance, prejudice, and irreligion. In this contest, however, he was always the victor, and it was a comfort, daily on the increase, when he saw his parishioners more and more united in reverence for the gospel and in personal regard for himself.

He was a man of great personal strength, and, on more than one occasion, he was compelled to use it against that opposition which a barbarous people presented to his ministerial efforts. There was a small proprietor in the parish who was known to be a libertine. Very much to the astonishment of his hearers, on one particular Sabbath, Mr. Sage, after divine service, intimated his intention to hold a diet of catechising at this man's house. His friends remonstrated with him. The man was, they said, such a desperate character that it would neither be decent nor safe to hold any intercourse with him, and they evinced surprise that he should propose, even for the discharge of pastoral duties, to enter his house. The minister would go, however. When he arrived at the house on the day appointed, the owner met him at the door, and with a menacing scowl asked, what brought him there? "I come to discharge my duty to God, to your conscience, and to my own," was the answer. "I care nothing for any of the three," said the man, "out of my house or—I'll turn you out." "Easier said than done," said my grandfather, "but you may turn me out if you can." This pithy colloquy brought matters to an issue. They were both powerful men, and neither of them hesitated to put forth upon the other his ponderous strength. After a short, but fierce, struggle the minister became the victor, and the landlord, prostrated upon his own floor, was, with a rope coiled around his arms and feet, bound over to keep the peace. The people of the district were then called in, and the minister proceeded seriously to discharge the duty of catechising them. When that was finished he set himself to deal with the delinquents present. The man was solemnly rebuked, and the minister so moved his conscience that an arrangement was entered into that he and the woman with whom he cohabited should be duly and regularly married. The man afterwards became a decided Christian.

It was about this period that the secession from the Church of

Scotland, headed by the celebrated Ebenezer and Ralph Erskine, took place; that is, in 1733, seven years after my grandfather's settlement at Lochcarron. This movement, which agitated the southern part of the country with the violence of a tempest, was almost unknown in the more remote parts of the Highlands. The truth is that, while the church in the south was long established, it was, in the mountainous districts of the northern counties, as yet in its infancy, while the livings were so small, the distance to Edinburgh so great, and the journey so expensive that few ministers attended the General Assembly. I am not aware that my grandfather was ever present at a General Assembly. Secession principles were not introduced into Ross-shire for nearly fifty years afterwards. During this period the moderate party in the church was rising into prominence, under the leadership of the celebrated Robertson, and developing a regularly organised system. The rise of this party was the real cause of the secession, and afterwards led to errors in doctrine as well as to laxity in the exercise of discipline within the church itself. In the north these influences were unfelt, and the very existence of the party was unknown. My grandfather received his appointment to the parish of Lochcarron, not through the presentation of a patron, but by the call and ordination of the Presbytery, which itself had been formed in the previous year.

On the 22nd of August, 1736, his third daughter, Flora, was born; she died in the following March. His daughter Anne was born on the 29th September, 1738, and was equally short lived; she died in March, 1739. John, the eldest son, was born on the 19th August, 1740, and died in his thirteenth year. Margaret, fifth daughter, was born on the 20th September, 1742, and died in her second year, and the second son, Murdo, born on the 10th of June, 1744, died in October following.

The year 1745 forms a striking and memorable epoch in Scottish history; a year of excitement, intrigue, battle, and bloodshed. The house of Stewart was deeply rooted in the national heart. That illustrious family grew with the growth, and identified itself with the progress of the people in every step of their advancement from incipiency to maturity, from barbarism to civilization, from absolute heathenism to pure Christianity. They fell into one great error, however; an error common to human nature in general, but common especially to kings; they forgot the existence of any authority superior to their own. It is true, they held the doctrine of the "divine right" of kings, but the source from which they drew this divine right was a divinity of their own device. The result of such a doctrine was obvious. The house of Stewart came to believe that Scotland was their own, her soil their personal property, to be disposed of as they saw fit. The lever which came at last to be applied, and which succeeded in overturning their throne, was forged by their own hands when they assumed arbitrary lordship over the conscience of their subjects. The blood of the Covenanters, which flowed so copiously under the sabres of Claverhouse and his ruffianly dragoons, cried aloud unto heaven, and drew down, at last, upon the house of Stewart that measure of Divine displeasure under which it finally sank; while those royal oppressors and persecutors of God's people, who had wielded at one time the whole power of the State against God's cause and His witnesses, became themselves in their turn, in the course of His wise and inscrutable providence, the persecuted and oppressed. Charles Edward, the last of the Stewart princes, and the Hero of the 45, was the elder son of the Chevalier St. George whom my grandfather had seen thirty years previously at Stonehaven. On the 20th of June, 1745, Charles, accompanied by the Marquis of Tullibardine, Sir Thomas Sheridan, Sir John Macdonald, Mr. Francis Strickland, the Rev. George Kelly, Eneas Macdonald, brother of Kinloch-Moidart, and O'Sullivan, an Irishman, embarked at St. Nazaire on board the Doutelle, went to Belleisle on the following day, and on the fourth of July was joined by the Elizabeth, having on board 100 marines and 2000 soldiers. On the fifth of July the whole expedition sailed from Belleisle, with a fair wind, and, after encountering many hair-breadth escapes from English ships of war, the Doutelle alone, with the Prince and his attendants on board, landed at Eriska in South Uist on the 23rd of July. Between that date and the month of August the Prince held interviews with many Highland chiefs, including Lochiel, Keppoch, Kinloch-Moidart and others, and gained them over to his cause. The arming went on rapidly; hostilities commenced; a skirmish, successful to the arms of Charles, took place on the 16th of August at Highbridge, near Fort-William, between a party of Lochiel's and Keppoch's men and a battalion of the Scots' Royals, under Captain, afterwards General, Scott. On the 19th of August, 1745, the Prince set up his standard at Glenfinnan in the parish of Ardnamurchan. From that day his progress was as that of a meteor, bursting at once upon the eye, brightening more and more as it rose into the sky, and, after attaining a certain height, disappearing suddenly.

On the 20th of August, at the head of an army of 2000 Highlanders, the Prince began his march to Edinburgh by the mountain pass of Corriarrock, and prepared to encounter the royal forces sent against him under command of Sir John Cope. From the head of Loch Lochy he, on the 23rd, advanced to Fassiefearn; on the 25th, arrived at Moy in Lochaber; on the 26th, encamped at Corriarrock, and there learned that the royalist general had avoided him and was in full march for Inverness. Continuing his march to the capital, he entered Athole on the 29th of August, supped at Blair Castle on the 30th, and on the 4th of September, at the head of his forces, entered Perth. After remaining there for several days, making preparation for the impending contest, and receiving considerable addition to his force by the adherence of the Duke of Perth and others, he left Perth on the 11th of September; passed the Forth at the Ford of Frew on the 13th, in the face of a strong body of dragoons, who were there posted to oppose him; advanced to Falkirk; next to Linlithgow; and, on the 17th, entered Edinburgh. On the 19th he left Holyrood Palace to join his army posted at Dudding-ston. On Saturday the 21st he fought the battle of Prestonpans, by which Scotland was laid prostrate at his feet. After remaining some time in the capital, he, on the evening of Thursday the 31st of October, proceeded on his daring expedition to England. On the 3rd of November, at the head of the second division of his troops, he left Dalkeith for

Kelso, and arriving at Lauder, took up his quarters at Thirlstane Castle. On the morning of the 6th he crossed the Tweed; entered England on the 8th; marched to Rowcliff, near Carlisle, on the 9th; was joined, on the same evening, by the first division of his troops, who had entered England by another route; and on the 10th proceeded to invest Carlisle. This city surrendered on the 15th of November, and on the 20th and 21st of the month, his army, in two divisions, left Carlisle for Penrith; marched to Kendal on the 23rd, and to Lancaster on the 25th; while, with his whole army, he arrived at Preston on the 26th of November. Still pressing forward, on the 4th of December he arrived at Derby, within one hundred and twenty-seven miles of London; but this was the limit of his progress. From Derby, on the 6th, he commenced his retreat into Scotland, and after a *rencontre* between his troops and those of the King, under the Duke of Cumberland at Clifton Moor, in which the Highlanders were victorious, he re-entered Scotland on the 20th of December, and arrived at Glasgow on the 26th.

On the fourth day of January, 1746, Charles left Glasgow with the view of capturing the Castles of Edinburgh and Stirling, and, on the evening of that day, surrounded the town of Stirling with his troops; captured the town on the 8th; besieged the Castle of Stirling on the 12th of January; and obtained a complete victory over the royal forces at Falkirk, under General Hawley, on the 17th. The siege of the Castle was again resumed on the 20th, but, after a considerable loss of his men, he was compelled to abandon it and retreat to the north.

On the 31st of January, the whole Highland army, under the command of Lord George Murray, began its retreat to Inverness. On the 4th of February, Charles arrived at Blair Castle. He came to Moy Castle, a seat of the laird of Mackintosh, on the 16th, and, on the 20th, entered Inverness, laid siege to the Castle, and took it. On the 8th of April, the Duke of Cumberland left Aberdeen for Inverness in pursuit of the insurgents, and arrived at Nairn on the 14th. On the same day Charles marched his troops out from Inverness as far as Culloden, and, on the 15th, arranged them in the order of battle on Drummossie muir. He marched his army to Nairn on the 16th of April, with the view of nocturnally surprising the Duke's army, but he utterly failed. The battle of Culloden was fought on the 17th of April, 1746, when his army was totally defeated by the Duke of Cumberland, and all his future prospects of sovereignty were buried in the graves of his devoted followers. From that period Charles's fortunes experienced a complete reverse. He was forcibly carried off from the last and bloodiest of his battles, and, escorted by a large body of horse, he crossed the river Nairn at a ford four miles from the battle-field. Dismissing his attendants, with the exception of three or four, he arrived about sunset at Gortuleg, and, after some refreshment, left it for Invergarry about ten o'clock. There his miseries began. The castle was inhabited but by a single domestic; and the Prince was under the necessity of sleeping in his clothes on a stone floor. The story of his wanderings afterwards, and of his hairbreadth escapes, of his miseries, heightened by tattered garments and food as coarse as it was scanty, and, at last, of his escape from Borrodale to France on board the L'Heureux, on the 19th of September, 1746, resembles romance more than reality.

This eventful year was the nineteenth of my grandfather's ministry. His parishioners were, when he first came among them, the genuine subjects of the House of Stewart. His near relatives, too, by his mother's side, such as Glengarry, Lochgarry, Barisdale, were all "out in the '45;" but I do not learn that he received any annoyance from either his relatives or parishioners on account of his anti-Jacobite principles. The Earl of Seaforth was peculiarly circumstanced. His father, who had acted so vacillating a part during the rebellion of 1715, under the Earl of Mar, had died in exile. The estate had been restored to his son, and this circumstance was a sufficiently strong and practical argument with that nobleman effectually to convince him of the folly of joining in the new rebellion. Whatever his private leanings were, he kept quiet; and his clan, the majority of my grandfather's parishioners, as a matter of course, kept quiet too. The only consequence to my grandfather, resulting from the disturbed state of the public mind, was an attempt which was made to murder him. The intending assassin · lived in Strathconon, through which the road then passed from Lochcarron to the Low country. He had seen my grandfather several times pass the road, and he formed the resolution, soon after the rebellion was suppressed, to take his life. Of any provocation, received or imagined, I am not aware. It was during the year 1746, when the Duke of Cumberland, under colour of quelling the rebellion, had been guilty of the most cold-blooded and revolting acts of cruelty towards the fugitives. It is probable that this man wished to make reprisals, having himself narrowly escaped the sabres of Cumberland's dragoons. He watched his opportunity, and it came. His house stood in one of the wildest and most secluded spots in the glen. My grandfather had occasion to travel to Dingwall and Cromarty; and of the day of his departure from the manse the intended slayer was promptly informed. Arming himself with a dirk, and posting himself in the hollow of a rock near the high road, he awaited his victim. My grandfather, on horseback, approached the spot, utterly unconscious of danger. As he drew near, the road being very rugged, and his horse tired, he dismounted, when, leaving the animal to graze, he, after his manner, retired to pray. The spot he chose for this purpose placed him directly in the view of the intending assassin, and the effect upon the ruffian's mind was irresistible. He had unsheathed his dirk, and advanced a step or two, with the full intention of perpetrating the bloody deed, by stabbing him on the left side, which happened to be next him. But when he beheld the powerful man prostrated in prayer, his arm was arrested, the dirk dropped to the ground, and he stood motionless. After finishing his devotions, my grandfather rose to pursue his journey, but as he turned round to look for his horse, his eye fell upon the man who stood before him. Ignorant of the man's recent purpose, my grandfather accosted him with familiarity and kindness. His face, betokening what passed within, was deadly pale, and my grandfather questioned him about his health; but to every question he returned an evasive answer. Disarmed, however, of all deadly intentions, the man accompanied my grandfather down the glen; and the conversation, fluctuating from the man's health to the weather, and from the weather to the news of the day, lighted at last on the moment-ous concerns of eternity, on which my grandfather spoke earnestly and to such purpose that the murderer in intention became the Christian in sincerity. He survived my grandfather, and on his death-bed, related the narrative of his dread intention towards him to whom he, under God, owed his conversion.

On the 15th of December, 1746, my grandfather's third son, William, was born. He attended college two sessions, but died soon afterwards, George, the fourth son, was born on the 27th day of November, 1748, and died on the 27th of December, 1752; and Thomas, the fifth son, was born on the 12th February, 1750, and died on the 16th day of December, 1752.

My grandfather's intercourse with his parishioners latterly became very different from what it was at the first. The light of that gospel which he had faithfully preached had arisen in full strength, and the gloom of ignorance and prejudice had passed away. Converts to the faith of the gospel became conspicuous, alike by their numbers and by their character, and constituted, if not the majority, at least the most influential portion of the parishioners. In connection with the real progress of the truth, my grandfather was zealous to promote the arts of civilized life. He fought against indolence and on behalf of house-hold economy. He also stood up as the uncompromising assertor of civil rights against all by whom those rights might be invaded. The parish of Lochcarron was almost wholly the property of the Earl of Seaforth. His lordship at the time had a factor named Mackenzie, known among the inhabitants as "Calan Dearg," or "Red Colin." This functionary was a not inconsiderable potentate. He had so much of bustling and ostentatious fidelity in the discharge of his duties as sufficiently to recommend him to his employer, and consequently had the Earl's entire confidence, and was the sole organ of communication between him and his tenants. Personally he acknowledged no higher power than the Earl's will, and no encouragement save his lordship's approval. Thus furnished he was the supreme authority in the parish of Lochcarron. With my grandfather, who was also a man in authority, this dignitary had many opportunities of measuring his strength. Red Colin had been collecting the rents for several weeks, and although he was fully aware that the minister's stipend was due, he took no steps to pay it; he treated with scorn a message from the manse on the subject; and, taking up his money, he secured it in his portmanteau, and posted off towards Brahan Castle. My grandfather, having got notice of the factor's departure, instantly followed him. The factor stopped for some time to refresh himself at Luibgargan, a place about fifteen miles distant. There, whilst regaling himself with a substantial breakfast, the room door was suddenly thrust open, and the tall muscular person of the minister stepped forward. "Colin," said my grandfather, "I come to get what you owe me; it would have been more civil and neighbourly if you had handed it to me at own fireside, instead of bringing me so far." Starting up, Colin drew his broadsword, "Let the issue," said he, flourishing his weapon, "determine whether you'll finger one plack of what you say is due to you." At some risk, parrying with his arm the thrust aimed at him by his opponent, my grandfather succeeded in closing with him. Seizing him by the collar, he threw him on the floor, shivering his broadsword, and thrust his head up into the chimney. Red Colin was sufficiently humbled, and, for the first time in his life, was reduced to the position of a suppliant. He shouted for quarter, and in the most earnest, but most respectful terms, declared that the stipend, to the last penny, should be paid. But Colin never forgot the encounter, and took many ways afterwards of showing that his pride and dignity had been wounded. Some time afterward, the parties again came into contact. The minister considered it his duty to interpose, in consequence of some arbitrary treatment to which his parishioners were subjected. Red Colin sought revenge in a new mode. He punctually paid my grandfather's stipend, but he did so in farthings. Poor "Callan Dearg" had a sudden and violent death. Lord Seaforth, accompanied by Red Colin, a retinue of servants, and a long train of baggage horses, on their way to Lews, passed the church of Lochcarron on the Sabbath day, close upon the hour when divine service was to begin. Aware of their approach, my grandfather went to meet them. He accosted Lord Seaforth with the respect due to his rank and station. "My Lord," said he, "you are on a journey, and I find you and your attendants prosecuting that journey on the Sabbath. Permit me to propose that you dismount, discontinue your journey for this day, unite with us in worship, and, after that is over, partake of my humble hospitality. My barn will contain your luggage, and my stable your horses." Lord Seaforth was about to comply, when Red Colin, who stood near, cried out, "Never mind what the old carle says, my Lord; let us continue our journey, we need all our time." As they moved forward, my grandfather said, "Colin, mark my words. You are now on a journey which you shall not repeat; you are going on a way by which you shall not return." And his words were fearfully true. A few months afterward, Red Colin, on his return-passage in an open boat from the island of Lews to the mainland of Ross-shire, was drowned. "Now, sir," said one of his parishioners to my grandfather, on hearing of the death of "Calan Dearg," "We knew you were a minister, but not until now that you were a prophet." "No," said my grandfather, "I am not a prophet, but judgment, I know, will follow upon sin."

My grandfather attained some celebrity by a marriage which he solemnized. A young and beautiful woman, named Matheson, had formed an attachment to a young man of her own age and rank. Her father forbade their uni n, as the young man was, though respectably descended, of limi ed me n ; and the father, moreover, had set his heart upon an aged but more wealthy, aspirant to his daughter's hand. He insisted, therefore, that as he had set his heart upon this individual as a son-in-law, his daughter should set her heart upon him as a husband. With this injunction the young woman could not comply, and for two reasons—first, that her affections were engaged ; and next, because the lover chosen for her by her father was not only not her choice, but, from his very ungainly person, the object of her aversion. Neither of these things, however, weighed with the father. He had made up his mind, and the marriage day was fixed. The lovers, in their distress, applied to my grandfather, who remonstrated with the father, but in vain. The young people now took the matter into their own hands. They eloped together, and in a boat landed on a small island in the bay of Lochcarron. Thither, by appointment, my grandfather went and married them. This conclusive measure made a considerable stir. The young woman's father was exasperated, and resolved to bring the celebrator of the marriage before his superiors. The case, however, was quashed by the interference of several influential individuals, and, among others, Macleod of Macleod, the renegade to the Stewart cause in 1745, who had been frequently a guest at the manse. A popular and highly-poetic song by a bard of the period, probably by William or Alexander Mackenzie, was composed on the occasion, "Floraidh Bhuidhe," or Flora the yellow-haired, as she is called from the colour of her auburn ringlets, is celebrated for her fidelity, and the elopement is minutely described. My grandfather, too, is honourably mentioned. His meeting with the father, his unsuccessful remonstrance, and, to the father's threats, his reply—all are graphically depicted :—

> " Thubhairt an sin an Saigeach liath,
> ' Tha mi tri fichead bliadhn' 'us sia,
> 'S cha'n fhac mi an duine sin riamh
> O'n gabhainn fiar 'is cainnt." *

At the advanced age of eighty my grandfather's tall athletic form was as straight as when in the prime of manhood. Several years before his death a total eclipse of the sun took place, and he lost the sight of one of his eyes by imprudently looking through a telescope at the sun, in order to notice the phenomenon. My father has told me that my grandfather one evening saw a vision. He was walking to the east of the church, on the shore side of the loch, in the dusk of the evening. He noticed, at a considerable distance, what he first took to be a thick dark mist moving slowly on the road. As it approached him, it assumed the more definite form of a crowd of people following a bier, which, covered by a pall consisting of a tartan plaid, seemed to be borne by four men. The whole passed by him closely. He saw their forms and faces, and could even recognise some of his acquaintances. The tread of their feet was also audible. The circumstance he mentioned when he returned home, but without expressing any anxiety or alarm. My father was his bed-fellow, and this, towards the close of his life, became the more necessary as he had the practice of walking in his sleep. My father told me that, one night in winter very shortly before his death, soon after they had gone to bed, he had himself fallen fast asleep, but wakening some time later, he found that his aged parent was not, as usual, beside him. Raising himself on his elbow, he remained for a

---

* From this verse it appears that " the grey-haired Sage replied, ' I am three score years and six, and I have never yet seen the man from whom I would take insolent language.' "—ED.

moment in that posture to listen, and soon heard a faint groan in the
direction of the door.   He went quickly towards the sound, and found
the venerable old man stretched on the floor.   With all the tenderness
of a mother for a child, my father raised him up, and replaced him in
bed.   But though the earthly house, once so strong, was dissolving, his
mind lost none of its vitality.   When his dissolution drew near, his
strength was so much exhausted that he was unable to speak.   The
frequent moving of his lips, however, and the uplifting of his hands,
intimated that his inward mental exercises were in accord with the
solemnity of a dying hour.   His wife, family, and friends surrounded
him.   There was a deep silence, interrupted only at intervals by the
half-audible sobbings of his daughter Mary.   This arrested his attention.   Slightly raising himself up, he looked at her.   "Mary," he said,
"weep not as those who have no hope, for if we believe that Jesus died
and rose again, even so them also which sleep in Jesus will God bring
with him."   He then said, "Lord Jesus receive my spirit."   These were
his last words.   In the course of a very few minutes afterwards he
expired.   He died on the 15th day of July, 1774, in the eighty-eighth
year of his age and forty-eighth of his ministry.   His burial was
attended by the parishioners—men, women, and children—who long
and deeply felt their bereavement.   For many of them had become true
and vital Christians through his ministry, and were themselves the
primitive fathers of the spiritual generations that followed them.

CHAPTER III.

ALEXANDER SAGE; HIS EARLY DAYS.
THE REAY COUNTRY.

1753-1782.

MY father, Alexander Sage, minister of Kildonan, Sutherland-shire, my grandfather's sixth son, was born at the manse of Lochcarron on the 2nd of July, 1753. After acquiring the first rudiments of his education under the paternal roof, he was sent to the school of Cromarty. The teacher, Mr. John Russel, was a man of great worth, an expert scholar, and a licentiate of the Church. The gentry, the clergy, and the upper class of tenants, in the shires of Ross, Cromarty, and Inverness, sent their sons to his school. His method of teaching had not perhaps the polished surface of those systems which are most approved of now, but it was minute, careful, and substantial. In the elementary rules his pupils received a training they could never afterwards forget. My father could, at the age of seventy, repeat the construction rules of Ruddiman's "Rudiments" and of Watt's "Grammar" as accurately and promptly as he was accustomed to do when the fear of Mr. John Russel was before his eyes. When the pupils began to read Latin, they were taught to speak the language at the same time. Among the more advanced classes not a word in the school did any of them dare address to the teacher, or to each other, but in Latin, and thus they were made familiar with the language. Mr. Russel was a most uncompromising disciplinarian. The dread of his punishment was felt, and its salutary exercise extended, not only within the four corners of the schoolroom, but over the length and breadth of the parish. The trifler within the school on week-days, the sauntering lounger on the streets or on the links of Cromarty on the Sabbath-days, had that instinctive terror of Mr. Russel that the beasts are said to have of the lion. The truant, quailing under his glance, betook himself to his lesson; the saunterer on the links, at the first blink of him on the brae-head, returned to his home. In addition to this peremptoriness, Mr. Russel exercised a spirit of vital piety. Profoundly versant in Scripture truth and in experimental religion, he was the companion of all who feared God. His love of discipline arose from a love of God, of moral duty, and of the sacred rights of an enlightened conscience.

A characteristic anecdote is related of him. Mr. John Cameron, a student of divinity and parochial schoolmaster of Tain, was on his trials before the Presbytery with a view to license. This young man possessed a fund of natural humour, and would not hesitate, for the sake of a jest, to sacrifice that which was important and sacred. He was afterwards minister of Halkirk in Caithness. Mr. Cameron and Mr. Russel were fellow-travellers on their way to the Presbytery seat where Mr. Cameron had some of his trial discourses to deliver before the court. They were at such a distance from their journey's end that they had to take up their quarters at an inn by the way. Mr. Cameron said that he had composed and committed to memory three Calvinistic prayers to offer before the Presbytery. Having fixed them in his memory, he kept them there *in retentis*, he said, to give them fresh to the Presbytery. Mr. Russel, however, contrived, much to poor Cameron's annoyance, to extract every one of them from him before they parted. When they came to the inn, and before they had their supper, Mr. Russel proposed family worship. To this Mr. Cameron did not venture to object; besides, as Mr. Russel was a preacher of some standing, he had no apprehension that there would be any demand for his personal services. He was mistaken. Mr. Russel asked him to pray, "and the end of it was," as Cameron himself told it, "that off went one of my best prayers." After supper they were shown to their beds, and were to be bed-fellows. Mr. Cameron was about to hasten to a corner of the room to his private devotions, but Mr Russel prevented him. "My friend, it is more becoming that we should pray together first, and then pray separately before we go to bed; and, as you are to be engaged to-morrow in prayer and preaching, you cannot any better prepare yourself than by being frequently engaged in social prayer." Mr. Cameron felt that an inroad had already been made on his stock of prayers, and to the new proposal he stoutly objected. But it would not do. Mr. Russel was peremptory—he must again pray; "so," as he related, "down I bent to my knees, and away went two-thirds of my stock." In the morning, when they were both dressed, Mr. Russel said, "We are entering upon our journey, and we ought to begin it with prayer together; let us kneel, and you'll proceed: it will suitably prepare you, and put your mind in a proper frame for the duties before you." Cameron resisted the proposal, but to no purpose. "I repeated my last prayer," said Cameron, "and where or how to get new ones in place of them I didn't know, unless I could splice them together."

Mr. Russel was a preacher of great power and unction. In 1774 he was settled minister of the High Church, Kilmarnock, and from thence he was, in the year 1800, translated to Stirling, where he continued until his death in the year 1817.*

* Mr. John Russel, minister of the second charge of Stirling, died on the 23rd February, 1817, in his 77th year and the 43rd of his ministry. Of somewhat uncouth aspect, with a stern and gloomy countenance, he was a fearless and most effective preacher. In his poem of "The Twa Herds," the poet Burns has celebrated him thus :—

> "What herd like Russel tell'd his tale;
> His voice was heard through muir and dale."

And in the "Holy Fair," in these lines —

> "His piercin' words, like Highland swords,
> Divide the joints and marrow;
> His talk o' hell, whare devils dwell,
> Our vera saul does harrow."—ED.

A contemporary of my father, under Mr. Russel's tuition at Cromarty, was Charles Grant, one of the directors of the E. I. Company, member of Parliament for Inverness-shire, and father of Lord Glenelg. He was then a shop-lad in the employment of William Forsyth, an enterprising merchant. How long my father remained at the school of Mr. Russel I do not recollect. His father came frequently to see him, and took a lively interest in the progress of his education and in the moral culture of his mind. He went to the Aberdeen University in 1776, and prosecuted his studies at King's College. One of the professors, Mr. Thomas Gordon, was a model of Scottish scholarship. Latin was his element, the classics his friends ; while his minute knowledge of the language of Rome, unbalanced by an enlarged mental quality, rendered him a pedant. He loved to express himself, not only to his students, but to his friends, in the correct and studied periods of Sallust, or Cicero, or Livy. The students called him "Jupiter." One of my father's class-fellows was Duncan Munro of Culcairn. This gentleman was pervaded with an inexhaustible fund of drollery, in which he was wont to indulge at the risk of a broken head. My father, on one occasion, was one of those who, for "value received" at the hands of Duncan, was able and willing to repay him. The students of King's College had a ball or dance in the College lobby every Saturday evening. At this dance, on one occasion, my father, a tall, gaunt lad, was practising his steps, when his activity, exhibiting far more strength than grace, attracted Munro's notice. He was holding an orange between his thumb and forefinger, when he cast his eye on my father ; the sense of the ludicrous got the advantage of him, and he sent the orange at my father's head with such dexterity that, after hitting him on the nose, it bounded to the top of the room, with the result that all the party laughed merrily. Calculating the consequences, Culcairn took to his heels, while my father gave chase—down the lobby stair, out at the entry, twice round the court-yard, until at last Culcairn, scrambling quickly over the court-wall, got off. This facetious gentleman was heir to the estate of Foulis. He was also connected with George Ross of Cromarty ; and his son, had he lived, would have succeeded, on the death of the present baronet of Foulis, both to the estates of Cromarty and Foulis. Culcairn sold his paternal property to clear off incumbrances on the estate of Cromarty, and lived at Cromarty House, where he died in 1820.

Having finished his classical studies my father, on the death of my grandfather, removed from Ross to Strathnaver in Sutherlandshire ; his mother went with him. His sister Catherine was there before him, married to Charles Gordon of Pulrossie. They took up their abode at Clerkhill, in the immediate vicinity of the Parish Church of Farr. Charles Gordon was a native of the parish, descended from that branch of the clan Gordon which originally came to Sutherland along with Adam, Lord Aboyne, second son of the Earl of Huntly. The place of Clerkhill he occupied as a farm ; he was besides factor on the Reay estate, and an extensive cattle-dealer. He was twice married ; by his first wife he had no family. By his second wife, my father's eldest sister, he had three sons and two daughters. John, the eldest, succeeded to the family estate; William, the second son, lived after his return from the American war at Clerkhill, and George at the farm of Skelpig, on the north bank of the Naver. His eldest daughter, Fairly, married James Anderson of Rispond, in Durness. His younger daughter married an Englishman named Todd, and thus gave offence to her friends, as her husband was obscure and indigent. But in London Mr. Todd got into business, and afterwards became affluent.

Charles Gordon took a lively interest in my father's welfare, and, being one of the most influential men in the Reay country, he had much in his power. To his friendship and influence, under God, my father was indebted for every situation which he held in that country. His first appointment was that of parochial schoolmaster of Tongue, a situation which he held until he received license. When he went to Tongue his mother accompanied him. There she died, and was buried in the tomb of the Scouries.

The Reay country, or "Duthaich Mhic Aoidh," extending from the river Torrisdale to the arm of the sea dividing it from Assynt to the west, was the territory of the clan Mackay, of which Lord Reay was chief. When my father first came to reside in that country, Hugh, sixth Lord Reay, had, six years before, succeeded to the title and estate on the death of his brother George. In early youth he showed no symptoms of that weakness on account of which it was found necessary to place him under a tutor for the efficient management of his estate. He made progress in his studies, and had a great taste for music. When his intellect gave way, he was lodged in the house of a clansman, a relative of my father, James Mackay of Skerra, where he continued until his death, which took place in 1797. His first tutor was his paternal uncle, Colonel Hugh Mackay of Bighouse, second son of George, third Lord Reay. On his death, George Mackay of Skibo, his brother, and third son of George, Lord Reay, was appointed. It was during the tutorage of Mr. Mackay of Skibo that my father came first to the country as schoolmaster of Tongue. George Mackay was a man of note in his time, but choleric and hasty in his temper—a propensity which has markedly characterised the whole race of the Mackays. He was also improvident and extravagant, while his wife, the grand-daughter of Kenneth, Lord Duffus, was not more careful. To be, during the nonage of the proprietor of a large estate, what was usually called the "Tutor," was, in those days, tantamount to being the actual owner. Yet, with all this advantage, George Mackay of Skibo died a bankrupt. At his death everything went to the hammer, and so completely stripped was his family that his children were conveyed from the castle of Skibo in cruppers on the backs of ponies. Mackay of Skibo, during the minority of Elizabeth, Countess and Duchess of Sutherland, was returned member of Parliament for that county. His Parliamentary career was distinguished by a persistent taciturnity. How he came to be proprietor of Skibo I cannot say. I am inclined to think that it was a part of the property belonging to the Reay family within the limits of the Sutherland estate, and was gifted to him by his father. After the present Lord Reay succeeded to the inheritance of his ancestors, it is said that he could never pass the manor of Skibo, then in possession of the Dempsters, without shedding tears. "It would have been my principal residence," he used to say, "and would have suited me so well, had my father had but common sense." But his lordship was at least equally deficient in common sense, as the recent sale of the Reay estate so clearly proves. Col. Hugh Mackay of Bighouse was elder brother of George Mackay of Skibo, and preceded him in the tutorship. He became proprietor of the estate of Bighouse in consequence of an arbitrary stretch of chieftain power by his father George, third Lord Reay. The estate of Bighouse for four generations was the hereditary patrimony of a family of the name of Mackay, lineally descended from William, youngest son of Iye Mackay of Farr, chief of the clan. The last of the proprietors of this family was George Mackay of Bighouse, who had a son, Hugh, and two daughters, Elizabeth and Janet. Hugh their brother died young, and his surviving sisters became co-heiresses of the estate of Bighouse. Elizabeth, the elder, married Colonel Hugh Mackay, and Janet espoused William Mackay of Melness, the lineal descendant and representative of Colonel Eneas Mackay, a younger son of Donald, first Lord Reay. On the death of George Mackay, last laird of Bighouse, the estate came to be divided between his two surviving children, Mrs. Col. Hugh Mackay, and Mrs. Mackay of Melness. Lord Reay, however, got the property settled on the elder sister, to the exclusion of the younger. This proceeding was resented by William of Melness, and being a man of as much resolution as he was hot and choleric, he resolved not tamely to submit to the injustice. Having ascertained that his chief was at home, Melness armed himself with his claymore, secured by a strong leathern belt round his loins, to which was added a pair of loaded pistols. Thus accoutred Melness crossed the Ferry below Tongue, and directed his course to the residence of his chief. Demanding entrance he was admitted to the parlour. His lordship received him with smiles, begged he would be seated, and asked him the news of the day. "My Lord," said Melness, "I have come to demand at your hands my just rights. My wife is co-heiress of the estate of Bighouse, and I know," he added, raising his voice to a wrathful pitch, "I know that you have the titles in your possession, and that—that—you're scheming to denude me and my wife of our share that your son Hugh may have it. I'll not allow this; I demand the title-deeds and the will of my father-in-law." Lord Reay attempted to parry him off with friendly assurances. At length, Melness got furious. "My Lord," said he, "I am not now to be trifled with," and, striding to the room door, securely bolted it. "Take your chance," said he, "either produce the will and the title-deeds or take this," and pulling out his loaded pistol, he placed it full cocked within four or five inches of his lordship's breast. Matters had become serious, and the chief waxed pale. "Melness," he exclaimed, "since you must have the papers you ask, will you allow me to go for them, they are in the strong box in my writing-room above stairs?" Melness assented, and his chief walked out at the parlour door and tripped upstairs. His lordship, however, had no sooner put a strong door doubly bolted, and a double pair of stairs between him and his kinsman, than he took other measures. Opening the window, he called to his footman, whom he

saw in front of the house, instructing him to request Mr. Mackay of
Melness, whom he would find in the parlour, to come out and speak to
him. The message was delivered, and on Melness making his appearance in the close, Lord Reay called from the window, " William, go
home and compose yourself, the papers you'll never handle." Closing
the window, he put an end to all further conference. Lord Reay's son
got possession of the property, and his removal from the Reay country
to reside at Bighouse took place soon thereafter.* These occurrences
happened long before my father came to that country. William Mackay
of Melness flourished in 1727, and must have been dead either before
my father was born, or when he was a child. During my father's
residence in the Reay country, George Mackay of Skibo was, as tutor
of Reay, succeeded by his brother, General Alexr. Mackay, after whose
death, George Mackay of Bighouse filled the office, and continued to do
so until Lord Reay's death. The leading men in the Reay country
were all members of the clan Mackay, and descended from the principal
family. They held farms by leases, or on *wadset*, that is, until the
proprietor redeemed the land by paying up a sum advanced on mortgage.

The most distinguished of the Mackays of that age was "Rob
Donn" the poet. This unlettered, but highly-gifted, individual was
born in the year 1714, at Allt na Caillich, Strathmore, parish of
Durness. From his early years his rich and original poetic vein was
strongly exhibited. His poetry was the plant, not in its improved and
cultivated, but in its natural state, growing in its first soil, in wild and
inimitable simplicity. Even Burns himself, high as his claims are,
must yield to Rob Donn. Burns and all his great poetic compeers
could read and rightly estimate the poetry of others. Rob Donn could
neither read nor write. He stood alone. With a poet's eye he looked
into the face of nature. Nature in its fairest or in its most abject
forms, whether animate or inanimate, rational or irrational, was at once
his theme and his study. In his poetry there is a variety of subjects
embracing all the incidents of common life. His poetry is history—a
history of everyone and everything with which he at any time came
into contact in the country in which he lived. His descriptions do not
merely let us know what these things or persons were, but identify us
with them; we behold them not as things that were, but as things that
are. They are all made to pass in review before us, in their characters,
and language, and peculiarities, and habits. His Elegies open a
fountain of sadness. They bring us to the house of mourning, they
place us by the dead man's bed, and compel us to feel a sinking of heart
iu sympathy with every member of the family at the breach that has
been made, His love songs are chaste and inimitably tender. In his
satires every vulnerable p n , whether a moral deformity or a bodily
defect, is seized upon, laid bare, and subjected to the lash, every stroke
of which draws blood, and not one of which misses its aim. Unlike
many poets of eminence, he is the advocate of religion. Then and for
many years after his death, the only library in which his poems were

---

* Rob Donn, on that occasion, composed one of the ablest effusions of his poetic
muse. It is one of the most graphic and complete hunting songs in any language.

to be found was the memory of the people. When he composed a song, he no sooner sang it than, with all the speed of the press, it circulated throughout the country. An edition of his poems was published in 1829, under the revision of Dr. Mackay of Dunoon; but it is singularly defective. The editor was anxious to ·give Rob Donn universal publicity in the Highlands by correcting his Gaelic; but being, unfortunately, no poet himself, he, in his attempts to improve the poet's Gaelic, has strangled his poetry. My father, when schoolmaster of Tongue, met with the poet. He invited him to dinner, an invitation which was accepted. The poet was pleased with his fare and still more with his host, and, at parting, offered to make his entertainer the subject of a poem. This offer my father declined, aware of those high powers of satire with which his guest was endowed, and which, like a razor dipt in oil, never cut so keenly as when intermingled with compliment and praise. Rob Donn died in 1778, at the early age of sixty-four. A monument of polished granite was, by subscription, erected to his memory in 1829, in the churchyard of Durness, his native parish. A monument far more in keeping with the originality and simplicity of his character was placed upon his grave by his surviving friends soon after his decease—a rude, unpolished slab, containing no other inscription than the two emphatic words " ROB DONN."

That which chiefly distinguished the Reay country in my father's time was its religious society. The ministers who constituted the Presbytery of Tongue were eminent for piety. The minister of Farr, Mr. George Munro, a man of great worth and Christian simplicity, was married to my father's maternal aunt Barbara, third daughter of John Mackay, minister of Lairg, by whom he had a daughter Mary. She was, after her father's death, housekeeper to her uncle, Mr. Thomas Mackay, at the Manse of Lairg, and after his death, resided at Dornoch. Her father, Mr. George Munro, was one of the most-honoured and useful ministers of his day. Previous to his settlement at Farr, he was missionary at Achness in the upper part of the parish, and there he began his ministerial labours at an early age. When he first came among the people of the district they were disposed to " despise his youth." A pious man applied to him for baptism for his child. Mr. Munro came to the man's house to celebrate the rite. While preparations were making for the ordinance, Mr. Munro began to play with one of the children. He fenced with the boy with a rod which he had in his hand, and chased him round the room. The pious father was so shocked at this apparent levity, that he had almost resolved not to receive baptism at his hands. The service, however, was commenced, and before the conclusion Mr. Munro so clearly and scripturally· laid down the nature of the ordinance and the sum of parental obligations, that the man declared he was overwhelmed with shame that he ever allowed himself to harbour any unworthy suspicions of his visitor's ministerial zeal. His ministry at Achness and afterwards at Farr was signally blessed. Some of the most eminent Christians who subsequently made Strathnaver another Bethel were the fruits of it.*

* Mr. George Munro was ordained minister of Farr in 1754 ; he died in 1775, at the age of seventy-four.—ED.

Two other eminent members of the Presbytery of Tongue were Mr. John Thomson, of Durness, and Mr William Mackenzie, of Tongue. Mr. Thomson was a native of the parish of Avoch in the Black Isle. When settled minister of Durness, he was deficient both in Gaelic and in sound theology. The former defect he never overcame; not so, however, with regard to his theology. He had not been many years minister of Durness when it underwent a decided change. His doctrine, at first, had been a mixture of law and gospel, grace and good works, not, however, placed in their proper and scriptural relation. Rob Donn, in a poem which he composed on the clergy of a former generation—the predecessors of those who have been named—remarks that " one of them may be found who on Sabbath day will assert that Christ is our Saviour, but who a week after will declare that there is no profit but in works; at one time he will fly so high and, anon, he will creep so low that, being like neither a bird nor a mouse, he makes of himself a filthy bat."

> " Gheibhear fear dhiu, la sabaid,
>   Their gur Slanaighear Criosd dhuinne ;
>   'S their e, seachduinn o'n la sin,
>   Nach eil' sta ach an gniomh'raibh ;
>   Bheir e' iteagan arda,
>   'S ni e magaran iosal ;
>   'S o nach eun e 's nach luchag,
>   Ni e trusdar do dh'ialtaig."

Mr. Thomson at first preached in such a strain as this, and, having neither the powers of oratory nor of mind to shape his doctrines into a regular system, nor anything like intelligible language to convey it, his preaching was rejected by the pious and scoffed at by the profane. Having preached a sermon on one occasion at Eriboll, a place within the boundaries of his parish, some of the best and most eminent Christians among his hearers were highly dissatisfied. At a fellowship meeting held at the same place next day, at which Mr. Thomson presided, they resolved to give out a question bearing on his doctrine. It was taken up and discussed. Mr. Thomson saw their device, and, highly offended, dismissed the meeting. The attack, however, led him to reflect and to test his own views by the Scriptures, the result being that, after many private conferences with his co-presbyter, Mr. William Mackenzie, he retracted his erroneous opinions, eagerly embraced the gospel, and preached it to his people. He became thereafter a zealous and devoted servant of Christ, and, to the close of his life, was a most exemplary pattern of that " simplicity and godly sincerity " by which the Spirit of Christ is most clearly manifested. He died in 1811, and was succeeded by his son-in-law, Mr. William Findlater, who was inducted in 1812.*

. * Mr. John Thomson was a man of great Christian simplicity, but very peculiar in his manner. When he preached, or when he expressed himself keenly in any argument, he had an odd habit of spitting in his fist. His powers of utterance, especially in the Gaelic language, being very limited, he made much use of his hand when he spoke to enforce what he did say. He was the immediate successor of Mr Murdoch Macdonald, the patron and warmly-attached friend of Rob Donn, with whom, however, Mr. Thomson was by no means such a favourite. The bard, though

In 1769 Mr. William Mackenzie succeeded Mr. John Mackay as minister of Tongue. Previous to his settlement in that parish he was missionary of Achness, having succeeded Mr. Munro of Farr in that charge. He was a lively, eloquent preacher of considerable talent and fervent piety, also of a fine personal appearance. He was much beloved at Achness, and no less so by the parishioners of Tongue, among whom he laboured for upwards of sixty years. While at Achness he married Jean, daughter of the Rev. William Porteous of Rafford, a near relative of the eminent John Porteous of Kilmuir-Easter in Ross-shire. She was a woman of considerable accomplishments, and a great talker. Her husband was also rather loquacious, and, when they were both present, whether at their own hospitable board or elsewhere, conversation was not allowed to flag. They not only engrossed the whole of it, but went full tilt against each other, for the purpose of talking one another down, especially when they both resolved to tell the same anecdote. It was the practice in those days for the people to bring presents to the minister, consisting entirely of eatables, such as butter, cheese, and mutton. Mr. Mackenzie was loaded with such gifts. On one occasion, when he was at Achness, as he used to relate, he had gone out in the forenoon to visit his people. Upon his return he came in to witness an amusing spectacle. The floor of their little parlour at Achness he found covered with six wedders, each of which was flanked with parcels of fresh butter, cheese, and baskets of eggs. Six honest housewives, the donors and bearers of these presents, were placed, side by side, on a form close by the wall. His wife stood in front of them, and laboured hard to do the honours of her house. It was, however, rather a puzzling task. She could speak no Gaelic, and not one solitary syllable of English did they know. But she was determined not to stop at this rather formidable obstacle. She produced meat and drink, the best the house could afford, and began and ended the repast by a round of kisses, beginning at the first and ending at the last of them, being the only way by which she could make them to know that they were heartily welcome to their lunch, and that she was grateful for their presents. Coming to her relief, Mr. Mackenzie spoke to them in language which they could better understand.*

As a teacher, my father had three distinguishing qualities—assiduity, fidelity, and, I must add, severity. The last of these arose from a hasty temper and his own early training. My father's temper was hot, but it was connected with that generosity which makes kind-hearted, hasty men the favourites of those who personally know them. His natural heat of temper too was the more formidable inasmuch as it was combined with a more than ordinary measure of personal strength. He was six feet one inch in height, with great breadth of chest and shoulders. To his scholars therefore his temper when ruffled was no trifle. Let me do him only justice, however, by saying that, it was

prejudiced against Mr. Thomson, could not but respect him. But the brother of the minister could not escape the wit of Rob Donn ; one of the bitterest of his satires is hurled at the head of poor Lewis Thomson.

* Mr. William Mackenzie was admitted to the parish of Tongue in 1769; he died in January 1834 at the age of ninety-six, in the 67th year of his ministry.—ED.

never called forth but by carelessness, disobedience to authority, or vice—in short, by any of those things which thoughtless youth are so ready to throw as obstacles in the way of their own progress or improvement. To remove these obstacles he subjected his pupils to strict discipline, and the heat of temper with which he did so was expressive, not of any ill-will towards the offenders, but of anxiety that the ends of discipline should be secured. On one occasion his severity excited a mutiny. His pupils combined to pay back in kind some very hard knocks which some of them had received. In those days scholars were not invariably schoolboys. Many attended his school who were nearly as old as himself, and some of them of considerable strength. At the head of the conspiracy were, of course, the strongest of them. They had agreed that on the first occasion when any boy was flogged, a simultaneous attack should be made upon the master. The occasion they anticipated soon offered itself. One of the scholars was called up to account for some misdemeanours, and was convicted. But just as the master was in the act of inflicting punishment, the mutineers rushed out of their seats and attacked him. The onset was so sudden, and on his part so unexpected, that, for a moment, he offered no resistance. But his apparent passiveness was but as the calm which is the prelude to the storm. With his ponderous arm he dealt heavy blows on his assailants, and, in a few minutes, cleared the schoolroom. The lesson of subordination which he so impressively taught was not forgotten so long as he filled the office, and he received from his pupils ever afterwards an implicit obedience. One of the ringleaders was Hugh Mackay, a native of the parish of Tongue, who, in 1793, became minister of Moy, Inverness-shire. Mr. Mackay was known as a decided and deeply-exercised Christian. He was the intimate friend in Christian fellowship and ministerial labour of my uncle, Dr. Fraser of Kirkhill. He died in 1804, amidst the lamentations of his flock.

Though my father's severity was resented by some, yet he was a favourite with others, and indeed ultimately with all his pupils. After passing the usual preliminary trials before the Presbytery of Tongue, he was by them licensed to preach the gospel on the 2nd of April, 1779. He now resigned the school, and was employed for several years as assistant to the Rev. Alexander Pope, minister of Reay, which office he held until Mr. Pope's death in 1782. When he assisted Mr. Pope, he resided, in the capacity of private tutor, in the family of his relative, by the mother's side, and the principal heritor of the parish, George Mackay of Bighouse. Mr. Pope was a native of Sutherlandshire. His father was the last Episcopal minister of Loth, and he was the lineal descendant of Charles Pope, Episcopal minister of the parish of Kirkmichael, now united with Cullicudden. Another of his ancestors, William Pope, was precentor of the Cathedral of Dornoch, of whom Sir Robert Gordon, in his history of the family of Sutherland, supplies some notices. Alexander Pope was the eldest son of a numerous family of sons and daughters. He had been most liberally educated, and being himself a man of more than ordinary talent, he made a corresponding use of his advantages. He was an accomplished classical scholar, an intelligent antiquary, and was intimately conversant with science.* When a young man he became acquainted with his namesake, Alexander Pope, the poet. He went to England purposely to visit this celebrated man. Their meeting at first was rather stiff and cold, arising, it is believed, from his having taken the liberty of calling in travelling attire. After he had come in contact with the strong and well-furnished intellect of his Scottish namesake, however, the poet relaxed, and their intercourse became cordial. Their correspondence was kept up. A copy of his poems, published in 1717, the poet sent to his friend at Reay, which, at the auction of Mr. Pope's books, after his death, was purchased by Mr. Thomas Jolly, minister of Dunnet. Mr. Pope was settled at Reay in 1734. He was a man of extraordinary strength, fervent piety, and unflagging zeal. His parishioners, when he was first settled among them, were not only ignorant but flagrantly vicious. Like the people of Lochcarron, they were Episcopalians in name, but heathens in reality. Mr. Pope soon discovered that they required a very rough mode of treatment, and being from his strength furnished with a sufficient capacity to administer any needful chastisement, he failed not vigorously to exercise it. He usually carried about with him a short thick cudgel, which, from the use he was compelled to make of it, as well as from a sort of delegated constabulary authority he had from Sinclair of Ulbster, the Sheriff of the county, was known as "the bailie." One Sabbath evening, after preaching to a small audience, he sat down on a stone seat at the west end of the manse. About a hundred yards distant stood a small hut used as a tavern. Mr. Pope soon observed that the inn was better attended than the church had been, and discovered among those visiting it a number of his parishioners, whose little measure of sense and reflection was overpowered by the fumes of the liquor in which they had indulged. As he was revolving in his mind what he should do to break up this pandemonium, two stout fellows from the crowd moved towards him. On coming up, they said that they were requested by their companions to ask him to come over and join their party. Mr. Pope declined the invitation, and told them that, while he commended their hospitality, he was very much grieved at their conduct in thus employing the day of sacred rest, instead of engaging in the services which God had enjoined. He accordingly exhorted them to disperse. "You are most ungrateful," said the deputies, "to refuse our hospitality, and if you think that we are to give up the customs of our fathers for you, or all the Whig ministers in the country, you'll find yourself in error. But come along with us, for if we repeat your words to our neighbours they'll call you to such a reckoning that you will be wishing you had never uttered them." Mr. Pope told them that he spoke the truth, that the truth he would never retract, that he was accountable to God, and that, in the path of duty, he never saw the man, or number of men, that would daunt him. Hearing this the men set off at a round pace to join their associates. In a few minutes after their arrival the inmates of the tavern turned out, and Mr. Pope saw nearly a dozen

* Mr. Pope was an accomplished antiquary ; he contributed materials to Mr. Pennant, in relation to Strathnaver, Caithness, and Sutherland, was a writer for "Archæologia Scotica," and translated a portion of the "Orcades" of Torfæus.—ED.

strong, able-bodied men advancing upon him, not so drunk that they could not fight, nor yet sober enough to refrain from so doing. Guessing their intentions, Mr. Pope rose from his seat, placed his back to the wall, grasped "the bailie," and stood firm. The foremost of the gang held in his hands a bottle and glass. When within three feet of Mr. Pope, he deliberately filled the glass, asked the minister to drink, and told him that it would be far better for him to warm his heart with a glass of whisky than, by refusing, to risk the safety of his head. Mr. Pope refused, and again renewed his remonstrances against such practices on the Lord's day. This was the signal for battle. The fellow now threw the bottle towards the minister's head, when Mr. Pope prostrated him by a stunning blow with his baton. Three or four strong savages next came forward in turn to avenge the fall of their companion, but these, one after the other, succumbed under the weight of "the bailie" vigorously applied. The rest of the gang soon beat a hasty retreat, carrying with them their wounded companions.

Mr. Pope visited his parishioners, when first settled amongst them, in the disguise of a drover, pedlar, or stranger on a journey, asking lodgings and hospitality, which in those days were never refused even by the rudest. On one occasion, after partaking of hospitality, he by main force compelled his host to allow family worship to be conducted. When the poor man discovered that his guest was his minister, he was much impressed; ever afterwards he kept family worship himself, became a devout man, and was subsequently ordained as an elder. Mr. Pope chose as elders, not only the most decent and orderly, but also the strongest men in the parish, the qualification of strength being particularly necessary for the work which they often had to do, and which was performed on what Dr. Chalmers would have called the "aggressive principle." A very coarse fellow, occupying a small farm, kept a mistress, by whom he had two children. Cited to appear before the Session, he obeyed the summons, and, in a few words, made his statement of the case. Mr. Pope pointed out to him the sinfulness of his conduct, and insisted that, in conformity to the law and discipline of the Church, he should make a public profession of his repentance, by appearing before the congregation on the following Sabbath to be rebuked. "Before I submit to any such thing," said the farmer, "you may pluck out my last tooth." "We shall see," replied the minister, dismissing him. This Session meeting was held on a Monday, and it was agreed, before the close, that three of the strongest elders should repair to the farmer's house next Sabbath morning, and forcibly bring him to church. When Sabbath came this was done. The elders went to the man's house about ten o'clock, and, after a stout conflict, he was mastered, bound with a rope, and marched to church. One of the elders now went to Mr. Pope for further instructions. "Bind him to one of the seats before the pulpit," said Mr. Pope, "and sit one of you on each side of him till the service is finished." His orders were obeyed. At the close of the service, before pronouncing the benediction, Mr. Pope rose to reprove the offender. "You told us," said the minister, "that we might pull the last tooth out of your head before you would submit to be where you are, but," pointing his finger in scorn at him, and uttering one of the most contemptuous sounds with his breath between his lips, which can better be imagined than described, he added, " Poor braggart, where are you now ? " The address was in Gaelic, and the peculiar expression is given below.* The fellow duly served discipline, but the epithet applied to him on this occasion stuck to him for life, and to his family for several generations.

During the course of his ministry, many of Mr. Pope's parishioners advanced in the knowledge of the truth, and also in the arts of civilised life. Ale and whisky drinking was discontinued on the Sabbath evenings, though too much indulged in on week days. One evening the landlady of the tavern came to him with the complaint that six men from a distance, who had come in the forenoon, had continued drinking ever since, that they refused to leave, and were now fighting with each other, and that she was afraid they would break all her furniture, and set the house on fire. After reproving her for keeping so disorderly a house, Mr. Pope directed her to get a ladder and place it against the back wall of her dwelling, to fill so many tubs of water, leaving them at the foot of the ladder, and to await his coming. All this was done, and in about half-an-hour thereafter, when the topers were holding high carnival within, Mr. Pope, seizing one of the tubs, mounted the ladder, and, sitting astride the roof, removed some thatch and turf, and emptied the contents of the tub upon the Bacchanalians below. This was followed by a second and a third down-pour as quickly as Mr. Pope could be furnished with tubs of water from below, with which he was readily supplied by the active co-operation of the landlord and his wife. The consequence of this ready method with the drinkers may be easily conceived. Their coats were drenched, and, like as many bull-dogs under similar treatment, they let go their hold of each other and rushed out. Coming to understand, however, that the landlord and his wife had a hand in the matter, they were about to deal with them rather roughly ; but Mr. Pope had already descended from aloft, and, with " the bailie" in his hand, stood beside them. It was enough, they all scampered off.

Mr. Pope made an annual practice of visiting his people and catechising them. When thus engaged he sought particularly to impress on his parishioners, especially the heads of families, the duty of holding family worship, giving them directions how they should proceed, and, in his subsequent visits, questioning them whether they had or had not followed his directions. Coming to the house of one William Sutherland, at a place called Caraside, he questioned him on this important duty. Sutherland answered that he was not in the habit of keeping family worship, as he had no prayers, " but my goot parson," he added, " gin ye give me a twelvemonths after this day, by the time ye're coming roun' amang us the next year, I'll pe ready for you." To this proposal Mr. Pope agreed, and at about that time next year he called at Caraside. " Weel, minister," said Sutherland, " I'm

"Faire ! faire ort ! a mhic a' dùd ! càit' am bheil thu a nis ? " This contains one of those idiomatic phrases of one language which cannot be literally translated into another ; but it may be rendered thus :—"Shame ! Shame upon thee ! bragging on of a beggar ! where art thou now ? "

ready for ye now," and, without further prelude, he went down upon his knees, and uttered aloud a long Gaelic prayer. Scarcely had the last syllable ceased on his lips, when he started up again, and said, " Now, sir, what think ye of that?"   " O, my friend," Mr. Pope replied, " it will never do; you must begin again if you would learn to pray aright." Sutherland was amazed. " It won't do, do you say, sir; I have spent a whole year in making up that prayer, and rather than lose my labour, if it winna do for a prayer, I'll break it down, and make two graces of it."   And Sutherland was true to his word; to the day of his death the blessing before meat was implored in the words of the first part of his prayer, and thanks returned in the words of the second.

Mr. Pope was a rigid disciplinarian, so much so as to induce many, who had rendered themselves liable to discipline, to become fugitives from it. On one occasion he had, at the close of the service, to refer to an individual, who, from his conduct, had fallen under the ban of his Session, but dreading the severity of the tribunal before which he had to appear, had absconded. Mr. Pope was very indignant, and said that, hide himself as he chose, he would find him out; " yes," he added, " and should he go to hell itself, I'll follow him, to get him back." Mr. Mackay of Bighouse was in the church, and, after the service, he called at the manse. Addressing Mr. Pope, he said, " I have called upon you to-day, sir, to bid you farewell, before you set out on your perilous journey."   " What do you mean, Bighouse?" said Mr Pope.   " Oh, you told us to-day," said Mr. Mackay, " that you were to set out in pursuit of an evil-doer, and that you would follow him even to hell." " Don't jest, my good friend, on a subject that eternity will make serious enough," replied Mr. Pope; " hell is the place appointed, no doubt, for all evil-doers in eternity, but the ways of sin and its delusions are hell on earth, and if I follow the sinner, with the word of God and the discipline of the church, into all his attempts to hide his sin, I go to hell for him, and, if successful, from hell I shall be instrumental in bringing him back."

Towards the close of his life, Mr. Pope lost the use of his limbs, and, for some time, was carried to the pulpit in a sort of litter. His son James, who had gone through the usual course of study for the church, was licensed to preach, and was, in 1779, admitted as his father's assistant and successor. He was a young man of very superior talents, and of decided piety, and gave every promise of being the worthy successor of so good a father. But he died soon after his ordination, sorely lamented by his father and all the parishioners. It was in consequence of this that my father became his assistant, which he continued to be until Mr Pope's death in 1782.

When the parish became vacant m   father's friends made every exertion to procure him the succession.y The living was in the gift of the Crown, and due application was made by his friends, Mr. Mackay of Bighouse and Mr. Gordon of Pulrossie, warmly seconded by a great majority of the parishioners. These, however, were not the days of popular settlements, and the application was not successful. George Mackay, a ferryman at Bonar, had a son, David, who was a preacher, and this young man was recommended to Mr. Mackay of Skibo, the

tutor of Reay and Member for Sutherland, who made him his protégé.
Mr. David Mackay was, through his interest, presented to the parish,
and admitted minister of Reay in 1783. He was a worthy, pious man,
but, during his incumbency of fifty-one years, he was unable to effect
much good in his parish. Soon after his settlement he became an
invalid. He suffered from a nervous disorder which, though it did not
interfere with his physical health, totally unfitted him for the discharge
of his ministerial duties with the exception of preaching every Sabbath.
He laid down some rules, however, whereby to regulate both his diet
and his hysical exercise, and, by a strict adherence to these, he
succeeded in turning his imaginary ailments into the most efficient
means of preserving his health and prolonging his life. He died when
upwards of eighty years of age.*

* Mr. David Mackay, minister of Reay, was noted alike for his piety and literary
industry. So early as four in the morning he commenced his studies daily. He was
particularly remarkable for fostering rising merit, and in bringing forward, from
humble life to stations of usefulness, young persons of ability. He died in 1835, at
the age of eighty-four years.—ED.

CHAPTER IV.

ALEXANDER SAGE IN DIRLOT, AND HIS CAITHNESS CONTEMPORARIES.

1784-1787.

M Y father was appointed in 1784 to the Mission of Dirlot, a wide and populous district within the boundaries of the parishes of Reay, Halkirk, and Latheron, and in the counties of Caithness and Sutherland. He officiated in turn at Dirlot, Strathhalladale, and Berriedale. His residence was at Dirlot, a most romantic spot on the banks of the Thurso river, which issues from a lake about twelve miles beyond it. This place was the property of his progenitor, John Mackay of Dilred in Strathy, who had obtained a . disposition to this and other lands in Caithness, from his brother Donald, first Lord Reay, in 1626, and in 1633, a charter of confirmation from John, Earl of Sutherland. The ruins of his castle consist of a small square tower standing on the top of an almost perpendicular rock jutting out into the river and nearly surrounded by it. Before the invention of gunpowder and the consequent use of artillery, it must have been impregnable. The savage wildness and extent of the district none but those who have seen it can accurately conceive. It extends from the shore of the Moray Firth to the ironbound coast of the Atlantic. The greater part was a heathy moor, full of quaking bogs, some of them extending ten and fifteen miles, and intersected with rapid mountain torrents, such as the rivers of Thurso, Halladale, Dunbeath, and Berriedale. The bogs were also studded with stagnant pools, some nearly twenty feet deep. It would be impossible for a stranger without a guide, to find his way through this region of mist and quagmire; and the only track, by which man or horse could be led, was along the banks of the rivulets, or on the tops of the small eminences by which the bogs were skirted. The breed of small horses then reared in the country showed a wonderful sagacity in threading their way through those dangerous morasses. These animals, in the coldest day in winter, unless during a severe snow-storm, were never housed; and when employed either in riding or bearing burdens indicated a know-ledge of the difference between hard and boggy ground which made a near approach to human intelligence. My father's house was a low, uncomfortable cottage of two rooms and a closet, not far from the old ruin of Dirlot. During his residence in the district he seldom rode on horseback. On foot he traversed the whole district, accompanied by his gillie or kirk-officer, and neither bogs, nor torrents, nor foul weather might arrest his progress. After preaching at Berriedale one Sabbath in spring, he cut across the mountains on his way homeward.   There was a rapid thaw, and the rivers were flooded.   When he came to the heights of Braemore the Berriedale river presented a formidable obstacle to his further progress.   It was over "bank and brae," and the stream, at the usual ford, raged and foamed and rushed with arrow speed.   The kirk-officer, who, according to custom, preceded him, no sooner cast his eye upon the flood than he made a dead halt.   "What is the matter now," said my father, coming up to him.   "O, sir," said the officer, "we must return; the big stone is two feet under water, and three men on the opposite side are waving their bonnets, warning us not to attempt the passage."   "What folly," said my father, and, seizing his attendant by the collar, he deliberately walked into the stream with him; then taking a diagonal course against it, amid the roaring of the torrent, and the warning and almost despairing shouts of the men on the other side, he pushed on, and, in less than ten minutes, placed himself and his gillie safely on the opposite bank.

I have often heard my father speak of those with whom he was on terms of intimacy during his ministry at Dirlot.   Marcus Gunn, his next neighbour, was a man of decided piety.   He lived at Dalmore, in the immediate neighbourhood, while his brother lived at Cattaich, also in the vicinity, and each had a large family of sons.   Marcus Gunn was lessee of the original estate of Dirlot, comprising Dirlot, Dalmore, Dalnaclaitan, Toremisdale, and Cattaich, and these pendicles of his farm he had sub-let to his own near relatives, presiding over them with all the simplicity and affection of a patriarch.   His lease he held of the laird of Ulbster, who, in the year that my father came to Dirlot, was created a Baronet as Sir John Sinclair.   Patrick, one of Marcus Gunn's sons, presented my father with a fine folio copy of Bishop Pearson's Exposition of the Creed, now in my possession.

Another of his acquaintances, Neil Macleod, lived at Braemore.   He had a good farm, and was one of the most substantial tenants in the county of Caithness.   He was subsequently appointed acting factor on the Braemore estate.   Moreover, he was a man of great personal strength, of much native humour, and of unbounded hospitality.   A native of Sutherlandshire, he in early youth left that country, and passed the rest of his life in Caithness.   An intimate acquaintance of his, Alexander Gordon, lived in his neighbourhood at Uäig, on the estate of Langwell, at the base of Scaraben, a high mountain which separates the estate of Langwell from that of Braemore.   Gordon was also from Sutherlandshire, and, like Macleod, was a very strong man.   In those days a sort of noisy feud subsisted between the Caithness Highlanders and those of Sutherland.   The embers of this quarrel were sure to be blown into a flame when the contending parties met at markets, and when, on such occasions, their tempers were heated by the ardent spirits which they drank immoderately over their bargains.   On one occasion, when a market was held at Dunbeath, an old feud between the Caithness and Sutherland men came on for decision.   The ringleaders in the fray were tenants on the estate of Swiney and Latheron.   These fellows had communicated their intentions to their landlord, Sutherland of Swiney, who, instead of checking them, went so far as to order some scores of hazel sticks from Inverness to furnish them with the means of attack. The business at the market had nearly closed when one of Swiney's tenants fastened a quarrel on Alexander Gordon, under pretence of having been unfairly dealt with by him in a matter of bargaining. From violent words they came to blows; Swiney's tenant struck Gordon with his cudgel, and this was the signal for a general onset. Gordon had no stick, and he was encumbered with the care of his son, a youth of nine, whom he held in his right hand. But forbearance was, in existing circumstances, out of the question. So, letting go his little son, he threw himself upon the foremost of his opponents, wrested his cudgel from his hand, and dealt out to him and two or three others such stunning blows as laid them prostrate at his feet. Their places, however, were soon supplied by others, and Gordon would have been overcome had he not, in his extremity, been observed by his stout friend, Neil Macleod. Placing themselves back to back, the two wielded their cudgels, striking down an assailant at every blow, until at last they got clear of the crowd, and their opponents surrendered. Macleod and Gordon came off with a few scratches, but a dozen of Swiney's tenants were carried home severely bruized. The case was tried before the Circuit Court, and the culpable part which Sutherland took in the matter being educed in evidence, he was so heavily fined as to be under the necessity of selling his estate. It was afterwards purchased by my uncle, Charles Gordon of Pulrossie.* From the manly and prominent part taken by Neil Macleod in this affray, and his successful defence of his friend, it was long afterwards known and remembered under the name of "Carraid Neil Mhicleoid," or "Neil Macleod's fight." He was twice married, and a son of his, by his second wife, was for a time minister of Maryburgh, near Dingwall [and afterwards of the Free Church in Lochbroom, in the west of Ross-shire.—ED.] Neil Macleod died at Berriedale in May 1814. His brother, James Macleod, kept an inn at Helmisdale.

Some of the members of the Presbytery of Caithness, during my father's residence at Dirlot, may also be named. Mr. Patrick Nicolson, minister at Thurso, kept a good table and stood high in favour of the gentry; but, in the discharge of his pastoral duties, he was certainly remiss and indolent. This inactivity laid him open to a severe censure by Rob Donn, the poet. "And what is poor Mr. Thomson doing among you?" asked Mr. Nicolson of Rob Donn. "Why, parson," replied the poet,, "Mr. Thomson is doing what you never did—he is doing his best." Mr. Nicolson inherited a small property from his father, whom he also succeeded as minister of Thurso; but his affairs got deeply involved, and the place was, after his death, sold for the behoof of his creditors.†

* Consequent on a long course of industry, Charles Gordon found means to acquire the lands of Pulrossie. He afterwards sold them to Mr. Dempster of Skibo, and in 1789 purchased, for £5500, the estate of Swinzie, or Swiney. The conveyance was taken to John Gordon, eldest son of the purchaser, who was represented by five sons and two daughters. By John Gordon, great-grandson of the original owner, the estate of Swiney was sold, in 1877, to the Duke of Portland.—ED.

† Mr. Patrick Nicolson, minister of Thurso, died on the 17th January, 1805, in the 48th year of his age, and 19th of his ministry.—*Ibid.*

Mr. John Cameron, minister of Halkirk, was my father's next neighbour and colleague, so that they frequently met. The same spirit of drollery, which he exhibited as a student of divinity, continued to be his characteristic feature when a minister. He married a Miss Lee, who was a governess in the family of George Sinclair of Ulbster, and who was recommended to Cameron by Lady Janet Sinclair, mother of Sir John. She was no beauty, and Cameron admitted that he married her simply because Lady Janet wished him to do so. One day, as he was writing an important letter, his wife looked over his shoulder and read what he had written. Aware of this, he dashed off the following couplet :—

> " Cameron is a pretty fellow;
> But, O, his wife ! she's dun and yellow."

On perusing this Mrs. Cameron went off in high dudgeon, and her husband was allowed to finish his epistle at his leisure. Mr. Cameron had a strong vein of poetry, particularly in the department of satire. Mr. Robert Mackay, a writer in Thurso, who published a history of the clan Mackay, carried on a poetical correspondence with Cameron, in which, after a "keen contention of their wits," and a most bountiful interchange of personal abuse, Mackay was worsted, and gave up the contest. Mr. Cameron had an only daughter, to whom he was very much attached, and he gave her every advantage for her improvement. She was a very elegant woman, and was married to James Dunbar of Scrabster, but did not long survive her marriage. In his ministerial capacity Mr. Cameron was a failure; his habitual levity effectually prevented any good being done by his ministrations.[*]

My father enjoyed some intimacy with Mr. Joseph Taylor, minister of Watten.[†] He was translated from Watten to Carnbee, in Fife, in 1805, by Sir Robert Anstruther of Balcaskie, who about that time became a proprietor in Watten parish. In the living of Carnbee he was succeeded by his son, the Rev. Anstruther Taylor.

Another of my father's friends when at Dirlot was Dr. John Morison of Canisbay, well known as a man of letters and a poet. He composed some of the most beautiful of our scripture paraphrases, such as the 19th, 21st, 27th, 28th, 29th, 30th, and 35th. He was a first-rate classical scholar, and possessed literary attainments of a very high order. Several poetical pieces he published in the "Edinburgh Weekly Magazine," with the signature of Musaeus. As a preacher, he was eloquent; but, as a divine, his theology was superficial and undecided. A native of Aberdeenshire, he was born about the year 1749, was settled in Canisbay in 1780, and died on the 12th June, 1798, in the 49th year of his age, and 18th of his ministry.

[*] Mr. John Cameron, minister of Halkirk, died 9th December, 1821, in his 88th year, and 53rd of his ministry.—ED.

[†] An alumnus of Marischal College, Mr. Joseph Taylor was ordained minister of Watten in 1779, and was translated to Carnbee in 1805. He died on the 29th November, 1815, in his 76th year. He married, in 1779, Jean Ross, eldest daughter of Duncan Forbes Ross, of Kindeace and niece of Lord-President Forbes. His grandson was the celebrated anatomist, Professor John Goodsir, of the University of Edinburgh.—*Ibid.*

With Mr. Alexander Smith, minister of Olrig,* my father had but little acquaintance. He was a very eccentric man, and his conduct, though unexceptionable, was somewhat defficient in consistency. His widow long survived him, and towards the close of her life was totally blind. Two of his sons became ministers in Caithness, William, who succeeded Mr. Oliphant at Bower, and James, who succeeded Dr. Morison at Canisbay.

During his residence at Dirlot, my father became a married man. On the 19th of March, 1784, he wedded Isabella, eldest daughter of Mr. Donald Fraser, minister of Killearnan, and afterwards of Urquhart, in Ross-shire. Their marriage contract, in the form of a letter addressed to her brother, Dr. Alexr. Fraser, by my father, thus proceeds :—

ALCAIG, 15th March, 1784.

REVD. DEAR SIR,—As your sister, Miss Isabella Fraser, and I have agreed to enter upon the married state, from a principle of mutual love and affection, and as I am not as yet possessed of an Established Church benefice with which to provide her as I would wish, I hereby oblige myself to bequeath to her all the subjects and effects belonging to me in case I should die before I am provided with a stipend on the establishment. I also hereby exclude any other person to intermeddle with any part of my subjects except the above Miss Isabella Fraser, my intended spouse alenarly. For the further security, I also bind myself to extend this security on stamped paper any time required. As I grant this, my obligation, from my special regard for your sister, so I hope she will be pleased to give a similar security to me in case I should survive her, and I am, Revd. dr. Sir, your mo. obedt. Servt.,

ALEXANDER SAGE.

I, the above-designed Miss Isabella Fraser, in consequence of the affection expressed for me in the above letter, do bequeath to Mr. Alexander Sage, my intended husband, all my effects that shall pertain to me at my death, in case I shall predecease him, and exclude any other person from intermeddling with them : in witness whereof I have subscribed these presents, at Alcaig, this nineteenth day of March, xvij. and eighty-four, in presence of these witnesses—Mr. David Denoon, minister of Killearnan, and Mr. John Grant, merchant in Inverness.

ISABELLA FRASER.

DAVID DENOON, *Witness.*
JOHN GRANT, *Witness.*

The marriage took place at Alcaig, a small farm in the parish of Urquhart, to which my maternal grandfather's widow and surviving family went to reside after his death. The union was solemnized by my grandfather's eminent successor, the Rev. Charles Calder, and among the witnesses present were my maternal uncle, the Rev. Alexr. Fraser, D.D., of Kirkhill, the Rev. David Denoon, of Killearnan, and Mr. John Grant, merchant in Inverness. And here I would record some particulars of the excellent individuals with whom, by his marriage, my father became connected. Superior to them all, not only by reason

* Mr. Alexander Smith, minister of Olrig, died 19th Decr. 1784, aged 47, in the 23rd year of his ministry.—ED.

of seniority in years, but also in gifts and graces, was my mother's father, the Rev. Donald Fraser. He was a son of William Fraser, a substantial tenant in the parish of Petty, near Inverness. The precise year of his birth I am not able to ascertain; it might be about the year 1711. During his attendance at College he was introduced to the chief of his clan, the well-known Simon, Lord Lovat, to whom he so strongly recommended himself by his capacity and acquirements that he made him private tutor to his sons, the late General Simon Fraser of Lovat, Archibald who succeeded him, and a third son who died before he attained to manhood. During my grandfather's residence in Lord Lovat's family, his time was spent partly in Edinburgh and partly at Beaufort Castle. It so happened that, when my grandfather and his pupils were in Edinburgh Lord Lovat was at Beaufort, and when they were at Beaufort his lordship was in Edinburgh. This must have arisen from his lordship's arrangements, but it certainly was not owing to any dislike to his tutor, or unwillingness that he should reside under the same roof with him. I mention the circumstance because it gave rise to a correspondence between them, which is preserved, and is in possession of the Frasers, ministers of Kirkhill, and lineal descendants of Mr. Fraser. The correspondence shows what Lord Lovat was at his own fireside, and exhibits him as possessing a shrewd and penetrating apprehension of what was right both in principle and conduct, as well as an anxiety that his sons should be trained up accordingly.

When my grandfather, after finishing his theological studies, was licensed to preach, his abilities speedily recommended him to public acceptance. The parish of Fearn in Ross-shire, becoming vacant, the parishioners, along with some of the heritors, made a joint application on his behalf, and they were on the eve of success, when suddenly, and from a quarter artfully concealed, arose a strong opposition. This opposition was based upon certain alleged irregularities, which were at once preferred against him before the local Presbytery. One witness only was brought forward, a woman, whose statements were proved to be false by an *alibi*. The charge was accordingly dismissed, but he lost the parish of Fearn, which was meanwhile given to another. In his letters to my grandfather Lord Lovat pretends to be very angry at this. He abuses the Fearn heritors, and expresses his determination to sift the matter to the bottom, adding that, "when the defamer of his dear Donald is found out, he would bring him to punishment though it should cost him a thousand pounds." Now Lord Lovat would have found himself in rather an awkward plight had the originator of the calumny been actually unveiled. For when the truth came out at last, it was ascertained that the instigator of the plot was none other than Lovat himself, who adopted this course in order to secure his tutor's services to his sons during the years of their minority.

On the 27th of March, 1744, my grandfather was ordained, by the Presbytery of Chanonry, minister of Killearnan. Three years thereafter, that is on the 8th day of June, 1747, he married Jean Fraser, daughter of Alexander Fraser, minister of Inverness. This Alexander Fraser, himself an eminently pious man, was son-in-law of a minister still more eminent, Mr. Angus MacBean, minister of Inverness. Mr.

MacBean,* whom it is refreshing to me to claim as my great-great-grandfather, was one of the many bright lights of the Church at the close of the seventeenth century. He was born in the year 1656, and was settled minister of Inverness in 1684. The subject of a popish sovereign, and an eye-witness of James's insidious efforts to restore Popery, Mr. MacBean bore an undaunted testimony against it; and, finding that even within the limits of his own charge at Inverness were to be found the abettors of Popery, he considered it his duty to resign his charge. This decided step surprised some, offended others, and filled all who derived benefit from his ministry with sorrow. After resigning his charge he preached in his own house to crowded audiences, and very soon thereafter he was cited before the Privy Council, and charged with insubordination and treason. After a long and grievous imprisonment, under which his bodily constitution, always weak, finally sank, he was, on the accession of William and Mary, at the Revolution of 1688, liberated, and restored to his charge. He died in Edinburgh in February, 1689, at the age of 33. A brief account of him, drawn up by Mr. Stewart of Inverness, was transmitted by Mr. Alexander Fraser at Urquhart to Wodrow the historian, on the 5th of August, 1723, and is published in the edition of Wodrow's History.

By his first wife, my grandfather had three sons and three daughters. Simon, born on the 4th April, 1748, went to India, and died at Calcutta in 1770. Alexander, the second son, born on the 4th of July, 1749, I shall notice afterwards. Isabella, the eldest daughter and my mother, was born on the 14th of January, 1751. Marjory, the second daughter, born on the 2ud April, 1752, married Mr. John Fraser, minister of Kiltarlity in 1773. They had a son and three daughters. The daughters emigrated to America. Donald, the third son, was born on the 10th December, 1756. During my grandfather's ministry at Killearnan, several occurrences served to distress his mind, and to impair his usefulness. The first was the rebellion of '45' in which he got involved in consequence of his personal connection with Lord Lovat. The artful part taken by Lovat in the national drama was as revolting to my grandfather's feelings as it was ruinous to Lovat himself. To my grandfather his conduct was wholly unexpected. He knew him to possess an ordinary share of sagacity; and therefore that he should have risked his family interests, his title, his standing as a chief, and his estate, not to say his head, in a political speculation was what, from his previous knowledge of him, Mr. Fraser could not conceive possible. Nothing, therefore, gave him more heartfelt sorrow than the sweeping ruin with which this unfortunate man was at last overwhelmed. His amiable and attached pupil, General Fraser, whom my grandfather had so carefully instructed in the principles of religion and loyalty, the

---

* Mr. Angus MacBean was arraigned before Arthur Ross, archbishop of St. Andrews, and eight presbyters, on the 27th February, 1688. When his health began to suffer by the imprisonment to which he was subjected, bail to the extent of a thousand merks was on his behalf offered by Sir Robert Gordon of Gordonstown and Duncan Forbes of Culloden, father of the Lord-President. The offer was declined ; and his liberation refused, but he was released by a mob in the following December, on the retirement of the Lord Chancellor, the Earl of Perth.—ED.

infatuated father compelled to head the clan, and lead them forth in arms against the laws and liberties of their country. When the political air-bubble burst on the field of Culloden, and when a Government, at first panic-stricken, but afterwards triumphant, entered upon the work of legal vengeance, my grandfather saw, with the acutest anguish, his aged chief dragged from his hiding-place, and hurried off to London, his castle burnt, his estate forfeited, and the wretched man himself, though at the utmost limits of human existence, put to death on the scaffold. Of this fearful consequence my grandfather had often warned him, but to no purpose, and two letters are to be found in his correspondence with Lovat, one to the father and the other to the son, full of the most earnest, forcible, and affectionate remonstrances with them both, on the dangerous courses they were pursuing. This most melancholy breaking-up of a family to whom he had such strong ties of natural affection bore heavily upon his mind, and rendered his residence at Killearnan, within view of the blackened ruins of the castle of the deceased chief, very painful to him.

Another circumstance, which did not contribute very much either to my grandfather's personal comfort as a man, or to his moral weight as a minister, was the active part he took in the extinction of a parish. The heritors of Scotland, in those days, were very active, not in extending the church, but in curtailing it. They did this wherever an opportunity offered. The parishes of Suddie and Kilmuir Wester were small, and that the heritors might not be burdened with the payment of a stipend to each minister, they entered into a plan by which the two parishes were to be united into one. This plan was readily countenanced by the Presbytery, and by none of the members more so than by my grandfather who was clerk. The Presbytery records on the subject are all written out in his own hand and occupy many pages. After this transaction he did not remain any time at Killearnan. He had little reason to be satisfied with the people of that parish. They were ignorant and obstinate, and although he was a powerful preacher, and unwearied in the exercise of all his pastoral duties, he found himself most unsuccessful in regard to the great end of his ministry. His health, too, was indifferent. His particular complaint was somnolency, which, before he left Killearnan, had reached such a height that, when in the pulpit, he often fell asleep between the singing of the first psalm and the prayer which followed. In what this singular ailment originated is not known; the country people ascribed it to witchcraft, and he himself thought so too. The tradition is that, in the public exercise of ministerial duty, he had given offence to two women in the parish who were dreaded as witches, and that they had, according to their diabolical art, made a clay effigy of him, laid it in the dunghill, and stuck it round with pins. On this Mr. Fraser got ill, and felt pains in his body which terminated in somnolency.*

In 1756, the neighbouring parish of Urquhart or Ferintosh becoming vacant, my grandfather, after an incumbency of thirteen years at Killearnan, was translated thither, and inducted by the Presbytery of

* Somnolency was formerly a common complaint in Scotland among those who lived in the fens and marshes. In some families the tendency became hereditary.—ED.

Dingwall on the 2nd of June, 1757. His ministry at Urquhart was more pleasant to himself and profitable to the people than at Killearnan. He very soon recovered his health. His stipend was very small, and, to increase it for the benefit of his family, he was induced to take on lease, from the proprietor of Culloden, the mills of Alcaig in the vicinity. This step did not please the parishioners; they thought it rather incongruous that the minister should also be the parish miller. One day he met with a parishioner, on his way home from Alcaig, a shrewd though quite an illiterate person. "Well, Thomas," said the minister, accosting him familiarly, "how are you, and what is your news?" "Very bad news indeed," said Thomas, "I am informed that our minister's wife has taken up with the big miller of Alcaig." My grandfather understood the innuendo, and so keenly felt the reproof, that, on his return home, he sent to the proprietor a resignation of his lease. In June, 1757, his daughter, Jane Forbes, was born. She married a man named Fraser, and had issue. One of her daughters, Margaret, wife of a sergeant in a Highland regiment, I recollect to have seen at Kildonan about the year 1799.

At Urquhart, or Ferintosh, as it is also called, my grandfather's ministry was much blessed. He was the honoured instrument of raising up some of the most eminent Christians in the north. Mr. Donald Mackenzie, for many years Society schoolmaster in the west end of that parish, was, at an early age, brought under the power of the truth through his preaching. He died at the age of ninety, having lived long enough to be a hearer of Mr. Donald Fraser's son, grandson, and great-grandson. After sixteen years of ministry at Urquhart, my grandfather died on the 7th of April, 1773. His son, Dr. Alexander Fraser, was settled minister of Kirkhill, Inverness-shire, about a month afterwards.

Of him I have some recollection, not from personal knowledge, but from that hearsay which so copiously flowed from his "praise" which "was in all the churches." I will relate a remarkable occurrence connected with his boyhood. A fierce cat had broken into the manse cellar at Urquhart, and committed great depredations. My uncle resolved to destroy the animal, and accordingly he and another boy of his own age pursued the creature, and having got it into a place whence it could not escape, they pelted it with stones until it was apparently dead. That night my uncle and his companion occupied the same room. For some reason his companion was unable to sleep, and, about an hour after he lay down, he heard my uncle's hard breathing as if in sound sleep, but this was followed by a stifled groan. Becoming alarmed, he got up, and, guided by the moonlight, walked towards my uncle's bed. There, to his horror, he saw the cat they had left for dead close at my uncle's throat, and in the very act of planting her fangs in it. He seized the animal, and strangled it.

Dr. Alexander Fraser was settled minister of Kirkhill in 1773. A Mr. George Mark had, on the death of the former incumbent, been presented to the living; but, owing to his ignorance of Gaelic, he was set aside, and by the choice of the people my uncle was appointed. As a preacher, Dr. Fraser was much approved. I have heard an intelligent hearer of his, who himself became afterwards a very distinguished preacher, say that he never felt more convinced of the infinitude and unfathomable depth of divine truth than under the preaching of Dr. Fraser of Kirkhill. He was an honoured and successful pastor as well as an able preacher. His literary remains are contained in two octavo volumes, and a small pamphlet. He was deeply versed in the higher walks of theology, profoundly read in Scripture truth, and an enlightened and judicious enquirer into prophecy. On the unfulfilled prophecies he wrote an admirable treatise, which he published in 1795, entitled a "Key to the Prophecies of the Old and New Testaments which are not yet accomplished." This work is now out of print. His "Commentary on the Prophecy of Isaiah, being a paraphrase with notes, showing the literal meaning of the Prophecy," was published in the year 1800, at Edinburgh. It is dedicated to Bishop Hurd of Worcester. None of his sermons have been published except one, which he preached at Tain, on the 27th August, 1800, at the opening and first institution of the Northern Missionary Society. My uncle united with his mental studies much bodily exercise. Kirkhill he found a wilderness, but, being a man of great taste, he left it an Arcadia. About the age of fifty, his health began to decline; this was ascribed by some to a fall which he got. However that might be, from being rather stout in bodily habit, he suddenly fell off, and became thin and spare, and without experiencing any pain, he lingered about three years after this, when his life and labours were finally closed on the 13th of January, 1802, in the 53rd year of his age, and 29th of his ministry.* He was succeeded in the living of Kirkhill by his son Donald.

After his marriage, my father continued missionary minister of Dirlot for some three years. During that time, two children were born to him, viz., Elizabeth, on the 7th December, 1785, and Jane, on the 21st of March, 1787.

* In the "Diary of James Calder, minister of Croy," an eminent contemporary, is the following passage:—"On Saturday young Mr. Fraser preached—a pious youth, greatly acceptable to the Lord's people—the son, the grandson, the great-grandson of eminent ministers of Christ. '*Filius, nepos, pro-nepos pastorum piissimorum Christi.*'"—ED.

CHAPTER V

ALEXANDER SAGE; HIS SETTLEMENT AT KILDONAN.
THE PRESBYTERY OF DORNOCH.

1787.

ON the 10th of May, 1787, my father was settled minister of Kildonan, Presbytery of Dornoch, Sutherlandshire. The living was procured for him by the interest of his steady and tried friend, Charles Gordon of Pulrossie. I have been informed that, on the death of Mr. William Gunn, minister of Golspie, that living was first procured for my father by Mr. Gordon; but, on considering that my father was not, by his natural capacity, well fitted for so public a place, Mr. Gordon waived his claim in favour of Mr. Keith, then minister of Kildonan, and, upon his translation to Golspie, my father became his successor.

His settlement at Kildonan was not an harmonious one. The causes of this lead me to state candidly what I conceive to have been his personal character. He was the sincere and uncompromising enemy of sin in every shape and circumstance. It might present itself under all its palliatives, alleviations, and recommendations, but his hostility to it remained unchanged and inveterate. Then he had naturally a beautiful and inimitable simplicity of mind, which interwove itself into his Christian character. There was an artlessness in all he said and did which no one could have assumed. It was in this natural simplicity of mind, under the guidance of the Divine Spirit, that he received his views of Divine truth. In the confession of his faith, there was a simplicity, solidity, and connection, all of which were characteristic of the structure of his mind. But while I state this as my deliberate conviction concerning him, I must also mention some things which contributed to obscure his Christian character and to limit his usefulness as a minister. His piety, though genuine and vital, was slow in its growth; divine truth had made a saving impression upon his mind, but that impression was not, at its outset or during its progress, accompanied by any very deep convictions. Then, again, he was not a man of intellectual force. He comprehended a subject after much and laborious investigation, but his mental progress was slow and tedious. His apprehension, too, was neither quick nor far-sighted, and he was defective in the *ars loquendi.* He had a difficulty in finding words to express his ideas or to convey his meaning, and he had a timidity amounting to shyness, which often crippled him as a speaker. Public observation his mind shrank from, and the effect of it upon him frequently was to make him confused in expressing his thoughts. When he felt himself in this uncomfortable state of mind, words invariably failed him. When settled minister of Kildonan, therefore, his parishioners, especially those eminent for piety, received him coldly. I may mention specially some of those who led the opposition. The first was an old man, an elder, who lived at Kinbrace, about six miles to the north of the manse. The next was John MacHarlish, who lived at Kildonan, and who was afterwards one of my father's tenants. Another was an old man who lived at Ulbster on the Strath at Helmisdale, about four miles to the east of the manse. Of his opponents, the most indomitable was the eccentric John Grant, who lived at Diobal. The opposition which all these men gave to my father's ministry was of the passive sort. They never attended church, but on Sabbath held meetings of their own. They thus succeeded in alienating the minds of my father's parishioners from his ministry, and to this might be traced the beginning of that disaffection to the Church of Scotland which afterwards, in my native county, prevailed so largely. This opposition, however, was not so persevering as it was strong in its first outset; it ultimately died away. My father's natural disposition and manners were, to the great body of his parishioners, irresistibly taking, and, in addition to this winning disposition, he had also those personal attractions which never yet were overlooked by, nor failed to have their due influence over, the mind of a Scottish Highland Presbyterian. My mother was eminently pious. Combined with a mild, equable temper, she possessed a deeply reflecting and intelligent mind. In these respects, she was to my father, who was of a temper directly the reverse, a true "helpmeet." Their circumstances were limited, as the salary of the Dirlot Mission never exceeded £40, and at Kildonan the stipend was under £70. At the outset they had difficulty in getting along. Furniture for a larger house, stocking for a considerable glebe, and a farm of very great superficial extent, which my father took in lease, subjected them to a far heavier outlay than they were able adequately to meet. My mother, who, to her mild temper, united a degree of humour, used to say, "is bochd so, is bhi bochd roimh," which was synonymous with the adage, "out of the fire into the embers." My father, however, had the faculty of keeping out of debt. He did not indeed succeed in avoiding it altogether, but, notwithstanding all his difficulties, he never contracted a debt which he could not ultimately discharge. This was owing, not to any special shrewdness in the management of his affairs, but solely to a native honesty, which was the leading feature of his disposition. The natural heat of his temper, however, was troublesome both to himself and others. His parishioners were not unfrequently scorched by it, and my mother often had difficulty in checking its violence. Like the foam on the water's troubled surface, it appeared only again to disappear. No judgment of my father's principles could be worse founded than a judgment resting on the transitory ebullitions of his temper, which, although too easily roused, somehow or other were invariably excited on the side of truth. His parishioners knew this, and when the more judicious and reflecting witnessed such a triumph of "the old Adam" over him, they neither resented nor were much surprised at its brief outbreaks.

D

The members of the Presbytery of Dornoch when my father became connected with it were, his maternal uncle, Mr. Thomas Mackay, minister of Lairg; Messrs George Rainy, of Creich; John Bethune, of Dornoch; Eneas Macleod, of Rogart; William Keith, of Golspie; Walter Ross, of Clyne; George MacCulloch, of Loth; and William Mackenzie, of Assynt. At Lairg, Mr. Thomas Mackay was appointed assistant and successor to his father on the 17th November, 1749; and at the death of the latter, four years after, the whole care of the parish devolved upon him. Of deep and fervent piety, he was profoundly versed, not only in Scripture doctrine, but in its life-giving influence on the heart. Prayer and the study of the Scriptures constituted the occupation of his private hours. When he preached, every intelligent hearer could see that "because he believed, therefore he spoke." He was recognised as an earnest Christian when he was but a very youthful minister, and his ministry was signally honoured in being made instrumental for bringing many to the knowledge of the truth. Yet with these bright features of spiritual character, Mr. Mackay was uneven in his temper, dogmatic in his opinions, and in his judgments, severe and harsh. My father, who was of different disposition entirely, could never agree with him, and felt uneasy in his society. Mr. Mackay had a family of five. His eldest daughter, Catherine, married Captain Donald Matheson of Shiness, by whom she had a numerous family of sons and daughters. His eldest son, John, was one of the clerks to the Commissioners for India, and in their service he lost his sight and retired on a pension. He purchased the small estate of Little Tarrel in the parish of Tarbet, to which he gave the name of Rockfield. Mr. Mackay's second son, Hugh, was a captain in the Madras Native Cavalry, and agent for carriage and draught horses to the Indian Army under General Wellesley, afterwards Duke of Wellington. He was killed in the battle of Assaye, assigning the bulk of his fortune to his elder brother, John. Mr. Mackay's youngest son, William, was a sailor, and commanded a merchant ship trading to India. In 1795 he was one of the survivors from the skipwreck of the Juno, on the coast of Arracan, of which he published an interesting narrative. He died in 1804. The youngest daughter, Harriet, married Mr. George Gordon, minister of Loth, by whom she had five children. Mr. Mackay lived to be an old man. Towards the close of his life, and when unfit to engage in his public duties, he employed assistants. The first of them was a Mr. William Ross, who was very popular among the humbler classes. The people called him, by way of respect, a "Lump of Love," but the higher classes called him "Lumpy." He died minister of the Gaelic Chapel, Cromarty. Mr. Mackay's other assistants were the late Mr. James Macphail, minister of Daviot; the late Mr George Gordon, of Loth; and Mr Angus Kennedy. The last of these succeeded him in Lairg, but afterwards went to Dornoch. Mr. Mackay died in 1803.

My father's next co-presbyter, in point of seniority, was Mr. George Rainy, minister of Creich; he was settled there in 1771. A native of Aberdeenshire, the Gaelic was not his mother-tongue, and even after practising it during an incumbency of 45 years he could not easily get his mouth about it. He was a truly pious man, and if he was not successful in adding numbers to the church, yet he was an honoured instrument in watering and refreshing the people who were committed to his pastoral care. His great defect was his deficiency in the language which his parishioners best understood. In other circumstances this drawback would have been fatal to his usefulness as a minister. But Mr. Rainy was the very model of a sincere, practical Christian; he preached the gospel by his life more than by his lips. What his tongue failed fully to explain to his flock his everyday walk clearly conveyed; and when they connected together the doctrines which he taught in the pulpit, his personal intercourse with each, his zeal, his sanctified dispositions, and the warmth and overflowing tenderness of his heart, they forgot the liberties which he took with their language and listened with attention, because they were convinced that they heard the truth from the lips of one of its most faithful preachers. Mr. Rainy married a daughter of Mr. Gilbert Robertson, minister of Kincardine. Mrs. Rainy was pious, the impersonation of motherly kindness, the *beau ideal* of a minister's wife.*

The next member of the Presbytery whom I would mention is Mr. Eneas Macleod, minister of Rogart. His father I have already noticed as the author of "Caberfeidh," the Gaelic satire, and well known in his native parish of Lochbroom as a poet, by the name of "Tormaid Bàn," or the fair-haired Norman. Mr. Macleod of Rogart was his second son. His eldest son was Professor of Hebrew in the University of Glasgow, and bequeathed his valuable library to King's College, Aberdeen, of which both he and his brother, the minister of Rogart, were alumni. The latter was admitted minister of that parish in 1774. Mr. Macleod was not a popular, nor a very evangelical preacher. He had a rich vein of humour added to great penetration and solidity of judgment, and, though not himself a poet, he possessed a high taste for the art, and ardently patronised it. With Rob Donn he was intimate, and he committed to writing the poems of that bard from the poet's personal recital. It is to this manuscript that we are indebted for the edition of Rob Donn's poems, edited in 1829 by Dr. Mackay. Mr. Macleod married Jane Mackay, the daughter of a respectable farmer who occupied the place of Clayside, now a part of the extensive ducal manor of Dunrobin. This Mr. Mackay was a connoisseur in card-playing, and was therefore recognised among his associates under the name of "Hoyle." By his wife Mr. Macleod had four sons, Donald, William, Hugh, and Wemyss, and three daughters, Esther, Jean, and Elizabeth.

---

* Mr. George Rainy was licensed to preach by the Presbytery of Chanonry in 1763, was ordained by the Presbytery of Tain in 1766 to be missionary in Kincardine and Creich, and was admitted as minister of Creich, 2nd April, 1771. His marriage took place on 17th Nov., 1772. He died 18th Oct., 1810, in the 77th year of his age, and 45th of his ministry. Mrs. Rainy died 13th Aug., 1833. They had two sons, Prof. Harry Rainy, surgeon, of Glasgow University; and Mr. George Rainy, merchant, Liverpool; and four daughters, Margaret, who married Charles Stewart Parker, Esqre., London; Christian, who married Mr. Hugh Tenant, manufacturer, Glasgow; Isabella, who married Mr. Angus Kennedy, minister of Dornoch; and Ann, who married Peter Brown, Esqre., merchant, Glasgow. (See Dr. Hew Scott's "Fasti," &c.)—ED.

He died on the 18th of May, 1794, and was succeeded by the Rev. Alexander Urquhart.

John Bethune, D.D., minister, first of Harris, and afterwards of Dornoch, and son of Mr. Bethune of Glenshiel, my grandfather's contemporary, "ministear na tunn" (the barrel minister) was my father's co-presbyter for upwards of thirty years. He was translated from Harris to Dornoch in the year 1778. He married Barbara, daughter of Mr. Joseph Munro, minister of Edderton in Ross-shire, by whom he had five sons, John, Joseph, Matthew, Walter, and Robert, and three daughters, Christian, Barbara, and Janet. Dr. Bethune was an elegant classical scholar, a sound preacher, and one of the most finished gentlemen I ever remember to have seen. His manners were so easy and dignified that they would have graced the first peer of the realm, and his English sermons, which he always read, were among the neatest compositions I ever heard. In preaching in the Gaelic language, he used very full notes, as his mind was of that highly-intellectual character that it could not submit to, nor indeed be brought to work in, mere extempore or unconnected discussions. With all his other qualifications he had a delicate sense of propriety, and from anything, even the slightest word, come from what quarter it might, that touched upon this *terra sacra*, he shrunk back as from something positively loathsome. He was a model Christian minister in the eye of the world; but with all his natural talents and acquirements, with all his orthodoxy and sentiment, and with his high sense of moral propriety, before the keen glance of Christian penetration, he sank at once to a much lower level. To the anxious and sincere enquirer after truth, his sermons presented only a dreary prospect of cold and doubtful uncertainty.

Mr. William Mackenzie was settled minister of Assynt in 1765. He was licensed by the Presbytery of Edinburgh, and preached his first sermon in the pulpit of Dr. Hugh Blair. Settled as the pastor of a rude and semi-barbarous people, in a wild secluded district, instead of setting before them the right path by his precept and example, he too became as barbarous and intemperate as the worst of them. His exhibitions in the pulpit were not only lame and unprofitable but absolutely profane, calculated as they were to excite the ridicule of his audience. His excesses reduced himself and his family to great indigence. On one occasion his shoes were fairly worn out. It was Saturday evening, and he had not a decent pair to wear next day in going to church. He therefore despatched his kirk-officer with all convenient speed to a David Macleod, a shoemaker, who lived at a very considerable distance off, and who had made many pairs of shoes before for the parish minister without having received one copper in the way of remuneration. Next day, after delaying the service as long as he could, his bearer per express to the shoemaker not having returned, Mr. Mackenzie was obliged to go to the pulpit slip-shod as he was. In his sermon, such as it was, he 1   occasion towards the close to refer to some incident in the life of David, King of Israel. "And what said David, think ye, my hearers?" He was, in due course, about to answer the question himself, but just at that moment his bearer to

David, the Assyut shoemaker, who had returned, was entering in at the church door. Hearing the minister's question he shouted out, loud enough to be heard by the whole congregation, "What did David say?— he said indeed what I thought he would say, that never a pair of new shoes will you get from him until you pay the old ones." Towards the close of his life he became quite helpless, and an assistant and successor was provided for him in the person of Mr. Duncan Macgillivray in the year 1813. Mr. Mackenzie died in 1816, at the advanced age of 82.

Mr. William Keith, minister of Golspie, my father's immediate predecessor in Kildonan, was admitted minister there in 1776. Previous to his settlement in that parish, he was first a missionary in the county of Argyle, and afterwards assistant to Mr. Donald Ross, minister of Fearn. Mr. Keith, with whom I was intimately acquainted, gave me many anecdotes of Mr. Ross. His narrow escape from a sudden and violent death, through the gigantic exertions of Mr. Robertson of Lochbroom (am ministear laidir), had in his latter days considerably impaired his judgment. Mr. Keith was not many years his assistant when, on the death of Mr. John Ross, he was settled minister of Kildonan. He was a man of good ability and sincere piety. His ministry as well as his temporal circumstances at Kildonan were successful and prosperous. Eminently practical, his doctrine did not enter very much into theological details, but it was sound, scriptural, and edifying. He was on the best ministerial footing with his parishioners. The living was very small, but his wants were few. He lived frugally, and the parishioners filled his larder with all sorts of viands, such as mutton, eggs, butter, and cheese. He had also, as minister of the parish, the right of fishing in the river of Helmisdale to the extent of seven miles down its course. He married Isabella, daughter of Mr. Patrick Grant, minister of Nigg, and had seven children, Peter, William, and Margaret, born at Kildonan; and Sutherland, Elizabeth, Sophia, and Lewis, born at Golspie. Mr. Keith was not very active among his people, being of an exceedingly easy temperament. He was also of a very social disposition; this indeed he indulged in to a fault. Society, good living, and the luxuries of the table, although they never led him into any excess, yet presented such attractions to him as often brought him in undue intimacy with the worldly and profane. After Mr. Keith had laboured for some years at Kildonan, the parish of Golspie became vacant by the death of Mr. Gunn; he then applied personally to the patron, who presented him to the living. His departure was universally regretted by the parishioners of Kildonan, who were much attached to him.

Mr. Walter Ross was admitted minister of Clyne in the year 1777. He was the immediate successor of Mr. Gordon. His admission was opposed by the parishioners, who had set their affections upon a Mr. Graham, a native of Lairg, and known to be a godly man. The then Countess of Sutherland was an enemy of God's truth, and her practice was to appoint, to every parish in her gift, men who in every way brought reproach on the ministerial character. The Countess, there-fore, indignantly rejected Mr. Graham, and Mr. Ross, whose principles were in strict accordance with those of his patron, was presented. As a preacher, he was nothing at all, for the reason that his sermons were not his own. As the prophet's son said of the axe, when it dropped into the stream, so might Mr. Ross say of each of his sermons, " Alas, master, for it was borrowed." He had a Herculean memory, and he used to say that he had often privately read, and afterwards, for a wager, publicly preached the sermons of his clerical friends. His private character, as an individual, had no moral weight, for not only was his conversation light, worldly, and profane, but it was characterised by exaggeration and absolute untruthfulness. He completely understood the art of money-making, and none could exceed him in domestic and rural economy. He was a farmer, a cattle-dealer, a housekeeper, and a first-rate sportsman ; and he knew how to turn all these different occupations to profit. He took a Highland grazing at Grianan, on the river Brora, about ten miles to the north of his manse, where he reared black cattle, and sold them to great advantage. He resided here during the summer months, and preached on the Sabbaths, in a tent, to the inhabitants of the more remote districts of the parish. His skill in domestic management recommended him to the late Sir Charles Ross of Balnagown, and so entirely did Sir Charles give up to him the economy of his household, and so much was Mr. Ross engrossed with this, that he was an almost constant resident at Balnagown Castle, to the total neglect of his parochial duties. Mr. Ross was, in short, like not a few clergymen of his party in the church of that day, such a minister as Rob Donn, in his satire on the clergy, has so graphically depicted :—

> Falbh 'n an cuideachd 's 'n comhradh,
> 'Is gheibh thu mòran do 'n *phac* ud,
> 'Dheanadh ceannaich no seòladair,
> 'Dheanadh dròbhair no factoir,
> 'Dheanadh tuathanach sunndach,
> 'Dheanadh stiùbhard neo-chaithteach,
> 'S mach o 'n cheard air 'n do mhionnaich iad,
> Tha na h'uile ni gasd' ac'.*

Mr. Ross married, some years after his settlement at Clyne, Eliza. beth. daughter of Captain John Sutherland, the occupier of the farm of Clynelish in the vicinity of his manse, by whom he had a son and daughter. He died in 1825, aged about 74 years.

My father's next neighbour and co-presbyter was Mr. George Mac. culloch, minister of Loth. With this short, keen, argumentative old man my earliest recollections are associated. His youth was spent at Golspie, of which he was the parochial schoolmaster. A native of the Black Isle. Ross-shire, he understood the Gaelic language but imper. fectly. When at Golspie, he was the stated hearer of Mr. John Sutherland, who afterwards became minister of Tain. Mr. Sutherland was an eminently pious man, and a truly scriptural and orthodox

---

* Join their clubs and society,
You'll find most of the pack of them.

divine.* To the doctrines of free grace he gave a more than ordinary
prominence, but this, instead of converting the schoolmaster, only had
the contrary effect of setting him to reason against such doctrines, so
that he ultimately settled down into a bigoted and rationalistic system
of Arminianism. He married Elizabeth Forbes, daughter of the gardener at Dunrobin, by whom he had sons and daughters. His sermons,
both in Gaelic and English, were intensely controversial. His Calvinistic antagonist stood continually in his "mind's eye," like a phantom,
and to this fancied opponent he preached, but not to his congregation.
They were entirely neutral, and listened to his arguments and repelling
of objections very much after the manner of Gallio, who "cared for
none of these things." He argued right on, and while he wearied himself by the "greatness of the way," he came at last to exhaust the
patience of his hearers. No friend, lay or clerical, who might casually
visit him, could remain for two hours under his roof without being
dragged into the "Arminian controversy." As he advanced in years,
although age did not cool his combative propensities, yet his views of
divine truth underwent a gradual but most decided change. In his
latter days he was much confined to his room, and there, under the
sanctified influence of bodily suffering, he applied for strength and
and patience to the volume of inspiration. In these circumstances, his
his arguments were exchanged for deep reflection, the pride of intellect
for self-abasement, penitence, prayer, and self-enquiry. Into this
ethereal fire, the favourite "Arminian Controversy" was at last
thrown, and reduced to ashes. He died on the 27th December, 1800, in
the forty-fifth year of his ministry.

> Fit for pedlars or sailors,
> Fit for drovers or factors,
> Fit for active shrewd farmers,
> Fit for stewards not wasteful;
> Their sworn calling excepted,
> Fit for everything excellent.

* Mr. John Sutherland was translated from Golspie to Tain on 23rd June, 1752.
He died 25th Nov., 1769, in the 39th year of his ministry. He was intimately
associated with the eminent Mr. Balfour of Nigg in the remarkable revival of true
religion which, under God, by their instrumentality, took place in Ross-shire at that
period. He also boldly contended for the rights of the Christian people in the calling
of ministers. His father was Mr. Arthur Sutherland, minister of Edderton, a man
of kindred evangelical spirit, who died in 1708, aged 54 years; and his son was Mr.
William Sutherland, minister of Wick.—ED.

CHAPTER VI

THE TOPOGRAPHY OF KILDONAN.

1800.

MY father was not a land improver, and consequently the actual surface of the place did not undergo any very material change from the day of his settlement to the close of his incumbency. The glebe consisted of nearly fifty English acres. The manse and its adjuncts were situated at its eastern boundary. The body of the house was built after the unalterable model for manses in those days, which had "the usual number of chimneys, namely two, rising like asses' ears at either end, and answering the purpose for which they were designed as ill as usual"—they drew the smoke down instead of conveying it upwards. It contained also the usual number of windows, namely, in front three in the upper flat, and two below or one on each side of the principal door. On the east gable there was, on the upper flat, a solitary window which looked out from the drawing-room, or rather dining-room, for drawing-rooms in manses were almost unknown, and then a small window at the summit of each gable to light the garrets, very nearly approximating in size and appearance to the loophole of the ancient fortalice. They served in the apartments for which they were intended to make "darkness visible." The whole was built of lime and stone, and the roof covered with blue slate—a matter not worth noticing at the present time, but of no ordinary consequence then in a Highland parish twenty-four miles long by seventeen broad, where it was the only residence so constructed. The arrangement within exhibited the infancy of architecure. The partitions were all "cat and clay," plastered over with lime, and finished with a coat of "white-wash," which was so made up as to be communicative to every one coming in contact with it. The rooms, including the garrets, were eight in number, namely, a parlour, bed-room, and an intervening closet, with a small window to the north, in the lower flat. On the second flat were a dining-room, bed-room, and an intervening back-closet of similar dimensions with its neighbour below, but accommodated with a larger window; and on the attic storey were two garrets, the one fitted up as a bed-room, the other a long, dreary apartment without plaster, used as a place for lumber. Two low buildings stretched out in front from each end of the manse. That to the west contained the nursery, the kitchen, and the byre, divided from each other by "cat and clay" partitions which very soon gave way, and brought the human and bestial inmates of each apartment within eye-shot of each other. The east wing contained the barn and stable, divided by similar partitions.

From the barn-door to the east extended a small rude enclosure which served as a rick-yard, and, from the stable-door in the same direction, was another, used as a cattle-fold. A few yards to the north-east of the rick-yard stood a flimsy clay and stone building fitted up as a kiln. The whole of the office-houses were roofed with divot or turf, finished off with clay and straw, which, in process of time, by the action of the weather, in so far as the winds permitted, got an additional coating of green fog or moss. The heavy rains, however, penetrated these miserable roofs, from the first moment of their construction to the last stage of their decay.

When my father was settled at Kildonan, the church used was a small popish building, thatched with heather. At its west end was the burial place of the chiefs of the clan Gunn, "MicSheumais Chattaich," as they were styled, and who, under the Earls of Sutherland, ever since the middle of the thirteenth century, had held lands in the parish, where they also had their principal residence. Their mortuary chapel was a small building with a Gothic window, attached to the church, and entered by a low arched door. About a year after my father came to Kildonan, this venerable fabric was taken down, and a new church erected on the same site according to a plan by James Boag, a church architect of repute. The building may be described thus. The front wall contained two large windows, reaching from half a foot from the eaves to within three feet of the foundation. On each side of these windows were doors leading into the floor of the church, and, within two feet of each of these southern doors, were two small windows. In the gables half-way up the walls were the gallery doors, each surmounted with a window nearly its own size, and separated from it only by a lintel common to both. In the back wall was another door entering on the gallery, merely to obviate inner passages. These gallery doors were furnished with flights of outside stone stairs, which had no parapet, and, instead of being built close to the side of the wall, projected at right angles from it, in the manner of a ladder. As to the inner furnishing of the building, it was regularly seated, and the pulpit stood against the south wall, between the two large windows. It was in the form of a pentagon, and panelled.* Below it, one on each side, were the only two square seats, the rest, both in the area and in the galleries, were pews. The fronts of the galleries were also panelled; the front gallery was three, and the east and west galleries six or seven seats deep. Directly in front of the pulpit below stood the elders' seat, or "lateron," an area of considerable breadth, which ran nearly from one end of the church to the other, and was accommodated with a seat all along its north side, intended for the poor. The elders sat at the south side of it, and when the communion was dispensed, it was fitted up for the table services. The walls of the church within, as well as the roof, were unplastered, and there was neither bell nor belfry.

Nothing could exceed the simple beauty of the locality; art had

---

* This pulpit is still preserved in the old, but now disused, church of Kildonan. Worn deeply into the wood of its floor are two distinctly marked hollows formed by the motions of the feet of the minister, Mr. Alexander Sage, who, as described, was a man of great bodily weight and stature.—ED.

done nothing, but nature had done everything to make Kildonan one of
the sweetest spots in northern Scotland. To the north, and almost
immediately behind the manse, a chain of round heath-covered knolls
rose in close succession, and, having every possible variety of elevation
and shape, each, under the slanting rays of the evening sun, cast its
shadow most enchantingly on the other. They lacked nothing to make
them like an Arcadia but a clothing of oak or weeping birch. Each,
too, had its separate interest and particular tradition. The greater
number were tumuli, or ancient sepulchres, wherein reposed the ashes
of those mighty men of renown who fought and bustled in the world
about seven or eight centuries ago. The most remarkable of them
stands behind the manse, at a distance of about twenty yards from it.
It was called, "Torr-an-riachaidh" (or the "scratching knowe"), but
this was a modern appellative, given it from a few stunted whin bushes
which grew on its south side; its ancient name is lost. In shape, it is
a perfect cone, about sixty feet high, the circumference at the base
being about ninety feet. That it is a work of art, and not a mere
natural eminence, the eye at once perceives, notwithstanding that it is
wholly overgrown with a thick sward of grass and stunted heather. A
few years ago, the top was laid open, when it was found to consist of a
huge pile of stones. The only key to its history is a standing stone,
about a hundred yards to the west of it, on a small eminence, having a
rude cross cut on one side of it. This is called "clach-an-éig" (or the
"stone of death.") According to tradition, a bloody battle was here
fought between the aborigines of the country and the Norwegians, in
which the latter were defeated, and their leader killed. On the spot
where he fell this rude slab was erected, and his remains were buried
on the battle-field, and "Torr-an-riachaidh" reared over them. To the
west of this mound, and elevated nearly a hundred feet above it, stands
"Torr-na-croiche" (or the gallows' knowe), which has been so called
from the fact that two noted thieves, or cattle-lifters who, after committing great depredations in the Strath of Kildonan, had been overtaken by a body of the Earl of Sutherland's men in a narrow dell about
a mile to the north of it, were tried by his Lordship, as hereditary
justiciary for the north, condemned, and executed upon the top of this
knowe. The spot where the free-booters were seized is still called
"Clais-nam-meirleach" (or the "dell of the thieves"), while their graves
are visible at the foot of the gallows' knoll. The eminence then
stretches to the west, where it abruptly terminates in the steep declivity
called "Badaidh-na-h' achlaise" (or tuft of the armpit), close beside
which are two other tumuli resembling that which has been described.
They are called "Tullach-mòr" and "Tullach-beag," simply signifying
"the great and little hillocks." At the base of this ridge lie the low
lands of the glebe, stretching southward to the river Helmisdale, which,
by a bend in its course from N.W. to S.E., embraces the western part
of the glebe, called Dalmore. About thirty yards from the base of the
eminence just described stand the ruins of "Tigh-an-Abb'" (or the
"Abbot's house", and a few yards below them, and to the south, is
"Loch-an-Abb'" (or the "Abbot's loch"), a pool of standing water
formed by the rills which ran down from the heights, and which cannot

escape to the river. The ruin and the lake have been so designated from a remote period. By Bishop Gilbert Murray's charter, between the years 1222 and 1245, the chapter of the bishopric of Caithness, including the whole of Sutherland, was reconstituted. The chapter of this extensive diocese consisted of nine canons, five of whom were dignitaries of the church. The abbot of Scone was one of these canons, and the church of Kildonan, or Keldurunach, as it was then called, was assigned to the abbot as the sphere of his pastoral labours, provided that, when absent, a vicar should officiate in his stead. The abbots of Scone had the charge of the parish of Kildonan until 1688, when the Reformation put an end to their rule. The mansion long survived its ancient owners. It was a long monastic building, low in the walls and steep in the roof, which was covered with gray flag, taken from the neighbouring mountain, Beinn Thuairidh. The river of Kildonan was, however, the finest feature in the landscape, and to describe it is to describe the whole parish, as this beautiful stream runs through its extreme length, extending to thirty miles. The ancient name of the river, and that which is still retained in the language of the natives, was the "Uilligh." The name Helmisdale it receives from a small village on the north coast of the Moray Firth, nine miles south-east of the manse of Kildonan, where the river enters the sea. The name Helmisdale—the "dale of the hemlet"—is of Icelandic origin. "Hialmasdal" is a term which occurs in one of the old Norse Sagas, and may be synonymous with Helmisdale, as the coast of Loth, about the year 1180, during the inroads of the Norsemen, was frequently visited by those bold adventurers, and they may have given the name to the village, as one of their temporary settlements, as well as to the river which ran through it.[*] The other name of this stream is much more ancient. The Helmisdale rises in the western heights of the parish; a small rivulet, the overflow of several wells, or "sùil-chuthaich," two or three miles within the parish of Farr to the north-west, is its chief source. This stream, after passing in its course through the defile separating Sutherlandshire from Mackay's country, called "Beallach-nan-creach" (the pass of the spoil), falls into "Loch-na-cuidhean" (or the "lake of the snow-wreaths." Another source of the Helmisdale flows through the "Lón-tarsuinn" (or, "cross meadow"), and, after passing through two lochs, empties their waters into Loch Badenloch, the largest lake in the parish, and the great reservoir from which the Helmisdale first issues with the strength of a river. On each side of this beautiful expanse of water arise lofty mountains—Beinn Chlibrig, about twelve miles to the south-west, in the parish of Farr, and Beinn Armuinn, in the south, are each between 2000 and 3000 feet high. To the north-west is seen, blue in the distance, the serrated top of Beinn Laoghal, in the parish of Tongue. To the north-east, Beinu Ghriammhór presents its extensive south front, nearly 2000 feet in height, exhibiting, on its shoulders, huge porphyritic blocks, from which all the mills in the parish were supplied with mill-stones. To the east,

---

[*] Hialmundalus, as the residence of Frakaurk, is made particular mention of by Torfæus, in his "Orcades," Book I., chap. 26, on the authority of the "Orkneyinga Sagas.".

and precisely on the boundary line between the parishes of Kidonan and Reay, is Beinu Ghriam-bheag, which scarcely yields in height to its greater namesake, although much less in breadth and extent. On the low grounds in the immediate vicinity of this loch northwards, was the place of Badenloch, a farm or township in which dwelt a number of small tenants, who each possessed some five acres of arable land, and a countless number of acres of heath pasture for their sheep and cattle; this they held in common. Their arable acres they held, according to the fashion of those times, in what was called "runrig," or, ridge about to each man. This place of Badenloch was a complete oasis, in the midst of a desert of heath. On the south side of the lake, situated on an eminence, was the farm of Breacachadh (or speckled meadow), which was for many generations in the possession of a family named Gordon. From the loch of Badenloch the river takes an easterly course, and after a short run of about five miles, enters Loch Achnamòine (or peat-field), a small lake, on each side of which are the farms of Achnamòine to the south, and Ach-na-h'uaidh (field of the graves), to the north. The latter was so called from a burying-ground which had been used from time immemorial. In the midst of this place of graves stood a rude and homely church, or meeting-house, as it was more appropriately called. The building was constructed of the simplest materials. The lower part of the walls, to the height of about two feet, was built of dry stone; the walls and gables were then brought to their full height by alternate rows of turf and stone. The roof was constructed of branches of birch laid on the couples, covered with divot, and thatched with a thin layer of straw which was secured with heather ropes. The windows were merely a few shapeless holes left in the roof and the walls for the admission of light, and were furnished with boards to prevent the ingress of sheep and cattle. The seating was originally a few planks of moss-fir, dug out of the bogs in the neighbourhood, and placed upon turf or stones. This was one of the preaching stations intended for the use of the itinerant minister of Achness. About three miles below, the river receives a considerable addition to its volume by the water of Strathbeag which, rising about eight miles to the N.E., there joins the Helmisdale. The place was called Duallach, and was the stance of a considerable cattle-market. This branch of the river, called the Amhuinn-bheag (or little river), has two principal sources. The first consists of two or three small streams uniting to form the loch Ach-an-ruathair. The river, after issuing from this lake receives, about a mile farther down, a large stream from the Cnoc Fhinn heights (1,416 feet high), on the Caithness boundary, and, a mile beyond it, the second, or western branch, at a place called Claggan. This stream also has its source in a lake called Loch Leum-a-chlamhain, which reposes its dark and mossy waters in a valley between the mountains Beinn Ghriam-mhor and Beinn Ghriam-bheag. The banks of this loch are noted in the history of the northern clans, as the scene of a bloody battle between the Mackays and the men of Sutherland. The Mackays, headed by their chief, had made an irruption into Kildonan, and forcibly carried off a number of cattle. As they were making all posible haste with their booty back to their own country, they were overtaken by a strong body of the clan Gunn, under the conduct of their redoubted chief Mac Sheumais Chattaich. After a conflict on the banks of this lake, the Mackays, although very severely handled and losing many of their best men in the action, succeeded in making good their retreat, carrying their spoil along with them. They directed their course to "Beallach nan creach," but were hotly pursued by the Gunns and Sutherlands, who at last came up with them in the pass. Here the action was about to be renewed, and the Mackays ran every risk of losing both their lives and their spoil; but, just as their opponents were rushing upon them in all the confidence of victory, the Mackays were suddenly reinforced by a party of the Clan Abrach,* and the Gunns were compelled to retreat. The cattle which the Mackays had carried off were, that evening, lodged in a pen-fold at Achness. Among them was a fierce bull who was very unmanageable, and who seemed to resent, at least as much as his owners, his being carried off from his native pastures. The pen-fold had no gate, and its place was occupied by the chieftain of the Abrachs, who stood there to protect the cattle. But the bull rushed suddenly upon him, gored him to death, and, with all the cattle following him, returned, ere morning, through the Beallach, to their favourite pasture land at Griamachdarry (or the shieling at the foot of Beinn Ghriam.

After leaving the lake, the Amhuinn-bheag passes through the places of Corrish and Bad-an-t 'sheobhaig (hawk's tuft), flows through the loch of Airidh-Chlinie, and issuing from thence, joins the other Amhuinn-bheag at the place of Claggan. The united streams pursue their course through a pretty rural strath, having the farms of Eilig on the west and Torghordstan and Achaneccan on the east, till they join the main river at Duallach. The Helmisdale now passes by the places of Seannachadh (old field), and Kinbrace, which lie close on its eastern bank. Here it receives a considerable stream, which rises in the hills to the north-east, and separates these two farms. A little above Kinbrace, the Helmisdale makes a beautiful bend, and moves so slowly as to assume the appearance, and almost the motionless stillness, of a lake; it is here at least six fathoms deep. The place of Kinbrace is of a rugged, stony appearance, but is venerable from its traditional history. As you enter it from the north-west, a number of cairns of various sizes meet the eye. Of these, the largest is the remains of a castle, once the principal residence, in Sutherlandshire, of the chief of the clan Gunn, known in 1489, under the title of the "Crùn-f'hear," or the "crown-laird." This potent baron, the lineal descendant of Olaf of Dungesby

---

* The clan Abrach was that branch of the Mackays descended from John Aberigh, second and natural son of the great chief Angus Dow Mackay, who flourished 1380-1439. John got his surname from the fact that his mother was a woman from Lochaber, and that he lived there some years. He returned north, and took his elder brother Neil's place while he was detained on the Bass Rock 1429-1437 In return for his honourable conduct and kindness to his father, Neil gave him the whole district of Strathnaver, where his branch of the family, the "Sliochd-nan-Abrach," became the most populous and powerful of the Mackays. He married first a daughter of the laird of Mackintosh, and second one of the Mackenzies of Gairloch. The Roys, MacPhails, Polsons, Morgans, Vasses, Bains, and MacNeils are other branches of the Mackays.—Ed.

in Caithness, a native of Orkney, had his principal castle at Halbury on the Caithness coast, but at the period mentioned, had obtained lands from the Earl of Sutherland. Those lands extended from the middle of the Strath of Kildonan, on the east side of the river, to the extreme limits of the present parish to the N.W. and N.E., where it marches with Lord Reay's country and the county of Caithness. As a sign of his rank under the Government, the chief wore on his breast a large gold brooch, the badge of his office; and in reference both to his office and to his dignity, the Highlanders styled him "Am Bràisteach Mòr," literally, "the dignitary of the brooch." His residence therefore in Kildonan came to be named after him, "Cinn-a'-bbràiste" (Kinbrace), or the "seat of the dignitary of the brooch." His castle, now a heap of stones, stood to the N.W. of Kinbrace. Seanachadh, a part of the township of Kinbrace, being near the castle, was consequently first brought into cultivation; it was therefore called the "old or first land." According to tradition, the Crowner "Guin," when residing here, received a great blow to his importance as an independent baron. The account is g en in many different ways, so that not only the locality in which the disaster took place, but also the causes and the events, are so differently stated as to land us in much uncertainty. I content myself with the tradition current among the people of Kildonan. ·It is as follows :—The Bràisteach Mòr," while quietly residing at Kinbrace one summer (for he lived in winter at Halbury), heard one evening, immediately before dinner, a bugle sounding at his gate.* The intimation was perfectly well understood both by himself and his attendants. It was a demand for hospitality. by a stranger, which was immediately complied with. The castle gate was opened, the stranger and his followers admitted, and, in a very few minutes thereafter, a tall elderly man, habited in a half-military attire, presented himself before the chief. The "Bràisteach Mòr" received the august stranger with much courtesy, and after some general conversation, the evening meal was served up. When the Baron's retinue took their places at the table, the guest being accommodated with a seat at the host's right hand, twelve young men, each six feet in height, and exquisitely formed, sat next to them, and their appearance and gallant bearing at once attracted the notice of the stranger. "Are these your sons?" said he to the chief. "They are," was the reply, "and I have no need to be ashamed to own them." "You may well be proud of them;" said his guest; "I don't

---

* The hospitality of the Highlanders was proverbial. It was a rule with them never to ask a stranger who craved hospitality his name. The breach of this rule they characterised as churlishness, because feuds being so common among them, the guest might thereby probably lose the benefit which, for the time, he greatly needed. Their Punctiliousness in this respect is alluded to by Sir Walter Scott in a note appended to the following descriptive lines of "The Lady of the Lake :"—

 "Every courteous rite was paid
 That hospitality could claim,
 Though all unasked his birth or name.
 Such then the reverence to a guest,
 That fellest foe might join the feast,
 And from his deadliest foeman's door
 Unquestioned turn, the banquet o'er."—Ed.

know a man in Caithness but may envy you such a goodly race—except one." "And who is that one?" said the Crowner. "That one is myself," replied the stranger, and removing his visor, he added, "You may know me now—I fear not your vengeance for our ancient feud as your hospitality protects me—I am the Keith of Ackergill. I will brag my twelve sons to your twelve sons, Crowner, gallant though they be, on any day you fix, in a fair field." The challenge was no sooner given than it was accepted. It was settled between them that the thirteen challengers should meet an equal number of the challenged, fully armed and on horseback, while the place of meeting was fixed within the limits of Caithness, in a spot so lonely as to preclude all interference. It was agreed that the Keiths would move forward on the appointed day to meet the Gunns, who would pass the limits of Sutherland, enter Strathmore in Caithness, and halt at any burn running into the river of Strathmore where they might see calves browsing on the banks. The Crowner and his gallant sons, at the appointed time, directed their course to a hollow through which flowed a burn with a few calves straying on its banks, a little below the Glutt of Strathmore, which has ever since preserved the name of "Alt-nangamhna," or "the brook of stirks." As they drew near, they descried in the distance their antagonists. The Crowner and the Keith, at the head of their respective followers, approached each other in full armour. But no sooner did both parties come upon the ground, than the treachery of the Keiths became apparent. Instead of twelve, the Keith had twenty-four followers, two men riding on each horse in his train. The chief of the Gunns saw that the destruction of himself and his gallant band was determined by their perfidious foes; but, scorning to retreat even before such fearful odds, he and his party dismounted, and the fray began. The great two-handed sword was wielded with pitiless ferocity by the enraged champions, each against the other. The combat was long, and for a time doubtful; for the superiority of numbers on the side of the Keiths was counter-balanced by the indomitable courage of their fearless antagonists. Henry, one of the Crowner's sons, greatly distinguished himself; under the fell sweep of his sword the bravest of the Keiths were laid prostrate. But numbers at length prevailed. The stout "Braisteach Mòr," and seven of his sons lay dead on the field, and the remaining five were constrained, from loss of blood, slowly to retreat. Keith with his train, scarcely less wounded or weary, was merely able to leave the scene of action with his banner displayed, and to carry off the slain and wounded of his followers. The Crowner's five surviving sons spent the night at "Allt Thorcuill," another stream flowing into the river Thurso further up Strathmore, where their wounds were dressed by Torquil, one of their number, from which circumstance the stream has obtained its name. The Keiths proceeded in the opposite direction on their way homewards, and arrived that evening at the castle of Dirlot, where they were received and hospitably entertained by the laird of Dildred, a vassal and relative of the Earl of Sutherland. There, after the bloody work of the day, they "kept wassail" far into the night. Not so, however, the surviving sons of the Crowner. Night closed around them, on the heathy banks of Allt Thorcuill, with a darkness in accord with the deep gloom which the death of their kindred, and their own disastrous defeat had cast upon their minds. Henry, the youngest, burned to avenge his father's death, and to recover his father's sword and golden brooch which the Keiths had carried off as their spoil. To his brothers, therefore, he submitted the proposal to follow the Keiths, and take them at a disadvantage when off their guard, and thus to repay them for their treachery. James, the eldest brother, refused his assent, and endeavoured to convince Henry that the attempt could only terminate in their own destruction, and not in that of their enemies. Henry, however, persisted; and leaving James and another of his brothers at Allt Thorcuill, he, along with the other two, arming themselves with bows and arrows and their formidable swords, set out in the silence of the night in pursuit of the Keiths. Having ascertained that they had gone in the direction of the castle of Dirlot, he concluded that they must be there; so Henry with his brothers silently clambered up the rock on which it was built, and placing them at the door, he himself took post at a window, the shutter of which chanced to be open. There he observed the Keiths seated around a large fire, quaffing flaggons of ale and talking boisterously. The Keith was seated at the right hand of the lord of the castle, wearing his helmet, but with the vizor unclosed. He loudly commended Henry, who had signalized himself above all his kin by his prowess, and remarked that, had all the Gunns fought as manfully as he, his own four-and-twenty followers would have been overmatched, " I propose a full cup to his health," said the Keith. But his last hour had struck. For just as he raised the cup to his lips, and threw back his head to swallow the contents, Henry bent his bow, deliberately took aim, and, whilst the arrow sped fast and drank deep of the old chief's blood, exclaimed, "Iomacharag Gunaich gu Kàigh," (literally, "With Gunn's compliments to Keith"). Keith reeled, mortally wounded, and his enraged followers rushed headlong to the windows and to the door to avenge his fall. However, as one by one, they leapt out, they placed themselves under the swords of Henry and his brothers who wielded their arms with terrible precision and irresistible force. The shouts of the assailants and the groans of the dying, added to gloom of night, produced such a scene of horror and confusion as enabled Henry to secure his father's armour and badge of office; with these, he and his gallant kinsmen contrived unscathed to escape. His brother James, however, but ill requited Henry's prowess. As the Crowner's eldest son, and therefore chief of the clan, James claimed his father's sword and badge of office. Henry scorned to dispute the matter, but, despising the despotism and cowardice which had entered so much into his brother's conduct on this occasion, he removed from Sutherland to Caithness, and vowed that none of his descendants should bear the name of Gunn. He is therefore the reputed ancestor of the Caithness Hendersons, or "Cheannraigich," as they are called in Gaelic. His brother James resided at Kinbrace, and to his descendants, from his name and residence, he gave the patronymic title by which, ever since, the chiefs of the Clan Gunn have been designated—"Mac Sheumais Chattaich," or "Son of James of Sutherland." This feud, so fatal to the political importance of this ancient race,* took place in 1511, during the reign of James IV., and while the earldom of Caithness was in the hands of the Crown. Such is the tradition which now renders so deeply interesting to the antiquary the otherwise obscure village of Kinbrace.

Leaving this interesting spot, the Helmisdale pursues its course, and about a mile farther on passes on the right the farm of Dalchairn (or dale of the cairn), a pretty rural place, which derives its name from an immense cairn situated in the centre of it, and about sixty yards from the right bank of the river. This place was, at the time of my father's settlement, occupied in lease by Alexander Gordon, whom I have already named. Here the Helmisdale receives one of its principal tributary streams, the water of Dalchairn, or Fridh, which rises about eight miles due west, and on the boundary line between the parishes of Kildonan and Clyne. This rapid stream is formed by the union of two burns, the one, flowing in a north-westerly direction, and surrounding in its course an old ruin or tumulus, from which it derives its name of "Allt-an-dùin" (or "the stream of the cairn or tower"); the other flowing from the N.W., and joining the former at the place of "Ach-an-dúin," unites with it to form the river Fridh, which flows through the strath of the same name. These last are so called because they are within the limits of the great chartered Sutherland deer-forest, which in Gaelic is called "Fridh." This strath presents, through its whole extent, a dull unvaried flat, the ground on each side of the stream seldom rising above twelve or twenty feet. The farms or inhabited spots upon it then were Ach-an-dùin, Rèisg, and Tomich at the upper part; Ceann-nabhaid, about the centre; and Feuranaich, about three miles above the junction of the river Fridh with the Helmisdale at Dalchairn. On the right bank of the Fridh, and opposite to Dalchairn, was the village or township of Borrobol, through which ran a burn of considerable size. This stream was the outlet of the waters of Loch Ascaig, about three miles to the S.W. of Borrobol. The loch of Ascaig lay to the south-east of the head of Strathfridh, and was so called from the township of Ascaig which, at the period of my father's settlement, was thickly peopled, and lay close on the S.E. shore of the lake. The burn of Borrobol drove a mill for the use of that township of a very peculiar construction.† About two miles further down the course of the Helmisdale, and on its eastern or left bank, was the place of Suisgill,

---

* Tradition is the only authority we have for the fact of this conflict having really taken place. While the different narratives vary in some of the details given, they all agree in stating that Keith of Ackergill was afterwards assassinated, and that George Gunn of Ulbster was killed in this affray. The former was the perpetrator, and the latter was the brave but unfortunate victim, of a base act of treachery. In his many engagements with the clan Gunn, Keith and all his male progeny perished. His only daughter inherited his estates, and made them, by her marriage with the Earl of Caithness, part and parcel of the Earldom; they finally passed into other hands.—ED.

† This was one of the old horizontal mills, once common in the Orkney Islands and especially so in the sister group of Shetland. As late as the end of last century they were also to be found in the northern mainland of Scotland, but are in use now only in the Shetland Isles. They were observed there by Sir Walter Scott, in his visit in 1814, and described as follows:—"The wheel is horizontal, with the

E

where, in my father's time, a very considerable number of the people of
the parish were congregated, although now it is a scene of desolation.
Here the river receives an addition to its waters from the burn of
Suisgill, which rises six miles to the N.E., in a deep morass, on the
S.W. shoulder of a hill situated on the borders of Sutherland and
Caithness, called "Cnoc-an-Eireannaich" (or "the Irishman's hill"),
from the tradition that an Irishman had there perished in the snow.
From Suisgill the river flows in a more southerly direction; its banks
for several miles are beautifully fringed with birch and hazel, and
about a mile below Suisgill, on its left bank, which becomes all at once
steep and high, is the little farm of "Ach-an-t'shamhraidh"—(*i.e.,*
"the summer or pleasant field"), embosomed in a thick wood. On this
spot is still to be seen the foundation of a Highland cottage of the
rudest simplicity, the abode of Domhuil direach, or Donald the just,
—one of the most eminent Christians of whom the county of Sutherland can boast, who flourished between the years of 1740 and 1768.
On the summit of this bank of the river stood the place of "Ach
nan nighean'" (maidens' field), where, for many years, was the only
blacksmith's shop in the whole parish. Near the smithy is the entrance
or opening of one of those singular subterraneous passages to be found
in some parts of the north of Scotland. This passage is a most
remarkable one. The entrance is built up on each side of solid and
regular mason-work, and finished at the top by a huge lintel which not
twenty men or more of modern times could raise a foot from the
ground. The door-way is half-filled with rubbish, but a sufficient
opening is still left to admit a person entering on his knees. A few
yards within the interior is a sort of chamber, wider by about five feet
than the entrance. Further progress is stopped by the falling in of
the roof, a circumstance which is made apparent by a deep hollow on
the surface of the ground outside. The passage is continued down the
bank, in a north-westerly direction, and carried under the bed of the
river, as was lately ascertained by the removal of a few flags at the foot
of the eminence, close by the river's bank, where the passage is again
discovered, about a quarter of a mile from the entrance.

On the opposite side of the river, and also on a wooded eminence, is
the township of Learabail, and, according to a tradition, at this place
the passage terminated. The story is said to be as follows:—Two
calves, browsing on a field near the eastern entrance of the passage,
began to skip about and chase each other, until at last the one after the
other ran in at the opening, and there being then no obstruction, the

cogs turned diagonally to the water; the beam stands upright, and is inserted in a
stone quern of the old-fashioned construction. This simple machine is enclosed in a
hovel about the size of a pig-stye—and there is the mill ! There are about 500 such
mills in Shetland, each incapable of grinding more than a sack at a time."

It is an interesting fact, however, that this particular form of mill at one time was
common over Great Britain and Ireland, and the whole of northern Europe, and was
found as far east as Syria and Persia, where it seems to have superseded the still
more primitive hand-quern. The last of these mills on the mainland of Scotland
were observed at Kirtomy and at Kinlochbervie in Sutherlandshire, as late as 1864.
For a detailed account of this whole subject see, "Proceedings of Soc. Ant. Scot.
1885-6."—ED.

animals pursued their course inside. Their entrance into the cave was noticed by two girls employed in looking after the cattle, and they both immediately ran after the calves for the purpose of bringing them back. The girls kept together until they had got to nearly the middle of the passage, when the foremost in pursuit, along with the calves, suddenly disappeared and were never more heard of. The other girl, horror-struck, went on groping her way in the darkness until she found her further progress prevented by the termination of the passage. Feeling about with her hands, she found that she was in a chamber of considerable size, but very low and roofed with flags. About the middle of the roof she found that one flag, was moveable by the pressure of her hand; she also heard the sound of voices above her. Exerting all her strength to raise the loose flag, she at the same time screamed for help. As the story goes, this subterraneous chamber was situated precisely under the hearth of one of the tenants of Learabail, who, at the time that the cry was uttered, and his hearth-stone thus disturbed, was, with his wife and family, quietly seated at the fireside. The cry from beneath, and the earthquake-like movement, came upon the tenant and his family like a thunder-clap. At once concluding that it was a domiciliary visit from the spirits of the deep, they all started up, and, in answer to the poor girl's cries for help, they only uttered a roar of terror and bolted from the house. The desperate girl at length succeeded in raising the hearth-stone and placing herself by the fireside. To the inmates of the dwelling, after their fears had subsided so far as to allow them to have speech with her, she gave an account of her appalling adventures. Her lost companion, it is said, was the daughter of a witch who, in a fatal hour, had promised her daughter to the devil. Under the semblance of the two calves the Evil One had come to claim his own. The place was, in memory of the event, called " the maidens' field."

Below the wooded bank on which it is situated, the bed of the river is one continued ledge of rocks, which extends for nearly three miles down its course. Surrounded with wood on the east side of the river, and just below the last-named spot, is a fairy-like plat called Achahemisgach, at the upper end of which is a rock with the form of a cross engraved upon it. This evidently must have been some place of sanctity in popish times, especially as the name of the adjoining wood is " Coille 'Chil Mer," or, " the wood of the cell of Mary." Learabail, on the opposite bank, was a township of considerable extent. At its east end a large and rapid burn, rising some miles distant, and making its impetuous way over many rocks which cross its channel, runs into the Helmisdale. The banks of the burn at Learaboll are romantic. In some parts they are fifty feet in height, and are composed partly of shattered rocks, and partly of abrupt precipices of gravel, here and there interspersed with clumps of tall birch trees and quaking ash. One place, where the burn tumbles over a rock into a deep pool, is said to be haunted by the vindictive spirit of a young woman who was forsaken by her lover, and died of a broken heart. At set times of the year, at the waning of the moon, her moan has been heard mingling with the hoarse murmur of the stream, imprecating woes upon her faithless lover. From the left bank of this stream and parallel to its course, Craig Dalangail, a huge rocky hill, suddenly rears up its majestic form. It rises from base to summit almost perpendicular, and all over its rugged front displays the channels of the impetuous torrents which fill them during the floods of spring and winter. This mountain forms the western barrier of the vale of Kildonan. At its base is the small farm of Dalangail, from which it derives its name. For upwards of a century this place was in the possession of a family named Gunn. A little below Dalangail, the river after flowing over a rocky bottom for upwards of two miles, is hemmed closely in between two rocks, and thence the whole volume of the stream rushes down with a slight fall and great impetuosity. This rapid is called " Leum Hennrig" (or "Henry's Leap"), from the following circumstances. Henry Gunn, a younger son of the tenant of Dalangail, a strong, athletic, and handsome young man, was in the habit, while the rest of his father's family went round by a wooden bridge to the church, of taking a short cut by leaping from rock to rock over the rapid. One fatal morning, when the family entered their seat, Henry to their surprise was not there; uneasy about him, they found on their return that their worst apprehensions were realized. Before leaping, he had as usual put off his shoes and hose, and thrown them to the rock opposite. There they were found by his sorrowing friends, while his dead body lay sixty yards below.

The river in its course now approaches the glebe. About a quarter of a mile above it is another picturesque fall about twelve feet in height, just at the angle where the river makes a rapid bend from N.E. to S.W. During the winter floods, the immense volume of water compelled, by the bend in the river's course, to turn suddenly off from its natural direction, the height of the fall, the rugged and shelving rocks over which the stream flings itself with such rapidity and violence, the stunning roar of the waters, and the spray shooting up from them as from a boiling cauldron, all combine to present to the beholder a scene of imposing grandeur and even of terror. In the drought of summer, however, the scene is entirely changed. The river then nearly disappears in its deep central channel, and in its wider bed which, during that season, is almost dry, are seen a number of holes scooped out of the rocks as with a chisel. During the summer the salmon may be seen trying to leap the fall, and after two or three attempts they succeed. Poachers made this cascade their principal resort for killing salmon, which they effected with spears and hooks as the fish leaped up the rocks. Below the " Slugaig," as this place of cup-like hollows is called, an immense block of whinstone, at least 12 or 14 feet high, rests in the middle of the river's bed. This was used as a river-gauge; if the water covered more than two-thirds of this boulder, the river was considered to be unfordable throughout its whole extent; but if, during a flood, the stone disappeared altogether, then it might be taken for granted that the river had overflowed its banks on the low grounds, and laid the lands of Strathuilligh under water. At the western extremity of the glebe a rocky islet stands in the centre of one of the deepest pools in the river, and from each side of it to the rocks on the opposite banks were thrown wooden bridges made of immense logs of fir found in the moss. This was the only part of the river crossed by a bridge; all the other crossings were fords. From the circumstance that two bridges were here necessary to effect the passage of the stream, the place was called " Poll-dá-chraig," or " pool of the two rocks." Its depth is above 30 feet. From this pool the river, in its course, forms the western and southern boundaries of the glebe. On its right bank, and close by Poll-dá-chraig, was a small farm called Dalbheag, so named from a stream which descended from the hill behind, and which, when in flood, laid the greater part of its soil under water. To the west and south, and rising abruptly from the margin of the river, is a wooded hill, Coille-an-Loiste, directly in front of the manse, and forming its south prospect; it extends from the southern limb of Craig Dalangail about two miles to the eastward. Right opposite the manse and church a waterfall is seen through the foliage, which produces an enchanting effect. Above the wooded bank, to the south-west, is the hill of Craggie, while over the ridge of Coille-an-Loiste appears the conical hill of Craggan-mór, 1581 feet high. Due east is a mountainous range, including Beinn-na-h' Urrachd, 2046 feet high; Beinn Mheulaich, 1940 feet high; and Cnoc Earnain and Cnoc Tuaraidh, the first of which may be about 1043 and the latter 1163 feet high; while still farther east on the south side of the Strath, and terminating the range within the limits of the parish, is Cnoc Eildirebail, 1338 feet in height. The topographical appearance of the sweep of the river around the grassy flat of the Dalmore, with its wooded bank just beyond, and this beautiful mountain range towering above all to the south and east, is one of the most attractive prospects in the highlands.

A little below the manse the river receives another of its chief tributaries in the Tealnaidh, or water of Loist (now Craggie burn). This stream rises to the west, in the hills which form the boundary between the parishes of Kildonan and Clyne. One of its sources is in the hill Innis mhòr, at the foot of which is the sequestrated spot of Tuaraidh. Another branch rises on the hill above Gordonbush in Strathbrora, and both streams uniting, flow through Strath Tealnaidh, in which are the townships of Halgarry, Achrintill, and Preaschoin. This strath is heathy and wild at its upper extremity, but, as the stream approaches its junction with the Helmisdale, it becomes romantic and beautiful. At the place of Craggie, the banks of the burn are thickly wooded; Achabhataich, a mile or two below, is a beautiful sylvan retreat. The stream afterwards enters a deep rocky dell, of which the precipitous banks nearly meet, whilst the stream far beneath, struggling and forcing its way over every rocky ledge that crosses its channel, is often rendered invisible by the shivering foilage of the aspens which grow luxuriantly from the face of the rocks. As it enters the farm of Loiste, almost a dead flat, the Craggie becomes a placid stream, a thick, close hedge-row of tall alder trees growing on each bank. During its course of nearly eight miles it receives about seven tributary streams, the last of which deserves to be named, not only from its size, but also from its source. It is a considerable body of water, and rises at the extreme

west point of Beinn h'-Urrachd. It there issues from a well, situated
at the bottom of an immense hollow or dell, called Coire-mòr, which
resembles a bowl or funnel, and which by an English sportsman many
years ago, from its singlar appearance, was fancifully termed "the
devil's punch-bowl." The Craggie enters the Helmisdale at a place
called Torr-daraicb (or the "oak knowe"), and here commences what
is usually called Strath Uilligh, or the Strath of Helmisdale, through
which that river flows for upwards of eight miles till it enters the sea.
I may name the townships on its banks, and its tributary streams from
Torrdaraich to its mouth. About a mile below is Bad-fluich (or wet
tuft), so called from the marshy ground by which it is surrounded, and
about half a mile below that is the place of Kilearnain (or the cell of
St. Earnan), through which runs a burn rising at the base of Cnoc
Earnain. The place of Kilearnain was a township of great extent,
accommodating about nine tenants. Another tributary stream of the
Helmisdale runs into it at Gaillebail (the township or farm of the
stranger); it rises out of the east shoulder of Beinn Mheulaich. As
it passes the place of Gaillebail, the river is of immense depth, and for
some miles assumes the appearance of a lake; this part of it was, therefore, called by the inhabitants Am-Bagh-mòr (or the great bay), and for
angling it was reckoned the best part of the stream. Below Gaillebail
three miles is the place of Ulbster (or in Gaelic Ullabisdale), a name of
unknown etymology, through which a foaming rapid burn, rising at the
west shoulder of Cnoc Eildirebail, rushes into the river. At the eastern
extremity of the hill is the place of Eildirebail, a most romantic spot,
situated upon an eminence about 50 feet above the bed of the river, and
thickly wooded. The burn of Eildirebail is almost one continued fall
from its source to its junction with the river. On this part of the
strath the sun is, in winter, never seen, owing to the height of this hill;
it has therefore been called "an taobh dorch (or the dark side). Other
two places on the south bank of the river, and within the limits of
Kildonan parish, are Gradsary and Marill, but at neither of them does
the river receive any addition to its waters. Such is the south side of
the Strath of Helmisdale; the north side begins at Kildonan. There
the river receives a large accession to its size in the burn of Kildonan,
which has its first source on the south side of Cnoc-an-Eireannaich,
and about two miles on its course passes through "Ach 'chroidh-
bhothan" (or the field of cattle booths), a hill grazing or shieling, so
called because the minister and tenants of Kildonan sent thither in
summer their milk cows and young cattle, attended by their cow-herds
and dairymaids, who then lived in booths. In its course from this
place to its junction with the river this stream receives many additions
to its waters. The largest of its tributaries rises in a deep dell to the
eastward named "Allt-uchdaraidh," formed by the junction at their
lowest points of two high hills. Of these the one to the north, on the
boundary line between Sutherland and Caithness, has on its summit a
pyramidal rock with two tops, called "suidh an fhir bhig," (or the seat
of the little man). The hill to the south is long and high, rising
abruptly from its base to about 1600 feet above the level of the sea, and
is called "Cnoc-leathaid-an-t' sholuis" (or the hill of the slope of light),

from its southerly exposure. On its right bank the burn of Kildonan is joined by a small stream at the pasture above mentioned, by another further down called "Allt-blàr-clais-a-choire," by still another called "Caochan-ri-nam-braoinan," and about two miles below that, on the left bank, by "Allt-clais-nam-breac," which runs from a valley where the tenantry of Kildonan cut their peats, called "Clais-nam-breac." As the burn approaches Kildonan, it considerably increases in size, and its banks become romantic and interesting. The whole of its course is through a dreary, heathy waste, but as it passes Clais-nam-breac, it flows far below the level of its banks, and then rolls at the base of the hill "Craig-an-rà'" (or the rock of defence). On the top of this hill the foundations may be seen of a number of enclosures running into each other, covering a surface of many acres, and exhibiting the appearance of an encampment. About the beginning of the 17th century many bloody conflicts took place between the Earls of Sutherland and Caithness, and it is probable that this spot was the entrenched camp of one of the hostile parties.

At the point where it emerges out of the deep dell, the burn tumbles over a rock, about fourteen feet high, forming a beautiful cascade, usually called Ath-struthadh. The place is also called "Eas-na-caoraich-duibhe" (the cascade of the black sheep), owing to the circumstance of a black sheep having been carried down the stream over the fall, and, after getting a hearty ducking at its foot, having yet escaped with her life. Nothing can exceed the beauty of this spot. To the north-west towers up, at least 800 feet, the shoulder of Craig-an-rà' rising like a huge wall from one side of the water-fall; on the other is a conical hill, much resembling an ancient tumulus, and exhibiting all its regularity. From the face of the rocky precipice on which this conical hill rests, a birch tree shoots out diagonally, throwing itself across the fall, so that in summer the foaming torrent is seen through its foliage. The base of the fall where it enters the pool below, is concealed by a ledge of rock, so that the water appears to be falling into a cavern in the earth. To the west of the cascade, and running at the base of Creag-an-rà' is the dell of "Clais-nam-meirleach." The burn of Kildonan then takes a south-easterly direction. On its east side is a high hill, at least 1000 feet in height, which terminates in an abrupt precipice about a mile to the east of the manse. This hill is called Coire-mòr, and the top of it, which, right above the place of Kildonan, rises into a conical point, is called "Cnoc-na-h' Iolair." (or the eagle's hill). The burn now enters another rocky dell, called "Creag-an-fhithich" (or the raven's rock), which is about a quarter of a mile in length from north to south. This craig forms the eastern bank of the burn, and presents throughout its whole extent a continued series of bold and rugged, but romantic precipices about thirty feet high above the margin of the burn, and exhibiting, by the tortuous course of the stream at its base, the appearance of the bastions of a garrison. About the middle of it, the rock rises to a point, on which are the remains of a castle. An affecting tale is connected with it. A huntsman started a fox from about the summit of Coire-mòr, and his gallant hounds instantly gave chase. The hunted animal took the direction of the raven's rock, and, arriving at the ruins of the "dun," precipitated himself headlong into an aperture in the walls. One of the huntsman's favourite hounds immediately followed him into the opening. The fox, being short and slim, made his way into a vault below, from which he afterwards contrived to escape; but the hound stuck fast, and his master could neither reach him nor employ any means for his rescue, so that death, in a few days, put an end to the creature's sufferings.

The raven's rock terminates to the east of Torr-an-riachaidh. The burn was there formed into a deep pool, called "Poll-na-h'ellich," by a strong stone barrier thrown across its channel, in order to convey the water to the mill of Kildonan, situated about 700 yards below. The burn, in its course to its junction with the river, forms the boundary between the glebe and the township of Kildonan. At the time of my father's settlement, this place was occupied by eight tenants, who, soon after his coming into the parish, became his sub-tenants. About 20 yards to the east of the church, the burn enters the Helmisdale, where, with a considerable declivity, its course turns from due east to south-east, forming a rapid called "Struthadh-an-fhuarain." On the banks of the river, from Struthadh-an-fhuarain, extending for a mile down its course, lay the lands, or "run-rigs" of the Kildonan tenants. The eastern extremity of their land was occupied by the "Eilean," a swampy, wooded marsh, covered with bushes of the black willow; where also, during the rainy season, a considerable quantity of water lodged, dropping from the neighbouring heights. A large cairn, upon an eminence, stood near the centre of it. In the vicinity of the "Eilean" was the place of Halgary, under the precipice which terminates the hill of Coire-mhòr. Below this place, and nearly opposite Loist, the river had, during the winter floods, cut out two channels, and formed an island. Here, by the division of the current, the river was fordable, and the ford was named "Athan-preas-na-suidheig" (or, ford of the raspberry bushes). Below Halgary was the place of Di-bail (want or robbery), lying close on the left bank of the river and opposite Badfluich. The road to Helmisdale from Kildonan lay along the left bank of the river, and passed through the several townships situated upon it. Close to Di-bail was a pool of water, formed by the rills which rush down from the braes above it, and which had an outlet into the river, fordable only at one point, called Stair-Di-bail (the steps of Di-bail). Immediately behind the townships on this side of the river, the ground is much elevated, presenting steep declivities fronting the south. Above Di-bail, rises Bein Dubhain, so called from its close resemblance to a hook, and at its base is the place of Costly. Farther down the river are Leodan and the township of Dalhalmy. The river, as it passes this last place, is very deep, and not fordable. Immediately below, it forms another island about 60 yards long and 20 broad. Balbheallach is the next township, and immediately to the east of it, a rapid torrent descends from the hill to the river, which in summer is perfectly dry, but during the rainy season comes down in spate, and not only cuts up the road so much as to render it impassable, but covers the arable land around it, to the extent of many acres, with shingle and peat. A mile or two below Balbheallach a burn of considerable size enters the river, having its head waters between Cnoc-Salaslaid (1581 feet high), and Beinn Dubhain, called Allt-breac. To the west of the influx of this burn into the river, near a small lake situated on a high bank, are two or three huge blocks of stone, in the form of a chair or seat, called "Cathair-Dhonain" (or, the the chair of St. Donan), after whom the parish has been called "Kil-Dhonian" (or, the cell of St. Donan). Donan was evidently the first Christian teacher who came to instruct the savage hordes inhabiting this district. Towards them he seems to have acted in the double capacity of a religious teacher and a civil magistrate. At his cell therefore he inculcated the truths of the Christian religion, and seated on his stone chair at this spot he administered the laws. In my younger days, there were many traditions of him afloat in the locality. One of these was that, after his death, none could be found to fill his place so as to exert the moral influence which he exercised over the minds of the people. His successor therefore caused a wooden image of him to be made, with features of countenance hideous and frightful. If any man proved refractory, he was immediately locked up in the church, or cell, at Kildonan, alone with this representation of St. Donan, during the silence of the night, and the consequences invariably were that, when brought forth from his confinement next day, the features of the saint, and the death-like stillness of the cell had reduced him to absolute obedience. The cell, as well as the whole parish,.from this circumstance was called "Kil-duranach," (or " the sullen cell," as it means in ancient Celtic). A few miles below Cathair-Dhonain, still on the north side of the river is the farm of Torruis, where another stream enters the Helmisdale. This is a large burn rising between Cnoc-Salaslaid and Creag-an-Scalmasdale. This latter mountain rises up to the height of 1819 feet, in the form of a truncated cone, and is composed of what appears to be one solid mass of granite, without vegetation of any kind. At the foot of this mountain, was the farm of Scalmasdale, on the edge of the lake of the same name. The burn, avoiding the high ground to the south of it, takes a south-easterly direction through a valley, and then turning south, after a course of about six miles, precipitates itself over a rock, thus forming a very picturesque fall. Quarter of a mile further down, it enters the river at west end of Torruis, called Torr-na-gaibhre (or goat's knowe). A streamlet also entered the river at the east end of Torruis, where the houses or cottages of the tenantry were built closely together. Here the strath becomes beautifully wooded with the black willow, oak, aspen, alder, and wild gean, the mountain ash, or rowan, the black flowering-thorn, and the birch tree. This tract of woodland extends about a mile-and-a-half down the course of the Helmisdale to the place of Kilphedder, a lovely spot, past which a rushing torrent breaks through the copse-wood on its way to the river. The burn of Kilphedder, a little further down, turned a mill, built there for the accommodation of the inhabitants of the lower part of the strath. The place of Kilphedder is interesting, not only from its romantic scenery, but from its historical associations. As the river flows past, it again divides its channel, and, nearly in the centre of the stream, forms a beautifully wooded island rising from the level of the water to a ridge about 20 feet in height. The mill was situated at the foot of a cataract, rushing over shelving rocks and huge blocks of whinstone, and all were embosomed in wood.

At the east end of Kilphedder, the foundation of a house is discernible. The stones are remarkable for their immense size, so much so, that it is difficult to conceive how they could have been placed there except by the aid of mechanical appliances—then, of course, unknown. These almost obliterated remains are associated with the domestic as well as the traditionary history of the Strath Uillidh Sutherlands, a nobly-descended and gigantic race. Their first ancestor was Alexander, son of John, 8th Earl of Sutherland, by his second Countess, a daughter of Ross of Balnagown. His sister Elizabeth, by his father's first marriage, on the death of her brother John, 9th Earl, who died unmarried, succeeded to the titles and estates, to the prejudice of her half-brother Alexander, on the plea-in-law that his father and mother being cousins-germain, their marriage, by the canon law, was illegal, and that he was therefore, illegitimate. Elizabeth married Adam, Viscount of Aboyne, second son of the Earl of Huntly. With him and his wife, Alexander, by force of arms, disputed the right to the titles and estate of Sutherland. He was killed in a battle fought at Alltachuilain, below Kintradwell, in the parish of Loth. Kilphedder was the place of his residence, and his descendants, for many generations occupied the lands on payment of a merely nominal rent to the Earls of Sutherland. With the melancholy and affecting death of one of his descendants, the ruins at Kilphedder are more immediately connected. This individual, a William Sutherland of Kilphedder, was a man of gigantic strength and stature. He repair-ed and extended the residence of his ancestors. In those primitive times, he himself had to execute the work, both as architect and builder. The largest of the stones he drew from the channel of the river. One huge block, however, which lay in the middle of the stream, after several attempts to remove, he gave up as too much for his strength. His wife noticed his attempts to remove the stone, and, when the build-ing was finished, said to him that it was a pity he had undertaken so difficult a work, as it had reduced him to the level of the insignificant persons around him. "That stone," she added, pointing to it, "will be a standing proof that William Mòr, of Kilphedder, is not the strong man which every one until now took him to be." Colouring with indignation, the redoubted William seized a crowbar, strode down to the river, placed it under the huge mass, and, exerting all his strength, turned it from its bed, rolled it out of the stream, forced it up the bank, and left it at last within a yard of his door. In this exertion he gave a fatal strain to his back, and he felt that the hand of death was upon him. He entered the house, and pointing, in his turn, to the ponderous mass, he said to his wife, "There is the stone, as a proof of your husband's strength, but its removal is the last act of his life." He immediately took to bed, and in three hours afterwards expired. A lineal descendant of his, a Mr. William Sutherland, died at an advanced age, about five years ago, in Edinburgh. He enjoyed a pension bestowed upon him by his relative, the late Duchess of Sutherland,

Below Kilphedder, and in its immediate vicinity, is Soluschraggy (or the rock of light). This place is right opposite the Taobh-dorch, or dark side of the strath. Here a conical rock, about 100 feet high, rises in the middle of the farm, and on this the sun shines during the very few hours in which it is visible in winter. This was the only ocular demonstration to the inhabitants of the Taobh-dorch, that it had risen at all, and hence its name. A small rill washes the base of this rock, and runs into the water. Below Soluschraggy is the place of Dalial, and behind where the farm-house stood, is a small loch about ten yards long and three broad. This loch is but a pool of stagnant water, and might very easily have been drained, but that the inhabitants regarded it with a superstitious dread. There is a tradition that a pot of gold lies in a vault below, guarded by a large black dog with two heads. It is said that a tenant once had attempted to drain the loch, and had succeeded, so that the water was all carried off. The only remuner-ation the unfortunate agriculturist received was to be aroused from his midnight slumbers by a visit from the black dog, which set up such a hideous howl as made the hills reverberate, and the poor man almost die with fright. Furthermore, with this diabolical music he was regularly serenaded at the midnight hour till he had filled up the drain and the loch had resumed its former dimensions.

The last farm or township on the banks of the Helmisdale is Cäen, a snug sheltered spot, surrounded with hills to the N.W. and E., and having a southerly exposure. During the earlier years of my father's ministry, this place contained nearly a hundred inhabitants. The river glides smoothly past it in an easterly direction, receiving from it a considerable stream; but when it attains to the precise boundary line between the parishes of Kildonan and Loth, marked by a small burn from the sides of a steep hill called the "Gearrlag," the river suddenly makes a bend to the south, and after falling over the Craobhdykes, about two miles below, it enters the sea at Helmisdale.

I have thus minutely delineated the local features of my native parish for two reasons: first, because with every one of those features is connected a crowd of associations of my early years, and then, because they are now, in so far as the hand of man could prevail, almost wholly obliterated. The townships in every strath and glen, and on every hill, which once teemed with life, are now desolate and silent; and the only traces visible of the vanished, happy population are, here and there, a half-buried hearthstone or a moss-grown grave-yard.

CHAPTER VII.

DONALD SAGE; HIS CHILDHOOD.

1789-1800.

J RETURN to the incidents of my father's life and ministry. Both my sisters were natives of Caithness, and were, at the time of my father's settlement at Kildonan, the one a year and a half and the other about two months old. On the 31st day of August, 1788, my elder and only brother Eneas was born at the manse of Kildonan. There, too, I was born on the 20th day of October, 1789. Six weeks after my birth I was baptised by Mr. David Mackay, the minister of Reay. I was named Donald, after my maternal, as my brother was called Eneas after our paternal, grandfather. My brother was nursed by one Marion Polson, the second wife of Donald Mackay, catechist of the parish. My nurse was Barbara Corbett, the wife of John Murray, who lived at a secluded spot in the parish of Loth, to the west of the rock of Marril, called Lonn-riabhach, or the speckled loan. Barbara took great care of me; her daughter Barbara was my foster-sister. She was latterly my servant when at Achness, and one of my first servants when I came to this parish.

I can now, at the intervening period of fifty years, distinctly fix upon the very first exercise of my memory. In the apartment in which I was born, and directly before the window, when I was about two years of age, I was asking something which I do not now remember of my mother. Like the usual demands of children, it was unreasonable, and therefore could not be granted. Yet three things are impressed upon my memory—the motherly tenderness with which my childish request was refused, and the petulance with which that refusal was received; connected with these comes the remembrance of my mother's personal appearance, especially the features of her countenance. My recollection suddenly stops here; but the memory which thus so suddenly slept was destined, in a few months afterwards, as suddenly to reawaken. The cause was my mother's untimely death. She died in childbed, of her sixth child. Of the circumstances connected with her illness I have no recollection; but I have been told that, about an hour before her death, we were all solemnly summoned before her, and ranged round her dying bed, to take our last farewell of her and to receive her blessing. She took particular notice of me, appeared deeply affected, and, in broken accents, prayed that I might yet be useful in the vineyard of Christ. Of this solemn scene I have no recollection, but of that which very soon followed my memory has, at this moment, a most distinct hold. On the evening of the 27th of November, 1792, when I was three years and a month old, I recollect entering in at the door of the room where my mother, but a few hours before, had breathed her last. It was the low caster-room of the manse. A bed stood at the north-east corner of the room, with dark curtains folded up in front. On the bed lay extended, with a motionless stillness which both surprised and terrified me, one whom I at once knew to be my mother. I was sure it was she, although she lay so still and silent. She appeared to me to be covered with a white sheet or robe; white leather gloves were on her hands, which lay crossed over her body. At the opposite corner of the room sat my father. He had, previous to my coming in, been indulging his grief in silence, and giving vent to the "bitterness of the heart" in half-audible sighs. My sudden and heedless entrance seemed to open up the flood-gates of his grief. I was the favourite child of her who now lay stretched in death—the last surviving pledge of their affection. It was too much for him. He sobbed aloud, the tears rolled down his face, his frame shook, and he clasped me in his large embrace in all the agony of a great sorrow. That sobbing still rings in my ears, although then my only feeling was that of childish wonder. · I gazed, now at my mother's body, especially at her gloved and motionless hands, then at my father, as I could not conceive that any but children could weep at all, or at least weep aloud. My mother died in the 42nd year of her age. Of the subsequent events—the freshness of my father's sorrow, the solemnities of my mother's funeral, the necessary arrangements in the household consequent upon her death—of these, with many other circumstances, I have not the slightest remembrance. But the scene I have just described retains its place like a framed picture in my memory.

When my recollections of these juvenile years again awaken, I find myself and my brother placed under the tutelage of a young man named Fraser, and under the care of one named Elspat Mackay, or "Eppy," as housekeeper. Hugh Fraser's attainments as an instructor of youth were as slender as could well be conceived. He knew all the letters of the alphabet, he could, without much spelling, read any ordinary English school book, and as for his pronunciation of that language, it would have warmed the heart of any Sutherland Highlander had he heard it on the banks of the Ganges, so strong did it smack of the "accents of the mountain-tongue." A slate-and-pencil knowledge of the four cardinal rules of arithmetic, too, was an essential part of the education which constituted Hugh's stock-in-trade. The only recollection I have of him is in connection with an object which, from the first consciousness that I had of the working of my mind, made an impression upon me, and that was the corn-mill of Kildonan. The *revolutions* of the *waterwheel* occupied far more of my waking, and even of my sleeping, thoughts, than the *revolutions* of *kingdoms* do now. The mill was distinctly visible from the manse windows, and its stillness or its activity were among the first unusual objects that attracted my attention. I was standing one day at the glebe dyke, right opposite the water-wheel, whilst it was in full career. I was intently gazing at it—at the rim, the spokes, and the circular shower of drops which, by the rapidity of its motion, it threw up around it. The spokes of the wheel were double, that is, four on each side of the rim, parallel to each other, and as the wheel revolved with great rapidity it seemed to my mind to present an interior chamber. Hugh Fraser tapped me on the shoulder. "What do you do here?" said he; "your dinner is almost cold, and Eppy is calling for you." "What would happen me," said I, "if I were within that wheel just now?" "You would get your crown cracked," said Hugh Fraser, "that would be all." This is the only information given me by Hugh Fraser that I can recall.

Eppy Mackay made a longer, as well as a more vivid, impression upon me. As a housekeeper, or upper and confidential servant, Eppy was a model. She had everything to do, and undertook to do everything. She was cook, chamber-maid, nurse, governante, and housekeeper, all in one. If things went on well, my father, who was an easy man, praised her; if things went in the contrary way, my father, who was also a hasty man, reproved and censured her. Both the praise and the blame Eppy received with the same placidity and imperturbable spirit. But in all this she did not act upon the abstract principle either of meekness or fidelity. There were certain advantages connected with the situation she held and the trust reposed in her, as the minister's housekeeper, which supported her under any irritability of temper, not to say fear, which she might occasionally have felt under the sudden but short-lived explosions of my father's anger. She possessed, for example, some little measure of parish patronage, and this she was careful to extend at least as far as on the occasion it would go. It was therefore reckoned advantageous for any of the tenants or their wives to have Eppy's ear. Then there was at her disposal, or under her charge, certain articles, such as soap, tea, or sugar, with which, after the family wants were supplied, she made herself gracious among her neighbours who could not come at such things in any other way. These articles, no doubt, were her master's property, but Eppy and her friends reconciled themselves to this rather questionable way of disposing of them, on a principle of Highland expediency of very old standing, namely, "that they would be the better for it, and he would not be the worse." By dispensing her favours after this method, Eppy succeeded in gaining for herself a "good name" among the old, and a goodly array of "cake-and-pudding" admirers among the young. Of the number of these last was John Ross, the miller of Kildonan, a stout young fellow who held the mill in lease from my father. He was Eppy's declared admirer, and to pay court to her, he had presented me with a windmill. His present rivetted my affections to him, and I followed him like his shadow. To put my attachment to the test, some of the servants one stormy evening, as I was seated by the kitchen fireside, told me that John Ross was dead—that he had been drowned in attempting to cross the burn when heavily flooded. I can even now remember the tumult which the intelligence excited within me. My breath came suddenly thick and short. With almost a feeling of suffocation, I appealed to Eppy for the truth of it. She sorrowfully shook her head, and pretended to be deeply affected. This to me was tantamount to proof positive, and, giving full vent to my feelings, I made the kitchen rafters ring with my roaring. As the instigators of the scene, however, were busily employed in soothing me, John Ross entered the kitchen. When he was told of the proof I had given of my childish fancy for him, he was much affected.

Of my father, at this period, or of my sisters, I have no recollection. My only brother, with whom 1 played all day, and slept at night, did attract my notice. I recollect one circumstance respecting him. We had both crossed the burn, and, for our own amusement, had called in at almost all the tenants' houses, where we met with a kind and cordial reception. We came at last to the schoolmaster's house, a Mr. Donald Macleod. I was a greater favourite with the people than my brother, and, as a proof of this, Mrs. Macleod, in treating us to a lunch, whilst she gave him some bread and butter, gave me as a very special delicacy, a half cake of oat-bread, larded over with cream. We were to remain at the schoolmaster's house until Eppy should come to bring us home. It was getting late and dark, and whilst I was quite content to remain until it was Eppy's pleasure to call for us, not so was my brother. He insisted upon being taken home, and all good Mrs. Macleod's remonstrances to the contrary were in vain. He was, from his earliest years of the most indomitable and determined resolution; and his will, in opposition to all that could be urged against it, he laid down by the usual arguments of a wayward child, that is by tears and bellowing. He carried his point, and Mrs. Macleod and her eldest daughter were under the necessity, not only of setting out with us both, but moreover, and in obedience to my brother's most sovereign will, of carrying us on their shoulders, and safely landing us at the kitchen-door. These comparatively trivial circumstances I merely notice as the terminating points of my memory at this distance of time. My father was at the period I speak of. much engaged in the discharge of his public duties, and frequently from home, so that he seldom came into such immediate contact with me as to make any impression on my memory, I was then in about my fourth year.

On the 11th day of December, 1794, my father married a second time. The object of his choice was Miss Jean Sutherland, third daughter of Major George Sutherland of Midgarty. This gentleman was the second son of Sutherland of Langwell in the county of Caithness. After having seen much service in the army, he retired on half-pay, and took in lease from the Earl of Sutherland the farm of Midgarty, in the parish of Loth. His lineal descent from the Sutherlands was ancient and respectable. His family had, not only the estate of Berriedale, but formerly also that of Swiney, which last came in process of time to be settled on a second son, from whom descended the Sutherlands of Swiney. Of the last of these, and of the circumstances which necessitated his selling the property, and of its purchase by Charles Gordon, of Pulrossie, I have already written. The last of the lairds of Langwell was the elder brother of George Sutherland of Midgarty. He lived on his property, at the beautiful and romantic place of Langwell, on terms of amity and friendship with all his relatives and fellow proprietors, and in the exercise of an unbounded hospitality. His estate furnished him with the choicest luxuries of the table, such as mutton, beef, salmon, venison, and game of every variety, while, from a well-stocked garden, he had the best fruits and vegetables which the soil and climate could produce. He was himself an epicure in no ordinary measure, but so social was his disposition that, even if his table groaned with good things, he could not eat a morsel with relish or comfort, unless he had one or more guests to enjoy them along with him. He was, besides, an excellent landlord, and, the desolating system of sheep-farming being then unknown, the straths of Berriedale and Langwell were the happy homes of a numerous peasantry, all of whom were ardently attached to their warm-hearted landlord. His eldest son and heir was, however, unworthy of his father and of his race. He was a determined prodigal. During his father's lifetime, he married Miss Sinclair, sole heiress of Brabster and West Canisbay, which, united with his paternal inheritance, afforded him the prospect of a very handsome income. But his extravagance and profligacy blasted his prospects. His loose habits so alienated the affections of his wife, that she felt herself compelled to sue for a divorce, whilst, by his extravagance after his father's death, he found himself so overwhelmed in debt that he was obliged to sell his fine paternal estate far under its value. Separated from his wife and family, and cast upon the world, he died in obscurity in London. His son George, inherited after his mother's death, the estates of Brabster and West Canisbay. Langwell was purchased by Sir John Sinclair, and when he too got unhappily involved, was by him forfeited, at a valuation of £40,000, to a Mr. Horne, the son of a blacksmith at Scouthel in Caithness, but who had prospered as a lawyer in Edinburgh.

Major George Sutherland of Midgarty was universally esteemed. He was twice married. By his first wife he had a family of eight daughters and two sons. By his second wife, whose name was Robertson, he had a son and a daughter. This lady was inadvertently poisoned. She had been invalided, and by her medical attendant she was recommended to take medicine. Instead of Epsom salts, a dose of saltpetre was accidentally administered, and the consequences were fatal. All Major Sutherland's daughters, with the exception of one who died at an early age, were well married. The eldest, Janet, married Mr. Gray of the Grays of Skibo, a West India planter, who amassed a fortune; the marriage, however, was an unhappy one, the parties separating by mutual consent. Mrs. Gray resided in London, and, after her husband's death, sued for a jointure, of which his executors contrived, in a great measure, to denude her. She lived to a great age, and died in rather limited circumstances. Esther, the second daughter, married, some years after her father's death, Lieut. Sutherland, son of Sheriff Sutherland of Shibercross. Their marriage was kept secret. Mr. Sutherland did not survive his marriage above a year; and it was after his death that it was publicly promulgated in order to secure to his wife her annuity as an officer's widow, her only means of support. During the years of my attendance at college in Aberdeen, where she then resided, I was intimately acquainted with her, and experienced much kindness from her. Major Sutherland's third daughter Jean married my father. Williamina, the fourth

daughter, married Robert Baigrie, who had been captain of a merchant-
man in the West India trade, and who, after realising a competency,
and after the death of his first wife, by whom he had one daughter,
took in lease, from the trustees of the then Countess of Sutherland,
the farm of Midgarty. It was at the time in the possession of his
sister-in-law, Mrs. Sutherland, previous to her marriage, and some
disagreeable altercation in consequence took place between them, which
produced a coolness that was not removed during the remainder of
their lives. Charlotte, the fifth daughter, married a Dr. Macfarquhar;
they resided in the West Indies, and had a son and three daughters.
They sent their son to Britain for his education, while yet a mere boy;
but while romping about on the deck during the voyage, he, unobserved,
dropped overboard and was drowned. His mother, who doted upon
her only son, when she heard of his death, suffered so severe a shock,
that it brought her to an untimely grave, and the loss of wife and
son terminated her husband's existence in a few months thereafter.
Elizabeth, Major Sutherland's sixth daughter, and one of the most
beautiful women I ever saw, married Joseph Gordon. This gentleman
was the second son of Mr. Gordon of Carrol, and younger brother of
John Gordon, the laird of Carrol. He was tacksman of Navidale on
the east coast of Sutherlandshire. He realised a few thousand pounds,
as a coppersmith in the West Indies, and resided for a considerable
period of his life, first at Navidale in the parish of Loth, and afterwards
at Embo, Dornoch. He died at Edinburgh in 1799. Roberta, the
youngest surviving daughter of Major Sutherland by his first wife,
remained for a considerable time unmarried; latterly she married
Robert Pope, son of Peter Pope, and nephew of the Rev. Alexr. Pope,
minister of Reay. The Major's only daughter by his second wife, also
called Janet, married, after her father's death, Captain Kenneth Mackay
of Torboll. The sons, by both his wives, all died unmarried. George
the eldest attained to the rank of major in the E. I. Co.'s service, and
died in India. James died in the West Indies. Robert the youngest,
and only son by the second marriage, went, at a very early age, to the
West Indies, where he succeeded in making a very large fortune as a
planter. He intended to purchase the parish of Loth, which the
Countess of Sutherland proposed to sell; but the sale being postponed,
Mr. Sutherland extended his speculations, and, sustaining great losses
in business, he soon found his whole fortune dissipated. He afterwards
went to St. Domingo, about the year 1810, and was the chief counsellor
of Christoph, king of Hayti, crowned in 1811. Mr. Sutherland only
survived his removal to St. Domingo a few years. He left a natural
son Robert, who was reared and educated at Torboll.

Major George Sutherland of Midgarty died at an advanced age.
His sons, at or before his death, had all gone abroad, and the farm was
managed, first of all, by his eldest daughter Mrs. Gray, and, after her
marriage, by her next sister Esther. It was during her management
that Captain Baigrie first got acquainted with Williamina, and afterwards became her husband. On his marriage with her, which might
be about the year 1784, he took the farm in lease for himself, and it
was owing to this circumstance, I am inclined to think, as well as to-

the division of Mr. Sutherland's property, that the permanent coolness arose, not only between him and Mrs. Sutherland, but between her and her three sisters, Mrs. Baigrie, my stepmother and Roberta, who were then residing at Midgarty, and supported Capt. Baigrie in the dispute. Mrs. Sutherland then left Midgarty, and never afterwards returned.

On the 11th day of December, 1794, my father was married at Midgarty by his co-presbyter, Mr. MacCulloch, minister of Loth. Weddings, or marriage-feasts, were highly in vogue in these days, and there was, in every case, a double feast, one at the bride's father's or friend's house, where the ceremony was performed; at this feast the bride and bridegroom sat as the principal guests, remaining one or more days. The next feast was at the bridegroom's house, on the arrival of the happy pair at their own home. This was called "a'bhanais theth," *i.e.*, the heating of the house, or, as the men of Sutherland literally rendered the phrase from their native tongue into English, "the wedding hot." At my father's marriage none of his children were present—we were too young. But all the particulars of their arrival at the manse, of the bustle of preparation to receive them, of our first and formal introduction to her who was henceforth to fill the place of our departed mother, of her looks and personal appearance, and of the feasting and dancing with which the whole scene was finally concluded, are still as distinctly within the reach of my remembrance as any past events of my life at a more advanced period can well be. First of all then, Eppy the housekeeper, in my memory's eye, occupies the foreground of the reminiscence. On that occasion all her varied tact was put into requisition. When the happy pair arrived in the close, we were, after a long previous drilling in the nursery, marshalled by Eppy to the kitchen-door, in breathless expectation of the great things that awaited us. There she left us to gaze, in dumb wonder for a time, whilst she herself, with all the solemnity of a Highland seneschal, moved forward to meet, and duly to receive, her new mistress —curtsying and bobbing at every third step of her progress in advance. Her measured movements filled me with wonder and admiration. My father was mounted on a strong grey horse, his bride on a long-tailed Highland garron. My father first alighted, then helped his spouse from off her horse, while Eppy stood bolt upright before them. I still remember my father's voice saying, " This is Eppy Mackay, my dear." She was acknowledged by her new mistress with a smile and a slight bow of the head, and then they all walked into the house. Soon afterwards Eppy made her re-appearance among us to usher us into the parental presence. But, before I mention our introduction by Eppy, I must notice the habiliments extraordinary in which we were clad. Both my sisters were dressed in tartan gowns of home manufacture, their hair was braided on the forehead, and saturated with pomatum, and they were made to look, upon the whole, just like two young damsels from a Highland nursery, making their first appearance in public life. My brother and I were clothed in the same identical tartan, but of a make and habit suited to our age and sex. This was a kilt after the most approved fashion, surmounted by a jacket, fitted tight to the body, and to which the kilt was affixed by a tailor's seam. The jacket and kilt, open in front, were shut in upon our persons with yellow buttons. Our extremities were prominently adorned, and Eppy, who was a first-rate Highland dressmaker, had exhausted her skill upon them, and even outdone herself. We were furnished with white worsted stockings, tied below the knee with red garters, of which "Malvolio" himself would have approved. Our feet were inserted into Highland brogues, while our heads were combed and powdered with flour, as a substitute for the hair-powder which was the distinguishing mark of all the swells of that fashionable age. Thus accoutred, we were all four marshalled by Eppy into the presence of our father and stepmother, and nothing is, at this moment, more vividly impressed upon my memory than the interview. I distinctly recollect the first impression which my stepmother's appearance made upon me. She had rather a fine countenance, full dark eyes, and regular features, expressive of intelligence, but also of quickness of temper. When we were all standing in a row before her, she received us very graciously. Her keen eye went over us all, until it lighted on the powdered heads of my brother and myself. So long as my sisters were the only objects of her scrutiny, an arch smile played over her face, but when we, with our white stockings, red garters, kilts and jackets, and, above all, our highly-powdered heads, met her eye, she could no longer contain herself, but burst into an incontrollable fit of laughing, in which my father, and even Eppy herself, were obliged to join. To the feast which followed, with its delicacies, all the sub-tenants on the farm of Kildonan, which my father held in lease, as also the elders of the parish, were invited ; and afterwards, to the heart-stirring strains of the Highland bagpipe, the guests, young and old, "tripped it heartily on the light fantastic toe." Below stairs Eppy was mistress of ceremonies. She danced with the elders and with the tenants, married and unmarried, each in turn. One of the elders, Roderick Bain, rises to my recollection ; he was turned of sixty. I was present in the low easter room whilst the dance was in full career. The room was crowded, and I was comfortably seated on a large meal-chest, placed in the north-east corner of it, near the chimney. From this elevated position I noticed a very amusing *rencontre* between Eppy Mackay and Rory Bain. Rory had participated largely in the merriment with the younger members of the group, and this was keenly observed by Eppy. The flour, with which she had already so profusely adorned my brother's head and mine, stood in a small barrel close at her hand, and she evidently was of opinion that what was good for the heads of the young would not be unsuitable for the old. Accordingly, as Rory was dancing with as much gravity as if he were engaged in something more important, Eppy served him such a plentiful goupen of good white flour, right on the top of his bald pate, as covered his head, face and eyes, and what was harder to bear, set the assemblage in a loud roar of laughter at his expense. Rory could not speak, as the flour had entered his nose and mouth, and had set him a-coughing ; but resenting Eppy's benediction, he immediately gave chase. One after the other flew out of the room, and their exit draws down the curtain between all

my present recollections and what subsequently took place at my
father's wedding. I recollect, however, the daily arrangements of the
family, as well as its amusements, soon after the marriage.

My reminiscences from 1794 to 1801, the year I went with my
brother to school at Dornoch, I may here introduce. Our step-mother
must necessarily occupy the first place in the record. She was a
person of no ordinary powers of mind. Her understanding was solid,
clear, and comprehensive. The conclusions to which she came,
respecting the dispositions and principles of those with whom she
became acquainted, were drawn with perfect accuracy, and she seldom,
if ever, was mistaken. She could discover moral weight and intrinsic
value of principle under the most disadvantageous outward appearances,
but she could also detect deceit and cunning under covert of the
most specious professions. She had a native generosity of spirit which
shone out with peculiar intensity when she came in contact with
kindred dispositions; and straightforward honesty of intention, even
when directed against herself, she acknowledged and respected. But
she had her failings. Her keenness of temper was, like her mind, of
more than ordinary strength. When thoroughly excited, it swept
down upon her with the force of a tempest. She was naturally a proud
woman, and cherished, especially, pride of family. It was not long
after the marriage when the sad fruits of this sharpness of temper
became visible to us children. At times our step-mother would absent
herself from meals, and even from family worship, and lock herself up
in a room for days, and even for weeks, together. I recollect on one of
those gloomy occasions that, whilst we were at dinner, I was sent by
my father with a pacific message to her. She at once entered warmly
with me on the whole ground of dispute between herself and my father
—a subject of which I could comprehend nothing but the painful
externals. The effect of all this upon the children was what is, I
believe, usual in such cases. Naturally looking up to those who
occupied the place of heads of the family, and leaning upon them, their
differences filled us with alarm. We all had an instinctive dread of
our step-mother's temper, and the measures of defence which we set up
against it were simply to do all what we could to please her, and to
deprecate her anger. My eldest sister Elizabeth, or Betty as we called
her, was remarkable for her good sense, and she viewed the differences
so often taking place between the heads of the house with apprehension
of the worst consequences. She was always planning some conciliatory
scheme by which my step-mother's irritable spirit might be mollified.
On one occasion, towards the close of spring, we happened to be very
scarce of fuel. The peat-stack was nearly exhausted, and the only fuel
to be had was wood. A fit of ill-humour had settled upon my
step-mother's mind for nearly a fortnight, when Betty proposed, as a
good deed that might propitiate her favour, that we should all turn out
after breakfast to the Dalmore, and gather sticks and rubbish which
the river floods had thrown upon it. This proposal was joyfully
adopted, the happiest consequences being confidently anticipated. We
had to gather the drift-wood in heaps, tie it up in bundles, and thus
carry it home on our backs. We toiled at this work for some five

hours. We were often on the point of giving it up, but the hope of being approved of cheered us on till we had finished our task, whereupon, exhausted with fatigue and hunger, we wended our way home. When we arrived we triumphantly threw down our bundles in the close, taking care to do so right before the parlour window, that they might be seen, and we entered the parlour with keen appetites, and full of expectation and hope. We found our father and step-mother finishing their dinner in moody silence. Plates, each containing little more than a spoonful of broth, and almost cold, were already set for us, to which we sat down without any recognition. No sooner had we finished this prelude to more substantial fare, than my step-mother asked my father to return thanks. This was accordingly done, and we perfectly understood it to be the signal that her dinner was ended, and that ours, scarcely begun, must end too. She rose from table, and so did we. I still remember the look which Betty gave us on this issue of our scheme of conciliation—a scheme which had cost her so much thought and us so much toil. My brother Eneas fell a-crying when the dishes were being removed, and my father, feeling for us all, said, "Give him some bread, poor fellow; I daresay he is very hungry." This I felt to be the most heartless act of my step-mother's life.

Comparing the years of my boyhood with those of my own children, under the tender sway of a mother, I can see that in many ways we were made to feel that our father's wife was not the mother of his children. Our food was but sparingly dealt out to us, and that at long intervals, and I often felt so exhausted before the dinner-hour that, like Jonathan in the wood, I felt my eyes grow dim from abstinence. But whilst I record these instances of hasty temper and of a spirit calculated to bring odium on the name of step-mother, it would be unjust in me not to add that they were but like the smart frosts and gloomy tempests of winter, preparatory to the genial warmth of spring. With all her asperity and heat of temper, none that ever stood in the parental relation to children discharged its moral duties more efficiently than did my excellent step-mother, and when her temper was stilled, none could be more agreeable and engaging in manner. Her advices and instructions, given when she assembled us in the parlour, remain engraved on my mind, and, by their plainness, perspicuity, and justness, made such a profound impression upon me at the time that I attached a sort of unerring perfectness to everything she said.

Soon after this marriage, we were sent to the parish school. The master, Mr. Donald MacLeod, was a native of Tain. He began life as a pedlar. I do not know when he first settled in Kildonan, but he married the widow of his predecessor, a person of the name of Gunn. I scarcely remember anything of my schoolboy days under his care, except his own personal appearance. Mr. MacLeod had a very grim visage and a long beard, and, with a leathern strap in his hand, he predominated in stern rule over a noisy assemblage of tatterdemalion, cat-o'-mountain-looking boys and girls. I remember my first effort at printing, for which, ever since, I have had a mechanical turn. On a leaf of my copy-book I had, and as I believed with success, printed the names of my brother and sisters and my own. My school companions were loud in their praises, and, not a little elated, I showed my work to the schoolmaster. He, however, gathering his brows into a frown, threw it from him, pronouncing me an idler and a blockhead. My father did not long leave us under the tutelage of the parish schoolmaster. He became our teacher himself, and the various branches which he taught us, as well as the room in which we assembled, are most vividly impressed upon my memory. The room was the little back closet upstairs, and in it were my father's library, his study-chair, and a large table placed close to the window, the view from which extended from Torr-na-Croiche and Clach-an-èig in the west to Torr-an-riachaidh, with a peep of Craig-an-fhithiche in the east. The elementary branches taught us were English reading and grammar, Latin and arithmetic. Our primer was all contained on the first leaf of the Shorter Catechism, and after it we were promoted to Fisher's spelling-book and grammar, and Mason's "Collection." Well do I recall the feeling of joy with which I received the intimation from my father that next day I was to begin the Latin language. He pulled out the table drawer and showed me a new copy of Ruddiman's "Rudiments" which he had purchased the week before at Brora. My sisters had been sent, sometime before, to reside at a Society's school in Strathnaver. With my father I read Cordery's Colloquies, Cornelius Nepos, Cæsar, Sallust, Ovid, Virgil, Livy, and Horace, and along with these I was so carefully instructed in the rules of Watt's Latin Grammar that I shall not forget them as long as I live. In addition to our week-day tasks, we all had our Sabbath lessons. At first they consisted of so many questions from the Shorter Catechism, and a paraphrase or psalm. After tea on Sabbath evening, we all assembled round our father, at the fireside in the parlour, and after we had repeated our tasks, he taught us sacred music. The psalm tunes of St. David's, St. Ann, Bangor, London New, Dundee, Stilt (York), Martyrs', and St. Mary's were amongst those thus learned. As I advanced in the knowledge of Latin, my father prescribed my Sabbath tasks in that language. I began with Castalio's Dialogues, and, when farther advanced, I learned Buchanan's Psalms. I still feel the salutary effect of the classical studies pursued under my father's tuition. The Latin authors which I read brought me into the knowledge of Roman history, as well as into that of their precursors and rivals, the Greeks. I attached a locality to all the various incidents recorded by the classic writers of Greece and Rome, placing them in the midst of the scenes around me. The place or township of Kildonan, with the tenants' houses grouped around, resembled a village. The round knoll, Torr-buidh, rose in the centre; on the east was the schoolhouse, with a green plat in the front of it. When therefore I first became acquainted with Greek and Roman story, local associations began immediately in my mind to stand connected with persons and events. The gay and elegant Athens, with its orators and heroes, its classic buildings, its Acropolis, and its thoughtless and polished mob;—Lacedaemon, with its double royalty, its abstemious citizens, its rigid and fantastic morals;—Thebes, raised to notice by the victories of Epaminondas ;—Corinth—literary, mercantile, and voluptuous—were all located in the village of Kildonan. Then also lordly Rome, with its Kings and Consuls, its Tribunes military and popular, its Decemvirs, Dictators and Censors, its Prætors, soldiers and Emperors, its wars abroad, its ferments and intrigues at home—all were to be found in Kildonan. The esplanade before the old school-house was the Forum ; there the popular assemblies met, there the Tribunes vetoed, there the infamous Appius Claudius seized Virginia, there the Decii devoted themselves to the fancied good of their country, there the Gracchi died, there "Tully spoke and Cæsar fell." The Roman poets, too, had their peculiar localities. Ovid's "Daphne in laurum," his "Io in vaccam," and many more of his fantastic scenes, I laid among the steeps of Craig-an-fhithiche, or the hazel groves of Coille-Chil-Mer. The scenes of Virgil's Eclogues—Tityrus' cottage and flocks, and his entertainment for his expatriated guest and countrymen Melibœus—my fancy laid at the foot of Tigh-an-Abb' ; Damoetas and Menalcas' singing match I placed on the summit of Craig-an-fhithiche, whilst the heifers, calves, goats and kids, contended for as the prize, browsed on the neighbouring steep of the Coire-mòr. I began the Georgics, with their antique lessons on husbandry, at the very time that my father's man, Muckle Donald, made his first bold attempt to plough the Dalmore, which for fifteen years had not been under cultivation. With a plough and harness scarcely less primitive than that with which Virgil himself might be familiar in his boyish days at Cremona, Muckle Donald turned up the green sward of the Dalmore, sowed it with black Highland oats, and finished it off with a scrambling sort of harrowing. This was in the month of May, and whenever I was done with my Virgil lesson, I became a constant attendant of Muckle Donald at his toil in the field. His team, three Highland horses and a cow, "groaned" most piteously while the ploughshare, pressed down by the hands of two attendants, "gleamed" as it opened up the furrows.* What wonder that, as in the tilling, sowing, harrowing, and ultimate growth, ripening, and reaping of the Dalmore crop of oats I realised the meaning, so there also I fixed the locality of these beautiful lines :—

> " Vere novo, gelidus, canis cum montibus humor
> Liquitur, et Zephiro putris se gleba resolvit,
> Depresso incipiat jam tum mihi taurus aratro
> Ingemere, et sulco attritus splendescere vomer."

> GEORG. I., 43-46.

To other incidents of "the days of yore" I must now refer. My brother and I, while still very young, made a journey under our father's guidance to the "Coast side," as we usually called that part of the

---

* The rude harness used was of the following description :—The collars of the animals were of straw, with hems of wood, to which were attached side traces made of horse-hair. The plough was a light wooden implement with an iron sock, on which two men had to lean with all their weight to keep it in the ground, if the land was stiff, while another guided it from between the stilts. The harrow was made of wooden spikes set in cross bars of native birch.—ED.

county of Sutherland which lay by the sea-shore. It was called by the natives ."Machair Chatt'" (or the Sutherland coast), extending from the Ord of Caithness to Dornoch, in distinction from the inland and mountainous part of the county which was generally designated "An Direadh" (or the ascending side). In this expedition, our object was to be introduced to our step-mother's near relatives at Loth. Two of her married sisters resided there, the one at Navidale, the other at Midgarty. This being the first time I ever was out of my father's house for more than a day, I have a vivid remembrance of the preparations for the journey, and all the incidents connected with it. My father, with saddle-bags manufactured not later than the year 1748, was mounted upon his grey horse—a noble steed for road or ford. My brother and I were seated on pillows behind two of the men-servants, mounted the one on a black garron, the other on a strong tun-bellied dun mare. Thus accoutred, we bent our way down the strath. When we approached Helmisdale, an object, unknown and extraordinary, suddenly presented itself to my view. Its first impression upon me was that which I could conceive might be produced by a miracle, or like the flitting of unearthly objects in the semi-consciousness of a dream. At the first glance, I was struck dumb with surprise, and in vain I tasked my childish powers to ascertain whether it belonged to earth or air. It had the appearance of a low but distant hill, its distance being particularly expressed by the deep blue colour. But then it had something about it quite different from any distant hill which I had ever seen. As we drew nearer, I thought I could perceive something like motion upon its surface, and then white specks appearing and disappearing upon it like spots of snow. I saw that it must be water, but, if water, why so blue? I could contain myself no longer. Riding close up to my father's side, I stretched out my hand in the direction of the object of my wonder, and eagerly cried out, " O, what's that long, blue, moving hill?" "O," said he, "Donald, that's the SEA."

At Helmisdale, we lodged under the hospitable roof of Mr. and Mrs. Houston. Mr. Louis Houston was an amiable man. He occupied the small farm of Easter Helmisdale, and the places of Scalbisdale and Suisgill in the parish of Kildonan, both of which he had sub-let to small tenants. The disorder of which in a few years he died had just begun, and he was very nervous. Now, for the first time, I met with Mrs. Houston, his kind and motherly wife, with whom my acquaintance continued for upwards of twenty years. During our stay at their house that evening, as we were all seated round the parlour fire, I was particularly struck with the substance which burnt so brilliantly, and sent forth so strong a heat from a low iron grate in the chimney. When it burned, it melted like resin or sealing wax, and every particle of it which lay untouched by the fire shone like so many pieces of polished iron. Being accustomed to see only peat, or moss-fir, and the wood rubbish of the Dalmore burned as fuel, I could not conceive what this new substance might be. In answer to my eager inquiries, I was told that it was English coal, and that it was used in England for fuel instead of our familiar peats. Next day we set out for Midgarty. There was then no bridge across the river at Helmisdale. Travellers got over it either by a boat or coble when the stream was in flood, or by a rugged ford when otherwise. At the mouth of the river stood the Corf House, a store built for the purpose of containing the corn-rents of the tenantry. It was almost surrounded on the south by the buildings of the salmon-fishery, a low tier of houses, roofed with red tiles, which particularly excited my wonder. I have a distinctly vivid recollection of our passage across the Helmisdale river by the boat, which was the first I had ever seen.

The distance between Helmisdale and Midgarty is three miles. The road then lay close by the shore all the way. It was a wretched, scrambling, bridle-road, scarcely fit for a horse to get through, and almost impassable to carriages, although it was at that time, and for many years afterwards, the only public highway through the whole county. As it passed Midgarty, access from it to the house was by a private path, which, at its junction with the main road, was shut in by a barred gate standing between two rounded stone-and-lime pillars, to which my youthful associations clung like ivy, under the name of the " gate of the shore." The path from the gate passed between two steep banks with a slight ascent, and afterwards through the centre of a corn-field straight up to the house. This path became familiar to me under the name of the "avenue." When we rode up the avenue, the house presented itself to view. I regarded it with awe as the finest house I had ever seen. It stood close to the base of a hill which rose up on the north to the height of 700 feet above the sea-level. The body of the house, originally erected by Major Sutherland, was a plain, ordinary building. Capt. Baigrie, who then possessed the farm, had added a large wing, and this addition contained two very handsome rooms, both being lighted by two large bow-windows, which gave the house an elegant appearance, whilst the rooms within, lighted in this manner, very much resembled the cabin of a large West-Indiaman. Indeed Captain Baigrie, who was master of a West-Indiaman, had planned the rooms in imitation of a ship's cabin. To the west of the house flowed a burn which issued from a well at the top of the hill. As it neared the house it was enclosed by a warren thrown across its channel, from which a considerable part of its waters were conveyed by leaden pipes to the house. The burn, after escaping from this monopoly of its current, wended its way through a rural dell, and passed through a plot of ground which had once been the garden and was now an orchard. The stream then passed between two very steep braes to the sea, which it entered through a bed of shingle, almost 200 yards to the west of the shore gate.

We were most hospitably and kindly received at Midgarty. My father, next day, went home, leaving us for a time to remain on the coast side. I rejoiced in my new quarters, and conceived myself to be in fairy-land. I may here introduce the heads of the family with whom I afterwards became so familiar. Captain Baigrie, a native of Buchan, had gone to sea as a cabin-boy on board a trader, and afterwards as a seaman on board a West-India-man. His voyaging was extensive; he had been, at one time, within a few degrees of the North Pole, where he experienced great privations, arising from scarcity of provisions and intense cold. He ultimately became captain of a West-India-man, and by several successful voyages realised a genteel competency of two or three thousand pounds. During his cruises from London to Jamaica, he married a Miss Hadden, by whom he had a daughter. His wife died, and he came to reside with his friends in Aberdeenshire, leaving his daughter with her maternal relations in London. How he first became acquainted with his second wife I know not; but after his marriage with her he took the farm of Midgarty, and resided there until his death in 1809. In his manners and habits he was the seaman out and out, generous, hasty, given to banning, and fond of diversion. In his diet he was singularly abstemious, and his privations at sea had so taught him to value food that he was not only systematically moderate in his meals, but he would also eat the coarsest food rather than have it wasted. He was bred a Scottish Episcopalian, and in his younger years he was inaugurated into that Christian sect by John Skinner, Episcopal minister at Langside, near Peterhead, better known to the Scottish public as the author of "Tulloch-gorum," and "The Ewie wi' the crookit horn," than as a gospel minister, or as the author of the theological works which bear his name. Captain Baigrie's second wife—my stepmother's sister—was one of the mildest and gentlest of her sex. She resembled one of the inland lakes of her native country, surrounded by giant mountains on every side, its smooth and placid surface seldom or never disturbed by the hurricanes which act so powerfully on the expanse of the ocean. Her pale countenance and spare, shadowy form gave but too sure and ominous indications of that insidious disease which, before the days of my boyhood were fully passed, consigned her to a premature grave. Captain and Mrs Baigrie had six of a family, three sons and three daughters. Robert, the eldest son, was now about sixteen years of age, and the idol of his parents, but, either from ignorance, or from culpable inattention to ultimate consequences, he was indulged to all the extent that an ardent temperament and youthful rashness might demand.

After spending some weeks at Midgarty, my brother and I left to go to Navidale, about four miles to the eastwards. On our way thither, we rested a day and a night at Lonn-riabhach, the house of my nurse, Barbar Corbet. We proceeded from thence to Wester Helmisdale, the house of Mr. Alexr. Ross. He was tacksman of the place; and although I knew but little of him then, I had occasion, as I advanced in years, both to hear and know of his eccentricities. He was the brother of Mr. Walter Ross, minister of Clyne; they were both natives of Ross-shire. Mr. A. Ross had come to Sutherland, and into possession of the farm of Wester Helmisdale, about the time of his brother's settlement at Clyne. He married Miss Pope, daughter of Mr. Peter Pope, brother of the minister of Reay, and by her he had a large family. "Sanny Ross," as he was usually called, was, in regard to all practical matters, abundantly shrewd. But whenever he indulged himself during fireside hours on abstract subjects, he was the living representative of Baron Munchausen. His brother of Clyne dealt pretty extensively in the marvellous, but compared with Sanny, he was but a tyro in invention. Mr. Walter, when "the cock of the club," loved with the incredible to embellish a story, but his brother carried matters much farther. With invincible gravity, and a solemnity of countenance which could not be surpassed, Sanny poured forth such a torrent of absurdities, that the most marvellous thing of the whole was how he could bring himself to think he could be believed. He was wont to tell a wonderful story about his passage of the river during a dark and stormy night. Sanny related that, coming to the brink of the river about midnight, he found the stream flooded over bank and brae, and the ferrymen were "all in their own warm beds, just where they ought to be on such a night and at such an hour." He had some thoughts of returning, but he said he was resolved "to trust in Providence," and accordingly, fixing his sagacious eyes on the roaring stream, he just waited to see what Providence would do in his behalf. "And 'deed," said Sanny, "He did'na keep me long, for as I was looking as I best could, what did I see, think you, but just the largest salmon that ever I saw, close by the bank of the river. So I threw myself stride-legs across his back, and he just brought me over the river as well as any two men with a coble in the whole country could do, so that, though with wet shoes and stockings, I got safely home!" He used also to tell a story about a turbot which the Helmisdale fishermen had hooked upon their lines and which drew after it the boat with twelve men in it for the space of twelve miles to the eastwards on the Moray Firth! These and many such marvellous incidents Saunders often related in a style peculiar to himself. He spoke with a lisp, and with a shrill, whining tone of voice, strongly marking his words with the Highland accent, which rendered his palpable absurdities irresistibly ludicrous. When my brother and I arrived at his house, we were most hospitably received. The house, a small cottage, stood on a considerable eminence, and I was much struck with the view from its windows. From the front might be seen the Helmisdale, pursuing the last two miles of its course, and making its embouchure into the sea. Just at its mouth, on a steep and elevated bank, stood the ruins of the castle of Helmisdale, with, as a background, the blue expanse of the German Ocean.

We next came to Navidale, a beautiful sequestered spot nearly surrounded with hills, while to the south it looks out on the Moray Firth. About three miles to the east is the celebrated Ord of Caithness, a bold, rocky precipice jutting out into the sea, and directly on the boundary line between Caithness and Sutherland. It is called the Ord because, on being approached from the west, it resembles a smith's or mason's hammer. The Gaelic name for this promontory is "an t'Ord-Ghallaobh," or the Caithness hammer.* The house of

* "Where the Norse element is strong among the Gaelic-speaking people in the north, O is commonly used for A, *e.g.*, Ord for Ard." (See paper on "Oghams on the Golspie Stone," by the Right Hon The Earl of Southesk, in Proceedings of Soc. Ant. Scot.) The mountainous and precipitous aspect of the coast of Caithness at the Ord presents a marked contrast to the sandy beach of Sutherlandshire extending immediately to the south, while the surface of the county of Caithness is flat or undulating.—ED.

Navidale was a plain building, too wide to be a single house, and too narrow to be a double one. It was furnished with the usual wings, extending outwards from the front, and forming a sheltered close or court. Mr. Joseph Gordon and his amiable and beautiful wife are, from the moment I crossed their threshold, indelibly impressed upon my memory. Never did I meet with any one, young or old, who could more readily command entrance into the mind of a boy than Mr. Gordon of Navidale. I became enthusiastically fond of him. "This world was made for Cæsar," and so, as I thought and felt, was Mr. Gordon made for me. First of all, he made a "totum" for me of a bone button-mould, which from its size, colour and rapid revolutions, I thought the most wonderful toy I had ever possessed. Then there was a parrot in the house. Its wooden cage stood at the upper stairhead window, close by the drawing-room door. It was the first I had seen, and its gorgeous plumage, its hooked bill, and outlandish screams riveted my attention. Mr. Gordon brought me one day close to the cage, and began to speak to the bird. I thought nothing of what he said, as there was nothing which I less expected than that the parrot should reply to him, unless by its usual harsh and unmeaning screams. But what was my astonishment and terror when I heard the parrot reply in words of human language to its owner, "No dinner, no dinner for pretty Poll!" Lawrence Sterne considered the starling in France, when it cried, "I can't get out, I can't get out," to be an incarnation of Liberty—I considered the parrot to be an incarnation of the Devil. Mr. Gordon did enjoy my fear and wonder as he saw me twist my hand out of his, and rush downstairs as if for dear life. I do not remember Mrs. Gordon at this time, although I had sufficient tokens of affection on her part warmly to recollect her afterwards. Miss Roberta Sutherland, her sister, lived with them at Navidale. She was there when we arrived, and being a gay, sprightly, good-humoured young lady, and very fond of children, she, my brother, and I got quickly and intimately acquainted.

CHAPTER VIII

BOYHOOD.

1789-1800.

THE particular incidents of our return from this juvenile expedition I do not now recollect, but between this event and the time we went to the school of Dornoch there are several characters and incidents which pass in review before me like objects in a mist. My father's serving men and women, first of all, present themselves. He employed as his principal farm-servant, during my boyish days, an elderly man called James MacThòmais. He lived at the west end of the glebe in a cottage built by himself. He kept a cow, for which a stall was fitted up close by his fireside; and as he had wrested from the moor on the glebe-land a few patches of ground on which he raised black oats, bere, and potatoes, he had also a barn attached to his cottage, the walls of which were built, from foundation almost to the top, with huge boulders of granite. James himself was a wrathful little body. His greed and selfishness and sharp temper have left a disagreeable impression upon my mind. He was married, and had a family of two sons and a daughter. His wife was a weak, silly woman, who, in the profoundest ignorance of the *power*, made strenuous exertions in her own way to keep up the *form* of godliness. These exertions consisted in a punctual attendance on the ordinances of religion, during which she watched the countenances and motions of those men who were reputed for their piety. If the preacher pleased or displeased them, Marsal, as she was called, shaped her course accordingly. If he displeased them, she knit her brows, shook her head, and appeared to be restless as a bird ready for flight. If, however, "the men" (na daoine) listened attentively, Marsal listened too; if they exhibited any outward emotion, or token of admiration, or approval of his doctrine, Marsal was instantly thrown into a devout ecstasy; she twisted her countenance into an absolute contortion, she groaned aloud, she threw up her eyes like a duck in a storm, and kept swinging back and fore like the pendulum of a clock. James' eldest son Thomas was considerably older than myself. He succeeded his father, and married, many years afterwards, a Janet Gordon, one of our servants, by whom he had a family. When minister of Achness, I baptised a child for him at his dying-bed side. He lived then at Kinbrace, and for some years before his death had given every evidence of having experienced a saving change. James' second son John was my more intimate acquaintance. He was about my own age, and all my recollections of my boyish amusements and pursuits are associated with him. My brother and I were, as boys, of a mechanical turn. We were always building houses and mills, in imitation of those at Kildonan. We built a clay house at the back of the manse, and below the bank of the mill-lade (or " Eileach "), we had mills as closely resembling their larger and far more useful prototype as our limited capacities could approach. We were also great fishers, or rather, I might say, trout butchers. We proceeded in two ways, first by a contrivance called a " weel," or " athabh," wide at the mouth, and tapering to a point, made of willow twigs. This sort of basket was placed in the middle of the stream, and on each side of it, a kind of warren was constructed across the burn to prevent the fish from getting down the stream. We roused the trout from their hiding, and drove them before us, hemming them in on every side, until we forced them into the mouth of the weel, which was then raised, carried out to the bank, and emptied of its contents. When the burn was in good order, we would have nine or ten at each haul. Another and still more barbarous method of killing trout was with a stick. We traversed the shallow pools, causing the fish to fly from us in all directions, and to rush under stones. We then, when an opportunity offered, struck our sticks under the stones where the trout had taken shelter with all our force; the wretched victims of our pursuit often came up in fragments! We fished with bait and with the fly, but that was at a later period. In all these youthful amusements, John MacThòmais was our constant companion, counsellor, and associate. He was a pleasing and talkative companion, and was furnished with an abundant store of old traditions, which he had rather a knack of telling, and which made many a day, like those of Thalaba, " merrily to go by." One of his many stories has puzzled me ever since by its similarity to the account of the fearful meeting between Ulysses and the one-eyed giant Polyphemus, described in the ninth book of the Odyssey. Can it be that the tradition has been handed down from the pagan ages of our Celtic ancestors? My father's other domestics, as they in succession, like Angus's vision of his royal progeny, pass before my memory's eye, were two young men of the name of Gunn from Costally, Robert and Adam. They were the grandsons of " John Happay," the frequent subject of Robb Donn's withering and merciless satire. Their mother's name was Annabel, who, the daughter of Ian Thapaidh, is mentioned by the bard in the celebrated song of " Tha mi 'n mo chadal, 's na dúisgibh mi." I do not know what became of Adam afterwards, but Robert, after leaving my father's service, enlisted as a soldier, and was killed, many years subsequent to this period, during the Spanish campaigns under Wellington.

The individuals who next present themselves to my recollection are my father's elders. The first, Rory Bain, I have already named as enjoying the festivities of my father's wedding. My father and he, as minister and elder, were much attached to each other. As his house at Killearnan was at a considerable distance from church, at which he was every Sabbath a most punctual attendant, my father very frequently asked him to dinner. On one occasion Rory was seated at table very much at his ease, and on a chair which, although it had seen much service, looked as if it could stand a little more. Rory had at the time finished his meal, and was earnestly engaged in some interesting conversation with my father, when, all at once, he began suddenly and rapidly to sink to the floor, until at last he rolled flat on his back. We were all alarmed, thinking that he had got ill. Rory, however, got up again all right, the cause of his fall being nothing else than the dissolution of the veteran chair, which was discovered lying in fragments on the floor. As an elder, he was a most rigid disciplinarian. A wretched woman, who had lapsed socially for the third time, had been appointed to appear before the pulpit in sackcloth. On that occasion Rory, on a cold frosty day, dipped the vestment in the burn, threw it over her head dripping wet, and caused her to wear it in this condition for three mortal hours! Rory considered himself the conservator of the congregation in respect of devotional decencies. An old, half-crazy man, named Donald Sutherland, or Donald Dalbhait, from the place of his residence, when he attended church usually sat in the poor's seat, on the north side of the area. Donald, sitting there one day, fell asleep, and the impropriety immediately came under Rory's notice. It was not a thing which, in Rory's estimation, was for an instant to be tolerated, and, accordingly, as only the breadth of the "lateran" area was between him and the delinquent, Rory pulled out his handkerchief, rose up from his seat, and stretching out his hand. smote Donald Dalbhait such a blow with the handkerchief across his bald pate as served suddenly to awaken him. Donald eyed his monitor with an angry look, and kept awake. Rory sat down in his seat, and as the day was hot, he himself, in his turn, fell fast asleep. This "weakness of the flesh" was eagerly noticed by old Donald, so pulling from his pocket a ragged napkin, he tied two or three knots upon it, rose up, and advancing stealthily and cautiously towards the "sleeper," returned the blow with such goodwill that Rory started to his feet. On turning round, he at once discovered his old friend Donald looking at him with all the proud consciousness of having discharged a debt. The congregation who witnessed this scene were sorely tempted to laugh aloud, and my father, under whose eye the whole was enacted, was compelled to pass his hand over the whole of his face, in order to prevent him participating in the mirth of his hearers. The other elders were Donald Mackay, John Gordon, Alex. Bannerman or Macdonald, Hugh Fraser, James Buidh or Sutherland, and George Mackay. Donald Mackay was an old man and the parish catechist, father of George Mackay who lived at Liriboll, and who, after his father's death succeeded him in his office. He was the husband of Marion Polson, my brother's nurse, was one of my father's tenants, and lived detached from the rest on an elevated spot to the east of the township of Kildonan. Donald Mackay was twice married. His son George was by the first wife; his succession to his father's office I distinctly remember. He was a man of deep and fervent piety, as well as of great natural ability; and, as a public speaker, was an Apollos, eloquent and mighty in the Scriptures. At his first outset in his catechetical office he was harsh in manner, and a terror to the timid and ignorant; but as he advanced in years, and in the Christian life he mellowed exceedingly, and became a most attractive Christian character. His father, by Marion Polson his second wife, had three sons and a daughter, Peter, Angus, Isobel, and John. Peter was my brother's foster-brother. Alexander Bannerman lived at Ulbster in the Strath. He was a truly pious man, but very hot-tempered. When he spoke at fellowship meetings he showed much devotional feeling and soul-exercise in the truth, but his spirit was vexed by sin in any one, as was shown by the warmth of temper with which he launched forth his reproofs against it. His eldest son and daughter were also pious, but subject to fits of insanity. He survived my father and lived to be a very old man. James Buidh or Sutherland, another elder, lived also at Ulbster. He was a native of the parish of Loth, and one of the loudest protestors against Mr. MacCulloch's Arminianism. He long was a follower of John Grant, and was an absentee from public worship in church, but he afterwards became one of my father's most attached supporters. When Lord Selkirk came to Kildonan in 1813, for emigrants to cultivate his North American settlements, James Buidh became one of them, and went to Canada, where, after experiencing much hardship, he died. My earliest remembrance of Hugh Fraser was as an old man, just on the very limits of human life. He lived at Halgary, within a mile of the manse, and the almost obliterated ruins of the cottage where he lived and died I could yet recognise. He was a tall, gaunt figure, and I distinctly remember his personal appearance at breakfast one morning when he had come rather late, but was, notwithstanding, plentifully served with broiled salmon and a basin of strong tea, which he seemed much to relish. I was particularly struck with his conduct in church. With the other elders he sat in the lateran, and, during the time of sermon, Hugh kept up an almost unceasing conversation in low whispers with his next neighbour. It was a practice among elders in these primitive times. The conversation was directly the reverse of anything in the slightest degree bordering upon levity or profanation. Their low, whispering conversation was nothing else than the communication of the impression made upon their own minds by the truths they were hearing. It must be admitted, however, that they very probably had a particular motive in making themselves so conspicuous. The principles upon which elders in a Highland parish in those days invariably were elected was, that they should be, not only the most advanced in years, but the most eminent Christians in the parish. To sustain the character of the office, and to act on the principle of their appointment to it by the tacit suffrages of the people, must be allowed, reasonably enough, to account for the rather ostentatious display which they made before their fellow-parishioners of their attention to the sermon.

Hugh Fraser was long confined to bed before his death. My brother and I attended his funeral, as our father was from home. It was in the dead of winter, a clear, boar-frosty, short winter day. The people assembled on the sloping green before his cottage, and were served with oaten cakes and whisky. When the procession moved off with the body, his wife and a female friend preceded us to the grave, " weeping aloud as they went." The grave itself exhibited the hard work of a winter day in that hyperborean climate. The sod, hardened by a mid-winter frost, had been pierced through with a mattock wielded with all the force of the stout arms of John MacPherson, the kirk-officer, and his assistant, Donald Gunn. The earth, thrown out of the grave, had become almost a solid mass when the burial arrived at its brink. The sound of the frozen earth falling in congealed fragments upon Hugh Fraser's coffin still rings in my ears—it was the first funeral I ever attended.

With the recollection of the elders of Kildonan I can connect the remembrance of incidents in which they along with my father were immediately concerned. The first of these are the sacramental occasions. The bustle of preparation, particularly in reference to "the things that are necessary for the body," has very specially left its impression upon my memory. In the north of Scotland a distinction prevailed in the annual administration of that ordinance which in the south was utterly unknown. That distinction was made between the public and the private or parochial administration of the Lord's Supper in any parish. The ordinance was considered as administered publicly when communicants from other parishes joined with those of the parish in its observance, and when, on that account, there were two distinct services, one in Gaelic and the other in English, and two different congregations, the one without, the other within doors. My father administered the sacrament for the most part publicly, and it was customary on those occasions for the minister on Sabbath to keep open table, as the services were much prolonged on that day, and a number of the parishioners lived at a distance from the church. To provide for such emergencies, the whole of the preceding week was occupied in receiving presents of mutton, butter, and cheese. On these occasions I have seen the whole range of a large cellar so closely laid with mutton carcases, that the floor was literally paved with them, and the gifts, like the offerings of ancient Israel, far exceeded the purpose for which they were intended. The sacramental occasions at Kildonan, which still fling their shadows upon my memory, are much associated with individuals who took part in them. First, I recall the ministers who preached on the Thursdays, the men who "spoke to the question" on the Fridays from Tongue, Farr, Loth, Clyne, Rogart, Latheron, and Reay; also the ministers who preached on the Saturdays, Sundays, and Mondays. Then I recollect the impression which the solemnities of the sacrament Sabbath produced more upon my imagination I fear than upon my understanding and conscience. On one occasion I distinctly remember that the congregation was assembled before the church, close by the banks of the river, and the communion table, extending to about 30 feet in length, was covered with a white cloth and surrounded by a dense multitude of between three and four thousand persons. On another and similar occasion, I recollect that we children had been seated with our step-mother near "the tent," or covered wooden pulpit used for the out-door services. When the communicants, at the close of the preliminary services of the day, rose to take their places at the Lord's table, we all followed her, and placed ourselves close by her side. The elders in attendance, with a smile of compassion, removed us, and conducted us back to our seats. It was on one of such

G

occasions that I first saw Mr. MacCulloch of Loth, whom I have already described. He was assisting my father, and in his ministrations, both in English and Gaelic, he was, as usual, hot on the Arminian controversy, alien as the subject was to the occasion. The consequences were that, when he left the manse for home on Tuesday, he was way-laid on his journey homewards by the notables of the parish, headed by John Grant, who called him to a reckoning for his heterodoxy. Mr. MacCulloch was as bold as a lion, but his antagonists were more than a match for him; they had better Gaelic and a more accurate knowledge of their bibles than he had, and he was at length but too happy to make his escape from them as fast as his horse could carry him. One Monday evening he entered into a controversy with Mr. Hugh Mackenzie, minister of Tongue. That gentleman was at the time a young man but recently returned from the army, where he had acted for some years as chaplain to a Highland regiment. He had preached on the Monday, whether in Gaelic or English I now forget; but Mr. MacCulloch was his hearer, and Mr. Mackenzie's views of doctrine, based as they were on the top stone of Calvinistic orthodoxy, were accordingly directly opposed to Mr. MacCulloch's Arminianism. Scarcely therefore had they both finished their dinner, than Mr. MacCulloch broke ground by impugning Mr. Hugh's discourse, whilst the preacher, thus assailed, vigorously returned the fire, both parties arguing without intermission for three weary hours.

The last sacramental occasion at Kildonan but one, of which I have any recollection, was connected with a circumstance which, childish and thoughtless as I then was, yet deeply affected me. It was a schism which broke out between my father and his elders in regard to the administration of that ordinance. My father wished to celebrate it privately, or rather parochially, about the middle of spring. This his elders resisted. They wished him to defer it till the middle of summer, and to have it publicly as usual. To this, however, my father would not agree, and matters ran so high that all the elders refused to assist him on that occasion. My father asked Mr. Mackenzie of Tongue to assist him, and his popularity, which was then very high, drew a far greater crowd than could be accommodated within the walls of the church. To the repeated and earnest demands for out-preaching my father would not listen, and on the Sabbath, during the fencing of the tables and the table services, I remember seeing about two hundred persons assembled on the north side of Torr-an-riachaidh, whilst Donald MacLeod, the schoolmaster, read a few chapters of the Scriptures to them, accompanied by prayer and praise. The elders, with the exception of Rory Bain, kept stoutly to their resolution to take no part. Although good old Rory was just as much opposed as any of them to the parochial sacrament, yet he attended every day and officiated, from his sincere regard and attachment to his minister. It was on a sacramental occasion that I first saw, and thenceforward became most intimately acquainted with Mr. Evan MacPherson of Ruthven in Badenoch. This gentleman, for justly might he be so styled, was the second teacher which the "Society in Scotland for Propagating Christian Knowledge in the Highlands and Islands" sent to the parish of Kildonan. His first commission from the Society directed him to teach at Badenloch, but in the course of time he migrated from place to place till, from the upper part of the parish, he ultimately settled at Caën, in the lower and eastern extremity of it. Here he died, and his memory is still venerated by all who knew him.

In bringing my reminiscences down to the beginning of the present century, there are a few things which occur to my memory, and which, although I know that they took place within this period, yet I cannot connect with any particular year. One of them is the marriage of John Ross the miller, Eppy Mackay's cake-and-pudding wooer and my early acquaintance. So long as Eppy's importance remained, which John could turn to advantage, he was all tenderness, love, and attention. But when, by my father's marriage, Eppy first lost her place, and then, as a matter of course, her influence, John drew off. He now became the thriving wooer of the eldest daughter of Rory Bain. Rory gave his consent and a hearty wedding, which I recollect, took place in the dead of winter. After feasting for two days at Killearnan, the young couple were accompanied to their own house by the greater part of their guests, and the ice was so thick on the river that, on their way to Kildonan, men, women, and children, horse and foot of the party passed safely over the river on the ice below Dalhalmy. At the house-warming in Kildonan we were all present, and I remember seeing John Ross, after the manner of the ancients, borne over his threshold.

Another incident which made a deep impression upon me, not eradicated by the sober reasoning of maturer years, I must now relate. A family, named Murray, lived at the place of Tuaraidh. The head of the family was Alexander Murray, one of Captain Baigrie's sub-tenants, as indeed he had been of his predecessor, Major Sutherland of Midgarty, who held Tuaraidh as a highland pendicle to Midgarty. Murray's wife was a sister of Barbara Corbet, my nurse, and an intimacy, in consequence of this connection, held between us children and the family. My brother, my sisters, and myself were often invited, and nearly as often went to spend days and even weeks at Tuaraidh, and the scenery, as well as names of hill and dale, in that wild and sequestered spot, are still familiar to me. The Innis mór, the Innis beag, the Lón, as also Tuaraidh-bheag and Tuaraidh-mhór—the site of Alister Murray's house, of his barn on the brow of the hill, of his swaggering corn-rigs, of his peat-moss on the banks of the Loist, which meandered through the Lón, and the houses of his sub-tenants, are all at this moment vivid in my memory. Two events arise as fresh to my remembrance as if they had happened but yesterday. These are the marriages of Murray's two daughters, Barbara and Janet. Barbara was married to Robert Mackay, a native of Clyne. At their wedding my sisters, my brother and I were amused and feasted for nearly a week, whilst our fellow-guests numbered about fifty. Her sister Janet, a few years later, also married a young man named Mackay, a younger brother of William Mackay in Ascaig,* who was one of my father's

* After the "Sutherland Clearance" of 1819, Mr. William Mackay of Ascaig, with many others, removed from Kildonan to Latheron in Caithness, where he died

elders, and as single-hearted and sincere a Christian as I ever knew. It was at Janet's wedding that this impressive incident took place. The marriage service was performed by my father in church at noon. As was the practice, after the day's festivities, the guests of both sexes retired to sleep in the barn. My brother and I were placed beside each other at the lower end of the building; the season might be about the end of autumn, as I remember that the nights were dark. So long as the sound of the voices, after we had all lain down, rang in my ears from all corners, I felt very drowsy; but when to the hum of speech, a deep silence succeeded, broken only by the hard breathing of the sleepers, I became wide awake. I felt an undefinable dread creep upon me, and, looking towards the upper part of the barn, the whole of which was enveloped in pitchy darkness, I noticed a white figure gliding slowly down from the upper to the lower part of the building, where it disappeared. It seemed to be a human form covered with some white garment hanging about it in loose folds, but although it passed within little more than a yard of me, I could neither see its countenance nor even hear the tread of its feet. On my way home the next day, I told the circumstance to those who accompanied us, and they accounted for it by saying that a young woman at Tuaraidh-bheag had long been confined to bed with consumption, and that she had been found dead in her bed that morning. Be that as it may, I never could satisfactorily account for the singular apparition. Had it been any of my bed-fellows rising in their sleep, and walking in their night-clothes, which, of course, were white, I could not possibly have perceived them without the aid of light, and light there was none, either shining from without through the chinks of the doors, or yet from within. Then how could the figure pass me without my hearing the tread of its feet. What it was I am as unable now, after the lapse of forty years, to account for as I was then.

The last event of this period of my life which I shall mention is the raising of the 93rd Highlanders, or Sutherland Regiment, better known under the name of "An Réismeid Cattach." This gallant body of men is favourably spoken of by the late General Stewart of Garth. "Not only in all those qualities," says he, "which constitute good soldiers are they not excelled by any regiment in the service, but in those also which make men in any profession valuable members of society. The light infantry company, for a period of twenty years, had not a single man of their number punished. After the regiment was completed in 1800, it embarked in September of that year for the island of Guernsay."

in 1843. He was buried at Mid-Clyth. Out of a family of ten, three sons and two daughters emigrated to Canada. Of these, his sons Joseph and Edward founded the wholesale firm of "Mackay Brothers" in Montreal. The former died on 2nd June, 1881, and the latter on 6th May, 1883—both unmarried, and each in the 71st year of his age. They have bestowed munificent donations on the Presbyterian Church in Canada, and the College in Montreal. The youngest son, Donald, has been in partnership with his late nephew, Mr. Gordon, as a wholesale merchant in Toronto. Their sister Euphemia was married to Mr. Angus Mackay of Grubmore in Strathnaver. Her three sons—Hugh, James, and Robert—continue to conduct the business firm in Montreal. It may here be added that some of the descendants of expatriated Kildonan people have been called to occupy positions of trust and honour in the Dominion of Canada.—Ed.

There is nothing more fresh in my memory than the enlisting of soldiers for this regiment. It was in May 1800, and Major-General William Wemyss of Wemyss, along with Major Gordon Cluness of Cracaig, and other gentlemen from the coast, came up to Kildonan. Their arrival was expected, and General Wemyss, to ingratiate himself with the Highlanders, sent up to the manse of Kildonan immense quantities of tobacco-twist and strong, black rapee snuff, together with the very suitable accompaniment of a large snuff-horn superbly mounted with silver, and having attached to it by a massive silver chain a snuff-pen of the same costly material. He had, however, mistaken the tastes of the Sutherland Highlanders, and had consequently put himself to unnecessary expense. Smoking was a luxury then utterly unknown and quite unappreciated by the men of Kildonan. What became of the General's supply I know not; but none of it was used, the old men contenting themselves with the light-coloured snuff which their fathers had used before them. I remember an assemblage on the green to the west of the manse; it was popularly called "the Review." The majority who assembled were tall handsome young fellows, who at the verbal summons of the Countess' ground-officer, Donald Bruce, presented themselves before General Wemyss, that he might have for the asking the pick and choice of them. But while the young men showed no reluctance to enlist, some manoeuvring became necessary to induce their parents to part with them. So two things were promised—first, that the fathers should have leases of their farms, and next, that the sons, if they enlisted, should all be made sergeants. The first promise was to a certain extent fulfilled; the second, it is needless to say, could not possibly be fulfilled.

I find that I have omitted to mention in its proper place a very serious illness which I had when about eight years old. It began with a hard, dry cough, which continued for nearly nine months, accompanied with profuse morning sweats and hectic fever, loss of sleep and appetite, shortness of breath, and an almost total prostration of strength. I was sent up to the garret to sleep alone, whilst another lay in the opposite couch to watch me. It was then that my excellent step-mother proved herself in possession of the skill of a physician in her treatment of my disease. She never allowed me to take anything cold—whether tea, or gruel, or soup—all must be warm; and this under God was the means of my recovery. The complaint, however, long and obstinately resisted treatment, so that on one occasion, when I was very low, I overheard my step-mother say to my sisters that she had given up all hope of my recovery, and that next week a bearer must be sent to the merchant at Brora to purchase linen for a shroud. The complaint, however, yielded at last, and of my step-mother's skill and tenderness I shall carry a grateful, sense to my grave. Alas, that I cannot feel equally grateful to Him in whose hands she was but the instrument.

Closely associated with all my recollections of olden times at Kildonan, is an individual who largely contributed to our amusement. She was a Mrs. Gordon who died at Golspie, a daughter of the Rev. Murdo Macdonald of Durness. She was then a widow with an only daughter called Peggy. Inheriting her father's taste for music, she played beautifully on the violin, and was a periodical visitor, and an almost constant residenter at the houses of the Sutherland gentry. Many a time and oft have we tripped it to her heart-and-heel-stirring reels and strathspeys in the low caster-room at the manse of Kildonan. She was universally known under the name of "Fiddlag." Her fiddle was her god. When on her death-bed nearly her last words were to "spread a cloth over the fiddle." When told that it was her soul that should then be her chief concern, and not her fiddle, she replied, "O I leave all these good things, as I ever did, to the worthy man, Mr. Keith."

My father, during an incumbency of nearly forty years, was only once a member of the General Assembly. I remember his return after an absence of nearly a month. He had brought a box from Edinburgh of many good and desirable things for his wife and children. What they were I forget, but on that occasion he secured the regular transmission of a London paper called "Baldwin's London Weekly Journal." From that paper we received information of the progress of the French Revolution, and of the determined opposition of this country to that reckless and fertile source of human enormities. I remember listening to my father reading aloud to us both the foreign and domestic intelligence of this journal—the atrocities of Robespierre and the whole Jacobin faction under the "Reign of Terror;" the subsequent fall and death of the miscreant; rise of Bonaparte; the victories of Lords Duncan and Nelson; and many other public and stirring incidents. The victory obtained by Admiral Duncan in 1797 over the Dutch fleet, off the mouth of the Texel, made the triumphant thunders of his cannon be heard throughout every glen in Scotland. Being himself a Scotchman of ancient descent, his countrymen were proud of him, as for many ages previously their country had produced no naval hero of whom they could boast. Lord Duncan's prowess made its way to my mind, however, merely through the instrumentality of a piece of printed cotton which had been purchased for dresses to my sisters. In honour of the Dundee hero the cloth was called "Camperdown," and I recollect when the parcel arrived, and the piece of print was spread on the table, I took it into my head to suppose that it came direct from the great Admiral, as a token of his regard to his friends at Kildonan. Lord Nelson's victory over the French fleet, under the brave but unfortunate Bruyes, in 1798, off the coast of Egypt, was the next note of war which reached us. Napoleon was then rapidly rising to that height of power from which in 1815 he fell "like lightning from heaven." His descent on Egypt was a blow struck at the very vitals of the British power in India, and Nelson's victory on the Nile was a blow still more deeply and mortally aimed at the power of Bonaparte. The only tidings of this great victory which made any impression upon my mind were conveyed by a pedlar who wended his way to the manse, and who, among other articles for sale, had a parcel of huge wood-cuts of Lord Nelson's battle of the Nile. One of them my father readily purchased, and it was immediately fastened up with wafers on the wall of the dining-room.

Mr. Gordon of Navidale, when his lease expired, took the Mains of Embo, in the parish of Dornoch, and resided there for a few years, after which he remained in Edinburgh. The farm of Navidale was taken in lease by Mr. Robert Pope, second son of Mr. Peter Pope, tacksman of Gartimore, younger brother of Mr. Alexander Pope, minister of Reay. This old gentleman I recollect to have seen at Kildonan, and I was much struck with his antique and venerable appearance. He must, when I saw him, have been close upon seventy years of age. He wore what was usually called a Welsh wig, and showed by his manners a rude and choleric temper. When I saw him on that occasion we had a few more guests at the manse, among others Mr. and Mrs. Mackay of Skerra in the Reay country. My recollections of them remain in my memory owing to a circumstance calculated to impress the mind of a boy. On the second day after their arrival, an excursion around the glebe was proposed and agreed to. My father and mother and their three guests, accompanied by us young folks, sat down in a circle on the grassy summit of the islet in the middle of the river. Having all assembled, Mrs. Mackay distributed several rich and highly-seasoned cakes of ginger-bread. In the round, however, I was forgotten, but Mr. Mackay, who was an exceedingly amiable man, noticed the omission, and immediately divided with me the portion he had got for himself. Old Peter Pope amused us on our return by stuffing his coat pockets with new-mown hay. His eldest son, William, whom I well knew, was then in the East Indies. His second son, Robert, had just returned from the West Indies, where, for upwards of twenty years, he had been engaged as a planter, and had realised several thousand pounds. On the expiry of Mr. Gordon's lease of Navidale, he took that farm at a lease of thirty-eight years. Besides holding Navidale, Mr. Robert Pope rented the Highland farms of Tiribol and Dallangal in the parish of Kildonan, and in looking after these possessions he had frequent opportunities of being a guest at the manse. He very soon afterwards had another and a far more interesting reason for being so often at Kildonan. Soon after Mr. Gordon's removal from Navidale to Embo, Miss Bertie, of whom I have already made mention, and who had resided with her sister whilst she was at Navidale, came to live alternately with her sisters at Midgarty and Kildonan. My step-mother had during one of these visits been confined to bed by a serious ailment, and while she was ill Miss Bertie had charge of the house, and her judicious and tender care of her sister as well as her lady-like accomplishments and her rich vein of wit attached us all so much to her that we almost idolised her. Mr. Robert Pope, soon after his arrival from the West Indies, had seen her at Midgarty, and at the very first interview, was smitten with the tender passion. He made no secret of his attachment, and was in consequence very much teased about it by the gentry of the parish of Loth, and very particularly so by the minister of Loth and his daughters, the Misses MacCulloch. Mr. Pope was annoyed at this, and even Miss Bertie was compelled at last, in order to escape their unceasing and clamorous raillery, to take refuge at Kildonan and reside there almost entirely. Mr. Pope followed her thither, and was all but her daily attendant. The event of their marriage is impressed upon my memory in connection with an amusement in which I was then engaged. It might be about the beginning of October, and a good deal of rain had fallen. I resolved to build a house with the mud which had collected during the rainy weather. Mr. Pope and Miss Bertie were in the house, and after dinner, leaving them all engaged in matters which, compared with mine, I considered secondary, I went out, laid the foundation of my house, and finding the mud quite plastic and ready to be formed into any shape, I was getting on with a success that exceeded my expectations. I had no thought about father, mother, sisters, or guests within—my house was everything to me. Most unwillingly was I called off from my employment at night-fall. I got up, however, in the morning with the very peep of dawn to continue my architectural labours. I was well enough acquainted with the internal arrangements of the manse to know where guests usually slept. I knew that since Mr. Pope and Miss Bertie had come to the house a few days before, Miss Bertie had slept in the little garret, and Mr. Pope in the principal bedroom. On passing the door of Mr. Pope's room, therefore, what was my astonishment to notice Miss Bertie's little shoes placed side by side with Mr. Pope's boots at his bedroom door. I thought this very strange, and one of the servant-maids, meeting me at the time, participated in my astonishment, but said with a sly leer, "'S cinnteach gu bhei liad pòsda," (Surely they are married). I came open-mouthed to my sisters, and told them what I had seen; but they were already initiated in the mystery, and told me that about 12 o'clock last night Mr. Pope insisted on being married to Miss Bertie, and that my father, after remonstrating upon the too great privacy and precipitancy of the measure, had yielded and married them. So I resumed my mud-building. Mr. and Mrs. Pope came often in the evening to look at my edifice, and I was much gratified with their minute examination of it and with their commendations. After remaining for some days at Kildonan, during which they amused themselves by strolling through the dells and woods, they went home accompanied by my father and mother.

About this time died Mr. MacCulloch of Loth, and was succeeded by Mr. George Gordon, of whom I have many recollections. Mr. Gordon, was the eldest son, by his first marriage, of Adam Gordon, tacksman of Rhenevy in Strathnaver, parish of Farr, and a nephew of Charles Gordon of Pulrossie. When a young man, and during his attendance at the University, he was tutor in the family of Mr. Gordon of Carrol, who resided at Kintradwell in the parish of Loth. Mrs. Gordon, sister of the late Donald MacLeod of Geanies, was an eminently pious woman, and took a deep interest in the spiritual and temporal welfare of the tutor of her children. George Gordon, after being a year or two in the family of Carrol, resigned his situation, as advantageous prospects of entering into the commercial line were held out to him by a near relative of his residing in London. Mrs. Gordon of Carrol strongly dissuaded him from availing himself of these prospects, and recommended him to pursue his studies as a candidate for the ministry. This, however, Mr. Gordon declined doing, upon the ground that he saw his call in Providence clearer to the one than to the other. " Well, young man," said the venerable lady, " I shall not live to see it, but, mark my words, you will die minister of Loth "—a prediction strictly fulfilled. Mr. Gordon's London prospects burst like air bubbles, and he himself, turning his attention to his theological studies, was licensed to preach by the Presbytery of Tongue. He then succeeded Mr. Alex. Urquhart as missionary of Achness, and after-wards became assistant to my grand-uncle, Mr Thomas Mackay of Lairg, whose second daughter Harriet he married. In 1801 he was settled minister of Loth, where he died in 1822, in the 26th year of his ministry. While missionary at Achness he used frequently to be at Kildonan, and he particularly arrested my attention by his inexhaustible store of anecdote, as well as by the hearty laugh with which he wound up every story he told, and into which he seemed to throw his whole heart. I always rejoiced when I saw him alight in the close on Monday evening after preaching at Ach-na-h'uaighe on the Sabbath. He was ever and anon accompanied by his servant, who followed him on foot like his shadow. What this man's name was I forget, but we never knew him by any other name than the "Gillie Roy." He was red-haired, and a young fellow of caustic, copious, and sterling humour. His master told anecdotes of him which made us laugh till we wept again, whilst he himself, at the very time, was setting the kitchen fireside in a continuous roar of laughter at his witty sallies.

Belonging to this period I have pleasing and painful recollections. Captain Baigrie's eldest son Robert was, ever since my father's second marriage, a frequent visitor at Kildonan. When I first began the Rudiments, he used to throw me into a perfect ecstasy by the fluency with which he read and translated the Latin language. He was naturally very clever, but his progress in letters was counter-balanced by the fatal progress which he made in those dangerous propensities which to ardent youth are the direct road to ruin. These propensities his affectionate, but inconsiderate parents greatly, though unin-tentionally, indulged, and they did so in two ways—first, they took him along with them in their visits to the first families in the county, where his youthful precocity drew upon him attention and applause by which he was entirely upset. Then they gave no heed to his choice of companions, and he certainly did not choose the best. Robert's introduction into genteel society gave rise to habits of extravagance and to expenses which at last he could not possibly meet. He had contracted "debts of honour" by card-playing at the tables of the " great," which he could not pay, and of which he was afraid to tell his father. In an evil hour therefore, and with one John Gordon, footman at Midgarty, as his accomplice, he, under silence of night broke open a shop in Wester-Helmisdale, and plundered the till of nearly £20. The robbery was discovered early next morning, and the hue and cry raised in the neighbourhood. Suspicion fell upon the perpetrators. Gordon was openly accused of it, but the charge against the man glanced directly at his master and associate. With aching hearts and streaming eyes did Captain Baigrie and his amiable wife hear the confession of guilt from the lips of their misguided son; the merchant's loss was refunded, John Gordon sent out of the country, and poor Robert Baigrie sent to the West Indies, where, in a few months after his arrival, he died of fever. Mrs. Baigrie died in February, 1798; she happily did not live to witness this painful termination of her son's career.

It was at this period that my mind received its first religious impressions, though when I look back upon the course of my life, I am almost afraid to call them such. But I remember that I used to take much delight in the historical parts both of the Old and New Testaments, more particularly the books of Samuel and Kings, and the four Gospels. The history of our blessed Lord made a vivid, if not a saving, impression upon me, so much so that I used to lie awake at times for the greater part of the night thinking of the Saviour, and in imagination following him with his disciples from city to city in Judea and Galilee. At his persecutors I felt a thrill of horror and indignation, and I often wished that I had been some potent prince strong enough to interpose in behalf of the meek and lowly Jesus. Peter's attempt to do so I applauded in my heart, and I could not understand the Saviour's reproof, nor his interposition in behalf of the high-priest's maimed menial. It was the act of too high and holy a spirit for me to have the slightest comprehension of at the time. These juvenile meditations set me often to pray, which I did with many tears. I thought I felt love to the Saviour in my heart, and this caused me to form many resolutions to reform my conduct, to be always praying and to keep myself in a serious frame. When such resolutions lay strong upon me, I was most assiduous in the performance of what I considered to be a religious duty. I dared not indulge myself so much at play, I was afraid even to smile, and I laboured hard to keep every vain thought out of my mind. But alas, these good intentions were one after the other soon forgotten, and only renewed with fear and gloomy anticipations of failure. If I now know the truth (and that is a question for eternity), these first impressions were so many initiatory lessons in self-knowledge, and led me eventually to see that salvation is not of debt but of grace.

CHAPTER IX.

SCHOOL-BOY DAYS AT DORNOCH.

1801-1803.

My brother impresses himself strongly on my reminiscences of this particular period of my life. I was warmly attached to him. Our fishing expeditions together on "the burn" to its very source, and along the bank of the river, and on one occasion to Loch Ascaig; our excursions also to Coille-an-Loist, Coill'-Chil-Mer, Cnoc-an-Eireannaich, Suidh-an-fhir-bhig, Cnoc-ant'sholuis-leathad, and Allochdarry for blae-berries and cloud-berries, all now recall to my remembrance my brother's intercourse and affection. It was about the beginning of November, 1801, I think, that we went together to the school at Dornoch. In the previous October some riot on the heights of Kildonan demanded the presence of the under-Sheriff of the county, to inquire into the particulars. The gentleman who then held office as under-Sheriff was Mr. Hugh MacCulloch of Dornoch, better known as an eminent Christian than as a magistrate or lawyer. His father, a respectable burgess of Dornoch, was one of the bailies of that burgh. His son Hugh, after receiving the rudiments of his education at his native town, studied law in Edinburgh. When a boy at school a remarkable event in his life took place. He had gone with one or two other youths of his own age to bathe. It was at that part of the Dornoch firth to the south of the town, called "the cockle ebb." Having gone into the water he attemped to swim, and, getting beyond his depth, sank to the bottom. His companions immediately gave the alarm, when two or three men engaged in work hard by plunged into the sea for his recovery. But he had been so long in the water that, when taken out, he was to all appearance lifeless. By judicious treatment, however, suspended animation was restored. This narrative I received from his own lips, and he further added that, if God were to give him his choice of deaths, he would choose drowning, for, he said, he felt as he was in the act of sinking, and when the waters were rushing in at his mouth and nostrils, as if he were falling into a gentle sleep. That choice, in the inscrutable providence of God, was given him, for about four miles above that spot, on that identical firth, he was, with many others, drowned at the Meikle-ferry, an occurrence hereafter to be noticed. The year of his appointment as Sheriff-Substitute of Sutherland I do not know. His character as a judge was ordinary. His administration of justice was free indeed from all sorts of corruption, but it was defective in regard to clear views of civil and criminal law. Sheriff MacCulloch, however, shone as a man of ardent and enlightened piety.

Saving impressions by divine truth and divine agency had been made upon his mind at an early age, and he advanced in the Christian life under the training, and in the fellowship, of the most eminent Christians and evangelical ministers in the four northern counties. On the evening of his arrival at Kildonan from the heights of the parish, on the occasion alluded to, he was drenched almost to the skin, as it had rained heavily through the day; he especially required dry stockings, and he preferred putting them on at the kitchen fireside. I was directed to attend him thither; bringing with me everything that was necessary to make him comfortable. Whilst thus engaged he took particular notice of me, and asked me many questions about my progress in learning, particularly in Latin. He was much pleased with my answers, and said that, if my father would send my brother and me to school at Dornoch, he would keep us for three months in his own house. He repeated the same thing to my father next day at parting, assuring him that the parochial teacher at Dornoch was resorted to as a teacher of ability and success. The proposal was entertained, and preparations were made for us to go thither in the beginning of November.

The morning of the day of our departure from under the paternal roof, to attend a public school, at last dawned upon us. My brother and I had slept but little that night. After breakfasting by candle-light, we found our modes of conveyance ready for us at the entry-door. My father mounted his good black horse Toby, a purchase he had lately made from Captain Sackville Sutherland of Uppat, while my brother and I were lifted to the backs of two garrons employed as work-horses on the farm. We set forward, and both my sisters accompanied us to the ford on the burn, close by the churchyard, whence, after a few tears shed at the prospect of our first separation, we proceeded on our journey accompanied by a man on foot. We crossed the Crask, and stopped for refreshment at an inn below Kintradwell, in the parish of Loth, called Wilk-house, which stood close by the shore. This Highland hostelry, with its host Robert Gordon and his bustling, talkative wife, were closely associated with my early years, comprehending those of my attendance at school and college. The parlour, the general rendezvous for all comers of every sort and size, had two windows, one in front and another in the gable, and the floor of the room had, according to the prevailing code of cleanliness, about half an inch of sand upon it in lieu of carpeting. As we alighted before the door we were received by Robert "Wilk-house," or "Rob tighe na faochaig," as he was usually called, with many bows indicative of welcome, whilst his bustling helpmeet repeated the same protestations of welcome on our crossing the threshold. We dined heartily on cold meat, eggs, new cheese, and milk. "Tam," our attendant, was not forgotten; his pedestrian exercise had given him a keen appetite, and it was abundantly satisfied. In the evening we came to the manse of Clyne. Mr. Walter Ross and his kind wife received us with great cordiality. Mrs. Ross was a very genteel, lady-like person, breathing good-will and kindness. To her friends by the ties of affection, amity, or blood, her love and kindness gushed to overflowing. Her father was a Captain John Sutherland, who, at the time of his daughter's marriage, was tacksman of Clynelish, within a quarter of a mile due south of the manse of Clyne. After the expiry of his lease he went to reside at Dornoch, and the farm was at the time I speak of in the possession of Mr. Hugh Houston, sometime merchant at Brora, and the brother of Mr. Lewis Houston of Easter-Helmisdale, whom I have named. Mr. Ross had by his wife a son and a daughter; the daughter died in infancy; the son, William Baillie, was of the same age with myself, and is, at the time I write (August 1842) a physician of repute in Tain.

After breakfast next morning we proceeded on our journey. After having passed the Bridge of Brora there soon burst upon our sight Dunrobin Castle, the seat of the ancient Earls of Sutherland, the view of which from the east is specially imposing; and here I may remark in passing, that the present excellent public road which runs through the county of Sutherland was, at the time I speak of, not in existence. In lieu thereof was a broken, rugged pathway, running by the sea-shore from the Ord Head to the Meikle Ferry, and at Dunrobin, instead of going to the north of the castle as the present line does, it descended to the sea-side, passing about two miles to the east of the castle right below it, and so round by the south. The building filled me with astonishment. The tower to the east, surmounted by its cupola, the arched entrance into the court, and then the simply elegant front looking out on the expanse of the Moray Firth, which rolls its waves almost to the very base, were to me an ocular feast. The garden too, on the north side of the road, over the walls of which towered the castle in ancient and Gothic magnificence, was another wonder. I was perfectly astonished at its extent. It stretched its south walls at least 300 yards along the road, and at each of its angles were rounded turrets, which gave it quite an antique appearance, in strict keeping with the magnificent edifice with which it was connected. The village of Golspie lies about a quarter of a mile to the west of the castle, close by the shore, and, as we advanced, the first object we saw was the manse, near which, on approaching it, we noticed walking towards us a low-statured, middle-aged man, dressed in a coarse, black suit, and with a huge flax wig of ample form. My father and he cordially recognised one another, and I at once discovered this venerable personage to be Mr. William Keith, minister of Golspie. We did not stop, but proceeded on our way to Embo, and reached the north side of the Little Ferry house at about two o'clock. As we dismounted, and every necessary preparation was made by the boatman to get us over, I felt a good deal alarmed. Except when crossing the Helmisdale river in a cobble some years before, I had never been in a boat or at sea; and I was particularly frightened at the idea of being a fellow-passenger with my father's large horse and our own lesser quadrupeds, lest they, participating in my own fears, might become unruly and swamp the boat. Matters went on, however, better than I anticipated; the horses, after remonstrating a little, were made to leap into the boat, and, with my heart in my throat, I followed my father and brother, and took my place beside them in the bow of the wherry. As we moved off I was horror-struck, on looking over the edge of the boat, to see the immense depth of the Ferry. It was a still, clear winter's day, and I could distinctly perceive the gravelly bottom far below. I could see, passing rapidly in the flood, between me and the bottom, sea-ware of every size and colour. The star-fish intermingled with the long tails of the tangle which by the under-swell of the sea heaved up and down, and presented the appearance of a sub-marine grove, retaining its fresh look by the greenish colour of the sea-water. It forcibly recalled to me Ovid's deluge; and as we mounted our horses after crossing and rode on, I repeated to my father these lines:—

> " Nec coelo contenta suo Jovis ira ; sed illum
> Coeruleus frater juvat auxiliaribus undis "

And again :—

> " Et, modo qua graciles gramen carpsere capella
> Nunc ibi deformes ponunt sua corpore phocae.
> Mirantur sub aqua lucos urbesque domosque
> Nereides."

My father reminded me that it was getting late, and that we must make the best use of our time, as Embo was still at a considerable distance. We arrived there, however, before it got dark, so that I had an opportunity of seeing in fair daylight the most elegant mansion I ever witnessed, with the exception of Dunrobin Castle. Embo House stood nearly half-way between Dornoch and the Little-Ferry, on the old line of road. It was the manor-house of a family of Gordons, scions of the Gordons, Earls of Sutherland ; and they had held it since the days of Adam, Lord of Aboye, the husband of the Countess Elizabeth. The estate was then in the possession of a collateral branch of the family of Embo. Robert Hume Gordon, having some years before canvassed the county, with the view of being its representative, in opposition to the influence of the Duchess of Sutherland, built this splendid mansion for the purpose of entertaining the electors. Mr. Gordon lost his election, yet by a narrow majority. He was supported by the most respectable barons of the county, Dempster of Skibo, Gordon of Carrol, Gordon of Navidale, Captain Clunes of Cracaig, and Captain Baigrie of Midgarty ; and most of those gentlemen, being tacksmen and wadsetters on the Sutherland estate, gave by their opposition to the candidate of the Sutherland family, almost unpardonable offence. Although Mr. Hume Gordon built the house at great expense, he never intended to reside permanently either in the mansion or in the county ; and Embo House and property were now rented by Capt. Kenneth Mackay, who also farmed the place of Torboll from the Sutherland family. Embo House was constructed very much after the fashion of the houses of the new town of Edinburgh, begun on the north side of the Nor' Loch on 26th Oct., 1767 ; the front was of hewn ashlar, and consisted of three distinct houses, the largest and loftiest in the centre, joined to the other two by small narrow passages, each lighted by a window, and forming altogether a very imposing front. The centre house was four storeys high—first, a ground or rather a sunk floor, then a first, second, and, lastly, an attic storey. The ground or sunken floor contained the kitchen and cellars, and in front of it was a wall surmounted by an iron railing, resembling exactly the fronts in Princes Street, Edinburgh. Outer stairs ascended to the principal entry door, and along the whole front of the building extended a pavement. The lesser houses, or wings, were each of them a storey less in height than the central building; and the attic storeys were lighted from the front wall, instead of from the roof, by windows about precisely half the size of the rest, which greatly added to the effect and beauty of the whole. Behind were other two wings of the same height with those in front, extending at right angles from the principal buildings. The interior of the mansion corresponded with its external appearance. The principal rooms were lofty and elegant, ornamented with rich cornices, and each having two large windows. Captain and Mrs. Mackay welcomed us, but not with that cordiality with which we were received by Captain Baigrie and Mr. Joseph Gordon. Mrs. Mackay, my step-mother's half-sister, was a neat little woman, with a pleasing expression of countenance. She was very lady-like, but she received us with that politeness which might be reckoned the precise boundary between kindness and indifference. Capt. Kenneth Mackay was in the prime of life. He was the lineal descendant of Col. Eneas Mackay, second son of Donald, first Lord Reay, and grandson of the redoubted William of Melness. He was therefore—failing the present family of Reay, descendants of the laird of Skibo, and after the Holland Mackays, descendants of General Mackay, second son of John, second Lord Reay —the next heir to the titles and estate of Reay. His father, John Mackay of Melness, married Esther, daughter and heiress of Kenneth Sutherland of Meikle-Torboll, in Strathfleet, parish of Dornoch, a small property which for generations was possessed by a family of the name of Sutherland, cadets of the noble family of Duffus, whose ruined castle of Skelbo we had passed on our way from the Little Ferry to Embo. Capt. Mackay's father, I believe, sold the property, and the family was, at his death, reduced to the greatest extremities. His eldest son, Kenneth, born in 1756, entered the army, where he never rose higher than the rank of lieutenant, and was under the necessity of retiring on half-pay, at his father's death, in order to take charge of his affairs. And never, indeed, it is probable, were affairs so involved more judiciously managed, or more successfully retrieved. With only his lieutenant's half-pay, the landless heir of Meikle-Torboll took his quondam property as a farm at a moderate rent, and at a time when agriculture was but little understood, and its produce turned to small account, he so successfully laboured that, in a very few years, he snatched his father's family from starvation, and for himself acquired a comfortable independence. At the time I first saw him he had the farms of Torboll, Embo, and Pronsy, in the parish of Dornoch, was factor for the estates of Reay and Skibo, and collector of the county revenue. His children at that time amounted to six—Harriet, Esther, Jean, Lexy, George, and John; they were afterwards increased to fourteen. We were both sent to sleep upstairs in one of the attics, but I scarcely shut an eye, being so much stunned with the noise of the sea, which, when excited by the east wind, is at Embo perfectly deafening. Next morning we rode into Dornoch. The road to the town lay on its south-east side, and, as we approached it, I was almost breathless with wonder at the height of the steeple, and at the huge antique construction of the church. My father brought us at once to the school. It was then taught by Mr. John MacDonald, A.M. (King's Coll.), who, in 1806, was ordained minister of Alvie, in Badenoch. The school was laid out in its whole length with wide pews, or desks, running across, while the master's desk stood nearly in the centre, so as to command a view of the whole. There were three windows in front, and at each of them a bench fitted up for reading and writing. The school was crowded, Mr. MacDonald being a very popular teacher. To my father's salutation he replied gruffly, and after being informed of the progress we had already made, he prescribed some books ; then, according to his usual custom, on any important accession to the number of his scholars, he gave holiday till next morning to the entire school. We then went to the Sheriff's house. He was engaged in court, but we were very kindly received by Mrs MacCulloch and her daughter, Miss Christy. Mrs. MacCulloch showed us to our bedroom. It was at the top of the house, an attic above an attic—a dreary, cold place, having all the rude finishings of a coarse loft. When the Sheriff returned in the evening he received us with the most fatherly kindness; and before supper the family were summoned to worship, which the Sheriff conducted with an unction and fervour which left a corresponding impression.

The next day my brother and I attended school; and, as we continued at Dornoch for about a year and a half—the first quarter at the Sheriffs, and the rest of the time boarded with a man named Dempster—I shall arrange my recollections with reference to the principal object for which we were sent there, namely—our education. Our teacher, Mr. MacDonald, was an excellent classical scholar, and highly qualified to teach all the ordinary branches. But his method was defective. He was a merciless disciplinarian, inflicting punishment for the slightest offences, not as part of a system, but in the gratification of temper. About a year before we came to his school he had been tried before the Sheriff for maltreating one of his scholars. The boy, Bethune Gray, son of Hugh Gray, a townsman, had committed some blunder in his lesson. MacDonald harshly corrected it, and the teacher's violence so stunned the poor fellow that, instead of getting out of his difficulty, he became wedged more deeply in his error. This rendered MacDonald more violent than before, and, coming out of his desk, he seized the boy by the neck, threw him on his face on a form, and with the knotted end of a rope so beat him that the boy fainted, and in that state was carried home to his father's house, where, for many weeks, he lay in bed dangerously ill. The father petitioned the Sheriff, and a Court was held to try the case, to which MacDonald was cited. During his examination he behaved most rudely to the judge. The matter would have gone hard with him, but for the interposition in his behalf of the leading persons in the town. MacDonald threatened to resign, and to prevent this the matter was compromised. Acknowledging that his discipline in the particular case had been much too severe, Macdonald came under the obligation that for the future he would inflict chastisement, not personally, but by substitute. To this resolution, except in one instance, of which I was myself an eye-witness, he strictly adhered. In all cases of delinquency, when matters between him and the delinquent came to a flogging, he acted by deputy, and the pauper, or janitor of the school, was appointed to inflict it. I was reading Cæsar and Ovid, with Mair's Introduction, when I first entered the school, but Watt's Grammar I had long before committed to memory. I was, however, sent back to Cornelius Nepos and the Latin Grammar. We were also set upon a course of English reading, but without parsing, or any knowledge of English Grammar. A grammatical study of the English language was at that time utterly unknown in the schools of the north, the rudiments of Latin being substituted in its place. To the school-hours of attendance we were summoned by the blowing of a post-horn, which the pauper, or janitor, standing at the outer porch, blew lustily. It was also the duty of the pauper, early in the morning, and especially in winter while it was yet dark, to perambulate the town, and, horn in hand, to proceed to the doors or windows of every house in which scholars resided, and blow up the sleepers. After this he proceeded to the schoolhouse to arrange it for our reception, by sweeping the floor and lighting the fire. For all this drudgery the only remuneration he received was a gratis education—whence his designation of the pauper or "poor scholar." MacDonald had instituted a system of disgrace, for the better regulation of the idle or disorderly among his scholars, which was, however, not judicious. The method was this : the first who blundered in his lesson was ordered out of his class and "sent to Coventry," which was the back seat, and there ordered to clap on his head an old ragged hat, the sight and smell of which were alone no little punishment. Under the hat, he was ordered to sit at the upper end of the seat, and, as the leader of "the Dunciad," styled General Morgan. If a succession of fellows, equally bright, were sent to keep him company, they held the next rank, were accommodated with head-pieces equally ornamental, and were named in order, Capt. Rattler, then Sergeant More, and the next was a fiddler, who, besides his head-gear, was furnished with a broken wool-card and a stick, wherewith to exercise his gifts in the line of his vocation. When lessons were done these unfortunate fellows were ordered out to go through their exercise. This consisted in a dance of the dignitaries of the squad, to the melody of him of the wool-card. On boys of keen sensibility, and on others, the first sight of this awkward exhibition, accompanied by shouts of laughter from their companions, produced some salutary effect; but custom soon made it lose its edge. The only premiums which he gave were confined to beginners, for good writing. They consisted of three quills, given publicly on Saturday to the boy who, during the week, had kept ahead of his class, by writing the best and most accurate copies. Such was the system of teaching pursued at the school of Dornoch. For me it was decidedly defective; as I only travelled over the same ground, and that far more superficially, on which I had advanced under my father's tuition. For any real progress I made, in any branch of literature, I was indebted directly to my father.

My recollections next bear upon the Sheriff's family, with whom my brother and I lived for three months. His house was situated to the south of the town, and at the foot of what was called the "Vennel," a small pathway leading from the churchyard. The house was of an antique cast. The parlour or dining-room had three windows, and on its wall hung several prints. In the north-west corner of the room and near the door, stood a handsome eight-day clock—a present which the Sheriff had received from the Sutherland Volunteers, of which he was Major. A large sofa stood on the opposite side, near the fire-place. The study was a small room upstairs, which was crammed with books and papers. The Sheriff's wife was a daughter of Mr. John Sutherland, minister of Dornoch, the immediate predecessor of Dr. Bethune. They had a considerable family. The surviving branches of them, when we were there, were three daughters and a son. One daughter was married to a Mr. Cant, a flour miller of Bishop Mills, near Elgin; another married George Munro, who first kept a shop at Wester-Helmisdale, and afterwards leased the farm of Whitehill in the parish of Loth. The Sheriff's son, William, was in the army, and had risen to the rank of captain. During our residence at the Sheriff's, his son was with his regiment in Ireland, and married; and before we left Dornoch he and his wife came to visit his father. Captain MacCulloch was as handsome a man as one could see; he much resembled his father, who was also a very genteel-looking man, and must have been very handsome in his youth. He so closely resembled Mr. Pitt, then Prime Minister, that once, when in London, Sheriff MacCulloch was mistaken for him on the streets, and addressed accordingly by several persons of distinction. His other daughter, Chirsty, was unmarried, and always resided with him. Family worship was regularly observed morning and evening in the Sheriff's house. On Sabbath evenings he examined all the inmates of his household on their scriptural knowledge, concluding with an exposition of the chapter which he had read. The people in the immediate neighbourhood usually attended; and as some of them had no Gaelic, particularly John Hay, a mason who lived close by the house, the concluding prayer was given partly in one language and partly in the other, which the Sheriff called "a speckled prayer." Every Saturday he went to Pronsay, where he presided at a fellowship meeting; and it was these occasions of Christian intercourse with his fellow-citizens, which they found peculiarly edifying, that embalmed his memory in the hearts of the survivors. He was a regular attendant at church; as, though Dr. Bethune's doctrine seemed to him to be dry enough, he, unlike others equally eminent for piety with himself, would not on that account become an absentee, all the more that he held a public office. He did not fail, however, by his restlessness of manner, to indicate when he was not being edified.

I shall here mention a few of my schoolfellows at Dornoch. My first acquaintances were Dr. Bethune's sons, Matthew, Walter, and

Robert. The last mentioned was not indeed a schoolfellow, being much younger that we. Matthew was in my class, and a most amiable fellow; he was naturally clever, but sickly from his early youth. I only saw him once after leaving school. At college he studied medicine, in the science of which he was not only a profound adept, but a perfect enthusiast. After finishing his medical course, and attending the Inverness Infirmary for a year or two, he set up in practice there for himself. He married Miss Jean Forbes of Ribigill, a celebrated beauty, the reigning belle of the four northern counties. She survived him, and is married again. He had several of a family, and one of his daughters, at least, was married. He died in 1820, in the prime of life. His brother Walter was not a class-fellow; he was dull and careless. I was not intimate with him; his disposition being just as cold and repulsive as his brother's was affectionate and winning. He did not go to college, but at a rather early age went to Australia, where, during the rise of the colony, he made an ample fortune, first, as a merchant, and then as a landholder. He afterwards came to England, where he married, and lived in receipt of an income of £1,500 per annum. Robert, the youngest of Dr. Bethune's sons, was spoilt by his mother. He, too, went abroad, and, marrying an American lady, returned to a farm in the Black Isle. Soon after, he, with his wife and family, emigrated to British America.

About the time I came to Dornoch, Hugh Bethune came to reside at the manse, to attend MacDonald's school. This young man was the second son of Mr. Angus Bethune, minister of Alness in Ross-shire, elder brother of the minister at Dornoch. Hugh's mental abilities were not of the highest order, but he had a good, working mind, suited not so much for the higher walks of literature, as for the business of the world. He was a forward, smart boy, and showed a precocity for bustling his way to the attainment of independence. Although he and I were intimate, yet my brother and he could not agree, nor in any way pull together. Hugh Bethune's disposition being such as I have described, it, naturally enough, was not very agreeable to boys of his own age, who considered themselves on a level with him. Smartness in a boy, when among his superiors, is often little else than arrogance when in the society of his contemporaries. Such precisely was Hugh's bearing toward his schoolfellows. He stepped at once, and without being asked, into the place of leader and principal adviser in all the amusements of our play hours. He considered such a place to be his due, and I and others were of his opinion. Not so my brother; to arrogance and undue pretension his natural disposition was decidedly opposed, and those bickerings at last ended in an open rupture. Now the ordinary way of deciding such differences between schoolboys is a boxing match; and in just this manner did the rupture come to be determined between Hugh Bethune and my brother. The challenge was given and received, the place appointed, and, in the presence of those only who had espoused Bethune's side of the quarrel, the combatants engaged. Hugh could count as many years as my brother, but he was far from being on an equality with him in muscular strength, and therefore, after exchanging a few blows, Bethune gave in, and his friends interfered to save him from more punishment.

Notwithstanding my intimacy with Hugh Bethune, I did not exactly relish his conduct towards my brother; and I must confess that I indulged this feeling, and deliberately laid down a plan whereby I thought I could avenge my brother's quarrel. Hugh, Matthew, and I were at the time reading Cæsar together; having gone over it before with my father, I understood it better than they did, and acted usually, when we were preparing our lessons, as their usher. Yet such was Hugh Bethune's influence over me that, although I could easily enough have kept the head of the class, I preferred that he should have it, and kept him and Matthew Bethune above myself, by prompting them when they were examined by the master. On the occasion alluded to, I changed my plan, and when Hugh faltered in his lesson, notwithstanding all his significant nods, I remained silent. His cousin, as next in place in the class, was appealed to by the master; but poor Matthew could not help him out. When it came to my turn, I answered correctly, and then, as a glorious revenge, I stepped above them both and took the head of the class! Hugh Bethune afterwards went to the West Indies, in the commercial line, where he set up as a merchant in Kingston, Jamaica. He married and had a family, but was early cut off by fever.

Another of my school-fellows was a ragged boy, who was an excellent arithmetician and a good reader—indeed, upon the whole, one of the cleverest boys at school. He was very quiet, distant, and rather unsociable. His name was George Cameron, and he is now Sheriff-Substitute at Tain. He studied law and practised as a solicitor at Inverness for many years; was a keen Whig in politics, and a very clear-headed public speaker. He was twice married, first, to a daughter of Gilbert Mackenzie of Invershin, and next to a daughter of William Taylor.

Angus Leslie and I once, most unjustly, got thirty lashes from the master. Beyond this fact, he made no impression on me as a school-fellow. Some years ago he was employed by the late Duke of Sutherland as one of his under-factors on the Strathnaver district of his large estate. While acting in that capacity, he behaved with great cruelty to a mason of the name of MacLeod, who was also a small crofter in Strathy, parish of Farr. Leslie turned him and his family out of his house and croft in the middle of winter, during a heavy snowstorm, and, at the same time, forbade any of his neighbours, for miles around, to give them shelter. This conduct led to a series of letters in the "Edinburgh Courant," and afterwards to a controversial pamphlet, which reflected very severely, not only on Leslie's action, but upon the measures taken by the late Duchess of Sutherland against her Highland tenantry in 1818. Leslie soon after resigned the bailiffship of Strathnaver, and took the farm of Torboll. He had a brother Robert, who was a good scholar, and very amiable and kind-hearted. He became a medical man, and went abroad.

George Taylor was only remarkable at school for his powers of endurance under discipline. He studied law, and for a time held the situation of county clerk. He married a beautiful woman, Christina, daughter of Captain John Munro of Kirkton, parish of Golspie. He is the author of two very able articles in the "New Statistical Account of Scotland"—those on the parishes of Loth and Kildonan.

Another of my schoolmates was Sandy MacLean. This youth was, through his father, respectably, and through his mother, nobly descended. His father, a lineal descendant of MacLean of Dowart, the gallant and the brave, rose to the rank of Captain in the British army, and fell fighting the battles of his country. He married Miss Sutherland of Forse, a lineal descendant of William, fifth Earl of Sutherland, and, after the Kilphedder branch, the next in succession to the titles and estate of that earldom. Previous to his death Captain MacLean had taken the farm of Craigtown, in the parish of Golspie, where his widow and her numerous family now reside. Sandy, their second son, was my contemporary. He had a fair face and a handsome figure. Although generous and warm-hearted, he was a wild and dissipated youth. His passion was the army, and he left school on receiving his ensign's commission in a Scottish regiment of the line. He was killed in the prime of life in a duel. The occasion of it was his warm espousal of the cause of a countryman and brother officer, who had received gross insult from a professed duelist, and, after a challenge, had fallen by his hand. Burning to avenge the death of his friend, poor Sandy challenged the murderer, and was himself mortally wounded.

Some of my schoolfellows, with whom I was most intimate when at Dornoch, were three young men of the name of Hay. They were natives of the West Indies; the offspring of a negro woman, as their hair, and the tawny colour of their skin, very plainly intimated. Their father was a Scotsman, but I never learned particularly anything more of him. Fergus, the eldest, was about twenty years of age when I was at school, and attended merely to learn the higher branches of mathematics, in order to fit him for commercial duties. Notwithstanding the disadvantages of his negro parentage, Fergus was very handsome. He had all the manners of a gentleman, and had first-rate abilities; but he had the indomitable pride of an Indian potentate, and over his younger brothers, John and Alexander, he exercised an absolute sway. Even MacDonald himself quailed before the lordly bearing of Fergus Hay. I was a great favourite of his, but our friendship had rather a hostile beginning. For the thirty lashes which I so unjustly received, I was indebted chiefly to Fergus. He it was whom the master in his absence had appointed censor; and—merely to save the skins of Walter Bethune, Bob Barclay, and others, who made the noise, but for whom both he and the master had at the time a favour—who caused Angus Leslie and me to be made the victims. Fergus Hay was conscious of the impropriety of his conduct towards me, although his pride would not allow him to say so; for, from that day till he left school, which he did about half a year after, he behaved to me with very great kindness. His brother John and my brother were sworn friends; John Hay was considerably older than he, and of more than ordinary strength. Alexander, the youngest, was a peaceable lad. Whilst at Dornoch we often made excursions, on Saturdays and other holidays, to many places in the neighbourhood together; particularly to the Ciderhall wood, and to the elegant place of Skibo, where we used to roam through the woods and not return till late. At the harvest vacation my brother and I usually went home, and on one of these occasions John and Sandy accompanied us, and remained a week at Kildonan.

When at school at Dornoch we had our holiday games. Of these, the first was "club and shinty" (cluich' air phloc). The method we observed was this—two points were marked out, the one the starting-point, and the other the goal, or " haile." Then two leaders were chosen by a sort of ballot, which consisted in casting a club up into the air, between the two ranks into which the players were divided. The leaders thus chosen stood out from the rest, and, from the number present, alternately called a boy to his standard. The shinty or shinny, a ball of wood, was then inserted into the ground, and the leaders with their clubs struck at it till they got it out again. The heat of the game, or battle as I might call it, then began. The one party laboured hard, and most keenly, to drive the ball to the opposite point or "haile;" the other to drive it across the boundary to the starting-point; and which party soever did either, carried the day. In my younger years the game was universal in the north. Men of all ages among the working classes joined in it, especially on old New Year's day. I distinctly recollect of seeing, on such joyous occasions at Dornoch, the whole male population, from the grey-headed grandfather to the lightest-heeled stripling, turn out to the links, each with his club; and, from 11 o'clock in the forenoon till it became dark, they would keep at it, with all the keenness, accompanied by shouts, with which their forefathers had wielded the claymore. It was withal a most dangerous game, both to young and old. When the two parties met midway between the two points, with their blood up, their tempers heated, and clubs in their hands, the game then assumed all the features of a personal quarrel; and wounds were inflicted, either with the club or the ball, which, in not a few instances, actually proved fatal. The grave of a man, Andrew Colin, father of one of my school-mates, was pointed out to me, as that of one who was mortally wounded at a club and shinty game. The ball struck him on the head, causing concussion of the brain, of which he died.

Among our amusements was our pancake-cooking on Pasch Sunday (or Di-domhnaich chàisg), and in February, the "cock-fight." This last took precedence over all our other amusements. About the beginning of this century there was perhaps not a single parochial school in Scotland in which at its season the "cock-fight" was not strictly observed. Our teacher entered, with all the keenness of a Highlander and with all the method of a pedagogue, into this barbarous pastime. The method observed at Dornoch was as follows:—The set time being well known (àm cluiche nan coileach), there was a universal scrambling for cocks all over the parish; and we applied at every door, and pleaded hard for them. In those primitive times, people never thought of demanding any pecuniary recompense for the birds for which we dunned them. When the important day arrived, the court-room itself, in which was administered municipal rule, and where good Sheriff MacCulloch ordinarily held his legal tribunal, was surrendered to the occasion. With universal approval, the chamber of justice was converted into a battle-field, where the feathered brood might, by their bills and claws, decide who among the juvenile throng should be king and queen. The council-board was made a stage, and the Sheriff's bench was occupied by the schoolmaster and a select party of his friends, who sat there to give judgment. Highest honours were awarded to the youth whose bird had gained the greatest victories; he was declared king, while he who came next to him, by the prowess of his feathered representative, was associated in the dignity under the title of queen. Any bird that would not fight when placed on the stage was called a "fugie," and became the property of the master. A day was appointed for the coronation, and the ladies in the town applied their elegant imaginations to devise, and their fair fingers to construct, crowns for the royal pair. When the coronation day arrived, its ceremonies commenced by our assembling in the schoolhouse. The master sat at his desk, with the two crowns placed before him; the seats beside him being occupied by the "beauty and fashion" of the town. The king and queen of cocks were then called out of their seats, along with those whom their majesties had nominated as their life-guards. Mr. MacDonald now rose, took a crown in his right hand, and after addressing the king in a short Latin speech, placed it upon his head. Turning to the queen, and addressing her in the same learned language, he crowned her likewise. Then the life-guards received suitable exhortations in Latin, in regard to the onerous duties that devolved upon them in the high place which they occupied, the address concluding with the words, "itaque diligentissime attendite." A procession then began at the door of the schoolhouse, where we were all ranged by the master in our several ranks, their majesties first, their life-guards next, and then the "Trojan throng," two and two, and arm in arm. The town drummer and fifer marched before us and gave note of our advance, in strains which were intended to be both military and melodious. After the procession was ended, the proceedings were closed by a ball and supper in the evening. This was duly attended by the master and all the "Montagues and Capulets" of Dornoch.*

The inhabitants of Dornoch next claim my recollection. Dornoch is the only burgh in the county, and although it is not less important than Tain as a seaport town, its trade has, for nearly half a century, been considerably on the decrease. My personal acquaintances among the inhabitants were to be found in all ranks and grades. I have described the Sheriff and his household. Mr. MacCulloch's eminent

---

* During the eighteenth century, cock-fighting was practised as an ordinary pastime in the parish schools of Scotland. It was observed on Shrove Tuesday, or Fastern's E'en, as it was called. The custom was condemned in 1748 by John Grub, schoolmaster of Weymss, in Fife, in a Disputation composed by him to be read by his pupils to their parents, but was continued in practice for eighty years later. The celebration which followed on the above occasion was usually observed on Candlemas, old style, or the 13th of February. (See Dr. Rogers' "Social Life in Scotland.") —ED.

piety and Christian fellowship have enshrined his memory in the hearts of all who knew him. It was during our stay in his house that my uncle, Dr. Alex. Fraser of Kirkhill, died. I had just come in from school, and found the excellent Sheriff in tears. I did not presume to ask him the reason, but he understood my enquiring look. "Ah," said he, "I mourn your loss as well as my own and that of the Church; a prince has fallen in Israel—your uncle, Dr. Fraser, is no more." My most distinct recollection of the Sheriff afterwards is when I saw him in the Major's uniform of the Sutherland Volunteers; he made a speech in Gaelic to the men, who were drawn up before him.

My next acquaintance of importance was with the family at the manse. Dr. Bethune's manners were most attractive to all classes, particularly to the young. His personal appearance and expression of countenance warmly seconded the amiability of his manner. He had piercing black eyes, and his nose, being what is usually called "cocked," gave a strong expression of good humour to his face. His hair was dark, and, although he was past fifty at the time, it was but slightly touched with grey. His conversation was humorous, interspersed with shrewd remarks, or lively anecdotes, at which he himself laughed with so much glee that others felt compelled to join him. Mrs. Bethune was a lively, pleasant woman. Quite the lady in her manners, her character was formed after the fashion of the world. To her husband she was an helpmeet in everything but in that which belonged to the sacredness of his office. From her father, Joseph Munro, minister of Edderton, she had imbibed such a measure of the chilling influence of Moderatism, as to repress any kindly ministerial intercourse between her husband and the pious and lower classes of his parishioners. Dr. Bethune would have been far more intimate with his people, and more useful among them, if this sort of home influence had not been brought to bear upon him. Their eldest son, John, died young; their second son, Joseph, was in the army. Their eldest daughter, Christy, married Capt. Robert Sutherland, H.E.I.C.S. His other daughters were Barbara and Janet; the former married Col. Ross, once of Gladfield, afterwards of Strathgarvie; Janet remained unmarried, and latterly resided at Inverness.

Among my other acquaintances were Mr. Taylor, sheriff-clerk; Mr. Leslie, procurator-fiscal; Hugh Ross, or "Hugh the laird;" and James Boag, the architect. Of Mr. William Taylor I had many pleasant recollections. He was a native of Tain, and the eldest of four brothers, all of whom I subsequently knew. He married a daughter of Captain John Sutherland, who by her mother was, through the Kirtomy family, a cousin of my father. Mrs. Taylor was a warm-hearted, motherly person, and lived to an advanced age. They had a numerous family. George, the eldest, was my contemporary at school. Robert, the second son, succeeded his father in all the public offices which he held in the county, acted as procurator before the Sheriff Courts, married Mary, youngest daughter of the late Colonel Munro of Poyntzfield, and was appointed Sheriff-Substitute, first, in the Island of Lews, and afterwards at Tain. Hugh Leslie, the fiscal, was both an innkeeper and the procurator in the Sheriff Court. All sorts of people frequented his inn; and often during the markets periodically held at Dornoch, fierce, disorderly fellows quarrelled and fought with each other there, like so many mastiffs. On such occasions Mrs. Leslie, who was an amazon in size and strength, came in as "third's man," followed by her ostler, "Ton'l," as we usually called him, a strong fellow from Lochbroom. When her guests were fixed in each other's throats, Mrs. Leslie made short work with them, by planting a grip with each hand on the back of their necks, tearing them apart, and finally by holding them until her ostler, by repeated and strong applications of his fists, had sufficiently impressed them with a sense of their conduct. Although Mrs. Leslie, however, thus so much excelled all males and females of her day in strength and resolution, and did not hesitate to exert both on pressing occasions, yet she possessed an amiable temper. Her expansive countenance had a mild expression; her height was at least six feet, and her person extremely robust. In her latter days she became a true Christian, and her death-bed was triumphant. Hugh Leslie's bodily presence was always made known by his cough. His legal attainments and appearance as procurator I still remember. During play-time I would frequently spend half an hour in the court-house, and I have often come upon Hugh Leslie in the midst of one of his forensic orations. He made use of no ingenuity of argument, or of special pleading; but he took up all the strong points of the case, and battered away at them, until, in ten cases for one, he was ultimately successful. His second son, Angus, was my fellow-scholar. "Hugh the laird" was another of the Dornoch lawyers. He was a highly-talented and accomplished, but most eccentric man. He had studied law with Sheriff MacCulloch at Edinburgh, and had evidently seen better days. In court, he was usually Leslie's opponent; and no two men could possibly present, even to those least capable of observation, a more complete contrast. "The laird" was cool, clear and eloquent. Abstract views of the common law, brought to bear upon the case of his client with far more ingenuity than solidity of reasoning, where the forensic weapons which he brandished in Leslie's face, much to his annoyance, and, not unfrequently, to his discomfiture. Poor Leslie's arguments, which he delivered with such heat and rapidity, that he could neither illustrate them with sufficient clearness of expression, nor very distinctly remember them when he had finished, his cool and more able opponent took up one by one, and demolished, with pointed wit and sarcasm. Ross held up all his words and arguments, from first to last, in a light so distorted and so perfectly ludicrous, that his fiery little antagonist could not recognise them again, but, starting to his feet, while "Hugh the laird" was going on, he would hold up both his hands, and, trembling with rage, cry out, "O, such lies! such lies! did ever you hear the like?" These explosions of temper Ross met by a graceful bow to the bench, and a request to the Sheriff to maintain the decency of the court. James Boag, the architect, a very old and a very odd man, then lived at Dornoch. He was a carpenter by trade, and was by extraction from the south country. In his younger years he had lived at a place called Golspie Tower, rented as a farm from the Sutherland family, where he got into an extensive business, having become contractor, almost on his own terms, for most of the public buildings, as well as for many gentlemen's houses, in the counties of Ross and Sutherland. All the churches and manses in Sutherland and Easter-Ross built between 1760 and 1804, were according to the plans, and were the workmanship of, James Boag. These plans were in almost all cases identical; that is, for churches, long, narrow buildings, much resembling granaries, in which convenience and acoustics were equally ignored. His manses we have already described in that of Kildonan. He built the church of Resolis, in Mr. MacPhail's time, in 1767; and the church of Kildonan, during my father's incumbency, in 1788. When a school-boy at Dornoch I never could meet Boag, or even see him at a distance, without a feeling of terror. He lived mostly at Dornoch, but spent a considerable part of the year at Skelbo, which he held in lease. He terrified all the school-boys, as well as every inmate of his own house, by the violence of his temper and his readiness to take offence. His son-in-law, Mr. William Rose, was decidedly pious, as was also Mrs. Rose. After Dr. Bethune's death, she was one of several eminent Christians who petitioned the Marchioness of Stafford, as patron, in my favour. They were not successful, and I was utterly unworthy of such an honour; but it is a consolation to think that, although I did not thereby become minister of Dornoch, I was, notwithstanding, the choice of those who were owned and honoured of God. Mr. Rose died at an advanced age. He was one of the elders of the parish, and his Christian character may be summed in this, that he was distinguished for simplicity and fervour, "a good man, full of faith and of the Holy Ghost."

Two antiquated ladies lived in the town, Miss Betty Gordon and her elder sister Miss Anne. I mention the younger first, because the elder sister was always ailing, and seldom visible to the outdoor public. Miss Betty herself was too feeble to walk out, but she usually sat in the window in the afternoon, dressed after the fashion of 1699, in an ancient gown, with a shawl pinned over her shoulders, and a high cap as head gear. Like all females, perhaps, in the single state and of very advanced age, she was very fond of society, and of that light and easy conversation otherwise termed gossip. When therefore she took her station at her upper window, a female audience usually congregated below it. These attendants gave her the news of the day; and she made her remarks upon it, as full of charity and goodwill towards all as such remarks usually are. These two old ladies were as ancient in their descent as they were aged in years. Daughters of the laird of Embo, they could trace direct descent from the noble family of Huntly, through Adam, Lord of Aboyne. Their brother was the last laird in the direct line, and was the immediate predecessor of Robert Hume Gordon of Embo.

The public fairs of this little county town made a considerable stir. From the Ord Head to the Meikle Ferry, almost every man, woman, and child attended the Dornoch market. The market stance was the churchyard. Dornoch was what might strictly be called an Episcopalian town; and the consecrated environs of the Cathedral was just the place which the men of those days would choose, either for burying their dead or holding their markets. The churchyard therefore became the only public square within the town. The evening previous to the market was a busy one. A long train of heavily-loaded carts might be seen wending their weary way into the town, more particularly from Tain, by the Meikle Ferry. The merchants' booths or tents were then set up, made of canvas stretched upon poles inserted several feet into the ground, even into graves and deep enough to reach the coffins. The fair commenced about twelve o'clock noon next day, and lasted for two days and a half. During its continuance, every sort of saleable article was bought and sold, whether of home or foreign manufacture. The first market at Dornoch that we attended took place six weeks after our arrival at the town. The bustle and variety of the scene very much impressed me. The master gave us holiday; and as my brother and I traversed the market-place, pence in hand, to make our purchases, all sorts of persons, articles, amusements, employments, sights and sounds, smote at once upon our eyes, our ears and our attention. Here we were pulled by the coat, and on turning round recognised, to our great joy, the cordial face of a Kildonaner; there we noticed a bevy of young lasses, in best bib and tucker, accompanied by their bachelors, who treated them with ginger-bread, ribbons, and whisky. Next came a recruiting party, marching, with " gallant step and slow," through the crowd, headed by the sergeant, sword in hand, and followed by the corporal and two or three privates, each with his weapon glancing in the sunlight. From one part of the crowd might be heard the loud laugh that bespoke the gay and jovial meeting of former acquaintance-ship, now again revived; from another the incessant shrill of little toy trumpets, which fond mothers had furnished to their younger children, and with which the little urchins kept up an unceasing clangour. At the fair of that day I, first of all, noticed the master perambulating the crowd, and looking at the merchants' booths with a countenance scarcely less rigid and commanding than that with which he was wont invariably to produce silence in the school.

Another incident of my school-boy days at Dornoch was a bloody fray which took place immediately after the burial of Miss Gray from Creich. The deceased was of the Sutherland Grays, who about the beginning of the last century, possessed property in the parishes of Creich, Lairg, Rogart, and Dornoch. She came down from London to the north of Scotland for change of air, being in a rapid decline, but did not survive her arrival at Creich longer than a month. Her remains were buried beside those of her ancestors in the Cathedral of Dornoch. The body was accompanied by an immense crowd, both of the gentry and peasantry. In the evening, after the burial, there was a dreadful fight. The parishioners of Dornoch and those of Creich quarrelled with each other, and fists, cudgels, stones, and other missiles were put in requisition. The leader of the Creich combatants was William Munro of Achany. I sat on a gravestone, at the gable of the ruined aisle of the cathedral, looking at the conflict. Broken heads, blood trickling over enraged faces, yells of rage, oaths and curses, are my reminiscences of the event. Dr. Bethune narrowly escaped broken bones. As he was walking up to obtain ocular demonstration of the encounter, he was rudely attacked by two outrageous men from Creich. They threatened to knock him down; but some of his parishioners, coming just in time, readily interfered, and his assailants measured their length on the highway.

Our visits to the manse of Creich were not to be forgotten. Worthy Mr. Rainy's face and figure, his grey coat, his fatherly reception of us, his motherly and amiable wife—ever "on hospitable thoughts intent" —his daughter Miss Bell, afterwards Mrs. Angus Kennedy of Dornoch, and his sons George and Harry, rise up and pass distinctly before me. Mr. Rainy made a most favourable impression upon me when I first saw him. He was a short, stout man, with full eyes and a most intelligent, expressive face, of which every feature was good, and every one of them said something peculiar to itself. His little parlour, for which he had a special predilection, had a small window in front, an old-fashioned iron grate in the chimney, and a whole tier of presses and beds, with wooden shutters painted blue, running along the whole extent of the north wall. This was his constant resting-place. Here he slept, breakfasted, dined and supped. The parlour was so much to his mind that it was with difficulty he could be got out of it. He lived in rather a genteel neighbourhood, and when, in the exercise of hospitality, and of a kindly interchange of civilities between himself and his people, he made provision for their entertainment, a well-furnished drawing-room came into requisition. But this room was, during his stay in it, little better than a prison. He sat by the fire, but there was no rest for him, not for a moment. He never ceased to paw the carpet with his right foot during the whole time he remained there; and nothing but a retreat to the parlour, and the settling of himself in his arm-chair, could put an end to his impatience. Mrs. Rainy was a very pleasant-looking woman, somewhat taller than her husband. The great attraction of her countenance was its unequivocal expression of kindness. If any child had missed its mother, and had met Mrs. Rainy, the conclusion in the child's mind must have been irresistible—that Mrs. Rainy could be none else than the "mother" so long sought for. She was never weary in well-doing, and had an ear to listen to, and a heart to feel for, every individual case, whether of joy or sorrow. It was during my visits whilst at Dornoch school to the manse of Creich that I first saw and became acquainted with James Campbell, a native of that parish. He afterwards was my class-fellow during my four years' attendance at college, my fellow-student at the hall, my fellow-probationer before the Presbytery of Dornoch, and ultimately, in 1824, my father's successor at Kildonan. James attended duly at the manse of Creich to be instructed by Harry Rainy in the Latin Tongue. He was, at the time, a full-grown man, afflicted with a more than ordinary measure of poverty. To teach him anything was no easy matter, the difficulty, on the part of the teacher, consisting entirely in his being utterly puzzled what method to fall upon so as to convey any kind of knowledge through the "seven-fold plies" of his pupil's natural stupidity. George and Harry Rainy, until they both went to college were their father's pupils. He was an accomplished classical scholar and, bating a little heat of temper, a first-rate teacher. Respecting the antiquities of Dornoch, I content myself with a very few remarks. The etymology of the name is Celtic, and means "the horse's hoof, or fist." The name was derived from the prowess of one of the family of Sutherland, at a battle fought between the Danes and the men of Sutherland, close by the shore, about a quarter of a mile to the east of the town. In the action the Danes were defeated, owing chiefly to the dreadful carnage of their men by this gigantic chief, who, Samson-like, had no other weapon than the leg of a horse, with the hoof of which he slew "heaps upon heaps." The hero of the day was himself unfortunately killed towards the close of the action. In memory of his heroism, an obelisk was erected on the spot, of open work, which still remains. When I was at Dornoch it lay on the ground in fragments; but it has been re-erected by the late Duchess of Sutherland, to perpetuate the memory of her ancestor. Dornoch, in point of extent, commerce and population, is the " Old Sarum " of Scotland. In ancient times, however, it was a place of considerable importance. It was the seat of a bishopric, in which stood the church of St. Barr, and the cathedral built by Gilbert Murray in 1222.* This cathedral, except the steeple, was burnt, in 1570, by the Master of Caithness and Mackay of Strathnaver, after a contest with the Murrays, vassals of the Earl of Sutherland; but it was reconstructed by Sir Robert Gordon, tutor of Sutherland, when it received its present form. It was originally built in the shape of a cross; the nave extended to the west, the transepts from north to South, and the choir to the east; and each of these four aisles met together under a huge square tower, surmounted by a wooden steeple. The last of its bishops was Andrew Wood, translated from the Isles in 1680, and ousted by the Revolution in 1688. After it became a Presbyterian place of worship, the west aisle was allowed to fall into decay, and was converted into a burial-ground, the other three being sufficient for a large congregation. In 1816 the roof was ceiled, and a gallery erected. But the last and most splendid renovation of this ancient fabric was that undertaken by the Duchess of Sutherland in 1835-7, by which it has become one of the most elegant structures, but one of the most unsuitable places of worship, in the Empire. The ruins of the west aisle were cleared away, and the nave re-erected, in chaste, modern-Gothic style, on the site, with a beautiful window and doorway in the gable; the other aisles were also renewed to correspond with it. Many additional windows were pierced, and filled with frosted glass; the bartizan of the tower was coped with stone; the steeple was built anew; and, instead of the old, crazy, one-faced, single-handed clock, a new one, of the best workmanship, was erected in the steeple, with four dial-plates, each furnished with an hour-and-minute-hand. As to the interior, the four

* Gilbert Murray, bishop of Sutherland and Caithness, was commonly called by the natives, "Gilbard Naomh," or Saint Gilbert, because he had been canonised by the Roman Catholic Church. He was bishop for 20 years, during which period he laboured with much energy and zeal to instruct and civilize the people of his rude diocese. The 1st of April, 1240, is given as the date of his death. The fragment of an ancient stone effigy, within the Cathedral of Dornoch, is believed to mark his grave.—ED.

aisles present one unbroken space within. The extreme height of the ceiling from the floor is upwards of 50 feet, and the distance from the pulpit, which rests against the north-east pillar of the tower, to the western door, is more than 70 feet. On the ceiling, at the spring of the roof, is a profusion of ornaments, interspersed with images both of men and animals; amongst the latter the cat of the Sutherland crest is conspicuous. The object of the Duchess, in this restoration, was to provide a mausoleum for the remains of her late husband, and for herself; and for this purpose she spared neither her own purse, nor the feelings of her people; for, in the course of the operations, she caused the very dead to be removed from their resting-place. More than fifty bodies were dug out of their graves in order to clear out a site for her own burial-vault, under the west aisle; the remains of the Duke having been deposited in a vault under the east aisle. The melancholy remains of mortality, consisting of half-putrefied bodies, bones, skulls, hair, broken coffins, and dingy, tattered winding-sheets, were flung into carts, without ceremony, and carried to a new burying-ground, where, without any mark of respect, they were thrown into large trenches opened up for their reception. The scene was revolting to humanity; but it was a fitting sequel to her treatment of her attached tenantry, whom, by hundreds, she had removed from their homes and their country.

The other remarkable relic of antiquity in Dornoch is the Castle, or Bishop's Palace. When I was at school these Castle ruins were the favourite resort of the more venturous among us, who went there in order to harry the nests of the jackdaws that built among the crumbling walls. The space which it enclosed still goes by the name of the Castle Close. The original structure seems to have consisted of two towers connected by a screen. Only one of these towers, with a fragment of the intermediate building, survives the ravages of time: the only part of the screen remaining being a huge chimney-stalk, containing the vent of the bishop's kitchen, which was below in one of the sunk floors. In the tower, access is gained to all its apartments by a spiral stone staircase, contained in a small rounded tower, projecting laterally from the side of the large tower, and running up its whole height. Below are subterraneous vaults, about ten feet high and arched at the top. A tradition among the people about the castle, for its site is now covered with hovels of the poorest of the inhabitants, was that it stood upon a "brander of oak." This meant, I suppose, that, as the soil was light and sandy, the castle was founded upon oaken piles driven deep into the ground. This castle was the bishop's town residence, or manor-house. He had besides two country residences, each of which were castles: Skibo, a few miles to the west of Dornoch, and Scrabster, in the immediate vicinity of Thurso, in Caithness. The Castle of Skibo was demolished in the last century, and that of Dornoch was, along with the Cathedral, burnt in 1567 by the Master of Caithness, in his conflict with the Murrays. It has since been partly rebuilt and fitted up as a court-house and prison. There were also two other ecclesiastical buildings, over the ruins of which I loved to clamber, and whose form and structure pointed to a remote origin. One stood at the east and the other at the west end of the town. That at the east had small vaulted apartments and a stone winding-stair. The people called it the "Chantor's house," and the farm in the immediate neighbourhood was called "Ach-a-chantoir." The ruin to the west was called "the Dean's house," and was a plain building with a jamb, or back wing, attached to it. It was tenanted for long after the Revolution, and, about twenty years before I was born, was occupied as an inn by a man named Morrison. The site has since been feued and built over, though when we were at school it was a ruin. For Mr. Angus Fraser, merchant, some years afterwards took it as a feu, pulled down the ruins, and erected his house on the site.

But the trade of Dornoch is at present a nonentity. Its markets, so flourishing in former times, have almost ceased to exist. Its population has decreased to about one-half the number it used to be. Its merchants, or shopkeepers, are not more than two or three; if a retailer sets up in any part of the parish or county he succeeds, but if he removes to Dornoch he almost immediately becomes a bankrupt. There seems, in short, to hang over the place a sort of fatality, a blighting influence which, like the Pontine marshes at Rome to cattle, is fatal to trade, house-building, mercantile enterprise, or even to the increase of the *genus homo* in this ill-starred and expiring Highland burgh. From the first it had to contend against its surroundings. The town is situated on a neck of land running out into the Moray firth at its junction with the firth of Tain. Around the town the soil is arid, sandy and unproductive, and so notorious for sterility was its location of old that, according to my earliest recollections, it went under the descriptive appellative of "Dornoch na gortai," or Dornoch of the famine. Its immediate locality, too, is bleak and bare as a Siberian desert. Though close by the sea, it has not only no harbour, but no natural capabilities for any possibility of having one. An almost stagnant burn flows slowly through it, but it vanishes in mounds of sand before reaching the sea. The estuary, which stretches to the west, is crossed at its embouchure into the Moray firth by a bar, formed by the lodgment of many centuries of all the sediment washed into it by the rivers Shin, Oykell, Carron, and Evelix. This bar, well known to mariners by the name of "The Gizzen Briggs" (called in Gaelic, "Drochaid an Aoig," or the Kelpie's bridge), is an insuperable *bar* to the development of Dornoch as a seaport town. But it might still have retained some of its former prosperity had it been held in kindlier hands. The greater part of it is the property of the family of Sutherland. They have purchased, of late, all the houses for sale, only to level them with the ground, and, by setting up villages and markets in other places, have destroyed its trade and reduced its population.

CHAPTER X.

HOME AND COLLEGE LIFE.

1804-1805.

MY brother and I left Dornoch to return to our paternal home in the spring of 1803; it was in autumn of the year 1804 that he left to go to sea. My worthy stepmother never could agree with any of my father's children but myself. My sisters and she had many painful *rencontres*, and Eneas, being of a bold, determined disposition, became as impatient and restive as they were. An open rupture had occurred about a month previous to his going to sea, and this was the circumstance which principally led to his departure. The matter was communicated to Capt. Baigrie, who made all the necessary arrangements. So widely acquainted was he with ship-captains and employers that he got my brother appointed as a seaman, at the age of sixteen, on board a West-India-man, in the employment of Messrs Forbes & Co., Aberdeen. The hour of his departure at last came. Capt. Baigrie had sent a bearer express to the manse to say that he must leave Kildonan next day, and be at Helmisdale about 2 o'clock in the afternoon to go aboard and sail to Aberdeen by a fishing smack, the master of which was Capt. Coy, in the employ of Mr. William Forbes of Echt. From Aberdeen he was immediately to proceed by the same conveyance to London, there to go on board the West-India-man on a voyage to the West Indies. The sudden message was as suddenly obeyed. My brother did not hesitate for a moment. His trunk was packed up on that same evening, and with scarcely three pounds in his pocket, and with hardly a tear in his eye, did he next day at 10 o'clock bid a last adieu to his father, stepmother and sisters. I acccompanied him to Helmisdale, but could scarcely speak to him on the road; for I felt, every step as we proceeded, as if my very life was gradually deserting me. At Helmisdale Capt. Coy was waiting for us—a gruff, harsh fellow, who said with an oath that we had been too long. The smack's yawl lay close to the shingly shore, bouncing up and down upon the waves which came in upon it one after another in rapid succession. My brother's trunk was hoisted into the yawl, the small anchor which bound it to the shore was unloosed and thrown with a crash into the boat. Coy sang out, "Step in, and all hands to the oars;" my brother grasped my hand, almost stupified with grief. "Farewell, Donald," were his last words, when, instantly obeying the summons, he placed himself by the side of Capt. Coy, the seamen stretched to their oars, and I parted with him for ever! I had not a tear to shed when he grasped my hand, not a word to say to him when he bade me farewell; but, as the yawl scudded through the waves and began to lessen in the distance, my heart sank within me, and it is likely I would myself have sunk also to the ground had not the flood-gates of sorrow been unclosed, and tears come to my relief. My eyes filled so fast with tears that the yawl and the loved being which it contained became quite invisible to me, and I saw not his arrival at the smack. When I recovered a little, I borrowed from Johnson, the salmon-boiler, a small telescope to take my last look. The sails were all set, the smack had veered round to proceed on her voyage, and I got the last glimpse of him as he stood on the deck.

My brother's arrival in London he intimated to us by letter. He particularly made mention of the kindness of Mr. William Forbes of Echt on his arrival at Aberdeen, in whose employ, as a seaman on board the West-India trader, he went out. Mr. Forbes gave him a strong recommendatory letter to the master of the trader, and, at parting, a pound-note. With this money he purchased a few prints of ships in gilt frames, which he sent as a peace-offering to his step-mother.*

I may here refer to my father's tenants and others who, at this time, lived in Kildonan. The first I notice is James Gordon or Gow, a blacksmith, who occupied the pendicle of Ach-nan-nighean. He could do everything to meet the demands and wants of the parishioners but one, and that was to shoe horses. He was not up to this, merely because the hoofs of the Highland garrons were so hard, and the greater part of the sort of roads so soft, that the inhabitants never thought of getting the feet of their horses cased in iron. When my father was settled at Kildonan, however, he got horses of a large size, which were accustomed to that safeguard, and, in fact, could not do without it; so that while all the smith-work of his kitchen, glebe, and farm was executed by the said James Gordon, he was under the necessity of sending his horses to be shod to the neighbouring parish of Loth. My first introduction to James Gordon was in the prepara-tions made for him by my father's servant. These consisted in making fuel for the smithy. Peat, or moss, was the *materiel*. It was subjected to a certain process by which it was converted into charcoal. Coals were not used by any blacksmith in the county, and the process by which the smithy fuel was prepared was simple enough. A large pit was dug in soft, friable ground; dry peats were placed in it, tier above tier, so as to burn when ignited, the whole being then kindled and allowed to burn almost to a cinder, when it was covered up with earth until the fire went out. The smith was a tall, slender man, with a countenance full of solemnity. He had a theory of his own upon almost every subject that came within his ken, and he was of the opinion that nothing ever could or should be done, within the four corners of the parish, without a previous consultation with him. He was always complaining of the state of his health, and these complaints were usually uttered when a more than ordinary arrear of parish work, in the way of his calling, lay unperformed on his hands. It came, therefore, to be a sort of a proverb among the people, if any one

---

* The next and last letter received from Eneas was dated from Philadelphia, U.S. In it he mentioned his having served for a short time on board a British man-of-war. What became of him afterwards was never known.—ED.

complained of the state of his health without any good grounds for it, that "he was a delicate person like James Gordon." (Tha 'e na dhuin' aumhuinn, mar tha Seumas Gordon." Poor James Gow, however, was upon the whole a kind and benevolent man, and of his hospitality my brother and I had often a bountiful experience.

George Dalangall lived on the farm of Kildonan. His house and garden originally stood close upon the bank of the mill-stream, and hence he was usually called "Seoras na h'ellich," or George of the mill-lade. His surname was Gunn, and as he was of the family of the Gunns of Dalangall, he was more frequently called "Seoras Dalangall." I recollect but little of him, as he died soon after our return from Dornoch. His widow long occupied the pendicle of her husband after his decease, and every one spoke of her under the designation of "Banntrach na h'ellich," or the widow of the mill-lade. Her son William and her daughter Kate were our constant play-fellows at the burn-side. William, who enlisted in the army, was in the Peninsular War, and returned scathless to his native country.

John Sutherland was a popular edition of "Isaac Walton," and to deer-hunting a perfect "Nimrod." Whilst returning home about midnight from an angling expedition on the river Helmisdale, his way lay through the churchyard. On entering it his attention was instantly arrested, and his rather hasty pace interrupted by two eyes like flames of fire which glared at him out of a new-made grave. Old "Ian Mòr" was not to be "*dantoned*" however. He walked up to the grave, planted his grip on some hairy, living thing which was in it, and which, in his grasp, jumped up and down with great activity. He succeeded at last in hauling it out, when it turned out to be a black ram belonging to one of his neighbours. Ian Meadhonach was his eldest son. He was surnamed "the middling" during his father's life-time because his younger brother was also called John, a rather unusual occurrence. Thus the father and two sons in the family were distinguished from each other by being called "Ian Mòr, Ian Meadhonach, and Ian Beag," or "John the big, the middling, and the little." John Meadhonach retained the appellative after his father's death among the parishioners, but in his own family he became Ian Mòr. He inherited his father's passion for angling and deer-hunting, and was also in his own way a bit of an antiquary. He could repeat almost all Ossian's poems, and, what I never saw in print, Ossian's tales.* I have still a faint recollection of

---

* According to Mr. Skene (see his introduction to the "Book of the Dean of Lismore," edited by Dr. Thomas MacLauchlan), the Ossianic poems, in their transmission, passed through three different stages. In the first and oldest form they were pure poems, of more or less excellence, narrating the adventures of those warrior bands whose memory still lingered in the country. Each poem was complete in itself, and was attributed to one mythic poet of the race which was celebrated. But as the language of these poems became altered, and the reciters less able to retain the whole, they would narrate, in ordinary prose, the events of the parts they had forgotten; thus the poems would pass into the second stage of *prose tales*, interspersed with fragments of verse. Bards of later times became imitators of the older Ossianic poetry, and made the tales, or intermediate prose narratives, the basis of their poems. This was the third stage, in which the names and incidents of the older poems were embedded in the new.—ED.

hearing John Meadhonach at our kitchen fireside, during the time that a log of wood of considerable length was consuming in the fire—about three or four hours—entertain his interested audience with long oral extracts from our Celtic Homer. My father not only held the township of Kildonan in lease, but had the right of fishing in the river, and John, as well as his two brothers, were some of the crew of fishers with the net on the glebe-pools whom my father employed. They were also poachers and smugglers. They and their next neighbour, Donald Gunn, were constantly in the habit of killing salmon, not only with the rod, but with clips and spears, at that particular part of it already described as the " Slagaig." They were so assiduous and successful that they kept their families, almost throughout the whole year, abundantly furnished with that savoury accompaniment to their vegetable diet. They were perfectly aware that in doing so they infringed on my father's fishing rights, and therefore, when they were thus employed, they set a regular watch to give due warning of the approach of the minister or either of his sons. At the first note of alarm they instantly threw down their fishing implements, and laid themselves prostrate under a huge rock above the Slagaig, where they remained perfectly secure from further observation. John was also a smuggler and a first-rate brewer of malt whisky. My step-mother often employed him in making our annual brewst for family use. We built a cow-house of stone and turf near the burn, at the east dyke of the corn-yard. The hovel was also employed for various other purposes, more especially for washing and brewing. There often, during the process of our whisky brewst, have I sat with John, watching the process and hearing his tales. He had five of a family, three daughters, Betty, Kate, and Jean, and two sons, John and Donald. They were all remarkably handsome, particularly the eldest daughter and youngest son. Betty "Mheadhonaich" married a Robert Bruce; Kate, an Alexander Fraser Beag; and Jane one Angus Mackay, son of Donald Mackay, the catechist. On his marriage with Jane, Mackay immediately emigrated to America, where he soon attained affluence; he left this country soon after our return from Dornoch. John himself, with his wife and two sons, long afterwards emigrated to the Red River, in Canada, under the direction of Lord Selkirk, but he died during the passage. Poor John had a strong attachment to my father, and a most profound veneration for him; and though his wife and sons came to bid us farewell, he, himself, after making four different attempts to come and take his last look of his minister, finally gave it up. His two brothers Donald and John had lived with him for a considerable time. Donald Mòr, as he was called, or "Muckle Donald," had, previous to our going to Dornoch school, enlisted with General Wemyss, and with his regiment had been in Ireland and England. But sometime before our return from school he had left the army, and come home, when he was soon engaged by my father as his principal farm-servant, at the rate of £6 per annum as wages. He afterwards settled in Kildonan, marrying Rose Gordon, where they both lived to an advanced age. His younger brother, John Beag, anxious after a while to do something for himself, became principal farm-servant of a well-doing sonsy widow in Glutt of Braemore, Caithness. He pleased her so well in this capacity that, in a very short time, she offered to promote him to the rank of a husband—an offer with which John instantly closed, and found himself very comfortable. These men had a sister of the name of Chirsty, better known among us as "Càirstean." She was unmarried, and was employed as a post-runner from Brora to Kildonan, a distance of about fifteen miles. This distance, twice told, Càirstean accomplished with much apparent ease, on foot, in the course of a day, once a week throughout the year, she being at the time about sixty years of age. She was for her years the most unwearied pedestrian I ever knew. On one pressing occasion she went and came from Kildonan to Dornoch, a distance little less than fifty miles, in a day. She long suffered from a malignant tumour in her arm, but finally repaired to the mineral well at Achnamoine, where, after using the waters freely, both externally and internally, at the end of two months she made a complete recovery.

Close by John Meadhonach's house stood that of Donald Gunn, one of the tightest and most active of Highlanders. Indeed, every possible element which entered into the structure of this man's mind, as well as into the size and make of his body, combined to constitute him the very model of a Highland peasant. He was exactly of the middle size, and well made, with just as much flesh on his bones as simply served to cover them, and no more. He had a face full of expression, which conveyed most unequivocally the shrewdness, cunning, acuteness, and caustic humour so strongly characteristic of his race. Donald Gunn surpassed his whole neighbourhood and, perhaps, the whole parish, in all rustic and althetic exercises. At a brawl, in which, however, he but seldom engaged, none could exceed him in the dexterity and rapidity with which he brandished his cudgel; and though many might exceed him in physical strength, his address and alert activity often proved him more than a match for an assailant of much greater weight and size. Then in dancing he was without a rival. With inimitable ease and natural grace he kept time, with eye and foot and fingers, to all the minute modulations of a Highland reel or Strathspey. He was also a good shot, a successful deer stalker, angler, smuggler, and poacher. Donald, however, with all these secular and peculiarly Highland recommendations was little better than a heathen. He was always under suspicion, and latterly made some hair-breadth escapes from the gallows, for he was, by habit and repute, a most notorious thief. His wife, Esther Sutherland, was a native of Caithness, and a very handsome woman. His daughter Janet married a man Bruce from Loist, and Jane married a Malcolm Fraser, who was afterwards drowned at Helmisdale. His son Robert went to America with Lord Selkirk's colony, and in an affray between these settlers and those of the North-West Company poor Robert Gunn was killed.

Mr. Donald MacLeod, parochial schoolmaster, was also one of my father's tenants. I have already mentioned him. At the fellowship meetings, both in the church where my father presided, and privately in the neighbourhood, Mr. MacLeod shone brightly in communicating his views and experience of the power of Divine truth on the heart.

He had also the gift and the grace of prayer; even the most careless and thoughtless could not but be affected even to tears by the fervency, the solemnity, and appropriateness of his prayers. Donald MacLeod had, however, as who has not, his failings and even peccadillos. He and my father were warmly attached to one another, and he and his family were invariably our guests on such holidays as Christmas and New-Year's day. On such occasions poor Donald used to indulge in rather deep potations of strong ale and toddy, much to the damage of his senses. On one of these festive occasions, as he was returning home, exceedingly unsteady in his movements, hobbling first to one side of the road and then to the other, he was noticed and pursued by a pugnacious old gander which we had at the time. The creature having made up to him, fastened upon his coat-tails, and kept dangling back and fore behind him, exactly in accord with his own movements, the poor schoolmaster himself being all the while quite unconscious of his follower. He was very useful in the parish, for he could let blood, and was a daily reader of "Buchan's Domestic Medicine," all whose instructions he rigidly, and often successfully, practised. He also, every Sabbath evening, kept what was called "a reading," the substitute in those days for Sabbath schools. Towards the close of his life, the contention between grace and corruption within him appeared to wax hotter and hotter, till at last, on his death-bed, he exhibited most clearly the magnificent moral spectacle of a great sinner, washed "white in the blood of the Lamb," entering upon the world unseen, triumphing through faith in the acceptance and hope of a free and eternal salvation. His wife was the daughter of "Ian Thappaidh," the target at which Rob Donn shot off his most envenomed shafts of satire. Widow of John Gunn, schoolmaster of Kildonan, the immediate predecessor of MacLeod, she had two children by her former husband, namely, Isobel and and Walter. Isobel married worthy Evan Macpherson. Walter, her brother, was the acquaintance of my earliest years, and the object of nearly my first recollections. I now remember many things illustrative of Walter's personal kindness to us, as well as of his own private history. Walter Gunn was a mechanic, something also of a naturalist, a gardener and a musician. He cultivated many varieties of seeds and flowers. His currants—red, black and white—were the best in the county. But his step-father and his brother by the second marriage and he did not very well agree. He took his resolution, therefore, and at last went to America. Donald MacLeod had four children—John, George, Margaret, and Christina. John, his eldest son, enlisted in the army, and his enlistment created, when known (for it was done secretly), a terrible sensation in his father's family. George remained at home, and became his father's successor. He married a daughter of Adam Gordon of Rhenivy, half-sister of the late Mr. George Gordon, minister of Loth. His brother, John, returned from the army, after many years' service, and lived at Tain. Margaret married one Fraser, or Grant, who lived at Fethnafall, in the heights of the parish. Chirsty married a Joseph Sutherland, from the parish of Loth. Mrs. MacLeod long survived her second husband; she died at the very advanced age of ninety-eight.

Thomas Gordon of Achnamoine held office as a justice of the peace, and was, moreover, a perfect enthusiast as a magistrate. He imagined that the cause of justice depended on his personal exertions. If the people of Kildonan did not furnish him with weekly opportunities of deciding in his worshipful capacity their various cases of dispute, Thomas Gordon put them in mind that justice was to be had for the asking. Quartering himself at the manse, he directed all disputants to repair to Donald Gunn's house, to have their disputes finally settled by his arbitration. I recollect, on one of these occasions, having had the special honour conferred upon me of being chosen clerk to his worship, and of having received his fee, the sum of one shilling! Of the farm of Achnamoine Gordon was tacksman, holding it in lease from the family of Sutherland. To his wife he was devotedly attached, and he never wearied of talking about her. She was a pious, amiable person, but she was always in bad health, and died many years before her husband. They had a large family of sons and daughters. Robert, the eldest, emigrated to America. Charles, their second son, held the farm after his father's death, but previous to that held a commission in the army; and, while on military duty at Portsmouth, got acquainted with the family of a gentleman named Russel, one of whose daughters he married. Having retired on half-pay, he came home with his wife, after his father's death, to reside at Achnamoine. On their way thither they spent two days at Kildonan manse. The wife accompanied her lord to a country, the localities, accommodations, and privations of which she had not thought or dreamed of. On the morning previous to their departure from my father's house to Achnamoine, she asked my step-mother what sort of a domicile might be found at Achnamoine, and whether it was like the manse. My step-mother led her to the gable window of the upper east room, and pointing very emphatically to John Meadhonach's long, straggling, turf hovel, which might be seen from the window, said, "It is. like that, but scarcely so good." The poor Anglo-Saxon burst into tears, and exclaimed, "Mercy on me," but, checking herself, added, "Well, domestic happiness is as sweet even in a cot as in a palace." And it was as she said. She lived with her husband many years in the turf-house at Achnamoine very happily. When Charles Gordon took possession of the farm, after his father's death, and his brother's departure to America, a better house was built by him; and I have been many a comfortable night there, as their guest, when at Achness. He retained the farm until after my father's death, when, on the expiry of his lease, he first resided at Avoch, in Ross-shire, and afterwards with his wife's relatives in Portsmouth. Hugh, the third son, also got a commission in the army, and retired on half-pay. Of him and his sisters more hereafter. Their mother was a sister of Mr. Gordon of Loth.

Alexander Gordon at Dalchairn I have already named. My acquaintance with him commenced at an early period. He was a wealthy and substantial tenant, as well as a most hospitable man. During any vacancy in the mission of Achness, in which the upper part of the parish of Kildonan was comprehended, my father preached at Ach-na-h'uaighe, and quartered himself at Dalchairn. Alastair Gordon and his wife, as well as the members of his family, were often Saturday and

Sabbath evening guests at Kildonan. Presents too of mutton, butter and cheese were frequently sent to the manse, and good old Alastair and his kind and hearty wife would not be content with an interchange of hospitality and friendship to this amount only; they insisted upon it that my brother and I should spend the Christmas holidays with them. I distinctly remember these festive occasions. To give us a more than ordinary treat tea was prepared for breakfast, a luxury almost unknown in these hyperborean regions. Gordon's second daughter Anne, who then had the management of her father's house, would insist on preparing it. She put about a pound of tea into a tolerably large-sized pot, with nearly a gallon of "burn" water, and seasoned the whole as she would any other stew, with a reasonable proportion of butter, pepper, and salt! When served up at the breakfast table, however, the sauce only was administered, the leaves being reserved for future decoctions. The old man had an unceasing cough, very sharp and loud, which was not a little helped by his incessant use of snuff. His wife was a lineal descendant of the Strath Uilligh Sutherlands. She had a brother, a kind, hospitable man, usually called Rob Muiller, with whom we often lunched on our way down the Strath. Alastair Gordon himself was a cadet of the Gordons of Embo. They had a numerous family. Gilbert, their second son, was a non-commissioned officer in the 93rd regiment, but afterwards went to Berbice, where he realised a few thousand pounds as a planter, came home, married a daughter of Captain John Sutherland of Brora, lost all his money by mismanagement, and ultimately emigrated to America. John, the eldest son, went to America about thirty years ago. He died leaving his family in easy circumstances. Robert also followed him three or four years after. William got a commission in the army, went to Jamaica, returned on half-pay, and lived in poverty at Rosemarkie. He was always a strange mixture of the shrewd wordling and the born fool. Another of Dalchairn's sons went to Jamaica, and died soon after his arrival. Their daughter Anne married one John Gordon of Solus-chraiggie; she lived with her husband at Dalchairn after her father's death, and afterwards took a lot of land in the village of Helmisdale, and a sheep farm in Caithness. Her husband died a few years ago, in consequence of cold caught in his winter journeys from his house at Helmisdale to his Caithness sheep-farm.* When they lived at Dalchairn, both before and after the old man's death, I was frequently their guest during my incumbency at Achness. Alastair Gordon's eldest daughter married John Macdonald, tacksman of Ach-Scarclet in Strathmore, Caithness, a noted Highland drover. After his death his widow and family emigrated to America.

George Mackay of Araidh-Chlinni, in the heights of the parish, was another of my acquaintances, and a frequent visitor at the manse. He was chieftain of a sept of the Clan Mackay which was coëval with, if not prior to, that of the chiefs themselves. George was a man of piety, wit, and natural shrewdness. For piety he had universal credit in the parish. On sacramental occasions he was one of the most pointed and lucid speakers to the question at the Friday fellowship meetings. His

---

* His widow died at Helmisdale in 1849.—ED.

wit was almost overflowing, and his sayings and doings are still remembered by his surviving friends. "A dry, ripe potato, well-boiled," he would remark, "was the only friend whom he would wish to see in a ragged coat." His Highland farm he rented from the family of Sutherland. He made an annual pilgrimage to Golspie to pay his rent to the factor, who resided at Rhives, a place in the immediate vicinity. On one occasion, going thither in company of a more than usual number of tacksmen on the same errand as himself, they were at night-fall rather hardup for want of lodgings. George, who was himself a man of unbounded and unceasing hospitality, applied to the keeper of a small inn, at the village of Golspie, for a bed and supper. His request was refused; he could neither get the one nor the other for love or money. Reduced to this extremity, Araidh-chlinni asked the innkeeper to allow him to sit by his kitchen fire during the night. This also was refused, so that he was under the necessity of mounting his nag and riding home on a cold frosty night. At parting he told his surly host that it was not altogether improbable that they two might meet again, and that the rude and inhospitable innkeeper might very possibly beg a night's lodgings from the man he had used so harshly. The landlord told him in reply that, if ever such a thing happened, he would give him full liberty to hang him up at his door. But, in thoughtlessly reckoning for the future, men not unfrequently become their own judges, and pronounce their own doom; so at least it happened with the Golspie innkeeper. He had a few stots grazing on the heights of Kildonan, and going about a year thereafter in quest of them, he was benighted at the foot of Beinu 'Ghriam-mhôr. Struggling hard for life through a swamp, long and large and deep enough to have summarily disposed of all the "men in the Mearns," he perceived a light glimmering through the gloom, for which he made straightway. On his arrival at the spot he found it proceeded from the window of a long straggling cottage, and, tremblingly alive to the value of food and shelter, he knocked at the door. His summons was instantly responded to; the door opened, and in a few minutes he found himself seated beside a huge peat fire, and a table in readiness for the evening meal. The landlord eyed his shivering guest with a smile of recognition, but the Golspie man did not recognise him in return. A blessing was asked on the bountiful meal, and the guest was cheerily invited to partake, which he proceeded to do. But, just as he was making himself comfortable, and vastly agreeable with his jokes and news and small chat, he was suddenly interrupted by his landlord calling out in a stentorian voice, "Get the halters; get the halters; this is my very civil Golspie landlord who wouldn't allow me even sit supperless by his fireside, but thrust me out at his door; and who told me that, when he ever came to ask such a favour of me, he would give me full liberty to hang him up." Completely prostrated, the innkeeper had not a word to say in arrest of judgment. After enjoying his triumph, however, and his guest's confusion, for a short time, during which some of the domestics became clamorous that the fellow should be hanged forthwith, Araidh-chlinni told him to make himself quite easy; that the rights of hospitality ought to be exercised, not on the selfish principles of corrupt nature, but according to the law of Christ—to do to others as we would that others should do to us. Araidh-chlinni had a family of sons and daughters; I remember three of them. Robert, his eldest son, was when a young man on marriage terms with one Chirsty Gunn, our dry-nurse during my mother's life-time, and a woman of eminent piety. She died, however, just when they were to be proclaimed in church. He afterwards got a commission in the army, and rose to the rank of captain. He married a Miss Medley Clunes, niece of Col. Clunes of Cracaig, parish of Loth, by whom he had one daughter. He retired on half-pay, and established his residence in the neighbourhood of Inverness. His daughter married Col. Mackay. She is a woman of piety and talent. Araidh-chlinni's second son George emigrated to America. His eldest daughter Catherine, well known to us when children as "Katie na h'àridh," married a George Mackay, or MacHastain, a native of Strath Halladale, and a wrathful man who, when he came to reside at his father-in-law's house during his declining years, quarrelled with all his neighbours, and then with his own wife, who endured his rough treatment with much forbearance. He had four sons. The eldest, George, was a grocer in Inverness, and very much like his father in character. He succeeded well in his trade, and dabbled not a little in politics and religion; in the former being a rabid Whig and making a great show of the latter. The second brother, John, was also a grocer at Inverness, and married a daughter of Mackay of Carnachadh, Strathnaver. The other two brothers went abroad and died, while their only sister married an Andrew Mackay, a grocer at Helmisdale.

Robert Gunn of Achaneccan was another of the old men of my youthful remembrance. He was the acknowledged lineal descendant and representative of the chiefs of Clan Gunn in the parish; although that landless and fallen honour was some years afterwards claimed by Hector Gunn of Thurso, whose only son became factor to the Duke of Sutherland. Robert of Achaneccan was, however, unquestionably nearer of kin. His farm, on which he had a number of sub-tenants, was scarcely two miles distant from Kinbrace, the seat of his renowned ancestor. He was a gentleman-like old man, who had been much in good society, and had received a somewhat liberal education. His descendants are still to be found here and there in the county of Caithness.

John Grant of Dioball, to whom I have already referred in connection with my father's settlement at Kildonan, was a truly pious man. No two things in one soul, however, could be placed in more direct, or even outrageous contrast with each other than all that there was of grace and all that remained of corrupt nature, in the soul of John Grant. As a vital Christian he was, for the depth and the extent of his knowledge of the truth, quite remarkable. His views were vivid, original, solid, and scriptural, and the language in which he expressed them was calculated, by its terseness, accuracy, and point, to do all justice in conveying them to the mind and comprehension of his fellow-Christians. He was also, although an illiterate man, yet unquestionably one of very considerable native talent. His life corresponded with his views and profession as a Christian in one respect, namely, in abstractedness from the every-day business and bustle of the world. But it was more the abstractedness of a hermit or ascetic, or of a naturally eccentric character, than that of a plain and practical Christian. His natural disposition, too, was not only hot and impetuous, but often ferocious. To indulge it he did not care whom he assailed, whether friend or foe. The one went down just as surely as the other before the explosions of his temper, and the merciless sarcasms which he launched forth against all, be they whom they might, who ventured to set themselves in opposition to his views or prejudices. I knew John Grant from my very earliest years. My brother and I, on our way down the Strath to meet our father on his way home, were very kindly entertained by him in his house at Dioball. Although he never attended church, he was a frequent visitor at the manse. He had a wide circle of admirers in Sutherlandshire and elsewhere, who liberally supplied him with everything that he needed. He left Kildonan, and lived afterwards at Strathy, then at Thurso, and lastly at Reay, where he died in 1828.

The other respectable tenantry in the parish I shall have an opportunity of describing when I come to record the particulars of my ministry at Achness.

It was intended that I should go to college, but as my father's stipend was small, and his circumstances consequently limited, all was to depend on my obtaining a bursary at either King's or Marischal College, Aberdeen. Mr. Ross of Clyne had gone to Aberdeen with his son, to attend the Greek class at Marischal College; and, as he was a warm friend of my father, he sought to be serviceable to me. No sooner, therefore, did he arrive in Aberdeen than he set himself to procure a presentation bursary for me at Marischal College. Through his address he got himself introduced to the Town Council, who had in their gift a presentation bursary (for one year) of £9 stg. His introduction to the Council was through the Lord Provost, Mr. Leys, a wealthy wine-merchant. With the Provost Mr. Ross had been acquainted many years before, and his acquaintanceship with him he renewed so much to my advantage, that the bursary was, by a majority of the Council, carried over the heads of twenty candidates, natives of the city, and granted to myself. This intelligence Mr. Ross immediately communicated to my father. The letter was received on a Friday; and, on Monday morning early, my father, Muckle Donald, and I set out for Aberdeen. My father accompanied me as far as Tain, where we arrived on Tuesday morning. The night previous we spent at Dornoch. At Tain we breakfasted at Turnbull's Inn, where we received great kindness and good cheer from Mrs Turnbull, a stout, jolly old lady, who, having buried her husband, an Englishman of the name of Combe, had solaced herself for her loss by taking his ostler of the name of Turnbull, in his place. After breakfast she stuffed my pockets with fine large apples; and my father parted with me to return home. Muckle Donald and I then tramped it on foot, from thence all the way to Aberdeen. The day we left Tain, crossing the Ivergordon ferry, we slept and supped at the Inn of Balblair in this parish, of which now I am minister. I was just fifteen, and the length of the journey proved too much for me. Within two miles of Inverury, I fairly broke down, and fell prostrate upon the roadside. There was a small farm-house, with a steading, hard by. By Muckle Donald I was borne into the house. The family received us with hearty and unsophisticated kindness. My whole story was soon told, and it was not told in vain. Some milk warmed and mixed with pepper was given me to drink, which at once revived me; and a fellow-traveller who had come in along with us partook of the same wholesome beverage, deriving from it also the same benefit. I was after all, however, too weak to walk; and this being understood, the good man of the house, with all the warm-heartedness of a Scotch peasant, went to his stable, saddled his horse, mounted me upon him, and brought me most safely and comfortably to the "Head Inn" at Inverury. My heart overflowed with gratitude to him. On our arrival I offered him a dram and he took it; I offered him money and a feed for his horse, but he refused it. He bade me adieu, mounted his horse, disappeared in the dark, and I never again met him.

I arrived in Aberdeen next day, and went at once to the house of my friend Mrs. Gordon, who received me with all the affection of a mother. Since her husband's death she had chiefly resided here, on her limited income. Her house was at the head of the Upper Kirkgate. I remained there until I got lodgings in Blackfriars Street Green, in the house of a man named Fleming. I met with Mr. Ross of Clyne, his son William, and William Houston, son of Major Hugh Houston of Clynleish. Both young men came to college under the care of Mr Ross, and they were all three lodged at the house of a Mr. Cantley, one of the town's officers, also in the Upper Kirkgate. I called upon Mr. Ross immediately after my arrival to thank him for his active friendship, and was received by him and by the two young men with much kindness. I also called upon and drank tea with Mrs. Sutherland, my stepmother's sister, who then lived in Aberdeen. Miss Jane Baigrie, eldest daughter and only child of Captain Baigrie of Midgarty by his first marriage, lived as a boarder with Mrs. Sutherland. I was much struck with her appearance. She was rather a pretty girl; but some years before, and just on the eve of her marriage, she, in running across a street in London, unfortunately came in contact with a window-shutter, and the violence of the blow broke the bridge of her nose. The consequence was that her betrothed ran off and left her. I shall mention her afterwards,

In the house in the Green I found before me a fellow-lodger and class-fellow named Gourlay. His father, an old man, was assistant minister of Arbuthnot, in the Presbytery of Fordoun, with a large family and an allowance of £50 per annum. Fleming, my landlord, let an upper storey to lodgers in order to better his condition. He was an industrious creature, and did all he could to procure a livelihood. His wife was the very model of an Aberdeenshire woman in three particulars—she spoke to perfection the vile lingo of her county, she was an inveterate smoker, and her loquacity was interminable. Their only son William, who was clerk in one of the banking offices of the

city, was a warm-hearted, generous fellow. Our landlady boarded us
for the very reasonable sum of eight shillings each per week, but our
fare corresponded with the rate. We were often dined upon what our
hostess called "milk-pothage." She was a shrewd, sensible woman,
and having a high sense of decorum, she made it a point to read every
night a chapter in the Bible. To this devotional act she attributed her
success in life. She would often take up the old quarto Bible from
which she read, and, wiping the dust from it with great reverence,
would say—"It's guid my part to tak' care o' that buik, for it has aye
keeppit me richt in the warld until noo."

Of my amiable friend Mrs. Gordon my recollections are vivid and
interesting. My personal attachment to her, and, I must add, my
short commons at Fleming's, made me a frequent visitor at her house.
After dining at my lodgings at 2 o'clock, I was often privileged to
partake with her at 4.30 P.M. Her servant-maid was a Christy Grant,
a native of Loth. Mrs. Gordon attended the West Church, but Christy
went regularly to the Gaelic Chapel, then under the pastoral care of
Mr. Neil Kennedy, of whom I was a frequent hearer. To accustom me
to the manners of good society, Mrs. Gordon introduced me to many of
her acquaintances, particularly to Dr. MacPherson of King's College.

I remember my first session at Marischal College more distinctly
than the succeeding ones. The college buildings which then existed
were in a state of rapid decay. They had been erected by George,
fifth Earl Marischal, in 1593; and the lapse of two centuries had
reduced them to what was little better than a habitable ruin. The
fabric consisted of a long, lofty, central building of four storeys, with a
wing of the same height at one end, and a huge, clumsy tower, intended for an observatory, at the other. In the front of the central
building, at the spring of the roof, was a clock; the windows were
small, and the mason-work was of the coarsest kind. On the wing
were two inscriptions, the one in Greek, namely: "*Areté aut' arkés,*"
or "virtue is its own reward;" the other was in broad Scotch: "They'll
say; quilk will they say, let them say." I have been told that the
latter inscription had a pointed allusion to the plainness of the
structure, and to the religion of its founder. King's College in Old
Aberdeen far excelled it in antiquity and splendour, and in the extent
of its revenue. Besides all this, King's College, which was founded by
Bishop Elphinston, was dignified on its first establishment, in 1494, by
a papal bull. Marischal College was built during the progress of the
Reformation, and was set up as a Protestant institution. The internal
accommodation consisted of a large hall on the ground floor of the
central building, called "the public school," where all the students, at
8 A.M., met for prayer. Nothing could be more mean or wretched than
this hall. It was a long, wide place, perhaps 100 feet by 20; the
windows, which were three in number, were short and narrow, and
were fitted with glass in the upper sash, and boards in the lower. The
floor was paved with stone, and along the walls ran a wooden bench on
which the students sat while the roll was called, and during prayers.
There were two raised desks in the centre of the hall, the one for the
principal and professors on Fridays, the other, right opposite, for any

student who had a Latin oration to deliver. In short, the whole gave one an idea of a hastily-built granary. Above the public school was the college hall; it was handsome, and worthy of a literary institution. The walls were hung with fine old prints, as well as full-length and three-quarter-length portraits of eminent men, more particularly of benefactors to the College. Among others was that of Field-Marshal Keith. In this hall the students met for the annual public examination. Above the hall, and in the upper flat, were the library, containing a very mediocre collection of books, and the museum, not remarkable either. The north wing, constituting the observatory tower, contained on the ground floor the Greek class-room, and above it was the divinity hall. In the third flat were apartments for one of the professors. On top of all was the observatory, or astronomical-room, reached by a winding stair. On the roof of the tower were placed philosophical instruments, rain-gauges, etc., and over this department presided the professor of Natural Philosophy, whose family lived in the apartments below. The south wing contained the Natural History, Natural Philosophy, and Mathematical class-rooms, and the apartments of the professor of Mathematics and Greek. Behind the college, to the east, was a garden, rendered interesting in connection with the early youth of James Hay Beattie, son of the eminent Dr. Beattie of Marischal College. It was here that young Beattie, then almost in infancy, feeling his ardent and precocious powers of observation directed to the sudden growth of some cresses which he had seen sown there a few days previously, asked his father what made them grow so soon, or grow at all. In reply to this simple question the moralist took that early opportunity of initiating in his son's mind the notion and belief in a God supreme and omnipotent.* The College Close, as it was called, was an open space, about an acre and a-half in extent, in front of the buildings and surrounded with houses. In the south-west corner of it stood Greyfriars Church, usually styled the College Church, not only from its immediate vicinity to that building, but because a gallery in the eastern wing was appropriated for the accommodation of the professors and students. Greyfriars Church was then only on the footing of a Chapel of Ease, its minister not having a seat in the Presbytery. Close by stood a low, mean-looking building, with a tiled roof, intended for the chemical class then taught by Dr. French.

The course pursued at Marischal College consisted in giving regular attendance at the University for four years, the first year at Greek; the second, at the Humanity, General and Natural History, and first Mathematical classes; the third, at the Natural Philosophy and second

* Dr. James Beattie was born at Laurencekirk, in 1735, and graduated at Marischal College in 1753. In 1760 he issued a volume of " Original Poems and Translations." He was shortly afterwards appointed Professor of Moral Philosophy in Marischal College. He published in 1770 his celebrated " Essay on Truth," in 1774 " The Minstrel," and in 1793 the second volume of " Moral Science." The University of Oxford conferred upon him the degree of LL.D. On his retirement from the professorial chair he was succeeded by his son James Hay, who died in 1790. Dr. Beattie died in 1803. He had sown some cresses in the garden to form the initials of his son's name. From this he taught him the argument for the existence of God, drawn from the evidences of design in nature.—ED.

Mathematical classes; and, in the fourth year, at the Moral Philosophy and Logic classes. Graduation for the degree of Master of Arts, at the close of the fourth session, was a mere matter of ordinary routine—a sort of literary masquerade for the pecuniary benefit of the College officials.

The Professor of Greek at Marischal College, in 1804, was John Stewart of Inchbreck, in the county of Kincardine. He was a frank and friendly man, and of his friendship I had a large experience during my attendance at College. Recommended to him as I was by Mr. Ross of Clyne, he took charge of my pecuniary affairs, and so managed them that I actually had more money on returning than I had on coming to College. It was chiefly by his means and influence that I enjoyed a bursary every year of my philosophical course. He married Miss Mowat of Ardo, in Kincardine, the last of an ancient line, which, by her death in 1823, became extinct. Her sister was the wife of Rev. Dr. Peters of Dundee. Prof. Stewart had five of a family, three sons, Andrew, Alexander, and Charles; also two daughters. Andrew studied medicine and went abroad. Alexander studied law in Edinburgh, where I met him during my attendance at the Divinity Hall. Of Charles and of the elder daughter I know nothing; but the second, some years after her parents' death, became the second wife of Mr. Glennie of Maybank, near Aberdeen.

To the method of teaching adopted by Prof. Stewart I may now refer. The books were Dunlop's Greek Grammar, written in Latin, also a small selection from the Greek writers, entitled a "Delectus." This compilation was edited by Prof. Stewart, and contained excerpts from Æsop's Fables, Lucian's Dialogues, Ælian, Isocrates, Demosthenes, with Libanius' argument; also from Anacreon, Sappho, Aristotle, Theocritus, and Bion, the whole comprehended in a small, thin volume of about 108 pages. He also used the Greek Testament and Homer's Iliad. His method of instruction was rather stiff and superficial. After mastering the Grammar, we proceeded to read, translate, and analyse the Greek Testament; then we got the Delectus to read, and, lastly, towards the close of the session, we studied a part of Homer's Iliad, Book xxiv. I may here observe that the particular book of the Iliad which we read marked the number of the years of our Professor's incumbency. He made it a part of his system to read with his class, every year, a book of the Iliad, commencing with the first, and going on to the next in order next session; so that the first session of my attendance at College was the twenty-fourth of Mr. Stewart's professorship.

Of my fellow-students, Peter Blackie attained some distinction. He was one of the many sons of a plumber, in Little John Street, His disposition was close, dogged, and sullen, and his countenance was a true expression of it. He studied medicine, went abroad as surgeon of a man-of-war, came into converse with Bonaparte, and, on his return, set up as a surgeon and lecturer in Aberdeen. He married a Miss Levingston, the daughter of a Col. Levingston, and one of the handsomest woman in Aberdeen. He died a few years ago. His brother, an Aberdeen advocate, was Provost of Aberdeen, and a man of weight and influence. His sister, a very beautiful girl, married Dr. Keith, of St. Cyrus, who has attained to such eminence as a writer on prophecy. Another of my fellow-students, Robert J. Brown, was third son of the Principal of the College, the Very Rev. William Laurence Brown, D.D., one of the most accomplished classical scholars in Europe. Robert made a respectable appearance in the classes. Soon after being licensed to preach, he was presented to the parish of Clatt, in the Presbytery of Alford, and on the demise of Prof. Stewart was appointed his successor in the Greek Class, in which he and I had been class-fellows. Another fellow-student, Thomas Fordyce, was the youngest son of Arthur Dingwall Fordyce of Culsh, Commissary of Aberdeen. His eldest sister was married to Professor Bentley of the Hebrew Class, in King's College, by whom she had two daughters, with whom I was well acquainted when residing there during my incumbency as minister of the Gaelic Chapel.

I returned home, at the close of the session, by sea. I took my passage for Helmisdale, on a salmon-fishing smack, which was in the service of Forbes and Hogarth, who then held the Sutherland rivers in lease from the Marchioness of Stafford. My friend Capt. Baigrie had given me a letter of introduction to Mr. William Forbes of Echt, who was so friendly to Eneas; and during my first session at college, I frequently called upon him at the quay-side. He was a kind, fatherly man, and received me with much urbanity. Mr. Forbes' eldest son James, the present proprietor, was in partnership with his father. Mr. James Forbes was then married, and had several children. His wife was a Miss Niven of Thornton, the sister of Sir Harry Niven Lumsden of Achindoir. I frequently met Mr. James Forbes in his father's office, and afterwards saw him at Midgarty.

The smack which bore me homewards was the identical one by which my brother sailed to London, but had a different master; Coy had been replaced by a rough fellow of the name of Colstone. I went on board about 2 o'clock in the afternoon, and dined before we set sail. Feeling hungry I partook largely of a coarse, greasy dinner at the skipper's table. It consisted of very fat broth and still fatter meat. Colstone, not content with swallowing the most enormous quantities of clear fat I had ever seen attempted even by a famished mastiff, after all was over greased his face with it, to keep out the cold as I supposed. This sappy dinner, as well as the remembrance of the skipper's face, served me for a strong emetic during the voyage homewards, which was both tedious and tempestuous. On going out at the pier-head the billows rose "mountains high," and as they rose, both my spirits and my stomach fell. The dinner with its associations presented themselves before me every half-hour, until I became grievously sick, and my very ribs ached again with the pressure of vomiting. The wind blew a hurricane from the west, and in the course of twelve hours we were close on the Sutherland coast, opposite Helmisdale, the place of our destination. But here again the wind chopped round in our very teeth, and we were for three days tossed back and fore on the Moray Firth in view of the harbour, without being able to enter it. The storm was so violent that even the skipper himself became sick. I was a Sabbath at sea; and although the wind blew contrary, the day was fine. The sailors observed the day with great decorum. There was nothing like social or public worship, but when any one of them got a spare hour, he laid himself face downwards on the floor of the cabin and conned over the New Testament. We left Aberdeen on a Friday, and landed at the mouth of the Helmisdale River on the Tuesday morning thereafter. I shall never forget the strong and penetrating feeling of joyous safety with which I leaped out of the ship's boat on the pebbly shore of the river near the Corf-house. Mr. Thomas Houston, now of Kintradwell, met me on the beach, and with him I went to the house of Mrs. Houston, his mother. After a cordial welcome and a hasty breakfast I walked up the Strath to Kildonan, where I found my worthy father engaged in the annual examination of the Parish School. He received me with a father's kindness, took me into his large embrace, and kissed me before the whole assemblage.

But it is high time to hasten to the close of this chapter. At the very time I am recording these reminiscences of early youth (January, 1843), the sky of Providence is darkening down with more than ordinary gloom on the Church of my Fathers. I do think that it has pleased God, in His inscrutable wisdom, to appoint my lot in life at the beginning of "troublous times," and times such as neither I hitherto, nor my fathers before me, have experienced. I shall, therefore, endeavour to hurry over the various incidents of my life till the period when these troubles began, so that while they are in progress I may, whether as a spectator or a sufferer, in any case as an eye-witness, record them.

CHAPTER XI.

ABERDEEN PROFESSORS. NORTHERN NOTABILITIES.

1805–1809.

*D*URING the summer of 1805 Capt. Baigrie's third son John became my pupil. He lived with us first at Kildonan; but latterly I resided with him at Midgarty, and our school hours were passed in Capt .Baigrie's bedroom, where we also slept in a small bed beside him.

My second session at college was in 1805-6. I again travelled to Aberdeen on foot with my father's man, Muckle Donald. I went this time by Inverness. We crossed the ferry of Invergordon, and then pursued our route through Resolis and Ferintosh to Kirkhill in Inverness-shire, crossing the Beauly at the ferry immediately below the village of that name. On our way to the manse of Kirkhill we were preceded by a funeral. That was the only time on which I saw or heard a bagpipe playing the Highland coronach on such an occasion— answering as it did the purposes both of the hand-bell at the interment of the lower classes, and of the "Dead March in Saul" at that of the upper classes of society. When we arrived at the manse our reception was what may be called very far north of kindness. Mr. Donald Fraser, my late cousin, was then a young man, his father's successor as minister of Kirkhill, and newly married. He had guests residing with him— a Mr. and Mrs. Munro from Inverness—who, like himself, were also newly married, and were there to spend their honeymoon. Mr. Fraser himself was scarcely twenty-one years of age, and exceedingly handsome both in face and figure. His wife looked ten years older than her elegant husband. Her brother, Mr. Gordon, had been in the West Indies, and making a fortune, came home and purchased the property of Drakies, near Inverness, but resided with his sister somewhere in the parish of Kirkhill. There Mr. Fraser got first acquainted with her. Succeeding his eminent father, he lived with his widowed mother and his sisters at the manse; and when he finished his theological course he paid his addresses to Miss Gordon, and their union took place when he was but nineteen. Under these circumstances the marriage much displeased his mother and the rest of his relations; but Miss Gordon proved an excellent wife. His brother-in-law, Mr. Gordon, died insolvent many years thereafter, and Drakies had to be sold. Unfortunately, owing to the legal peculiarities of the case, Mr. Fraser got somewhat involved with the creditors—a circumstance which much encumbered him during his whole life.

My man and I left Kirkhill early on Monday for Inverness, where we both breakfasted in the same room, after a weary tramp under a

K

heavy downpour of rain. At Fochabers we fell in with a returning hired horse, belonging to a man of the name of Campbell, an innkeeper and horse-hirer in Aberdeen. This lucky cast made our journey comparatively easy. Muckle Donald and I rode alternately, the horse carrying our baggage also.

On arriving at Aberdeen, rather late in the evening, I went to Mrs. Gordon's, Upper Kirkgate, where I was received with unabated kindness. Next day I took lodgings in the house of one Alexander Brown, a wheelwright in North Street, where I had as my fellow-lodger my friend James Campbell. He and the landlord's son George were again my class-fellows.

During this session I attended the classes of Civil and Natural History, as well as the Humanity Class, all taught by Prof. James Beattie, nephew of the well-known Dr. Beattie; and the first Mathematical class, taught by the eminent but eccentric Dr. Robert Hamilton. "Humanity" was usually taught at eight in the morning. Professor Beattie was one of the first classical scholars of his day. Latin he both understood and spoke, and when the disorderly conduct of the students called it forth, *scolded* in it with fluency and force. He was of keen passions and a hasty temper. As a disciplinarian, he carried matters as far as they could go, seeing that his reproofs, pointed enough in themselves, were sometimes rendered terrible by the external accompaniments of his warmth of temper and extraordinary bodily strength. To such of the students, however, as were naturally slow and dull, but at the same time diligent and anxious to learn, he curbed his temper, and showed the noblest forbearance. His plan of teaching was as follows:—In the morning hour we read the classics, both Greek and Latin. In the forenoon the professor carried on his course of civil history. He commenced by a few preliminary lectures on chronology and geography, on oral tradition, historical poems, and other methods employed before the use of letters for preserving the memory of past events on the stages of civil society and the principal forms of government. In entering more immediately on his subject, he treated of the first four monarchies, viz., the Assyrian, the Babylonian, the Persian, and the Egyptian. He then gave a course of lectures on what he called "the two leading objects" of ancient history—the Revolutions of Greece and of Rome—pursuing first the history of Greece till its subjection to Rome, 164 B.C., and concluding it with a view of the state of literature, philosophy, and of the fine arts among the Greeks. He then took up the subject of Roman history, which he pursued till the accession of Augustus, when he lectured on the Roman constitution, manners, military discipline, and on the progress of Roman literature. He then resumed the history of Rome, and carried it on to the final settlement of the northern nations in Italy towards the close of the 6th century, concluding the whole with a few lectures on the manners of the northern nations, and on the history of the Christian Church down to that period.

The course of Natural History next followed. That science the professor divided into six great branches. These were—Mineralogy, Geology, Hydrology, Meteorology, Botany, and Zoology. He also dictated to the class, at occasional meetings, the outlines of his course of lectures, which each engrossed in a MS. book. It gave him peculiar pleasure to see these outlines neatly written out. A copy of the MS., which I wrote to his dictation, of the outlines of his lectures both on civil and natural history, I have still in my possession. His lectures on mineralogy contained a short system of chemistry; and when on the subject of acids, most of us had our fingers soiled and considerably burnt by trying experiments on the various properties and effects of sulphuric and sulphurous acid, nitric and nitrous acid, muriatic acid, and so forth. When he entered upon mineralogy itself, he divided all the subjects of the mineral kingdom into six classes, viz., Earths, Inflammables, Saline bodies, Metals, Petrefactions, and the Impregnations of water. He adopted, in botany and zoology, the systematic arrangement of Linnæus—the more modern and improved systems being then unknown.

Dr. Hamilton's first Mathematical Class we attended daily. He began the course by putting us through the cardinal rules of arithmetic, and explaining to us, in his own summary way, the abstract principles of arithmetic as a science. Then we went on to the Elements of Euclid, or what may be considered the first principles of mathematical science, such as Algebra, mensuration, etc. The mathematical course, however, taught by Dr. Hamilton during that and the ensuing session I may here dismiss at once, by mentioning that he published, for the use of his class, a mathematical treatise, entitled, "Heads of part of a course of mathematics, as taught at the Marischal College," comprehending the following subjects, viz., use of scales and sliding rules, plane trigonometry, practical geometry, doctrine of the globes; perspectives, navigation, projection of the sphere, and spherical trigonometry. These, to the best of my recollection, were the subjects taught by Dr. Hamilton during the two sessions I attended. But I must here frankly confess that, under the tuition of this learned and excellent, but most eccentric man, I never could understand anything of the subjects he taught. This might, no doubt, arise from a natural deficiency to comprehend mathematical science. But if my natural capacity had been more extensive than it really was, it would have but little availed me under the worthy doctor's method of teaching. For, first of all, he made himself both the master and the scholar, both the teacher and the taught. If the points of instruction were arithmetical questions, he chalked them out and worked them all himself; if the propositions of Euclid, he drew the figures, marked the letters, took up the demonstrating-rod, and, after, uttering or rather muttering, with great rapidity a few hasty explanations, went on to demonstrate the proposition or problem, step by step, with all the hurry and assiduity of a tyro, while the class had only to listen. His personal appearance, the odd intonations of his voice, the quizzical contortions of his countenance, the motions of his hands, his fidgety impatience, and the palpable absurdity of the whole man, with his little scratch wig awry on his head, and his gown flapping around him, and ever and anon in the way of his feet, or his hands, or his eyes—all taken together really held out a premium to every student, from the lightest to the gravest, to look on and laugh. When he entered the class, it was with the bustle of one who felt that he was too late, and had kept people waiting for him. With this impression, he would walk up to his desk with his hat on; after jumping about here and there, and handling this thing and the other, it would at last occur to him that his hat should be taken off; but, in the hurry of the removal, both hat and wig would come off at once, exposing his bald pate and setting the class in a roar. Stunned by the noise, he would clap his wig on the nail and his hat on his head; and then, on discovering his mistake, would make the hat and wig immediately exchange places. When he noticed any of the students trifling, he rose from his desk, ran up to the offender with neck out-stretched, and, clapping his hand upon his chin, first preluding his reproof with two or three short coughs, he mentioned the offender by his name in Latin, in the vocative case, and exclaimed, "Take your hat and go away," or, "Take your hat and leave the skule" —looking at him the meanwhile like an ape who had ensconced himself aloft out of the way of a parcel of curs baying at him. The insubordination of his class came to such a height that he felt himself compelled at last to summon the aid of the Senatus Academicus, or the "Faculty," as he called them, with which he had often threatened the more disorderly. Responding to his complaint, the Senatus deputed Prof. Beattie, the most thorough disciplinarian at college, to pay us a visit. Prof. Beattie did so accordingly, and, entering the class-room one day with the port of Ajax—"earth trembling as he trode"—he made us tremble too by the wrath of his countenance, the stern severity of his reproofs, and by the movements of his herculean person with which every threat was enforced. The effect of all this, however, was not permanent. The *origo mali* was to be found, not so much in any peculiar propensity in the students to turbulence as in the total incapacity of the teacher to maintain his authority.[*]

Brown, my landlord during this session, was something of a religious character. He could not be curbed within the limits of any particular sect, but, on the contrary, was continually wandering from chapel to chapel, and from one sect to another. He was first an Antiburgher, and decently went with his wife and daughters to be edified under the plain and pithy, but rather homely, ministrations of Mr. James Templeton, the Seceder minister of Belmont Street. But he soon tired of this, and walked off alone to wait upon the ministry of Mr. Lawrence Glass, a burgher minister of the Old Light. He did not remain long under the ministry of Mr. Glass, who was both a profound divine and a preacher of great unction and power, but he finally joined the Independents, and became the regular hearer of Dr. Philip of the Laigh Kirk, one of their ablest and most talented preachers, who afterwards went as a missionary to Cape Town.

[*] Robert Hamilton, LL.D., was born in Edinburgh in 1743. After having been ten years Rector of the Perth Academy, he was, in 1779, appointed to the Chair of Natural Philosophy, in Marischal College, which he afterwards exchanged for that of Mathematics. He is the author of a book of reputed merit on the "National Debt of Great Britain," and also of a posthumous work, entitled, "The Progress of Society." He died in 1829.

During this session, too, some of my fellow-students and I made an expedition to a manganese mine, near Grandholm, when we were interested to note, close by, the site of the great battle of Harlaw.

The only public event during this session was the death of William Pitt, on the 23rd of January, 1806. The recent defeat at Austerlitz, with its disastrous consequences on the health, and finally the life, of this illustrious man, was the conversational topic with every one, and, among others, with the students of the colleges. I recollect talking of it with a simple Sutherlandshire student from Invershin, who, not knowing exactly the difference between a minister of State and a minister of the Gospel, gravely asked me what parish in England had become vacant by the Prime Minister's death.

On the closing day Professor Beattie, in giving his last lecture, was so deeply affected, that he could scarcely articulate his parting word, "valette." Next day a number of the students from the north began their journey homewards, starting about six o'clock in the morning. James Campbell, John Anderson from Elgin, and a fellow-townsman of his, one James MacAndrew, a very young man little more than twelve years of age, but who, notwithstanding, had that year finished his college course, and James Bayne, eldest son of the late Dr. Ronald Bayne of Kiltarlity, and myself, all set out together. Our first stretch was from Aberdeen to Keith, a most overwhelming journey for one day, being little less than 50 miles. I was most grievously tired before I reached my resting-place for the night, and, when, I did, could neither eat nor sleep. The present turnpike road from Aberdeen to Thurso, the Ultima Thule of the five northern counties, did not then exist, and no part of the old road could be more rugged than that from Huntly to Keith. After leaving the little dram-house of Benshole in the glen of Foudland, the wretched, floundering track crossed a bleak hill, and then came stumbling down a steep, miry slope immediately to the east of the straggling village of Keith. On this road, in the olden times, horses have sunk to the very girths in mud.

During the summer I was · appointed parochial schoolmaster of Loth. I resided with Mr. Gordon the minister, whose wife was my second cousin, and the daughter of the venerable Thomas Mackay of Lairg. I remember yet my scholars, my difficulties, my weariness, and longings for home, to which I made many Saturday journeys across the Crask, and where I often remained too long into the ensuing week. It was in this year that the great county roads were begun, and I had great interest in tracing their progress through Sutherlandshire. Instead of straggling along the sea-shore, the new line swept along the base of the hills in an almost straight course.

My attendance at college during the third session I shall dismiss in a few sentences. Patrick Copland, the professor of natural philosophy, under whom I chiefly studied this year, was the most efficient of the public teachers of Marischal College. He was a very handsome man both as to face and figure; his wife was a neat, demure, pretty little woman. They had three sons and one daughter. His knowledge of the beautiful and extensive science which he taught was rather superficial. He was, however, both an elegant lecturer and an expert mechanic, and thus made the study most interesting to us. The science he divided into four great branches, viz., the mechanical philosophy, chemistry, the animal economy, and the vegetable economy. The first of these constituted the substance of his lectures; this subject he subdivided into six subordinate branches, mechanics strictly so called, hydrostatics or the doctrine of fluids, comprehending hydraulics and pneumatics, electricity, magnetism, optics, or the doctrine of light and astronomy. He did not dictate a syllabus of his lectures as the other professors did; but I took very full notes whilst he spoke on each of these branches, as well as copies of his drawings, diagrams, mathematical figures, machine models, etc., all which I digested, when at leisure, into a very full manuscript of three large 8vo volumes, with plates of my own drawing.

After my third session at college I resumed my labours at the school of Loth, but I did not long continue there. I must confess that I had not been very assiduous in the discharge of the duties devolving upon me, having ever had a natural repugnance to the drudgery of teaching and being neither attracted nor reconciled to it by the circumstances in which I found myself placed. The accommodations provided, the small amount of salary, and the irregularity with which the fees were paid, and above all, the character of my patron, the parish minister, combined to increase my dislike to my calling. Mr. Gordon was, as a preacher, sound and scriptural, and a lively and animated speaker, but his mind and spirit were thoroughly secularised, and this great moral defect palpably exhibited itself in his week-day conduct. My remembrance of him is both painful and bitter. He was even then indulging in habits which brought him to the grave about the close of the year 1822. The only one of his family who survives is his eldest son Charles, at present minister of Assynt.* Among my acquaintances at Loth were Colonel Cluness of Cracaig, Mrs. Gray of Kilgour, and George Munro of Whitehill.

Colonel Cluness was the lineal descendant of a family of that name who were formerly proprietors of a small estate in the Black Isle of Ross-shire. After the sale of his property the colonel's grandfather came to Sutherlandshire, and, being a man of skill and experience in country business, became the Earl of Sutherland's factor. His residence was at one of Lord Sutherland's seats, the castle of Cracaig in the parish of Loth. That baronial mansion was demolished and burned during one of the rebellions, and a less imposing manor-house was built in lieu of it, which the factor's descendants, down to my day, continue to occupy. Colonel Cluness' father was usually styled "Bailie Cluness," and flourished during the Scottish troubles of 1745. A passage in his life, during these turbulent times, handed down by popular tradition, now occurs to me. In the glen of Loth, and nearly at the centre of it, two burns meet almost at right angles. The larger stream runs through the whole length of the glen, the lesser joins it at the angle already mentioned; the mountains tower up on all sides of the streams, and in every direction, to the height of nearly 2000 feet. On an eminence close by the junction of the streams are three or four

* Mr. Charles Gordon was ordained minister of Assynt on 22nd Sept., 1825. —ED.

standing stones, grey with the moss of ages, the memorials either of the rites of the Druids or of the invasions of the Norsemen. A spot about a quarter of a mile above these monuments, at a bend of the burn, was the scene of a deed of blood and treachery, perpetrated during the memorable year of 1745-46, with which Bailie Cluness was innocently associated. Two young men, one the son of an Episcopal minister, the other of a Highland chief, both of whom were engaged in the rebellion, had escaped from the field of Culloden, and directed their flight northwards towards the counties of Sutherland and Caithness. They had gone as far as Thurso, when, understanding that the vigilance of Government in the pursuit of the fugitive rebels had relaxed, they ventured to return through the mountains homewards. The Government, however, had held out a reward for the apprehension of the insurgents, and the course of these unfortunates, ever since they crossed the Ord of Caithness and entered the county of Sutherland, was dogged by two or three men from Marril and Helmisdale. These fellows, under pretence of being their guides, took them to this fatal and gloomy spot where, rejecting all overtures of escape, or of surrender on condition of sparing their lives, the ruffians murdered them in cold blood. After these ruthless homicides had perpetrated the bloody deed, they came to Cracaig, and gave some dark and mysterious hints to Bailie Cluness of the tragedy which they had enacted, with a view to receive the promised reward. The humane and right-minded magistrate, however, no sooner penetrated into their design than, after expressing his abhorrence of their cold-blooded ferocity, and warning them of the moral consequences of what they had done, he ordered them out of his presence. Bailie Cluness left a numerous family, but of only two of them have I ever heard anything, and these were his eldest two sons, Gordon and John. Gordon was the Col. Cluness of Cracaig of my day. He married a daughter of Gordon of Carrol, by whom he had three sons and five daughters. Their eldest son was Archibald, who went to the West Indies, where he died. William, their second son, was in the army, and rose to the rank of Major, when he sold out, and lived at Cracaig after the death of his brother, and subsequently of his father, of whom, of all his sons, he was the only survivor. Major William Cluness was a gigantic, handsome, soldierly-looking man, of a truly noble countenance. After his father's death, he was among the first who took extensive sheep-farms in the parish of Kildonan, on account of which hundreds of the natives of the soil were all summarily expelled during the first Sutherland clearances. That whole extent of country, from the lower part of the Strath of Kildonan to Cnoc-an-Eireannaich on the boundaries of Caithness, constituted the store-farm of Major Cluness. He never married, and died in 1829. His nephew, Innes of Thrumster, succeeded to his lease of Cracaig. Col. Cluness' youngest son, Gordon, rose in the army to the rank of Captain, but he too sold out, and came to reside at his father's farm. He afterwards leased the farm, and commenced working it according to the new system. Poor Gordon Cluness died a fearfully sudden death. The local militia were embodied at Dornoch under the command of Lieut.-Col. the Earl

Gower, and in it Gordon Cluness held rank as Captain. When they were disbanded for the year he, in company with William Gordon of Dalcharn, a brother officer, proceeded homewards. They left Dornoch after breakfast, and in the afternoon arrived at Uppat House, the seat of William Munro of Achany, where they remained for dinner. After dining, Captain Cluness rose to go away. His intention to leave that evening was strenuously resisted by his host and by all present. Not only had he indulged too freely after dinner, but he rode a full-bred English hunter which, without being urged by whip or spur, would of his own accord devour the way. Resisting all importunities, he insisted on having his fiery steed led to the door, when he mounted and set out at full gallop. Gordon, intending to follow, could scarcely come within sight of him. Coming full speed down upon Brora bridge, which crosses the river at almost a right angle with the road, and the parapets of which were then scarcely a foot and a half in height, Cluness was flung from the saddle over the parapet into the river, there at least 50 feet deep. He sank to rise no more. The overseer of the salmon-fishing at Brora had uniformly made it a practice, as well as a pastime, every evening to pass and repass with his coble under the bridge. On that fatal evening, however, he had remained at home, busily engaged in perusing the newspaper. Had he been present he might easily have saved the wretched man's life, as the overseer was one of the best swimmers in the north of Scotland.

Col. Cluness' eldest daughter married one Innes, an officer of excise, or gauger. By the death of several wealthy relations, he realised a considerable fortune, resided for many years at the Castle of Keiss, which, with the farm, he rented from Sir John Sinclair, and ultimately became the proprietor of Thrumster. When at Loth I saw several of his sons, particularly William and Gordon, both of whom were afterwards killed during the Peninsular war. Cluness' second daughter married John Reid, surveyor of taxes for the counties of Caithness and Sutherland; and his third became the second wife of Mr. Robert Gun, minister of Latheron. His fourth daughter, Elizabeth, died at Clynemitton in 1837, unmarried; she suffered from kleptomania. Anne Cluness, the youngest of the family, was, during my residence at Loth, a dashing young woman, the reigning belle of the coast side of Sutherland. She married Joseph Gordon of Carrol [who died in 1854, at the age of 80.—ED.] and has a throng family. The old couple, Col. and Mrs. Cluness, when I was in Loth, lived in ease and affluence, and kept open table. The Colonel himself retained his rank as honorary commander of the Sutherland Volunteers. He was a chatty, kind old man, very much afflicted with gout, and very much addicted to swearing, both in Gaelic and English; an old chum and acquaintance of the late Sir Hector Munro, and a profound admirer of Elizabeth, Marchioness of Stafford. He died in 1818. Mrs. Cluness was a most kind, hospitable, and warm-hearted old lady. Her husband was as enthusiastically fond of her as she was of him, and as an helpmeet, for this world at least, he had every reason safely to trust her, for a more skilful manager of a household never existed. She ruled her servants with a prudence and sagacity beyond all praise—only now and then

she was a little hot-tempered. Like Queen Bess, too, she not unfrequently let out the occasional sallies of her temper in something more
tangible than words. Her usual weapon was her slipper, which she
put in requisition against any of her female attendants who offended
her, by throwing it directly at them. An Eppy Campbell was an
important personage in the establishment, and enjoyed the confidence
and approbation of her mistress, but even Eppy herself could not at
all times escape the discipline of the slipper. On one occasion the old
lady got very angry on some point of domestic management, and, as
Eppy maintained her own side with not a little obstinacy, Mrs.
Cluness' slipper was forthwith hurled against her. The old lady
expected Eppy to do in such a case what all her women were enjoined
to do on these occasions, viz., to pick up the slipper, and very respect-
fully return it to its owner. Eppy, however, adopted another method.
Coolly taking up the missile, she bolted out at the door with it, and
left the old lady to tramp shoeless through the house in quest of it.
After her husband's death, Mrs. Cluness left Cracaig and came to
reside in Edinburgh, where she died in 1830. My first recollections of
her are seeing her, with her daughter Anne, at Kildonan when we
were all children. Mrs. MacCulloch of Loth accompanied them, and
one evening we were, along with Anne Cluness, busily employed in
taking out of the river, immediately below the church, fresh-water
mussels in quest of pearls.

Of John Cluness, who lived at Whitehill and Kilmot, and who died
before I was born, I only know that he was the father of Medley, who
married Captain Robert Mackay of Hedgefield, near Inverness, Araidh-
chlinni's eldest son.

Mrs. Gray at Kilgour was another of my acquaintances at Loth.
She was then a widow, but her maiden name was Nicholson, and she
was a native of Shetland. Her father was the proprietor of Shebister;
during the first year of my attendance at the hall in Edinburgh, I
recollect seeing at her house there her nephew, Arthur Nicholson, the
heir to the estate. Her husband, whom she survived for many years,
was connected with my native county. He was a Mr. Walter Gray,
whose ancestors had lived in the county of Sutherland for centuries.
They derived from John, second son of Lord Gray of Foulis, who,
having killed the constable of Dundee for insulting his father, fled his
country, and came as a refugee to Ross-shire. There he succeeded by
marriage to certain lands belonging to a branch of the clan Mackay,
the "Siol Thornais"—who also were proprietors of the lands of
Spinningdale, and others in the county of Sutherland lying on the
Dornoch Firth. His descendants were subsequently, for generations,
proprietors in that county. There were at least four different branches
of them; Gray of Skibo, Gray of Criech, Gray of Lairg, and Gray of
Rogart and Ardinns. The Grays of Creich and of Rogart were the
subjects of two of Rob Donn's most withering satires, and with them
Walter Gray, who was their contemporary and near relative, was connected. But he and his elder brother, Captain John Gray, were men
of probity and honour; both were therefore exempted by the bard
from the sweeping sarcasms with which he so mercilessly demolished

the character of their near kinsmen, Robert of Creich and John of Rogart. I have a distinct, though distant, recollection of seeing Captain Walter Gray in his house at Kilgour. My acquaintance, Mrs. Gray, was his second wife. His first was a Miss Elizabeth Sutherland, daughter of James Sutherland of Langwell, Caithness, my step-mother's cousin-german. To her memory after her death, for she died at a premature age, the Reay Country bard composed a graphic and beautiful elegy. From the poet's description of the lady she must have rivalled at least, if she did not excel, in her personal attractions, my beautiful aunt and her cousin, Mrs. J. Gordon of Navidale. The only one of Walter Gray's family by this lady was his daughter Dorothea, whom I often saw at Kildonan, and who died at Wick unmarried. In regard to his domicile, Captain Gray was continually shifting. He resided at Rian, parish of Rogart, and, after his first wife's death, went to Langwell, the property meanwhile having been sold, and purchased by a brother, or a near relative of his own; then he went to Skibo, and at last to Kilgour, where he died. When he was at Langwell, the late eminent Mr. Hugh Mackay of Moy, already mentioned, who was missionary minister at Berriedale, Dirlot, and Strathhalladale, resided at his house.* During my last year's residence at Loth, Mrs. Gray was residing at Kilgour with a numerous family of daughters. Her lease having expired, the Marquis of Stafford refused to renew it to her, but let it to Mr. William Pope, elder brother of Robert Pope of Navidale, who had lately returned from India. Mrs. Gray then went with her family, in 1808, to reside in Edinburgh.

William Pope, on taking the farm of Kilgour, began by projecting many improvements, few of which he was able to carry into effect. He had little capital with which to stock it, and at last he was under the necessity of resigning his lease. After his return from India, he lived at his brother's house at Navidale. He was a well-informed man, generous and kind, but rather extravagant and free in his life. After he left Kilgour, he came again to reside at Navidale till after Mr. and Mrs. Pope's death, when, reduced to poverty, he went to live at a small cottage at Gartymore, where he died in 1815.

The circle of society of the better classes in Loth at this period was, perhaps, as respectable as any of the same kind in all Scotland. They were the tenants or tacksmen, to be sure, of the Marchioness of Stafford, but they were more on the footing of proprietors than of tenants. They were all, without exception, gentlemen who had been abroad, or had been in the army, and had made money. They had each of them, too, their sub-tenants, and their long leases or wadsets, in virtue of which they each had a vote in the county. Such, indeed, was the state of society throughout the whole county, more especially on the coast side of Sutherland, then and long previously, particularly so in the parish of Loth, which might not unjustly be regarded as an "urbs in rure." Their farms were not of very great extent towards the coast, so that their respective houses were in sight of each other. As in all human societies, however, under similiar circumstance, but too

* Mr. Hugh Mackay, A.M., was ordained minister of Moy on 25th April, 1793. He died 7th March, 1804, aged 42 years.—ED.

much strife and petty jealousy existed among them. Capt. Baigrie and Mr. Pope, for example, although nearly connected by marriage, quarrelled, and during the whole course of their lives never made it up. The inland parts of the county, too, abounded with tenants equally respectable in their own sphere, such as Mackay, Araidh-chlinni; Gordon, Dalcharn; Gunn, Achaneccan; Gordon, Griamachdary; Mac-Donald, Polley; Mackay, Achoull; and many more whom I could mention. These men, though dwelling in houses or rather hovels of stone and turf, and speaking their native Celtic, yet had their sub-tenants, were the subsidary owners of vast tracts of moorland, were given to hospitality, were enlightened by divine truth, aud knew their Bibles well, and to all comers and goers, from the highest to the lowest, could furnish a plentiful and hospitable table and lodgings. But, as I shall soon show, this high-souled gentry and this noble and far-descended peasantry, "their country's pride," were set at nought, and ultimately obliterated for a set of needy, greedy, secular adventurers, by the then representatives of the ancient Earls of Sutherland.

The widow and daughters of Mr. MacCulloch, former minister of Loth, lived at Kilmote when I was at Loth. The old lady was very feeble, very good-natured, very much addicted to tea, and exhibited all the loquacity incident to "narrative old age." Her daughter Bell was equally loquacious, and, although considerably advanced in years, had lost none of her tact in holding fast by the one side of an argument. Her sister Anne was an obsequious and zealous assentor to any side of an argument which to her appeared to be the strongest.

Mrs. Pope of Navidale had, as a family, two sons, Peter and George, and three daughters, Elizabeth, Isobel, and Roberta. The three young ladies reside at Navidale.* Peter married his cousin, Miss Mary Mackay of Torboll; George also married a cousin, Miss Charlotte Baigrie of Midgarty, and both brothers, with their wives, went to India. Mrs. Pope died under an operation in Edinburgh, and her husband only survived her a few months. Mr. Pope, by his will, settled the lease of Navidale on Alexander Ross, his brother-in-law, until his eldest son Peter should come of age. Mrs. Gordon took charge of the orphans at Aberdeen, where they were educated.

In 1808 I left Loth to reside at Kildonan. About the end of November I went to Aberdeen, where I found almost everything subjected to change. Mrs. Gordon had removed from Upper Kirkgate Street to the opposite side of Denburn, then consisting merely of a straggling house here and there, but now grown up into a very elegant street called Skene Terrace. I boarded in a house situated at the angle between Broad Street and the Upper Kirkgate. John Baigrie from Midgarty was my fellow-lodger. My attendance at college was, during this my fourth session, most uninteresting. I attended the Moral Philosophy class taught by Prof. G. Glennie, D.D. This reverend and learned person was possessed of the least possible measure of talent or imagination. Whatever knowledge he might possess, he was totally destitute of tact in so conveying it to others as either to arrest attention or excite interest. His lectures were the very essence of dulness, and

* Elizabeth and Isobel died there in 1887.—ED.

were an ill-digested compilation of the sayings and discussions of more eminent men, particularly of Dr. Beattie, whom he had succeeded, and to whose daughter he was married. He also taught the second Humanity class, both Greek and Latin. His class, at the close of the session, received each of them the literary distinction of A.M. The graduation, as it was called, was a mere literary farce. The students were examined in Latin or some branch of moral science, but the questions and answers were dictated to us by the professor a week previously. On our repeating this well-conned catechism the Principal, Dr. Brown, rose up solemnly, and holding an old dusty piece of scarlet cloth in his right hand, whilst we all stood like so many wooden images before him, he went the whole round of us, and, touching our heads, dubbed each of us a Master of Arts. For this piece of literary mummery we had each of us to pay double fees to the professor of Moral Philosopy as the promoter, double fees also to the sacrist and janitor of the college, and half a guinea for a piece of vellum, on which a skilful penman had written the diploma in Latin for our academical honours, and to which was attached in a tin box the college seal.*

I returned home by land, and had as my fellow-traveller George Urquhart, only son of Mr. Alex. Urquhart, minister of Rogart. This young man was my second-cousin by his mother, who was the niece of the Rev. Thomas Mackay of Lairg, my father's uncle. Mrs. Urquhart's father, a Mr Polson, had the farm of Easter-Helmisdale, previous to its occupation by Louis Houston. Miss Polson and her sister lived in it while Mr. A. Urquhart was missionary-minister of Achness, and it was during her residence there that she was married to Mr. Urquhart. They were a very odd couple. Mr. Urquhart, who died in 1812, was the the immediate successor of Mr. Eneas Macleod, minister of Rogart. Their family were short-lived. His son George succeeded him, in 1813, as minister of Rogart, but falling into bad health, he went to Italy. There feeling himself dying, he started for his native land, but died at

---

* The text of the diploma is as follows :—

Omnibus et Singulis quorum interest. S.

"Nos Gymnasiarcha et Artium et Linguarum, Moderatores Universitatis Marischalanae Abredonensis; candide testamur probum ac ingenuum adolescentem Donaldum Sage filium legitimum viri Reverendi Alexandri Sage Ecclesiae Pastoris in Parochia de Kildonan : Studiis Philosophicis Literisque humanioribus, per quadriennium apud nos feliciter incubuisse ; et post exactum studiorum currriculum ingenii sui ac eruditionis luculento specimine edito : Gradum Magistri in Artibus liberalibus merito consecutum fuisse : Quapropter eum omnibus bonorum morum et liberalium Scientiarum fautoribus sedulo commendatum habemus : ut eum humaniter amplecti ac benigne promovere dignentur. Quam gratiam oblata occasione, libentissime referemus, nos qui chirographis nostris publicoque Universitatis Sigillo Diploma hocce muniendum curavimus.

"Datum Abredoniae,   }   "Geo. Glennie, Mor. P.P. Promoter.
"quinto die Aprilis, A.D., 1808. }   "Gul.Laur.Brown,S.S.T.D.&P.Gymnasiarcha.
                                  "Pat. Copland, Math. P.
                                  "Ro. Hamilton, LL.D., P.P.
                                  "Jo. Stuart, Lit. Gr. P.
                                  "Jas. Beattie, P.P.
                                  "Gul. Levingston, M.D., M.P.
                                  "Geo. French, M.D., Chem. P.
                                  "Jac. Kidd, LL.OO.P."

sea off Marseilles in 1821. James Campbell, "mine ancient," was employed as his assistant during his absence, and married his youngest sister Johanna. On my father's decease, in 1824, Campbell was settled minister at Kidonan, and his mother-in-law, with her two only-surviving daughters, Mrs. Campbell and Elizabeth, went to reside at Kildonan. He had a family of three children. Mrs. Campbell died of consumption, and Elizabeth, always weak in her intellect, was found drowned, after being amissing for several days, in a pool in the upper end of Craig-an-fhithich'. George never married. Mr. Campbell demitted his charge in 1845, and died at Pictou, N.S., in 1859.

I had been only two months at home when proposals were made to me by Mr. William Smith, minister of Bower,* who was long acquainted with and attached to my father, to become schoolmaster of his parish. Some time thereafter I accepted of the situation, and accompanied by Robert Gunn, my father's servant, went to Bower round by the Ord of Caithness. We came the first night to Latheron manse, where I first saw and became acquainted with Mr. Robert Gun, the minister of that parish.† He was a thin, spare man, and at that particular period of his life, was fast falling into a gentle but decided and growing decline of nature, of which, in 1819, he died. His manners were those of a gentleman of the old school. He always met his guests at his entry door with his hat off to usher them into his house. He was not much of a favourite either with his parishioners or his heritors. He was rather a stiff, uninteresting preacher, peevish in his dispositions, and not a little fond of litigation, on account of which his heritors usually styled him Mr. Robert McProcess. He was, however, a sound although not an attractive preacher, and a strict disciplinarian; while it is but doing him justice to say that his peevishness and love of litigation were in a great measure wrung from him by his people and heritors, consequent on their frequent disorderly and improper conduct. His heritors were, with one exception (Mr. Sheriff Traill), unruly and profligate. My cousin-german, John Gordon of Swiney, was at the very head of them. Mr. Gun prosecuted one and all of them, not only for repairs of church and manse, and augmentation of stipend, but also for the fines laid upon them in course of parochial discipline. The parishioners also were disorderly in their own way. They were much given to battery and bloodshed at markets, and afterwards to religious dissensions—particularly as the followers of Peter Stewart, who was a native of that county, and whose leading tenet was that the public ordinances of the gospel, as administered by the pastors of the Church of Scotland, should be openly and universally renounced by the people, on the ground that the Spirit of God had left

---

* Mr. William Smith, A.M., was ordained minister of Bower on 6th May, 1789; he died 3rd June, 1846, in the 79th year of his age and 58th of his ministry. On 16th Jan., 1813, he married Ann Longmore, third daughter of Mr. John Sinclair of Barrock. She died in 1856.—ED.

† Mr. Robert Gun was ordained minister of Latheron 27th Sept., 1775; he died 29th Nov., 1819, in the 70th year of his age. His son Thomas, after having been schoolmaster of Latheron, was ordained minister of the *quoad sacra* parish of Keiss, near Wick, 24th Sept., 1829; in 1844 he became Free Church minister of Madderty in Perthshire, where he died at an advanced age.—ED.

the Church, and that it was doomed to destruction. On my arrival at his house that evening Mr. Gun received me with great kindness. He lived in the old manse whilst the new was building. He had been, for many years before, married to his third wife, and the children of his three wives were residing with him at the time. Their names were Cecilia, by his first wife Miss Henderson of Stempster; Gordon, William, and Mary, by his second wife Miss Cluness of Cracaig; Thomas, and Adam, by his third wife Miss Gun of Forres. On my telling where I was bound for he shook his head doubtfully, and said that he much feared I should not find myself very comfortable when I arrived. His shrewd predictions were fully verified. When I arrived at the manse of Bower I found, first of all, that the minister was not at home. He had gone to the Assembly, and nobody could tell when he would return. I quartered myself in the meantime at his house until he should arrive. Nothing could be more dreary than the manse of Bower. Although considerably advanced in years, Mr. Smith was still a bachelor, and his domestic arrangements corresponded with his condition. The internal economy of the manse was placed under the absolute control of a still *older maid* than the owner was a *bachelor*. The agricultural authority was vested in—a bachelor also—a genuine Caithnessman, or it might be the descendant of a Norwegian boor. He was a vinegar-visaged, club-footed, conceited fellow who, without very well knowing why, assumed in his own proper province all the ignorant but absolute authority of a German innkeeper in the 15th century. I next discovered that my appointment to the school of Bower was a mere thought or capricious suggestion of Mr. Smith to my father in a private conversation, and that he had taken no legal steps nor even once consulted the heritors about the matter.

As there was no preaching at Bower, I walked on the Sabbaths to the neighbouring parishes. My first " Sabbath-day journey " was to Thurso. My relative and future father-in-law, Mr. Mackintosh, was minister of this parish. I arrived about 11 o'clock, A.M., had no place to which to go but the inn, and, when the hour for public worship arrived, I went along with others into the church. Mr. Mackintosh preached first in Gaelic and then in English, within the old church, for the present elegant building was not then in existence. During the Gaelic service I got a seat, but when the English service commenced I was ousted from one seat to another until, at last, I found no rest for the " soles of my feet " but at the outside of the church altogether, so I walked off that afternoon to Bower. During the week-days I called upon the resident heritors, Mr. Sinclair of Barrock, Mr. Henderson of Stempster, and Col. B. Williamson of Banniskirk, as trustee and factor on the estate of Standstill. They all, without exception, told me that they knew nothing of my appointment as a parochial teacher, yet, with all the liberality of gentlemen, they assured me that they would neither cancel my appointment nor refuse to pay me my salary when demanded.

It was then I got acquainted with the late Mr. John Sinclair of Barrock, father of the present Sir John Sinclair, 6th Baronet of Dunbeath. The Sinclairs of Barrock are the oldest and most respectably descended of all that name in Caithness, being nearly connected with the noble family of Caithness, the powerful family of Freswick, and, as they have lately proved, with the knights-baronet of Dunbeath. When I first called at Barrock House, I was civilly and even kindly received. It was about the dinner hour, and I was hospitably invited to partake. The old gentleman, a little before dinner, came into the parlour, saluted me politely, and after expressing his utter ignorance of my appointment, and his long and intimate acquaintance with Mr. Smith's peculiarities, entered warmly into politics, declared himself a Whig and a firm adherent of Mr. Fox, to whom he was attached from personal acquaintance, and personal favour with which the Right Honourable Secretary had honoured him. His family consisted of two young ladies arrived at their bloom, and two or three more of them below their teens. When dinner was served up a rather vulgar-looking person bustled in, moved to the head of the table, and set herself down in the hostess' chair. The young ladies eyed her with looks of scorn, and the old gentleman introduced her as Mrs. Sinclair. During dinner she spoke but little, for she had been a servant in the family establishment of Barrock house. In that humble sphere, however, she was able to attract the eye of her laird and master, and with such powerful effect as to make his attentions remarkable during his first wife's life-time, who was then in declining health, and but too soon after her death the menial became the second Mrs. Sinclair of Barrock.

I called at Stempster House. The laird was not at home, but was expected to dinner. His lady and eldest daughter, after a very polite reception and the offer of a glass of whisky, invited me kindly to wait his arrival. He did come, and I dined with him. I found him to be a plain, frank, and most gentlemanly man, full of kindly feeling, totally unaware of my appointment as parochial teacher, but utterly unwilling to give me any opposition. After calling upon Col. Williamson, who was my dear stepmother's near relative, and getting his consent also to my otherwise vague appointment, I returned home until Mr. Smith should come back from the Assembly. About the middle of October thereafter I was informed of his arrival, and again set out for Caithness by a short rugged track across the mountains, and, again accompanied by Robert Gunn, arrived at Bower on the evening of the same day. It was a distance of at least 36 miles, and in the course of this long journey we called at Braemore, at the house of one Jean Gunn, who had been for many years dairymaid at Kildonan during the days of my boyhood, had afterwards married one MacDonald from Skye, and resided in this place. Jean received me with tears of joy. The best viands were immediately produced, consisting of very thick cream mixed with oatmeal, which Jean called an "ollag."

I resided with Mr. Smith that winter and spring teaching the school. The winter and spring which I passed at the manse of Bower was to me perhaps the most disconsolate and disagreeable of any portion of the years of my life. Mr. Smith was capricious and eccentric, "unstable as water" also in all his plans, conferences, and habits. His meals were most extraordinary. To breakfast we had porridge and milk, and mustard seed mixed up with them. I now rather think that he furnished me with this extraordinary beverage in order the more speedily to weary me of living with him at the manse, which I perceived he neither relished, nor had at all calculated upon.* But the matter was brought at once to the issue in the ensuing summer when, one morning, having taken down a book placed on the mantel-piece to read it, I neglected to put it back again precisely in the place I had found it. He flew into a passion, and said that if I had nothing else to employ me at his house but to put matters into confusion, the sooner I shifted my quarters the better. The hint was too broad not to be taken, and that day I took my lodgings in the house of his neighbour, Peter Keith, tacksman of Thura, where I remained until I got happily rid of the school of Bower.

My reminiscences at Bower go back to two or three individuals. The first is Mr. Stewart, whom I found a guest with Mr. Smith on the first night of my arrival. The young man was a preacher, and came to the county in the capacity of assistant to Mr. James Smith, minister of Canisbay, brother of the pastor at Bower. Mr. James had got disordered in his intellect, and therefore required an assistant. Mr. W. Smith, who was himself a most accomplished scholar, had a tolerably well-furnished library of books. Among others, he had "Whitaker's Life of Queen Mary," a strong defence of that unfortunate princess. As a devoted adherent, Stewart devoured the book, and afterwards quarrelled with many on the guilt or innocence of Queen Mary. Mr. Smith of Canisbay recovered in the course of a few years, and Mr. Stewart was consequently parted with. He afterwards became private tutor in a family at Gairloch, Ross-shire, when, in a fit of despondency, he drowned himself in Lochewe.

Dr. William Sinclair of Freswick was also another visitor at the manse of Bower. This most eccentric but highly-ingenious man was a relative of my own and of Mr. Smith of Bower. He was bred to the medical profession, and, had he turned his attention to it, would have attained eminence. His father was also a physician, and the country people, who recollected them both, called the elder "the Red Doctor," and the younger "the Black Doctor," from the respective colours of their hair. Dr. William, "the Black Doctor," was an impersonation of erudition and eccentricity. He and Mr. Ross of Clyne were fellow-students, and also fellow-combatants against the mob both at Aberdeen and at Thurso. On the death of John of Freswick, who lived at Dunbeath, and was famous for the gift of second sight, Dr. William Sinclair succeeded as heir to his estates in Caithness. By living long the life of a bachelor, and by penurious habits, he saved so much money as greatly to augment his already extensive property. At one time, and in some one of his numerous manors, he used to lie in bed for weeks and even months, sleeping away the most of his time, and living on cold sowans, having no other attendant but an old woman, as eccentric as himself, and well known in the neighbourhood of Dunbeath

---

* It is more probable, as those acquainted with Mr. Smith's frugal habits know, that this was one of his usual, favourite diets. Another Scotch dish in great favour was *sowans*—"a thick soup or jelly made from the husks or millings of oats —a very nutritious food, called in England *flummery*." (*Stormonth*).—ED.

as " Black Nance." When he chose to eat, the meagre diet of sowans was served up to him, and what he left of it, which often was little enough, for he had a voracious appetite, Black Nance got, and this she gobbled up at the fireside in his bed-room, whilst he again betook himself to his slumbers. Her very slender portion, however, of the meagre fare Black Nance often attempted to increase by a secret application to the cask where the sowans was stored up, on the presumption that her master was asleep. She was, however, very frequently and rather unpleasantly convinced of her mistake in this last particular. Freswick shut his eyes but kept awake, all the while watching the movements of his house-keeper, and having at his side in bed a black stick of more than ordinary length; so that when Black Nance had arrived at the cask, and was in the act of stretching out her hand to denude it of so much of the contents as might eke out what she lacked of her evening meal, she was promptly reminded of the illegality of her attempt by a sudden and rather smart application on the crown of her head of the black stick, by her apparently slumbering master. Foiled in this attempt to better her commons, she went out among the people, complaining most bitterly to them of her master for starving her. Some of them used to give her heels of old cheeses which she most thankfully received, and carefully secreted from her master's eye, but which, after he fell asleep, she roasted at the fire, and joyfully regaled herself with. One evening, after making a very tolerable repast on the heel of a kebbuck, just as she was about half through with it, she herself fell asleep. Freswick smelt, if he did not exactly see, what was going on, and getting up whilst she was asleep, took it out of her lap, and ate it. When she awakened her first search was for the cheese, but it was gone. "Ah," said she, shaking her fist at the sleeper, "I even dreamt that the black dog was upon me." At other times Freswick could travel all over the country on foot, and quarter himself on every family whom he thought he could impose upon. With Smith of Bower and old John Cameron of Halkirk he lived at free quarters for many months. At last he took a fancy for the married state, and, being often at Barrock, the whole country had it that Miss Jean Sinclair, Barrock's second and very handsome daughter, was to be his wedded wife. But going to Edinburgh, he there fell in with a Miss Calder of Lynegar, whom about three weeks after their first introduction to each other he made his wife. He had three children by her, the eldest of whom was a son and heir to the estate of Freswick. Mrs. Sinclair died soon after the birth of her last child, and her husband was inconsolable. He soon rallied, however, and in a very few years turned again to her whom everyone concluded to be his first choice, viz., Miss Jean Sinclair of Barrock. They were married; and whilst Mrs. Sinclair insisted that he should reside permanently at Dunbeath Castle, he insisted on repairing his father's old domicile at Thurso, and residing there. There they did reside, and there both Mrs. Sinclair and he terminated their earthly existence. Mrs. Sinclair died first. Freswick, and one of his daughters by her, as also his eldest son by his first marriage, survived her. He lived to the age of 90. During his last illness he continued to be active and anxious about the passing things of time. All the inland and mountainous parts of Dunbeath he converted into a sheep-walk, took it into his own hands, and turned out a numerous tenantry. Whilst on his death-bed, and conscious of the injuries he had inflicted, he used to say, " Sandy Gair, the godly man, has been telling the people that 'the earth is the Lord's and the fulness thereof,' but I'll show him and them that Dunbeath is not the Lord's but mine." The hour of his dissolution, however, at last came. He himself, from his medical skill, was fully aware of its approach. His more intimate friends were assembled around his dying bed. He told them that he had not full ten minutes to live, but that he was resolved as he had lived so would he die. He called for a glass of port wine. "Now," said he, "gentlemen, I wish you all a good night." He swallowed the bumper of port, leaned back on his pillow, and, after a few strong convulsive struggles, expired. Freswick was, in his personal appearance, above the ordinary size, exceedingly handsome, with a fine open countenance, but over which had been superinduced an expression of recklessness. The last time I saw him was at Thurso, at my father-in-law's house in 1828. He wandered up about 10 o'clock at night, anxious to have a chat about matters bygone, for he was a great antiquary. Mr. Mackintosh did not wish to encourage him, and, after a few civil words, left us both, and went to bed. About an hour afterwards I got him away, and accompanied him to his own door.

Another of Mr. W. Smith's visitors, whilst I lodged with him, was Captain Wemyss of Standstill. He dined one day at the manse. He was then unmarried and very handsome. His mother, the heiress of Southdun, was living and residing at Standstill. Afterwards he formed an attachment to, and subsequently married, a Miss Harriet Dunbar, second daughter of Sir Benjamin Dunbar of Hempriggs. They had a son and two daughters, the one married Mr. Sinclair of Forse, the other Mr. Robert Innes of Thrumster. Poor Captain Wemyss got deranged, from which he never fully recovered, except at brief intervals. Having retired to private life, and taken lodgings on the banks of the Solway, he went out one day, in a fit of insanity, to walk on the sands at ebb-tide, but, neglecting to return in time, before the tide came in with its usual well-known speed, he was overtaken and drowned.

I left Bower in 1811, and went to Stempster in the capacity of private tutor. I do not remember the length of time I resided at Stempster, but of my intercourse with the family, and of the public and private events involved in that period of my life, I have a distinct recollection. Mr. Henderson of Stempster and his lady were a very amiable couple. Mr., or Captain Henderson, as he was usually called from his holding that rank in the local militia of the county, was a plain, unassuming, upright country gentleman, the proprietor of an estate which realised between £300 and £400 per annum, the best part of which he personally farmed. In his younger years Mr. Henderson served as midshipman on board the "Royal George," afterwards lost in port. His father died, not an old man, and he succeeded to his patrimonial inheritance when comparatively young. He married, in the year 1787, a Miss Duthy, daughter of Mr. Duthy of Arduthy in the "How of the Mearns." Soon after his marriage he took the farm of Tister in his immediate neighbourhood, and on such terms that he could easily enough have become the proprietor. By the profits of the farm he was enabled to improve his estate, to build a manor-house, and to lay up the balance as bank stock at Thurso. A bank-agent of the neighbourhood was, before his appointment, obliged to find securities. Unfortunately for Captain Henderson he became one of them, and in consequence his money was lost. Mrs. Henderson was amiable and good-looking. While fond of argument on any subject, she had a tender conscience on religion. They had nine children—sons and daughters. David, the eldest son, was then in the army and in Spain. Alexander, their second son, also got a commission in the army, and having, with many of his brother officers, been put on board an old leaky transport, he was wrecked and drowned. William got into the navy, and has, since then, by his merit and gallantry, risen to distinction. Margaret, the eldest daughter, was then a lively young lady of nineteen, the image of her father. The rest of the family, Mary, Johan, James, and Peter were my pupils. My recollections of the treatment I met with from members of the family of Stempster are most pleasing. As parents they were both judicious and affectionate, as children docile and submissive. In the discharge of my duties as teacher, however, I never had reason to be satisfied with myself. I regret how little I then made the instruction of my pupils a matter of conscience before God, and how my natural heat of temper disqualified me from being a successful teacher of youth. Indeed, I must note this period of my life as that during which I was least under the influence of divine truth. It was not merely that I was not religious, but I was an enemy to religion, and my hostility to it rested solely on the ground of the stern and uncompromising opposition which its pure precepts uniformly gave to my own corrupt nature and propensities. In this hopeless state of mind, too, I was confirmed by everything around me. Religious truth, as publicly taught in two of the neighbouring parishes at which we attended on alternate Sabbaths, rather confirmed me in, than convinced me of, my moral obliquities. Mr. Smith, the minister of one of these parishes, was both a talented man and an accomplished scholar. But his religion, both in the pulpit and out of it, was, at best, but the mere caprice of the moment. He had, in his public prayers, a volubility and variety of words and expression, and even of ideas, such as they were, which had nothing of the spirit of devotion. No one could ever have conceived that he was addressing his Creator, but rather that he was exhibiting like a mountebank on the boards of a platform. Then, in his sermons and expository lectures on scripture, he was always straining after something curious, or sarcastic, or puzzling, or even profane. There was no unction, no edification, no solemnity, not even sound scripture doctrine, but a sort of nondescript jumble of everything that might be said or fancied on the text, however in themselves either absurd or contradictory. Then his private devotions, as well as conversations with his people, were equally frivolous and flighty. He had an odd habit of marching down from his house to the church, at a certain fixed hour in the evening, both in summer and winter, for the purpose of reading, or rather chanting aloud and alone, the Hebrew Psalter, concluding the whole with a long prayer, which he uttered aloud. The locality about the manse and church was exceedingly wet in winter, and cut up in all directions with quagmires of very considerable depth. On one occasion, and in the pitchy gloom of a December night, I saw him coming in at his door, covered over from his crown to his feet soles with slime, and exhibiting the most grotesque and ludicrous appearance imaginable. The cause of the mishap was that, whilst engaged in church in the dark, he had been suddenly interrupted by some urchins who had crept up on the church couples, and in the love of fun had, right above him, uttered some unearthly yells. This so terrified him that he rushed out at the church door, and in passing through the gate of the churchyard, he stumbled headlong into a deep ditch crossing it at the threshold, whence, after floundering about in order to get to his legs again, he came home at last in the plight already mentioned. If any of his parishioners conversed with him on light or secular subjects, he changed the conversation at once into that of a grave and solemn cast ; and if any of them spoke to him about the state of their minds, or the concerns of their souls, he turned the whole at once into a jest. His co-presbyter, Mr. John Cameron of Halkirk, was his twin brother in levity and folly. I have already twice made mention of him. But whilst at Stempster I was often his hearer. Nothing could be more irreverent or unedifying than his appearance in the pulpit. He had a stuttering, rapid utterance, slurring his words so much as to make them unintelligible, or, if they were understood, they were so perfectly ludicrous as often to set his audience a-laughing. He usually read his English sermons. The manuscripts were at least 40 years old, the crude lucubrations of his younger years, whilst the deep yellow hue of the leaves, and their tattered and rounded corners, bore occular testimony to their antiquity. He was diminutive in person, had an ill-combed shock of grey hair coming down on his forehead and shoulders, with a countenance strongly expressive of levity, drollery, profanity, and folly. He died at the manse of Halkirk, on the 8th of Dec., 1822, at the advanced age of 88. Under the ministrations of two such men, from the existing state of my own mind, I had no prospect or opportunity of improvement, and religion, distasteful to myself, was thus presented to me in the very light which of all others was most calculated to make it more so. Besides, the family at Stempster, although naturally as amiable, kind, and hospitable as all their intimates and friends could wish them to be, were destitute of even the forms of either personal or family devotion. They did not relish their parish minister; their discontent did not arise from any want which they discovered in him of fidelity and spiritual power as a preacher, but because they considered him, as the laird often pronounced him to be, " a wrong-headed man." The society in which they moved was also worldly and secular. Religion was never mentioned except to sneer at, or to argue against.

The families and individuals with whom I became acquainted at Stempster I can but cursorily mention. All the clergy without exception I both knew and visited. Mr. Sutherland of Wick, a hospitable landlord, his amiable wife, and their two daughters, Misses Mary and Margaret; Mr. Macintosh of Thurso, my future father-in-law, his wife, and then very young family, of whom my present wife was one; Mr. Jolly of Dunnet, whom I often visited on Saturday, remaining until Sabbath afternoon to meet John Dunn, my old college companion whom I had formerly known in Sutherland, when tutor at Wester. Helmisdale, and who, afterwards, became parochial schoolmaster at Dunnet. Mrs. Jolly brought her husband a large family of sons, with each and all of whom I became acquainted. The late Mr. George Mackenzie of Olrig, Mr. David Mackay of Reay, Mr. Alexander Gunn of Watten, and Mr. James Smith of Canisbay were acquaintances at whose manses I was often kindly received and hospitably entertained. The laity whom I met as guests at Stempster or elsewhere were, the present Earl of Caithness, then Lord Berriedale, Sheriff Traill, his sons and daughters, Col. Williamson, who then resided at Oldfield, near Thurso; Mr. Innes of Sandside; Mr. John Miller, merchant at Thurso, who was married to a sister of the minister of Bower, and his brother, Donald Miller, tacksman of Skinnet. I also met Captain Swanson at Gerston, a laughing, jovial fellow; John Horne of Stirkoke; Bailie MacLeay at Wick; Major Williamson at Reiss; George Sinclair Sutherland at Brabster; and Dr. Henderson of Clyth. With Mr. John Gordon of Swiney, my cousin-german, I often spent days and weeks at his house in Caithness, and afterwards at Fortrose. Of Mr. Gordon my recollections both at Swiney and at Fortrose, are most vivid He was well-informed, and had travelled much on the continent. He resided at Fortrose for some time to get his children educated. Whilst there his second daughter Catherine died, and his third daughter Fairly married one Young, then Town-clerk, and in good circumstances. Swiney himself died at his own house in 1825. I remained about two years at Stempster. My father visited me whilst there. He spent a day at Stempster. His sound, Christian advice to me on that occasion I still reverentially remember. Mr. Milne, then schoolmaster at Wick and a preacher, who afterwards married a daughter of Mr. Sutherland of Wick, often officiated for Mr. Smith during his absence. Mr. Milne was a dull, evangelical, but unmeaning preacher—a mere gospel parrot. He afterwards, on the death of Mr. James Smith, became minister of Canisbay. Mr. Wm. Munro, schoolmaster at Thurso, also frequently officiated for the minister of Bower. He was a native of Reay, and had, with many others, been aided in the prosecution of his studies by the worthy and philanthropic Mr. David Mackay, minister of that parish.

The public events during my residence at Stempster were the Spanish war and the campaigns of the Duke of Wellington. Stempster's eldest son was in the Duke of Wellington's army, and the progress of the campaign, its bloody contests, and its doubtful issue. filled his parents with the most intense anxiety. Col. Williamson's two sons were also there—Donald and James; both of whom were killed, the one at Burgos, the other at Badajoz. Captain Donald Williamson, the elder son, I have seen at Stempster, a most elegant youth, but thoughtless and extravagant. He soon afterwards joined his regiment in Spain. His brother was killed as he was cheering on his men to the assault at the seige of Burgos. He himself fell at Badajoz in a forlorn hope expedition for which he volunteered his services. Captain Sinclair Davidson, the eldest son of Mr. Davidson of Bukkies, Sir John Sinclair's quondam factor, fell in the Spanish war, with many more of the natives of Caithness.

CHAPTER XII.

ABERDEEN AND EDINBURGH; DIVINITY HALLS.

1809-1813.

DURING the period of my residence in Caithness, I attended the Divinity Hall in Aberdeen, and after I left Caithness entirely, I attended the Hall in Edinburgh. My first session in Divinity was in the winter of 1809, during my sojourn at Bower. My first outset was very unpropitious. I set off from Bower in company with John Dunn as my fellow-student and travelling companion. My half-year's salary to clear expenses I had collected from the heritors; this amounted, with as much of school-fees as I could gather, to £10. The better to secure it, I sewed up the notes between two pieces of pasteboard, and deposited the packet in my waistcoat pocket. Mr Dunn and I travelled on foot all the way to Aberdeen, and it was about the latter end of December that we arrived, on the first night of our journey, at a small inn on the Causewaymire road, called Achavannaich, through a perfect tempest of drift and snow. In the evening, after dinner, I went out to view the night, and, totally unconscious of my loss, dropped my cash-case in the dark, and came in again. We set off next morning very early, and, owing to the heavy fall of snow, with great difficulty we arrived at Berriedale inn. Just as we were going to bed did I miss my case. I searched my clothes, it was not to be found. I appealed to John Dunn in my perplexity; he knew nothing about it, the subject not having been hinted to him before. My last resource was to search my recollections, and at once it occurred to me that I had lost my money in my night ramble, and that I had nothing better for it than to start for Achavannaich at peep of day, whilst John Dunn was to await my return. After passing an almost sleepless night I did so. But it was labour in vain, and I came back, on the evening of next day, to Berriedale, only just as wise as I went, minus my ten pounds. What was to be done I knew not, but, at my fellow-traveller's suggestion, it was arranged that both of us should proceed on our journey as far as Helmisdale, and that there he and I should separate for a time; I to proceed to my father's at Kildonan to get the money replaced, and he to wait for me at the house of his former host, "Sanny Ross," at Helmisdale. This plan was strictly put in execution. We proceeded next day, notwithstanding the continuance of the storm, and in spite of a hard frost during the night, which put us both in the morning in imminent peril of our lives. It was in crossing the Ord in Caithness where the road in those days crept along the very edge of the precipice. Both my fellow-traveller and I lost our footing, slipped upon the ice, rendered still more slippery by a coating of snow which it had received that morning, and fell flat on the very brink of the precipice. We gathered ourselves up again in fear and trembling; it was certainly one of those occasions during the course of my life in which I felt the fears of death upon me. We parted at Helmisdale, and, on my arrival at my father's, my pecuniary embarrasment was soon removed by the friendly interposition of kind Captain Baigrie, who, on my application, gave me an order on his friends the Forbeses in Aberdeen. In company with old Henry, the carrier at Helmisdale' John Dunn and I met and prosecuted our journey, without further interruption, to Aberdeen.

The Divinity Chair at Marischal College was then filled by Dr. William Laurence Brown, Principal of that University; whilst that of King's College was occupied by Dr. Gilbert Gerard. I had, in some measure, become acquainted with Dr. Brown during my attendance at the philosophy classes. He was a learned man. Previous to his appointment at Aberdeen, in the threefold office of Principal of Marischal College, professor of divinity, and minister of Greyfriars' he lectured in Latin in some University in Holland.* His father, one of the profesors of St. Andrews, was remarkable for a rather clever *bon mot* which he uttered at one of the University dinners. One of his colleagues, after dinner, with all due gravity, having proposed as a toast " the Arts and Sciences," Dr. Brown responded by drinking to " *their absent friends.*" His son was inflamed with a love of ostentation —Dr. Campbell, his predecessor, was a great controversialist, Principal Brown must be so too—Dr. Beattie was a poet, and immortalised himself by his " Minstrel " and " Hermit," Principal Brown must outdo him, and accordingly he composed his poem of " Philemon." The idlest striplings about college attempted to vie with each other in the perfection with which they mimicked the Highlanders. but they too had a formidable rival in the Reverend the Principal of the College, who endeavoured to equal and excel them. His lectures on theology were vague and indefinite. He had a course of lectures on the whole system, measured out so as to meet the course of the students' atten- dance at the hall, viz., four full successive sessions. I attended his lectures for four sessions, two partial and two full, but I never yet could precisely ascertain where they began or where they closed. I never heard from his lips three consecutive sentences illustrative of any of the doctrines of the Bible; and I can conscientiously say that I never heard him pronounce, even once, the name of Jesus Christ in his lectures during my four years' attendance at the hall; a wordy torrent of controversy, a mere " beating of the air," uttered with an ostenta- tious display of oratory and fine writing, was perpetually his mode of dealing with his theme. Then he had other exercises in the hall, viz., to pronounce judgment on the sermons of the students. The practice in the theological seminaries of Scotland in those days was that, when

* William Laurence Brown, D.D., was born in Utrecht in 1755. He became minister of the English Church, and professor in the University of Utrecht. In consequence of the war which followed the French Revolution, he was obliged to leave Holland, and in 1795 was appointed Professor of Divinity in Marischal College and Principal of the University. He died in 1830.—ED.

a student of theology delivered any piece of trial, whether homily, lecture, exegesis, or exercise and addition, not only the professor, but the divinity students were called on to give their opinion on the manner and ability with which he had handled his subject. To this practice Dr. Brown rigidly adhered. The remarks of the students were usually on those pieces of trial delivered in their vernacular which they could best understand, and were in general very superficial, suggested more by prejudice or partiality than by knowledge or sound judgment. The Rev. Doctor himself brought up the rear. His remarks were chiefly, if not entirely, strictures on composition or pronunciation, in which he prided himself as having exquisite taste. The doctrine of the discourse, however, the learned professor seldom noticed. One solecism, or two or three ill-pronounced words, were sufficient to put the doctrine, whether Scriptural or anti-Scriptural, Popish or Protestant, entirely out of his head, and to make him pass it over as of comparatively little moment. The students who, year by year, constituted his class, presented a melancholy and dreary prospect as the rising generation of ministers. Their attainments, their exhibitions, their habits and conduct, as aspirants to the ministry, were, particularly during my first year at the Hall, miserable in the extreme. Many of them could not put three consecutive sentences together in prayer without having them written down, and placed in the bottom of their hats; they then read them aloud with all the outward semblance of devotion. When an exegesis was delivered—usually on some given subject of polemical theology, illustrated in the Latin tongue—Dr. Brown, observing the usual practice, called upon the students to deliver their opinions. But as these opinions could only be expressed in the language in which the exegesis was delivered, the doctor's call was usually responded to by a prudent silence. He then proceeded to pronounce upon the subject his own verdict, characterised indeed by its usual want of depth, but expressed in Latin which was at once fluent, classic, and elegant. This latinity had all the native ease of a living language, and George Buchanan could not have expressed himself more accurately. The invitation to the students of theology to deliver their opinions in Latin I never knew to have been complied with but once, and that was by Mr. Robert Gordon, one of the teachers of the Perth Academy, who, at once accepting the challenge, for it was little less on the part of the learned Principal, in a short, luminous and pointed criticism, far exceeded the doctor in depth, and almost equalled him in the elegance of his style. This Mr. Gordon also delivered a discourse—a close and most consummate piece of reasoning—but the most perfectly free from the slightest allusion to the gospel of anything of the kind. Afterwards he became minister of Kinfauns, in the neighbourhood of Perth, and there, through the instrumentality of his excellent wife, he experienced a thorough change of views and of heart. He is now advanced in years, and is the eminent and pious Dr. Robert Gordon of Edinburgh. Dr. Brown, not content with the three offices which he already held, conjoined with them a fourth, *suo sponte*, viz., that of teacher of elocution. For this purpose, after his theological prelection was concluded, he made the students by turns read a piece of English in order to correct them in pronunciation, attitude, tones of voice, etc.; and after the student had read the piece prescribed, the doctor himself read it over again in order to hold up to our view the faultless model which it would be our duty to imitate. He had a peevish expression of countenance, and an unceasing cough. In church politics, he was of the evangelical party, but in his preaching he was a genuine Arminian moderate.

Dr. Gerard, Professor of Divinity in King's College, was associated with Dr. Brown in teaching the theological classes, and the students attended his lectures on Tuesdays and Fridays during the session. The attendance at both Halls was rendered imperative by church law, but the prescribed pieces of trial were not on that account doubled, it being optional with the students to take out their discourses and deliver them before either of the professors. During the years of my attendance Dr. Gerard was in the decline of life. He succeeded his father in the theological chair—a man of considerable eminence, the author of some theological works, chiefly approved of for their literary merit.*

My attendance at the Aberdeen Hall was of no benefit whatever to me; I knew nothing at all of theology or of the Bible, nor was I made to know anything of them by my public teachers. I am deeply to blame for this, but they are nearly as much so. The divinity session was only for three months, beginning about the end of December and terminating with the philosophical courses. Of my fellow-students I have now scarcely any recollection.

I attended the Divinity Hall for six sessions; the last two were at Edinburgh. I left Kildonan about the beginning of November to go to Edinburgh by land, and from Inverness to Perth I took a seat in a stage coach which had been started on that line of road. The Highland road by Drumuachdar was then in a wretched state, being the mere skeleton of the military line made in 1746 by General Wade. The coach took two days from Inverness to Perth, a distance which the improved modes of travelling of modern times enable a stage-coach to perform in one. I had picked up as a fellow-traveller Mr. MacPherson of Belleville in Badenoch, nephew of the celebrated James MacPherson, translator of Ossian. He had occasion to go to Edinburgh, and the coach waited for and took him up at his own porter's lodge. We travelled together to Perth, stopping the first night at Dalwhiunie. When we arrived next evening at the " Salutation Inn " I prudently parted with my fellow-traveller, and decamped to a less costly hostelry. Next morning getting up early, with stick and bundle in hand, I began my journey to Edinburgh. Forty miles, however, on a short November's day, was something considerably more than a mere walk. Taking the old line of road from Perth to Kinross, for there was then none other, after breakfasting at the latter place, I did not arrive at Queensferry

---

* Gilbert Gerard, D.D., born in Aberdeen, was for a few years minister of the Scotch Church, Amsterdam. In 1791 he was elected Professor of Greek in King's College; in 1795, appointed successor to his father in the Chair of Divinity; and in 1811, inducted to the 2nd charge of Old Machar Church. In 1808 he published his principal work, entitled " Institutes of Biblical Criticism." He died in 1815.—ED.

until near sunset, and after crossing the ferry, which occupied a considerable time, it was dark. The moon rose, however, as I advanced on my way to Edinburgh, but its light only served to increase my apprehension of assault and robbery. The road through which I passed was edged on each side, in one portion of it, with clumps of wood of considerable extent, at another with hedge-rows, and as I advanced, with palpitation of heart, at every new opening of the road I fancied I saw a fellow with fustian jacket and stern face, with pistol or cudgel in hand, advance upon me from the right or left. But it was all imagination. I was permitted to wend my weary way without molestation. When late at night I entered the suburbs of the city, I met a young fellow idling about, of whom I asked where I could get quiet lodgings at an inn. The honest fellow by a sort of instinct appeared at once to comprehend my case. " Ou," said he, " ye'll be ane o' the puir stoodents comin' to Edinberry. There's kindly folk in the High Street that keep a public in a sma' way; no stylish folk, ye ken; a' the horse-coupers and carriers put up at the hoose, and ye'll find yourself quiet and comfortable." " Well," said I, " but where is the High Street?" " Ou, ye ha' na been in Edinberry afore, then; weel, I'se gang wi' ye mysel'." So we trudged off together, and he showed me in at the door of the hostelry. It was exactly as he had described it—not stylish indeed, either as to the apartments, the furniture, or the fare. The house was the general resort of mechanics for that quarter of the town. They came hither to drink, and their beverages appeared to me not a little extraordinary. They began the potations by swallowing a glass of whisky, as a *heater* as they called it, and then, as a *cooler* after it, drank a bottle of twopenny or small beer. I remained at the hostelry over Sabbath, and on Monday took lodgings in Rose Street. That day I entered the Divinity Hall.

The professor of theology was Dr. William Ritchie, formerly one of the ministers of Glasgow and an extreme Moderate. When in his parochial charge, from some probable leanings towards Episcopacy, he had introduced an organ into his church, for which he was so roughly handled, both by his congregation and his presbytery, that, like the mariners in a storm, " he wished for the day" in which a prospect of earthly emolument might take him elsewhere. The Moderates having then all the influence in Church and State regarding such appointments, he was made professor in room of Dr. Hunter. On his appointment being made public, a ludicrous caricature was put forth by the celebrated Kay, in which he was represented as trudging on foot from Glasgow to Edinburgh with an organ on his back; and then stopping on that part of the road where Glasgow is seen for the last time, he is shown in the last part as playing on his organ, " I'll gang nae mair to yon toon." When I came to Edinburgh he was both professor of divinity and one of the ministers of the High Church. On my entering the Hall the first day, after hearing his preliminary prayer and his lecture, both of which were very neat pieces of composition, I witnessed at the close a rather unusual scene. The doctor had just pronounced the apostolic blessing, when a fellow stood up and intimated that a meeting of the students was to be held within the hall

on most important business *immediately.*   Dr. Ritchie stared and
appeared for the moment rather brow-beaten; but rallying immediately,
he rose up in his desk, and authoritatively said, "Gentlemen, I hope
you will all retire." The great majority of the students then moved off
in a body.   Not knowing at the time anything about the meaning of
all this, I just joined with the majority, and walked out with them
accordingly.   As we were moving off, however, the insurgent student,
availing himself of the time we took to get out, emptied his bile in
most abusive terms against Dr. Ritchie; so much so, that the doctor
was compelled to mingle with the retiring crowd to make his escape.
As the last of us were wending out at the door, we came in for a liberal
share of the abuse and censure for the side we took.   Next day the
matter was committed to the Senatus Academicus, at a meeting called
expressly for the purpose, and a decree of expulsion from the University
was summarily pronounced upon the delinquent.   The individual in
question was an old acquaintance of mine, a John Ross, a native of
Contin.   I had first seen him at the house of Mr. Neil Kennedy; late of
Logie, when minister of the Gaelic chapel, Aberdeen, and he then made
ardent professions of piety.   I afterwards travelled on foot to Aberdeen
in company with him, the late Dr. Hugh Mackenzie of Killin, and
Daniel Forbes, son of the late Daniel Forbes of Ribigill.   I then
particularly remarked the conduct and bearing of John Ross.   He was
considerably older than any of us, and he lectured us on the importance
of scriptural knowledge and personal piety.   In all this I could clearly
enough see a great deal of ostentation, a love of argument, and not a
little arrogance.   He afterwards became schoolmaster of Fodderty,
where, under the superintendence of the parish minister, he quickly
got rid of all his "fanatical" notions of religion, and drank deeply of
the Castalian font of Moderatism.   To exhibit his new-fledged views on
the subject, he entered the lists with Mr. Robert Findlater, dyer at
Drummond, parish of Kiltearn, in a keen controversy about the nature
and character of forced settlements, or what we would now call non-
intrusion.   Mr. Findlater advocated the principle in a pamphlet
entitled "The Old Seceder," and Ross replied, *contra,* in a furious
effusion entitled "A Lash for the Old Seceder."   His dispute with Dr.
Ritchie was Moderatism *v.* Moderatism, of all such quarrels the most
relentless.   The Moderates of those days were indivisible in their
opposition to Christ in the Government of His church in Scotland, but,
when they fell out with each other on minor and secular points, their
quarrels could only be compared to the merciless onset of enraged
mastiffs.   After his expulsion from Edinburgh University Ross went
to London in the capacity of reporter to the *Times* newspaper.   Before
his departure for England he was, however, in defiance of his sentence,
licensed to preach by the presbytery of Lochcarron.   As Professor of
Theology Dr. Ritchie's exhibitions were grave and becoming, but
somewhat meagre and artificial.   His preliminary and concluding
prayers were first carefully written, and then committed to memory.
He had composed just three forms, on which he "rung the changes"
during the whole session.   What these forms lacked in unction was
compensated for by elegance of diction and by the well-knit structure

of the sentences. One of these rounded periods I yet remember—and so well I might, it having been every third day of two sessions at the Edinburgh Hall stamped and re-stamped upon my memory, if not upon my devotional feelings. The mellifluous sentence was as follows:— "We adore that goodness of Thine which is infinite—we venerate the wisdom that cannot err—we tremble at the Providence to which nothing is impossible," etc. Dr. Ritchie, however, was a rigid Calvinist, That scriptural system of interpretation of revealed truth he adhered to, and supported in his lectures and criticisms in the Hall and in his sermons in the pulpit. He was the first professor of theology in Scotland who successfully resisted the practice, until then observed in all the Scottish Universities, of asking the students to give their opinions on the pieces of trial delivered at the Divinity Hall. All his public exhibitions were premeditated, and when he made the slightest attempt to speak extempore, he stumbled and broke down. He had occasion to intimate a very liberal invitation by Professor Jameson to the students of divinity, to attend the Natural History Class gratis; and Dr. Ritchie was so much impressed with his colleague's generosity that he ventured to make an extempore speech in praise of the Natural History professor. "And, gentlemen," said the doctor, "we do accept of this most liberal offer, and—we—of this offer do accept—and, gentlemen, we do, and that most thankfully— gentlemen—that is—close with Professor Jameson's offer, with, with thankfulness and"—but here the worthy doctor's feelings were too much for his powers of utterance, and—he summed up the whole by lifting up his hands, pronouncing the apostolic benediction, and dismissing us.* He was succeeded in the Theological Chair by the far-famed and illustrious Dr. Thomas Chalmers.

The general character of my fellow-students at the Edinburgh Hall resembled that of those whom I left at Aberdeen. A very considerable number were from Argyleshire and the Border counties. My acquaintances were but few, and my reminiscences are scanty. Andrew Bullock was the Divinity Hall librarian, in which capacity he erred both in principle and practice. Dr. Ritchie had set on foot a sort of close system by which he had contrived to place the whole institution of the library under his control. Bullock lent himself to Dr. Ritchie's plans until his employer found it no longer convenient to retain him. Bullock, when in his turn dismissed, became quite obstreperous, holding evening meetings with the students to rail at Dr. Ritchie on account of the very measures which he had himself so long supported. Bullock became, afterwards, a subject of divine grace. He died minister of Tulliallan in 1836, at the age of 47, and for a considerable time before his dealth had exhibited all the evidences of the Christian spirit. Another of my contemporaries at the Hall was Robert Story,

---

* Dr. William Ritchie was translated from St. Andrew's Church, Glasgow, to the High Church, Edinburgh, and on 10th May, 1809, was elected Professor of Divinity in the Edinburgh University. which position he held in conjunction with his parochial charge. He died at Tarbolton, where his ministry began, on 29th Jan., 1830. His statement before the Glasgow Presbytery "as to the use of an organ in St Andrew's Church" was printed and circulated.—ED.

afterwards minister of Roseneath. He impressed himself on my notice
by a discourse which he delivered. It was. as Dr. Ritchie characterised
it, "a tissue, from first to last, of trope upon trope and metaphor upon
metaphor." As an illustration of his text it could only be compared
to Macbeth's vision of the weird sisters who, at first, showed an array
of hideous, unearthly countenances, but who, ultimately, became thin
air into which they evanished. George Urquhart of Rogart, another
student, was at Edinburgh either during the first or second year of my
attendance. His father had just died, and as he had the promise of
the succession, he came to finish his theological studies preparatory to
licence. His ordination took place the following summer. George
Mackay, the only son of David Mackay, minister of Reay, was tutor in
the family of the eminent Dr. James Gregory, professor of the Practice
of Physic, for which he had the very handsome salary of £100 per
annum.   I had frequently met George Mackay at my aunt Mrs.
Gordon's during my second session in Aberdeen, then at his father's in
the manse at Reay, and afterwards at Stempster. He delivered both
an English and a Latin discourse at the Hall when I was there. The
exegesis was expressed in classical and elegant Latin, and showed,
according to Dr. Ritchie, very considerable ease and practice in Latin
composition. The subject, too, was suitably arranged and illustrated.
The English discourse, which was a homily, was equally unexceptionable.   In 1816 he was presented to the parish of Rafford in
Moray-shire.*

To my other acquaintances in Edinburgh, during my two sessions
there, 1 may now briefly refer. My cousin John Mackay of Rockfield
lived in a house, his own property, in Princes Street, right opposite the
Castle. He married Miss Isabella Gordon, youngest daughter of John
Gordon of Carrol, and my earliest recollections of him are during his
honeymoon, when I dined with him at the house of my kind old friend
Mrs. Houston of Easter-Helmisdale. I also saw him at the house of
his brother-in-law, Mr. Gordon of Loth, soon after he had become the
proprietor of Rockfield. He always showed me great kindness, particularly so when in Edinburgh. He was specially instrumental in
procuring for me a bursary from the funds of the Society for the Sons
of the Clergy ; he also advanced money for me during the second year
of my attendance, which I repaid to him when I got the living of
Resolis. Whilst in Edinburgh I was not only a frequent visitor at his
house, but I went there daily as his amanuensis to write his letters,
and keep his accounts, in return for which he gave me lessons in
French, and in English reading. For these he was peculiarly well
qualified, being a most accomplished man. When I left Edinburgh for
the north he accompanied me. He had. in an evil hour, taken the
sheep-farm of Shiness, once occupied by Captain Donald Matheson, his

---

* Dr. George Mackay, minister of Rafford, was son of the minister of Reay, and
received his elementary education at the parish school, Reay, under Mr. John
Tulloch, who afterwards became Professor of Mathematics, King's College, Aberdeen.
He connected himself in 1843 with the Free Church of Scotland, of which he became
the minister at Rafford, and died 19th Jan., 1862, in the 71st year of his age and
46th of his ministry. His son David succeeded him.—ED.

brother-in-law, and after his death held by his son Duncan, then an advocate at the Scottish bar. Duncan Matheson was but two happy to get rid of it, and his uncle, without once counting the cost, as readily took it along with the stock of sheep. The inevitable consequences of this bargain soon became visible. His shepherds milked his cows, ate his sheep, rode his horses, and, in short, turned all the profits of the farm to their own account, leaving him to pay them their wages and the landlord his rent. He was, therefore, compelled to resign his lease, though at a loss. Both the horses which we rode were his property, purchased at the Grassmarket for the farm. On our way north we stopped at Perth, and spent a day at the house of an early acquaintance of his, Mr. Josiah Walker, afterwards professor of Humanity at Glasgow. On arriving at Kingussie, we breakfasted with the late excellent Mr. John Robertson, the minister of the parish, who very kindly received us, and who, at family worship, offered up a very striking and most impressive prayer. I parted with Mr. Mackay at Kessock, Inverness, and went home.

Dr. Brunton of the Tron Kirk was appointed professor of Hebrew the first year of my attendance at the Edinburgh College. I was a hearer of his preliminary lecture in the Hebrew Chair, when he first opened it on his appointment to fill the office. The chief object of the lecture was to prove that the Hebrew points had neither authority nor common sense in support of their use or practice. They were a mere modern invention—quite absurd—some of the sounds he could only compare to "a calf calling to its mother." This sparkling witticism elicited from his accompanying friends an unanimous smile of approbation. As a teacher he was superficial, and as a preacher he was equally shallow and uninteresting. I occasionally went to hear him and his superannuated colleague Dr. Simpson,* when their pulpit lucubrations forcibly reminded me of the dull old minister's remark to his equally dull but younger assistant, "Ou man, may the Lord tak' pity on the puir folk that's been to hear us baith." Dr. Brunton's manner was kind and affable ; he loved popularity, and to obtain it he was smoothness and plausibility personified. He watched the students as they passed him on the street, and the slightest movement of their hands to their hats drew from him the most graceful bend of the body and wave of the hand. His wife, Miss Balfour, was a native of Orkney. She was an authoress, and composed two novels, somewhat of a religious character, entitled "Discipline," and "Self-Control," which excited considerable interest, especially as she concealed her name from the public. I supped, along with a number of my fellow-students, at Dr. Brunton's, about the close of the session.† One of the

* Dr. Wm. Simpson had been translated from Morebattle to Lady Yester's, and from thence, in 1789, to the Tron Kirk. He died 24th Jan., 1831, in the 87th year of his age and the 60th of his ministry.—ED.

† Dr. Alex. Brunton was translated from New Greyfriars to the Tron Kirk on 23rd Nov., 1809, and elected professor of Oriental Languages in Edinburgh University on 19th May, 1813. He became a moderator of the General Assembly, and for 13 years in succession was convener of the Assembly's Committee on India Missions. He died near Cupar-Angus 9th Feb., 1854, in the 82nd year of his age and 57th of his ministry. His wife was the only daughter of Col. Thomas Balfour of Elwick.

students there that evening was John Paul, a nephew of Sir Harry Moncreiff, and the son of Sir Harry's former colleague in the West Church, who, in the course of a few years thereafter (1828), became in his turn Sir Harry's successor.

Principal Baird, one of the ministers of the High Church and also the head of the chief University of Scotland, was raised to fill that double charge through private favour. He was not a man of talent, and had a very ordinary education, but through his marriage he acquired an immense amount of personal influence. Money, indeed, had in those days everything to say. It was the pass-key to open up the way before all aspirants to civil, religious, or literary distinction. Whoever could command the four-wheeled vehicle of money, influence, patronage, and moderatism, was sure to be wafted onward from one step of promotion to another.*

With Dr. Davidson I was personally unacquainted, but his character was well known to me. He was an eminently pious man who preached the gospel in its purity, and who took a deep Christian interest in young men who were candidates for the ministry. He was the representative of an ancient and opulent family of landholders in the county of Midlothian, the Davidsons of Muirhouse. His own family name was Randall, but on the failure of the direct line, being next of kin, he succeeded as heir-at-law, and changed his name to Davidson. He lived a life of opulence and ease, but in the exercise of every Christian virtue.†

I was personally, but slightly, acquainted with his colleague in the Tolbooth, Dr. Campbell. He was a pious man and a profound divine, but of a very sour and dogged natural disposition.

Sir Harry Moncreiff was one of my favourite preachers when at the Hall. In the forenoon he always lectured first, and then preached, and nothing could exceed the ability, the clearness, and comprehensiveness of his expositions. He himself remarked, and the remark was worthy of his judgment, that the commentator, Matthew Henry, "had carefully compiled all the *sense* and all the *nonsense* ever written on Scripture." No man living could have more accurately conveyed the precise meaning and all the leading points of a chapter in the Bible, excluding all extraneous matter, even to a single superfluous remark, than Sir Harry Moncreiff. He was truly a master in Israel. His intellect flowed out on every subject with the irresistible force of some mighty engine which either presses down or breaks into shivers

---

A third work of hers was entitled "Emiline." She died 19th Dec., 1818, aged 40 years.—ED.

* See note, Chap. xxi.—ED.

† Dr. Thomas Davidson was born in 1747 at Inchture, Perthshire, of which parish his father, Thomas Randall, was minister. Educated at Glasgow and Leyden Universities, he was appointed to succeed his father at Inchture. In 1773 he was translated to the outer High Church, Glasgow; he afterwards became minister of Lady Yester's, and, in 1785, of the Tolbooth Church, Edinburgh. Though extremely modest in his demeanour, he exercised a powerful influence for good among all ranks in Edinburgh by "the elevation of his Christian character, and his diligence in pastoral work." His second wife was a sister of Lord Cockburn. He died in 1827. (See "Dictionary of National Biography," edited by Mr. Leslie Stephen.)—ED.

everything that presents even a momentary resistance to its progress. The greatest minds, however, have their corresponding weaknesses, and the vigour of Sir Harry Moncreiff's intellect on abstract subjects made him, on ordinary matters, arbitrary and punctilious to absurdity. In common with the other city ministers, Sir Henry read all his discourses. He was also a most laborious minister among his flock, and a rigid disciplinarian. On one occasion a sailor's wife, her husband being at sea, applied to Sir Henry as her minister for the baptism of her child. He proceeded to examine her on her religious knowledge, asking her in his double bass tone, "What is baptism?" The poor woman was dumb. Sir Henry repeated his interrogation, when the catechumen summoned courage to say that she could not repeat the answer from memory. "Then, good woman," replied the minister, "you must just go home and learn it before I can baptise your infant." Away she went, and at the hour appointed presented herself again before Sir Henry. "Have you now got the questions?" "Yes, sir." "Well, what is baptism?" In reply, the woman, putting her hand into her pocket and pulling out the Shorter Catechism, began very deliberately to read the answer there printed. "Stop, woman; what are you about?" exclaimed Sir Henry, "that will not pass with me; you must say the answer by heart." "Ey, Sir Harry," replied the sailor's wife, "wull ye no lat me *read* the question—Ou, sir, bonnily do ye read yersel', Sir Harry." The child was baptised very soon thereafter. During my last year's attendance at the Hall, I was ordered by my father to call upon the baronet, who was for many years collector for the Widows' Fund, in order to pay the annual rate. I found Sir Henry in his office, made my raw obeisance, and tabled the money, viz., a round sum in notes, from which a balance of six shillings and threepence was expected to be returned by the collector. But Sir Henry was in one of his punctilious moods. "What, young man," said he, "you expect the balance, and do you suppose that I have nothing to do but to trudge up and down the streets to find your balance for you; you ought to have provided yourself with it, and paid down the exact sum without giving yourself or me any further trouble." It so happened, however, that considerable quantities of silver and copper were, in the meantime, exhibiting themselves quietly, but very visibly, on a side-table, disposed each after its kind in so many rows or stalks from which it would have been easy enough for him to have handed me my balance without betaking himself, or sending me, to the streets for it. My eye mechanically turned to the provision of the side-table. I presumed not, however, to say anything, but in the most humble and respectful manner possible, assured the lofty baronet that I would instantly go for the change, return, and pay down the exact sum as he wished. This mollified him not a little, and he condescended to say in a much milder tone that such always was his method.*

* Sir Henry Moncreiff Wellwood of Tullibole, Bart., D.D., was translated from Blackford to the West Kirk (St. Cuthbert's), Edinburgh, 26th Oct., 1775, and was appointed joint convener of "Ministers' Widows' Fund" in 1784, to which he rendered important services. He died 9th Aug., 1827, in the 78th year of his age and 56th of his ministry. He took a prominent part in all schemes devised for the

Mr. Andrew Thomson of Greyfriars was then scarcely known,· although afterwards he became so celebrated as a minister and a controversialist. Mr. (afterwards Dr.) Henry Grey, a native of England, and minister for only a few years of some Scottish parish on the borders, was appointed, during my last year at the Edinburgh College, to the Chapel of Ease connected with the parish of St. Cuthbert. I heard him preach his first sermon after his induction; it was evangelical and ingenious.

Dr. Fleming was the minister of Lady Yester's;'I was his hearer now and then. He was a plain and unsophisticated, but the very reverse of either a lively or a powerful, preacher of the pure evangel. He had been translated many years before to the city from a country charge in Fifeshire.*

At the Edinburgh Hall I only delivered a lecture, and this, together with a homily which I delivered at Aberdeen, were the only pieces of trial I ever gave during my six years' attendance at the theological classes. The courses of study were not in those days so strictly looked after, either by synods or presbyteries, as now. I attended the Church History Class when in Edinburgh, then taught by Dr. Hugh Meiklejohn of Aberdeen. Discourses were delivered by the students in his class also. He received the student's manuscript, brooded over it for about a week, and then read aloud in the class a carefully composed, written critique which he had concocted upon it. His criticisms and lectures, however, were uninteresting, tedious and prosing, as he evidently had the art of speaking, utterly irrespective of the art of thinking.

But reminiscences of my student life in Edinburgh are not very pleasant to recall, owing to a nervous disorder from which I then suffered. I could not sleep at night. To the very top of Arthur's Seat at two or three o'clock in the morning was my usual stroll in quest of health and an ordinary appetite; there I would remain sitting on one of its highest peaks, and watching the dawn of day.

true welfare of mankind. The title and estates were inherited by his son, Mr. James Moncreiff, advocate, an influential and powerful debater on the evangelical side in the church until he became a Lord of Session; he died in 1853. Lord Moncreiff had two sons, who also rose to eminence, viz., Sir Henry Wellwood Moncreiff, Bart., D.D., of the Free West Church, Edinburgh; and the Right Hon. James Moncreiff, who became Lord Justice Clerk and a Peer of the realm.—ED.

* Dr. Thomas Fleming had been minister of Kirkcaldy, from which he was translated, in 1806, to Edinburgh; he died 19th June, 1824, in the 70th year of his age and 46th of ministry. Benevolent in disposition, he interested himself chiefly in the charitable institutions of Edinburgh. He translated the "Westminster Shorter Catechism" into Gaelic.—ED.

CHAPTER XIII.

SUTHERLANDSHIRE; "FIRST CLEARANCE."

1813-1815.

*A*FTER returning to abide once more under my paternal roof nothing particularly occurs to my recollection but my studies in the garret which my brother and I had so long tenanted as our waking and sleeping room. There, long after his departure, I studied alone, preparing myself for my respective courses at college, my discourses for the hall, and my trial exercises for the presbytery. About the middle of summer, after I returned from Stempster, two young female relatives of ours paid us a visit, Miss Alexa Anderson and Miss Fairly Gordon. Lexy Anderson was the daughter of Mr. James Anderson, brother of the overseer of the salmon-fishings at Invershin. He first held the farm of Rispond in the Reay Country, where he not only carried on agricultural but also commercial speculations, dealt much in the cod fishery, in which he employed much shipping, and for the accommodation of which he built a pier and formed a village at Rispond. Mr. Anderson afterwards leased the farm of Ausdale in Caithness from Sir John Sinclair. After building upon it a most substantial dwelling-house, office-houses, sheep-fanks or folds, and cultivating not a little of the surrounding moor, he gave it up in disgust and took a farm in the Orkneys, which, in a few years thereafter, he also relinquished and then retired to his native county to end his days. He was thrice married. Of his first wife I know nothing. His second wife was my cousin-german, Fairly Gordon of Clerkhill, daughter of George Gordon of Pulrossie. By her he had a son Charles who entered the army, also a son Thomas who resides at Stromness, a decidedly pious man. Mr. Anderson's only daughter by this marriage was Alexa, who, along with Fairly Gordon, second daughter of Captain William Gordon of Clerkhill was our visitant at Kildonan. She was exceedingly good-humoured, and in her manners very pleasing and attractive. After they had resided nearly a week at Kildonan, my eldest sister and I accompanied them to Clerkhill. It was on a beautiful summer day that we set out upon our journey. Our visitors had their own horses and a Clerkhill servant; my sister rode one of my father's garrons, and I was provided with a good, stout, Highland pony by Alastair Gordon of Dalcharn. Our progress was such as might be expected; the extent of moor and moss, and the depth of the fens, bogs, and peat-bags are almost inconceivable. A stranger wending his way through these all but interminable wastes, without often so much as a sheep-track to guide him, might just sit down and die. But with all its marshy mazes the natives were just as familiarly acquainted as is the post-boy with the high-road which he daily perambulates. We did not know the road or even the direction which we were to pursue; but the Clerkhill man knew every step of it, and guided us through fell and fen with unerring skill. Our route lay through the heights of Kildonan, by Suisgill, Kinbrace, Ach-na-h'uaighe, Garvoll'd, until we came to the boundary line between the parishes of Kildonan and Farr, which consists of the celebrated pass of Beallach-nan-creach, through which we passed, and struck in upon Strathnaver at a place called Ravigill. The day, which was fine, showed the moors and mountain tops of the Ben Griams close beside us, and of Ben Loyal (Loaghal) and Ben Hope blue in the distance. But as towards evening we entered Strathnaver the weather suddenly changed, and a cold wind, with that sort of drizzle called a " Scotch mist," blew behind us from the east, and so with heads and hearts equally light and thoughtless, we put our nags to their full speed, and cleared the Strath at the gallop, till we reached the celebrated Loch Mo-nair, within three miles of Clerkhill. This lake, little better than a horse-pond, was as much celebrated among the northern Highlanders as was Bethesda among the Jews in the time of our Lord. Deranged and fatuous persons were conveyed from the extremities of the five northern counties, at no matter what risk and expense, to this muddy pool for cure. The method was to come there on the evening previous to a certain day of the year—I think the first day of February. The unfortunate victim of this "freit" was, on the previous evening and on the ensuing appointed day, kept bound, and very sparingly fed until sunset. No sooner did the "ruler of the day" settle below the blue wave of the Atlantic (visible from the spot) than the patient was immediately unbound, led forth to nearly the middle of the pool, and hurled head foremost under its dusky waters. Then he was dragged out, stripped, and dried, and conveyed home by his attendants, in the confident expectation of his recovery.

Our reception at Clerkhill was most cordial, and my sister and I remained there about a week, after which we went on a visit to Tongue manse, along with Captain Gordon. My venerable acquaintance, Mr. William Mackenzie of Tongue, is impressed on my recollections. His manse was noted as the headquarters of hospitality, and Mr. Mackenzie was "the wale of old men." He had entered the territory of "narrative old age," and his narratives were fluent and almost interminable. He knew all my maternal ancestors, and he described them to me so minutely that I groaned for weariness. Mrs. Mackenzie, besides her other good qualities, was a poetess; her verses, which very much pleased her friends, were hung in black frames on the parlour wall. The good old man of Tongue could never be happy without, not only all his family, but even his nephews and grand-children filling each a place in his establishment. Two were then at the manse. One was the late Dr. Hugh Mackenzie, minister, first of Assyut, next of Clyne, and lastly of Killin, in Perthshire. He was the second son of old Hugh Mackenzie, tacksman of Creich, the minister of Tongue's eldest brother. Young Hugh was a special pet of his uncle. His recommendation to the old man's favour consisted in three things, viz., his natural talents, his evangelical sentiments, and the fact that Hugh was at the time on marriage terms with Nelly, his cousin, Mr. Mackenzie's second daughter. Miss Helen was not a fool's fancy. She had passed her prime, and to look at was hard-featured and sallow, and wore a wig. I shall afterwards notice them. Another relative of the family whom I saw there at this time was Miss Barbara Gordon, only daughter of Robert Gordon, tacksman of Langdale, in the parish of Farr. She was Mr. W. Mackenzie's grand-daughter, by his eldest daughter. Miss Barbara was a very shy, pretty, young woman of about seventeen. She afterwards became the wife of her cousin, David Mackenzie, eldest brother of Dr. Hugh Mackenzie, who was latterly successor to the Rev. James Dingwall, minister of Farr. I returned to Clerkhill, and while I remained there I called once or twice on the parish minister, Mr. Dingwall. Of this thin, spare, old man, I have many recollections. He was the immediate successor of Mr. George Munro, of whom I have already made mention. Mr. Dingwall was a native of the parish of Tarbat, and descended of an ancient family of proprietors in that part of Ross-shire. He was himself of humble parentage, but having received a liberal education at the parish school, he studied at college and the hall, and was licensed to preach, in the meantime filling the office of parish schoolmaster at Tarbat. From this post he was transferred to officiate in the pulpit at Farr. On the day of his settlement there by the Presbytery of Tongue, he told them that, if they asked him to answer the usual question, " Did he use any means, directly or indirectly, to procure the living," he should give no reply ; and, strange to say, the Presbytery resolved to waive the question and proceed to induct him. Mr. Dingwall, during nearly the whole course of his life, was the *Moderate* minister of Farr ; that is, like all of that " caste," he was not respected as a minister by his parishioners, but regarded as a mere stipendiary, and quite a secular character ; and his pulpit ministrations were considered, not as the faithful discharge of ministerial duties, but as a mere serving of the time being. I have often seen him at Kildonan, on his way to the Synod. He seemed to me, then, to be a shuffling, swaggering, tough, grey-headed, old carle. He nearly lost his life on one occasion on his way home from Golspie with his stipend. He lodged at Kildonan the night before, and started next morning at break of day. It was during the very height of a winter storm, his stipendiary aliment was lodged in his portmanteau, on which he had rested as a pillow during his slumbers, and which he placed behind him on horseback when he set out on his perilous journey. After beating up the whole day against the storm, which drifted in his teeth, and floundering through fens, quagmires, and wreathes of snow, he was overtaken by night whilst wending his way through Beallach-nan-creach. There he was seized with an inclination to sleep, and, accordingly, dismounting from his horse, he twisted the bridle round his arm, laid himself down on a wreath of snow and slept. When he awoke he felt benumbed with the cold, but he walked his horse to Ravigill, and on his arrival narrated his hairbreadth escapes, also some extraordinary dreams he had had during his repose on the Beallach.

Worthy Charles Gordon, his host, proposed, first of all, that his feet should be bathed, which was accordingly done, but, unfortunately, it was with warm water instead of cold, the consequence of which was that the majority of Mr. Dingwall's toes were thereby, to the day of his death, put *hors de combat.* He lived most penuriously, and saved some money. His wife was like himself; they had two sons and a daughter.

But it is most refreshing to me, on looking back on the past, to be enabled on highly respectable authority here to record that Mr. Dingwall gave decided evidence at the close of his life of having died the death of the righteous. To a few select Christian friends who visited him during his last illness, and who remarked that he must now look to Christ alone for help, he replied, with much solemnity and fervour, " I look to Him now, not for *help* only—that were comparatively nothing—but that He would be pleased, as He only is able, to do *all* for me." This was the language of faith and experience. But, indeed, the general tenor of his life, when viewed apart from the prejudices excited by the weakness of his intellect and the extreme levity of his manner, would lead us to conclude that, notwithstanding his infirmities, he had " the root of the matter " in him. He was ever most assiduous in the discharge of his ministerial duties; he was conscientiously just in all his dealings; and his apparent levity, or, rather, rapidity in the expression of his thoughts, was more the result of the character of his mind than of vitiated principle or habit. Mr. Dingwall will, in all probability, on the great day of reckoning be numbered among those who then shall verify the words of our Lord— " Many that are first shall be last, and *the last* shall be first."*

I left Clerkhill after a few days to return home, and as I proceeded on my journey, mounted on Dalcharn's horse, I felt unwell. Whenever the horse attempted to trot I felt a violent pain and dizziness in my head. I attempted to shake it off, but it wouldn't do, and all my attempts to do so rather increased than diminished it. In passing through the Beallach my illness had increased to such a height that three times successively I was obliged to dismount and stretch myself on the ground. The last time I did so I fell into a feverish slumber, and after some wild fantastic dreams I awoke, far more weakened than refreshed by my repose. I came to Dalcharn in the evening, where I lodged for the night. I was sent to sleep in an outhouse, cold and damp even then, in the middle of summer, which added not a little to my distemper. I left next morning on foot without food, for which I felt an utter loathing, and old Gordon convoyed me from his house to the ford on the river, which I crossed, and bent my steps to Kildonan. On reaching home I went to bed, from which I did not rise for nine weeks thereafter. My complaint was evidently a low fever acting upon my nervous system. My bed was made up at first in my father's

* Mr. James Dingwall, A.M., a native of the parish of Tarbat, was ordained missionary at Achness on 30th Oct., 1772, and admitted minister of Farr on 30th March, 1789; he died 16th Sept., 1814, in his 72nd year and 42nd of his ministry. He became unable latterly to stand in his pulpit, but preached regularly, in a sitting posture, down to the last Sabbath of his life.—Ed.

bedroom. Whilst I was still there, Harry Rainy of Creich, at present Dr. Rainy, Professor of Forensic Medicine in the University of Glasgow, along with one of his sisters, paid us a visit at Kildonan. The sister who accompanied him is now married to Mr. Robert Brown of Glasgow. This gentleman was one of the great Glasgow merchants engaged in the West India trade. He afterwards retired, and now lives at Fairlie in Ayrshire. Harry Rainy was then a student of medicine, very talented and very argumentative. My case was by my stepmother brought under his notice. In the art of healing the sick, the lovers of it, in every successive age, have fancied that they have attained to the acme of perfection. The advance of the science then reached was, that the sprinkling of cold water in cases of fever was a sovereign antidote; and I was accordingly, by Mr. Harry Rainy's prescription and manual operation, subjected to that newfangled treatment. The consequence was, that the complaint, after taking its own independent course, settled at last in the back of my head. Dr. Ross of Cambusmore, the only medical practitioner in the county, was also called in. He was a better sick-nurse than a medical adviser, and, consequently, had great sympathy for his patients'. sufferings and peculiar fancies. I fancied a fresh herring during the height of my illness, and Dr. Ross most cordially allowed me to have it. After nine weeks' confinement I arose, but the effort was too much for me. I almost fainted. I yet remember the sudden sinking of my energies, the tender but skilful treatment of my excellent stepmother, and the alarm of my father, of my sisters, and of John Baigrie, who also was present. I recovered slowly.

Previous to my illness I had engaged to become private tutor in the family of Mr. Robert MacKid, Sheriff-Substitute of the county, who lived at Kirktown, parish of Golspie, and no sooner was my health re-established than I went thither. Mr. MacKid rented the farm of Kirktown from the family of Sutherland, and on it he built a new house and a square of offices. His family consisted of three sons, Joseph, Alexander, and Robert, and three daughters, Catherine, Anne, and Sophia. None of these are now living but Sophia, who, along with her father and husband, Mr. Gillanders, now lives at Fortrose. Joseph died in the West Indies, Alexander at sea, and Robert at Fortrose. Catherine and Ann were both married; the elder to a merchant at Redcastle, who afterwards became manager of a distillery at Tarbat; there he died, and she soon followed him to an untimely grave. The younger daughter, Anne, was married to Mr. Thomas Jolly, minister of Bowden, son of the old minister of Dunnet already mentioned. Her husband had been tutor to the present Duke of Roxburgh during his father's life-time, and was, in consequence, presented to the parish of Bowden. He had a large family. Mr. Mackid himself was a lawyer by profession, and made money in the way of his vocation, first at Fortrose, and afterwards at Tain. While he was at Tain, Sheriff Mac-Culloch met with his death at Meikleferry, and Mr. MacKid became his successor.

Perhaps it would be as well here to introduce the particulars of that mysterious dispensation of Providence which cut off this valuable life.

On a market-day at Tain the worthy Sheriff left his own house at Dornoch in the morning, and crossed the Ferry to Tain, intending to return home in the evening. When he came to the Meikleferry, late in in the day, the shore was crowded with people returning home from the market. On his arrival they all made way for him, and he was quickly seated at the stern of the wherry; but afterwards the multitude pressed into the ferry-boat—the more earnestly, as they would thus have the privilege of crossing in the same boat with the Sheriff. Apprehensive of the issue, Mr. MacCulloch turned away at least two score of them from the boat. There still remained on board, however, too many for safety. It was a dead calm, and the wherry was pushed off from land. But when it had nearly reached the middle of the ferry, and the deepest part of it, the boat gave a sudden jerk, the water rushed in, and, with the exception of two or three who escaped by swimming, the whole of those on board sank to the bottom and perished. About 70 persons were thus drowned. This fearful event took place during the darkness of night in the year 1809, and created a deep sensation all over the country. The Sheriff's body was among the last that was found. The particular spot where it lay "under the flood" was discovered in a dream. A fellow-Christian and an acquaintance, deeply affected by his death, dreamed of his departed friend. In the dream the Sheriff appeared, spoke of his sudden call to the other world, and told him where his earthly remains lay, adding that, whilst the fish of the sea were permitted to mangle at their pleasure the bodies of his fellow-sufferers, they were restrained from putting a tooth upon his, which would be found entire. The dream was realised in every particular. The Sheriff's wife and daughter long survived him, and they, together with the rest of the surviving relatives of the victims of the catastrophe, were ample sharers of a fund set on foot for their support, and called the "Meikleferry Fund." Captain Robert Sutherland, Dr. Bethune's son-in-law, was one of the leading members of this charitable association.

I remained for about a year in the capacity of tutor in the family of Mr. MacKid. I shall briefly sum up what I remember of this period. I was very nervous, and was continually adopting one quack remedy after another for the bettering of my health. Tea, ardent spirits, and animal food I entirely renounced. My bed was furnished with the usual accompaniments which administer to repose, but all this was thrown away upon me, and the experience of a single sleepless night convinced me that a feather-bed and English blankets were rather the means of suffocation than of comfort. I therefore got rid of them. The coverings I exchanged for a single fold of a blanket, and for the feather-bed I substituted a chaff mattress. Thus furnished I slept soundly. I adopted also the nostrum of early rising, both in summer and during the gloom of winter; and, as in Edinburgh so also at Kirktown of Golspie, two or three o'clock in the morning found me seated quietly on the top of a hill—in the present instance, Beinn-a-Bhraggie, near Dunrobin, some 100 feet higher than Arthur's Seat.

It was a very short time previous to my residence in Mr. MacKid's family that the first "Sutherland Clearance" took place. This consisted in the ejection from their minutely-divided farms of several hundreds of the Sutherlandshire aborigines, who had from time immemorial been in possession of their mountain tenements. This sweeping desolation extended over many parishes, but it fell most heavily on the parish of Kildonan. It was the device of one William Young, a successful corn-dealer and land-improver. He rose from indigence, but was naturally a man of taste, of an ingenuous turn of mind, and a shrewd calculator. After realising some hundreds of pounds by corn-dealing, he purchased from Sir Archibald Dunbar of Thundertown a small and valueless property in Morayshire called Inverugie. It lay upon the sea-shore, and, like many properties of more ancient date, it had been completely covered with sea-sand which had drifted upon its surface. For this small and worthless spot he paid a correspondingly small price—about £700—but, tasking his native and vigorous genius for improvement, he set himself at once to better his bargain. Making use of a plough of peculiar construction, he turned the sand down and the rich old soil up, and thus made it one of the most productive properties in the county. This, with other necessary improvements, however, involved him in debt; but, just as it became a question with him how to pay it, his praise in the north as a scientific improver of land reached the ears of the Stafford family who, in connection with their immense wealth, were racked with the anxiety to improve their Highland estate. As William Young had been so successful on the estate of Inverugie they thought he could not but be equally so on the Sutherland estate. Young introduced the depopulating system into Sutherland.* This system, during his tenure of office as commissioner on the Sutherland property, was just at its commencement. It was first brought to bear on the parish of Kildonan. The whole north and south sides of the Strath, from Kildonan to Caen on the left bank of the river, and from Dalcharn to Marrel on the right bank, were, at one fell sweep, cleared of their inhabitants. The measures for their ejectment had been taken with such promptness, and were so suddenly and brutally carried out, as to excite a tumult among the people. Young had as his associate in the factorship a man of the name of Sellar, who acted in the subordinate capacity of legal agent and accountant on the estate, and who, by his unprincipled recklessness in conducting the process of ejectment, added fuel to the flame. It was said that the people rose almost *en masse*, that the constables and officials were resisted and their lives threatened, and the combination among the peasantry was represented as assuming at last so alarming an aspect that the Sheriff-Depute of the county was under the necessity of calling in the military to quell the riot. A detachment of soldiers was accordingly sent from Fort-George, a powder magazine was erected at Dornoch, and every preparation made as for the commencement of a civil war. But the chief-magistrate of the county, shrewdly suspecting the origin of these reports, ordered back the military, came himself

---

* "Clearances" had, however, been effected in some parts of Sutherland previous to this period, although to a smaller extent. From along the banks of the river Oykell, for instance, many families were evicted, in the year 1800. (Statement by the Rev. Dr. Aird of Creich.)—ED.

alone among the people, and instituted a cool and impartial enquiry into their proceedings. The result was that the formidable riot, which was reported to have for its object the murder of Young and Sellar, the expulsion of the store-farmers, and the burning of Dunrobin Castle, amounted after all only to this, that a certain number of the people had congregated in different places and had given vent to their out-raged feelings and sense of oppression in rash and unguarded terms. It could not be proved that a single act of violence was committed. Sellar laboured hard to involve my father and mother in the criminality of these proceedings, but he utterly failed. The peasantry, as fine as any in the world, were treated by the owners of the soil as "good for nothing but to be cast out and trodden under feet of men," while the tract of country thus depopulated was divided into two large sheep-farms, one of which was given in lease to William Cluness of Cracaig, and the other to a Mr. Reid from Northumberland.

While I was resident in the parish of Golspie my acquaintances were—worthy Mr. Keith and his family, Captain and Mrs. Sutherland of Drummuie, Mr. and Mrs. Mackay at Ironhill, John Mackay and his sister Chirsty, who lived at Craigton, and Mr. Peter Sellar, already mentioned, who then lived on his farm at Culmailie. Of Mr. Keith's numerous family, three only resided with him—Elizabeth, who after-wards married Charles Sutherland, merchant in Golspie, Sophia, and Lewis. Mr. Keith had been a widower for many years. His ministry was solid and edifying. He was a pious man, but his advanced age had not unnaturally impaired his ministerial usefulness. Captain Sutherland lived at Drummuie, a farm on which he had expended a very considerable sum in improvements and buildings. He had no family, but being very wealthy, he and his wife exercised an unbounded hospitality.

The Mound, across the estuary of the Fleet, a work of immense labour and expense, was begun during the time I remained at Kirk-town. The Stafford family, during their summer residence at Dunrobin, I frequently saw passing and repassing Kirktown on their way to the Mound, or returning from it.

Leaving Kirktown, I went home to commence my probationary trials before the Presbytery of Dornoch. I delivered one exercise, after which, being importuned by my friend Mr. John Mackay of Rockfield to go in capacity of private tutor to a family, his near relatives and mine, that of Mr. Matheson of Attadale, in the parish of Lochcarron, I went thither in 1815, and got a transference from the Presbytery of Dornoch to that of Lochcarron, in order to prosecute my trials.

CHAPTER XIV.

LICENSED AND ORDAINED TO PREACH.

1815-1816.

THE laird of Attadale, in whose family I was to reside, had arranged to send a horse as far as Dingwall for me to ride. I arrived there on Sabbath morning, and at the usual hour attended church. The late Dr. Stewart of the Canongate Church, Edinburgh, was then minister of Dingwall, to which he had been translated from the parish of Moulin. I was deeply impressed by his Gaelic discourse. His elegant and beautiful dialect of the Gaelic language, and what was worth all the languages on earth, his pure and vivid views of gospel truth and Christian experience, left upon my mind, I dare not say a saving, but certainly a lasting impression. I rode in the evening to Muirtown, then the property and residence of a Mr. Reid, an exceedingly plain, unsophisticated, downright sort of a man. His wife, a very pretty-looking woman, was a native of Gairloch, and sister of the present minister of Golspie, Mr Alexr. MacPherson. When I arrived at Muirtown it was rather late in the evening, and, on alighting at the door, a demure, serving-looking man met me, of whom I enquired if his master, Mr. Reid, were at home. He replied that he was, and, moreover, that he himself was that identical master in his own proper person. I stammered out an apology, but he cut me short by saying that 1 was by no means the first who had, in his case, mistaken the master for the man, and at once ushered me into his parlour. We had tea, and, immediately thereafter, Attadale arrived from Inverness. I left Muirtown on the Monday, in company with him and Mr. Reid, and arrived that night at Luibgargan, the identical inn where my grandfather, nearly a century before, had his rencontre with Red Colin. Next day, Mr. Reid returned home, and the laird and I, proceeding onwards, arrived at Attadale about two in the afternoon.

My cousin, Mrs. Matheson, received me very kindly. The family consisted of five sons, Alexander,* Hugh, Farquhar, Donald and John, and two daughters, whose names I now forget. Attadale's mother and sister also resided in the family, but soon afterwards he built a cottage on his property for their accommodation. All the boys were my pupils. The place of Attadale is very romantic, but almost entirely inaccessible, except at low water by the sands to the east, and by a break-neck, scrambling road over the edge of a precipice to the west.

Mr. Lachlan Mackenzie was then minister of Lochcarron, a man of genius, but of great eccentricity, and distinguished as one of the most eminently pious ministers of his day. As such his praise was in all

* Afterwards Sir Alexander Matheson, Bart., M.P., of Ardross.—ED.

the churches. I was his stated hearer during my residence in his parish. We had to cross the bay of Lochcarron to reach the church. It was built towards the close of my grandfather's ministry, and was, every Sabbath, crowded to the doors. This worthy and eminent servant of God was by this time in the decline of life. He was much afflicted in body by one of those nervous disorders which, undermining his constitution, terminated in paralysis; he died in 1819. His sermons exhibited the most profound views of divine truth. His expedients to re-establish his health were very peculiar. At one period of his life he bathed, often many times but always once a day, and that too both in summer and winter. He literally loaded himself with clothing. I have seen him on a hot summer day, in the church which was crowded with people, wrapped up in three vests, over which were two coats, a great-coat, and a cloak. His elders were weak and injudicious. They filled his ears with all the idle, gossipping complaints against this individual or that, which floated on the breath of the common people, and this both grieved and irritated him. These he introduced into the pulpit, so as often to excite his own mind, and very little to edify his audience. There was one individual, a stated hearer, against whom he frequently pointed some awful and crushing denunications. He was a sheep-farmer, who resided in the immediate vicinity of the manse. This man rose from a humble origin to be a prosperous and wealthy holder of stock. During the days of his obscurity, and when he lived in a humble hut, he made a profession of godliness, frequently communicated with Mr. Lachlan on the state of his mind under the hearing of the Word, attended the prayer and fellowship-meetings, kept family worship, and, in short, was apparently a decided Christian. But, as the world began to smile upon him, a change came over his spirit. He gave up family worship, absented himself from all meetings held for prayer and Christian conference, exchanged the society of the prayerful people for that of the profane, and finally crowned his apostacy by railing against the venerable pastor whom he had formerly professed to love and revere. Mr. Mackenzie first endeavoured to regain him by private admonition, but this having only a hardening effect, he took up his apostacy and publicly denounced it. Those denunciations, some of which were truly predictive of what afterwards took place, were uttered frequently in my hearing and were singularly appalling.

Of all his nine co-presbyters Mr. Mackenzie was the only minister who preached the gospel with purity and effect. Mr. Morrison of Crow-Kintail adopted the evangelical strain, but he was more remarkable for his blundering than for any actual efficiency. Dr. Ross of Lochbroom was an able man, and a sound and talented preacher, but his love of controversy and of litigation destroyed his ministerial usefulness, and was withering to his soul. Dr. Downie of Lochalsh was a man of wealth and of gentlemanly manners, a princely landlord, an extensive sheep-farmer, a good shot, but a wretched preacher. Mr. Russel of Gairloch, Mr. Macrae of Glenshiel, Mr. Macqueen of Applecross, and Mr. Colin Macivor of Glenelg, were complete and respectable specimens of Moderatism in those days.

I was introduced to Mr. Mackenzie, and not a little recommended to him by my lineal descent from the first Presbyterian minister of that parish, of whom he often made honourable mention in his pulpit doctrines, repeating in the way of illustration certain anecdotes of him, or pithy sayings, which he was reported to have uttered. These references, because of my close relationship to the person referred to, drew upon me the eyes of the whole congregation, among whom my ancestor's memory was still fresh, and many of whom had both seen him and heard him preach. I was often a guest at Mr. Mackenzie's table, and although myself, at that time, very careless and ignorant of divine things I felt that my host was truly a man of God. There was a simplicity and heavenliness, in all that he said and did, that both impressed and overawed me. Mr. Mackenzie never married, but he was a great admirer of the fair sex. He was known to have had, for many years, a predilection for a young woman, a near neighbour of his; but there was nothing in her spirit or conduct to induce such a man as Mr. Mackenzie to marry her, as she and all her family were destitute of any sense of vital godliness, and he was not the man to put himself under an "unequal yoke." He died in the 66th year of his age and the 38th of his ministry.

Having as a candidate for licence, been transferred from the Presbytery of Dornoch to that of Lochcarron, I delivered before the latter my remaining trial discourses, and was accordingly, by their moderator, Mr. Morrison of Crow-Kintail, licensed to preach the gospel. This was in 1815. How ignorant of that gospel was I then, and how callously indifferent to the great charge with which I was then entrusted! The day on which I was licensed I left Attadale somewhat early, to cross the river Carron at its junction with the sea at low water. The day was dry, and the river very low, so that I had not the slightest difficulty in getting over, and I arrived at the church of Lochcarron in full time to witness the commencement of the Presbytery's proceedings. It was so late in the evening before they could take up and fully go through my trials, that I was under the necessity of remaining in the inn at Jeantown over night. Early next morning I set out for Attadale. It had rained heavily during the interval, but had cleared up about daybreak. Being well mounted I directed my course to the ford on the Carron, which I had crossed on the previous day, when the water was not deep enough to reach much past the horse's fetlock. The river, however, on my return was greatly flooded. Unaware of this fact, and unconscious of my danger, I entered the ford. But I had not ridden ten yards into the stream when my horse suddenly lost his footing, and we were both at once swept down by the strength and rapidity of the current into the tide below, which was making at the time. I was about to give up all for lost, but had the presence of mind to wheel my horse round, when after swimming for the distance of ten or fifteen yards, he reached the beach with me in safety. My condition there was, however, by no means a secure one, as the tide was advancing around me. A man, accidentally passing, guided me out of my perilous position. He said that although no man nor horse could have crossed the river where I had attempted it, he would undertake to lead me over a little farther down, where, he assured me, the water would scarcely be knee-deep. Accordingly, coming with me to the very point where the current of the stream entered the tide, and going before me himself on foot, he led me in a diagonal direction across, following closely the bank of sand which the force of the stream had thrown up before it on its entrance into the sea, and thus we reached the opposite bank in perfect safety. I thought so little of this incident at the time that I never even mentioned it, but on looking back on it from amidst the vicissitudes of after-life, and the many difficulties and subsequent deliverances which I have experienced in the course of my ministry, I have frequently had reason to acknowledge the goodness of God towards me on that occasion.

Mr. Dingwall of Farr had died in the previous year (1814). His successor was Mr. David Mackenzie, missionary-minister of Achness, to whom the patron presented the living, on which he entered in May 1815. The vacancy in Achness was soon afterwards filled, the Assembly's committee appointing me to that place. In consequence of this I left Attadale, and once more came to reside under my father's roof.

Previous to my departure from Attadale, it might be about a week or two, I was, as a licentiate of the Presbytery of Lochcarron, asked to preach within their bounds. My first attempt to address a public audience was made at Lochalsh, and in the pulpit of Dr. Downie, the parish minister. My exhibition was an almost complete failure. I was wretchedly deficient in the Gaelic language, and I entered upon the ministry with a conscious dependence upon myself. Both the Gaelic and the English sermons which I preached at Lochalsh were the result of a whole week's study, and I had closely committed every word to memory. Dr. Downie, for whom I officiated on this first occasion, was one of my early acquaintances after I came to reside in that part of the country. I had been frequently a guest at his house, and he treated me with uniform kindness. But careless and ignorant as I then was, I could not fail to notice the glaring deficiencies of his ministerial character. His sermons were literal transcripts from Blair " et hoc genus omne." These he read in English, and translated into the purest and most elegant Gaelic. Dr. Downie's respectable neighbour, Coll MacDonnell of Barrisdale, a cadet of the family of Glengarry. claimed cousinship with me as the great-great-grandson of MacDonell of Ardnafuaran. This gentleman was. in personal appearance, size. and manners, a genuine specimen of the Highland " duan' uasal;" he lived at Actertyre, a farm which he held from Hugh Innes of Lochalsh.

Dr. Downie had four daughters and three sons. His eldest son attended college; he afterwards went to the West Indies. Charles, the second son, is now minister of Contin, and Alexander, the third son, is a medical practitioner in a foreign country. His eldest two daughters. Flora and Margaret, about the time I resided in that country, 1813-15, were at a London boarding-school. During the visit of the allied sovereigns of Europe to the Prince Regent in 1814, after

Napoleon's banishment to Elba, these young ladies were spectators of a public demonstration made by the Regent in honour of his Imperial and Royal visitors. Poor Margaret, a very beautiful girl, caught cold on that occasion, which threw her into a consumption. She and her sister came home, and her death took place a few months after her arrival. It was the second Sabbath thereafter that I preached at Lochalsh. Dr. Downie walked with me to church. When we entered the churchyard gate, one of the first objects which met our eyes was the new-made grave of his daughter. A convulsion passed over his face, the tears started over his eyes, but he quickly regained his composure.*

Leaving Attadale early in the morning, I breakfasted at Luibgargan, proceeded on foot down Strathconon, and rested during the night at Garve. Next morning I met with a clansman, the only one outside my own family I had ever seen. He was a John Sage, an excise officer in that district. We breakfasted together, and setting off immediately thereafter, I arrived at Kildonan on Thursday. The communion was to be administered on the Sabbath following, and I found my father, with his assistants, Mr. John Munro, missionary-minister of Dirlot, and Mr. Duncan MacGillvray, minister of Assynt, busily engaged in the preparatory duties. The services were conducted in Gaelic, and in the open air. The spot selected for the meeting of the congregation was about a mile to the north of the manse, on the banks of the burn, and about two or three hundred yards below the waterfall of " Ess-na-caoraiche-duibhe." My father preached the action sermon in Gaelic, and I succeeded him in the evening. I selected for my text the same passage I preached from at Lochcarron. I uttered a few preliminary sentences with considerable boldness and facility. But all at once my memory failed me, and I made a dead pause. My father sat behind me in the tent, and groaned aloud for very anxiety. The congregation, too, among whom were a number of my future flock at Achness, all on the very tiptoe of curiosity and attention on my first appearance, were agitated like the surface of one of their own mountain lochs when suddenly visited with a hurricane. After a pause of some minutes, however, during which I felt myself pretty similarly circumstanced as when carried away by the river Carron, I pulled out my manuscript, and stammered out the rest of my sermon with much trepidation, and in the best way I could. I returned home totally disconcerted, and seriously meditated the renunciation of my licence, my mission, and all my ministerial prospects. Mr. Munro, however, came to comfort me in my distress. It would appear that he himself had had a personal experience of the very difficulty with which I had then to grapple. He had been requested by Mr. Bethune to preach at Dornoch, but although he got through the Gaelic service without much difficulty, when he attempted to preach an English sermon without his manuscript, he had to stop short in the middle of a sentence, and was under the necessity of having recourse to his paper, much to his own confusion no less than

* Dr. Alexr. Downie died in May, 1820, at the age of 55, having been minister of Lochalsh for 29 years.—ED.

to that of his audience. He could thus the more readily sympathise with my feelings, and I was not a little cheered and encouraged by his truly Christian and fatherly admonitions. I think, indeed, that upon the whole I was no loser by this very severe trial of my natural feelings. It read me a most humbling lesson respecting myself, and struck a telling blow also at the very root of my self-confidence, then my easily besetting sin.

I may here record some notices about my father's assistants at that communion. Mr. John Munro was a native of Ross-shire.* His more immediate ancestors were tinkers—not of the gipsy race, however, but native Highlanders—who gained their livelihood by the manufacture of horn-spoons and vessels of tin or white iron, and by mending broken stoneware, and who wandered about from place to place in pursuit of their vocation. They were therefore called, in their native tongue, "ceardaidhean," or craftsmen. Mr. Munro, although sprung from so humble a race, was yet destined by the All-wise Ruler for far higher ends. At a very early age he felt the power of the truth upon his heart, through the instrumentality of his mother's instructions. He received the first rudiments of his education at Kiltearn parish school, and afterwards, during his attendance at the College and at the Hall, became parochial schoolmaster, first of Resolis, and afterwards of Tarbat. While in this latter place he married Miss Forbes, sister of the minister of the parish. After finishing his course at the Hall he was licensed to preach by the Presbytery of Tain. Although a man of great moral weight, and of faith unfeigned, his natural capacity was limited, as were his literary attainments. He understood the first principles of Latin and Greek grammar, but abstract views of a subject, the logical arrangement of it, and the bringing out of his views in a regular and consecutive form, were qualifications of which he was destitute. When on his trials before the Presbytery he delivered a homily, on which all bestowed most unqualified approbation. It was clear and concise, and, in short, a masterly performance. But Mr. John Ross of Logie, one of their number, who well knew the extent of Mr. Munro's abilities, and the very much more than mere help which he received from his parish minister, added with much emphasis, after highly commending the performance, "But, young man, is not the hand of Joab with thee in all this?" Soon after being licensed, about the year 1812, he was appointed missionary-minister of Dirlot, and it was during his ministry there that he regularly assisted my father when he annually administered the sacrament at Kildonan. He was missionary at Dirlot when I was at Stempster, and I noticed that although he was universally respected by the pious among the lower classes, yet, by the higher and better-educated who knew not the truth, he was known in Caithness by the epithet of "Munro of the hills." He was elected minister of the Gaelic Chapel, Edinburgh, on Mr. Macdonald's translation to Urquhart, or Ferintosh, as successor to the eminent Charles Calder. On the death of Mr. Cameron at a very

* Mr. John Munro died 1st April, 1847, in the 41st year of his ministry. He was for 25 years minister of Halkirk, where his memory is much revered.—ED.

advanced age, he was, as the choice of the people, presented to the church and parish of Halkirk.

Mr. Duncan MacGillivray, now of Lairg, was a near relative of the venerated Dr. Angus Mackintosh of Tain.* He was a native of the parish of Moy, Inverness-shire, and an original member of the Northern Missionary Society, being present at its first meeting held at Tain in 1800. The first charge to which he was appointed on being licensed to preach was that of Achness. I have even now a distinct remembrance of seeing him at Kildonan on his way to enter upon his labours. My father and step-mother were from home, and he stepped in upon us on the evening of a raw, cold, misty day in spring. He was the immediate successor of the late Mr. Gordon of Loth, and like him was a frequent visitor at my father's when he preached at Ach-na-h'uaighe, and was always his assistant during sacramental occasions. During his visits to Kildonan he had often been my instructor in Latin. Both as a preacher and a well-educated man Mr. MacGillivray was highly respectable. His sermons were well-composed, and exhibited throughout clear, comprehensive and impressive views of divine truth. His delivery was peculiar. He had a sort of paralytic affection in his throat which, at frequent intervals, interrupted his elocution, not only during the utterance of a sentence, but even of a single word, and he had a rather awkward habit of holding up his left hand, folded almost double, close at the root of his ear. Soon after his settlement at Achness, which was then a most populous tract of country, he married a daughter of Mr. Robert Gordon, then tacksman of the farm of Achness, a very handsome, high-spirited woman, by whom he had sons and daughters. On the death of the late Mr. Wm. Mackenzie, minister of Assynt, Mr. MacGillivray was, by the patron, appointed as his successor. His appointment to Assynt was a personal arrangement between himself and Lord and Lady Stafford. The people of Assynt were not consulted in the matter. They, however, took the liberty of thinking for themselves in the case. They had formed a strong attachment to the late venerable Mr. John Kennedy, minister of Killearnan, who was still officiating among them at that time in capacity of assistant to the late Mr. William Mackenzie. The parishioners wished to have Mr. Kennedy settled among them as Mr. Mackenzie's successor. Their request, however, was peremptorily refused, and Mr. MacGillivray was appointed. The Presbytery of Dornoch, therefore, met on an appointed day to settle the presentee. They reckoned, however, without their host. As they were all assembled in the manse parlour, with the exception of my father and Mr. Keith, and were about to proceed with the settlement, their

* Dr. Angus Mackintosh was translated from the Gaelic Chapel, Glasgow, and admitted minister of Tain 11th May, 1797 ; he died 3rd Oct., 1831, in the 68th year of his age and 39th of his ministry. He was one of the originators and secretary of the Northern Missionary Society. In 1800 he married Anne, youngest daughter of Mr. Ch. Calder, minister of Urquhart. She died 23rd Jan., 1857. He was succeeded by his son Dr. Charles Calder Mackintosh, who was ordained (assist. and suc.) 19th June, 1828 ; translated to Free Church, Dunoon, in 1854 ; and who died at Pau 24th Nov. 1868, in the 62nd year of his age and 41st of his ministry. (See his Memoir and Sermons, published and edited by the late Rev. William Taylor).—ED.

N

attention was directed to a strong body of Assynt Highlanders, each armed with a cudgel, who presented themselves before the manse windows. As if significantly to express the purpose of their assemblage, each pulled off his neckcloth with one hand, and wielded his cudgel with the other, and loudly demanded the compearance of the Presbytery. The members resolved to go out and remonstrate with the rioters, but it would not do. The mob which now assembled told them through their leaders that the only way by which they could escape broken bones was that each should get to his nag with all convenient speed, nor slack bridle till they had crossed the boundaries of the parish, for that they were determined that the presentee should not on that day, nor on any other day, be settled minister of Assynt. To this peremptory condition the Presbytery members were compelled to submit, and each and all of them, together with the presentee, his wife, family and furniture, were sent back the way they came, closely followed by the men of Assynt. This affray was productive of consequences obstructive to the subsequent usefulness of Mr Mac-Gillivray in the parish. The ringleaders were discovered, tried before the Justiciary Court at Inverness, and, in spite of the earnest entreaties of their pastor, sentenced to nine months' imprisonment. Shortly thereafter, the parish of Lairg becoming vacant by the translation of Mr. Angus Kennedy to Dornoch on the death of Dr. Bethune, Mr. MacGillivray was settled minister of that parish, with the unanimous consent of the parishioners, and there, as I write, he still labours at a very advanced age.*

For the first half-year after my appointment to the Achness mission I remained at Kildonan, and went to both stations to preach almost every Sabbath. Indeed my commission from the Assembly's Committee of the Royal Bounty had not, from some unaccountable delay, been forwarded; and therefore, although I preached in the mission, I was not ordained by the Presbytery until they had received my written appointment, which was not till the month of November, ·1816, nearly six months after my return from Lochcarron. It came at last, and I went to Creich, where the Presbytery held a meeting. I was then ordained by Dr. Bethune, the Moderator, to the pastoral charge of the mission at Achness. I went home that evening with my ecclesiastical father, and, if I remember well, preached for him at Dornoch on the following Sabbath.

I yet remember my first visit to Achness to preach my first sermon there. I lodged at Breacachadh, in the parish of Kildonan, on the Saturday evening. Thomas Gordon was then tacksman of that farm. He was the lineal descendant of a race of Gordons transplanted from Banffshire to Sutherland during the days of Adam, Lord of Aboyne, who, on his marriage with Elizabeth, heiress of Sutherland, became titular Earl of Sutherland. I was long and intimately acquainted with

* Mr. Duncan MacGillivray, A.M., was ordained minister of Assynt at a meeting of Presbytery held at Dornoch on 24th Aug., 1813, and was translated to Lairg 12th Aug., 1817. He was a native of Inverness-shire. His two sons, Angus Mackintosh and Alexander, have been ministers of the Free Church of Scotland. He died 11th Feb., 1849, in the 48th year of his ministry.—ED.

Thomas Gordon, and had also seen his father, old William Breacachadh. The Gordons of Breacachadh and of Ach-na-moine were of the same race. Their original ancestor, a Thomas Gordon, was a man of gigantic strength. His descendant, William Gordon, was a low-statured, broadshouldered, square-built man, the model of a Highlander, with keen black eyes, and most respectable and consistent in point of character, but peculiar in temper, and of a somewhat sordid disposition. About eight or ten miles farther on, and in the same parish, resided a neighbour, George Mackay, Halmindary, already mentioned, a man of wit, humour, and piety, who not unfrequently indulged his native poignancy of wit and sarcasm at the expense of William of Breacachadh. Old William was a man of frugal habits, and George of Halmindary had all the thoughtless prodigality of the Sutherland Highlanders. Both strictly maintained the terms of good neighbourhood with each other; but although they often exchanged the rights of hospitality, they never met or parted without their "miffs." Halmindary could not possibly keep his caustic humour against Breacachadh within the bounds of civility when they met, and this Breacachadh both felt and resented.

With Thomas of Breacachadh I lodged on the Saturday evening before my first Sabbath at Achness. He provided me with a horse, and accompanied me the next morning, after an early breakfast, to the place where the congregation met. The rural church, or meeting-house as it was called, at Achness was at the time almost ruinous, and until it was repaired the people were obliged to meet in the open air. After addressing them both in Gaelic and English, I returned in the evening to Breacachadh. The terms of my commission enjoined upon me to preach two Sabbaths successively at Achness, and the third at Ach-na-h'uaighe. My incumbency at Achness lasted for three years. My reminiscences of that period involve, first of all, a description of the nature and the locality of my ministerial labours.

Missions, particularly in the Highlands and Islands of Scotland, were of very long standing, for I was the seventh and last in succession of the missionaries appointed to officiate at Achness. My aboriginal predecessor in office was the revered and truly pious George Munro of Farr, married to my grand-aunt.[*] The object of the Church in establishing these missions was to supply the almost total lack of ministerial service in the extensive parishes of the north. Parishes of forty, fifty, and even sixty miles in length are there of frequent occurrence, and both the larger and smaller parishes are absurdly divided. The principle adopted in settling the bounds was not, evidently, to take into account the distance from, or proximity of, the population to any place of worship erected for them, but solely so as to include the landed property of the heritors of the district. This was called a parish, and in many cases it exceeded in extent many whole counties in the south.

[*] Mr. George Munro was ordained successor to Mr. Skeldoch as minister of Farr 23rd May, 1754. On 16th December of the same year he married Barbara, daughter of Mr. John Mackay, minister of Lairg. She is said to have been a woman of masculine understanding, but of feminine amiability and Christian piety; while Mr. Munro was a guileless character, but an honoured servant of the Lord. He died 1st May, 1779, aged 74, and in the 25th year of his ministry.—Ed.

Missions were established for the accommodation of such of the parishioners for whom it was a physical impossibility to attend the parish church. For the support of the missionary-ministers there were two sources of funds, the Christian Knowledge Society and the Assembly's Committee for managing the Royal Bounty. The Christian Knowledge Society was established by Royal Charter in the year 1701, and gradually, I presume, it extended its efficiency over the sphere of its labours, establishing itself as it best could. To send forth ministers. catechists, and schoolmasters, each in their respective departments of moral and religious usefulness in the Highlands and Islands of Scotland, was the peculiar province of this Society. It began its labours when moral and religious education, as a popular and efficient system, was but little understood. The management of the Society, therefore, was not progressive; and although its schools and missions were, at the first outset, productive of considerable benefit to the rude and benighted Highlanders, yet upon the whole it was very inefficient, and at the time I write it is almost defunct.* The Assembly's Committee for managing the Royal Bounty was of more recent origin, but was evidently intended for a similar purpose to that of the Society. A grant of £2000 annually from the last Sovereigns of the House of Hanover was presented in due form by their commissioner to the General Assembly, in order to be bestowed in sums of from £45 to £50 upon missionary or itinerant ministers in the five northern counties. Achness was one of the stations. The minister's right or authority to enter upon his duties, and to draw the salary, which was £50, was the Committee's letter, called his "commission," which contained instructions directing him how to proceed. He had to keep a journal of his preachings every Sabbath, whether within the bounds of his own charge or elsewhere, and to send it up to Edinburgh half-yearly, duly attested by the Presbyteries within whose bounds his charge lay.

The mission at Achness, in regard to locality and surface, of very great extent. It lay within the bounds of the neighbouring presbyteries of Tongue and Dornoch, comprehending the extreme heights of the parish of Farr, from Moudale down to nearly the middle of Strathnaver, towards the north-west, and from Halmindary down to Kinbrace, in the parish of Kildonan, towards the south-east. A very considerable portion of the population had already been removed by the Stafford family, and their tenements given to sheep-farmers, so that the peopled part of that vast district was comparatively limited. The whole population in the Strathnaver district lay apart from the missionary's house, being divided from it by the Naver, a river of such volume and breadth in the winter months as completely to preclude the

* The S.P.C.K. was at first supported by persons of all Protestant denominations in the country. But in 1846 the Court of Session decided that all its agents must belong to the Church which was established by law. Since this decision, the funds of the Society have been diverted from education to the support of missionary teachers and catechists belonging to that particular denomination. The Commissioners on Educational Endowments have lately, however, prepared a scheme by which it is to be restored to its original and catholic constitution. (Statement by the Rev. J. C. MacPhail of Edinburgh.)—ED,

attendance of the people at their wonted place of worship during that season. That part of the mission which lay within the parish of Kildonan extended from the boundary line between the parishes to Kinbrace and Borrobol, on either side of Loch Badenloch and of the river Helmisdale which issued from it. The population here lived, like that of Strathnaver, in detached townships. Those in Strathnaver were Moudale, Tobeg, Grumore, Grumbeg, Ceannachyle, Syre, Lang-dale, Skaill, and Carnachadh—all possessed by small tenants, and lying on the north and west banks of the loch and river of Naver. Those in Kildonan were Gairnsary, Breacachadh, Badenloch, Bad.'chlamhain, Ach-na-moine, Ach-na-h'uaighe, Dalcharn, Borrobol, and Kinbrace. All these townships were more or less densely peopled, and lay alternately either at the head of Loch Badenloch or on each side of the shores of the lake and of the river Helmisdale. The great majority of the population was to be found in the Strathnaver district; and, consequently, it was incumbent on the missionary, for once that he preached at Ach-na-h'uaighe in Kildonan, to preach two Sabbaths successively at Achness in the parish of Farr. There were three more townships in the Kildonan district, viz., Griamachdary, Knockfin, and Strathbeg.

The rural church at Ach-na-h'uaighe I have described in a previous chapter; that at Achness was scarcely better. When I entered on the duties it was in a wofully dilapidated state, but it was soon afterwards repaired by the people, and made merely habitable. It consisted of a long low house, with a large wing stretching out from the north side of it. The walls were built of stone and clay, the roof covered with divot and straw, and the seats were forms set at random, without any regularity, on the damp floor. The house of the minister was erected at the foot of a steep brae, and in the middle of a fen. Its walls were of stone and lime; it was thatched with divot and straw, and contained four apartments, a kitchen in an outer wing, a parlour with a bed in the wall, a closet, and a bedroom. The minister also rented, for the sum of £5 annually, a small farm from the sheep-farmers, Messrs Marshall and Atkinson, which afforded corn, straw, and hay for a horse and two cows. The place of Achness itself, once densely peopled, was in my time entirely depopulated, and the only one left was a miller, who resided at its northern extremity.

The people of the districts in both parishes were much fewer during my ministry than under that of my predecessors. I mention this par-ticularly in reference to what has been called one of the Sutherland clearances, which took place in 1815, nearly a year before I went to Achness. A vast extent of moorland within the parishes of Farr and Kildonan was let to Mr. Sellar, factor for the Stafford family, by his superior, as a sheep or store farm; and the measure he employed to eject the poor, but original, possessors of the lands, was fire. At Rhimis-dale, a township crowded with small tenants, a corn-mill was set on fire in order effectually to scare the people from the place before the term for eviction arrived. Firing or injuring a corn-mill, on which the sustenance of the lieges so much depends, is or was by our ancient Scottish statutes punishable by imprisonment, or civil banishment, and on this point of law Mr. Sellar was ultimately tried. The Sheriff-Substitute, Mr. R. MacKid, hearing of the case, proceeded in his official capacity to the spot to make a precognition of the circumstances. The Sheriff's enquiry fully established the fact, and elicited many aggravating particulars, so that he considered himself called upon to issue a warrant for Sellar's apprehension and incarceration in Dornoch jail, and to prepare the case for the Inverness Circuit Court. That MacKid was at the time not on good terms with Mr. Sellar, was well known. But though his procedure may have seemed harsh, it did not alter the particulars of the case. The trial took place, but the final issue of it was only what might have been expected when a case came to be determined between the *poor*, as the party offended, and the *rich* as the lordly and heartless aggressor. Sellar was acquitted, while Sheriff MacKid was heavily censured. Indeed, the latter was threatened with an action for damages at the factor's instance. To ward off this blow, MacKid threw himself on the other's mercy—a submission which was readily accepted, as Sellar was only too happy to escape incurring any further public odium. The whole matter, however, left a stain on the memory of the perpetrators which will never be removed.

After residing for nearly seven months at my father's house, I went, about the beginning of the winter of 1816, to reside permanently at the manse of Achness. My furniture was scanty and my books were few. Some articles of furniture I got from the manse of Kildonan, and some, such as a bed and bedding, a carpet, and some chairs, I purchased at the roup of Kirktown in Golspie. For, consequent on the proceedings in Mr. Sellar's case, MacKid felt that he could no longer act as Sheriff, nor very comfortably dwell at his farm of Kirktown, which he held in lease from the Stafford family. He therefore resigned his office as Sheriff-Substitute, and his lease as tacksman of the farm, selling off his farm stock and household furniture by auction. He went to reside at Thurso, and practised as he could in his legal profession, but without much success. His wife died there, and he soon afterwards returned with his family to Fortrose, where, having lost all his money, he died at a very advanced age.

CHAPTER XV.

PROMINENT PERSONS IN SUTHERLAND.

1816-1819.

MY father, in the prime of his life, was both strong and healthy, but as he approached his grand climateric, and in immediate consequence of a fall from his horse, he began to feel unusual pains in the lower part of his chest, which at first entirely confined him to bed, and filled him with apprehensions of approaching dissolution. My step-mother, at first, feared dropsy. It turned out, however, to be "the stone," from which complaint, by the use of very simple remedies, such as soda-water and the decoction of black currant leaves, after passing some calculi, he completely recovered some years before his death in 1824. It was during the earlier stages of his illness, however, that my step-mother first incurred that fatal disease which, in 1819, at the age of sixty-five, brought her to her grave. Her complaint was cancer. During my residence at Achness she daily got worse. The Strathpeffer mineral water was recommended, and I accompanied her thither by sea from Helmisdale to Dingwall. We slept at Cromarty, and next day arrived at the Spa, where I took lodgings at the place of Achdermid. She remained there for some weeks, and returned greatly benefited. But her recovery was temporary. During the last year and a half of my residence at Achness she was entirely confined to bed. The illness was eminently sanctified to her. I have often, on a Sabbath evening after preaching at Ach-na-h'uaighe, arrived at Kildonan and preached in her bedroom, when she would listen with intense interest.

My sister Elizabeth came to reside with me and keep my house at Achness. Our sister Jean had for some years before been the wife of Mr. William Forbes, minister of Tarbat. They were married during my absence at the Divinity Hall on the 26th of November, 1813, by Mr. Munro of Halkirk. Both my sisters had, many years before, given the most decided evidences of the power of Divine grace in their hearts. Elizabeth, the elder, was a most decided, deeply-exercised, progressive and consistent Christian, and during her life, which was comparatively a short one (for she died at the age of 52), the excellency and purity of her Christian character were remarkably conspicuous. I only wish that I had derived the benefit which I might have done from her converse and example while she stayed with me. During her residence at Achness, she fell under the influence of a highly nervous disorder, superinduced by the loneliness of the place, by my frequent absence from home, and by her apprehensions about my safety when, in winter, I had to cross the burns and fens of immense extent, so abundant in that Alpine region. Her fears were, on one occasion, well-nigh realised.

I had procured from a friend, Mr. Gordon of Breacachadh, a Highland pony, very strong and sure-footed. Having been bred in that district, the animal, with the instinct for which horses in general are so remarkable, could find his way through the most sequestered and intricate morasses to his stall, or to the house of his owner, whether by night or by day. This creature was instrumental, on this occasion, in saving my life. I had left Achness on a Saturday, in order to officiate on Sabbath at Ach-na-h'uaighe. It was in winter, and the day was bitterly cold, so that the showers of hail, blowing directly on my face, pierced the skin in many places and drew blood. I had to cross a small rivulet in going to Breacachadh from Achness, which then scarcely wet my horse's hoofs. A great deal of rain had fallen, however, during Sabbath, and on my return on Monday the rivulet was flooded. I heedlessly entered it, without thinking of the circumstance, but the force of the stream almost immediately carried both horse and rider down with the foaming current into the lake, into which it emptied about thirty yards below, and from which the stout pony only made his escape, with his rider, by swimming about forty yards onwards to the other shore. During the summer months my sister usually went to Ross-shire, not only to visit her sister at Tarbat, but to attend the sacraments, administered at that season of the year almost weekly, by rotation, throughout the district of Easter-Ross and the Black Isle.

I never administered the sacrament to my flock, as there was no accommodation for that purpose at either station, but I regularly catechised and visited in both districts, and, owing to their large extent and the amount of their population, this occupied me five months of the year. A catechist was appointed who officiated in each district, but while these men were themselves pious, and most conscientiously discharged their duties, there were some things decidedly wrong in the system at that time adopted. For example, in Strathnaver the catechist came from another parish where he had his residence, and made his appearance only once a year among the people. In the discharge of his public duties, he collected whole townships together at each respective diet, including ten or fifteen families, and then asked three or four of them merely to repeat each a question of the Shorter Catechism, after which he lectured to them for the remaining time of the meeting. But there was another defect, or rather I might call it a practical abuse of the system, which was exceedingly prevalent in the northern counties. Catechists often held the catechetical charge of three or four parishes at once, solely for the sake of the emoluments, and thus estabished a system of pluralities exactly similar, although on a small scale, to that of the English and Irish establishments.

I shall now mention some of the individuals among my flock at Achness. About the middle of the 18th century there lived a generation of very godly men all over that district, though when I came amongst them but few of their type of Christian character remained. I shall particularly mention William Calder, John MacIan, William Mackay, and Alexander Mackay, as with them I became personally acquainted during my ministry at Achness.

William Calder was a native of Ardclach, Nairnshire, and came to Strathnaver about the year 1786 as a teacher in the service of the Society for Propagating Christian Knowledge. His school was, during the days of my childhood, at the place of Rhiloisk, a pendicle on the east bank of the Naver, about four miles from Achness. After our mother's death, my father sent both my sisters as pupils to his school, boarding in his house. In course of time the Society removed their school from that station, when Mr. Calder, who was then out of employment, went to reside at Tongue. Some years thereafter he was appointed catechist of that parish, and subsequently of Strathnaver, Durness, and Strathhalladale. William Calder was a man of considerable strength of mind. His judgment was solid, his powers of perception clear and comprehensive, and his knowledge of divine things extensive, accurate, and profound. He could express himself with great terseness, both in Gaelic and English, on subjects of Scripture doctrine and Christian experience. But he was chiefly distinguished for his fervent piety; it was a fire ever burning, a light ever shining, a pure limpid stream never ceasing to flow. He was often my guest at Achness, and his conversation was edifying and refreshing. On one occasion he visited, along with me, the sick-bed of a dying woman. He knelt at her bedside and prayed, and words of supplication more suitable, comprehensive, and earnest are rarely heard in such circumstances. His peaceful and peace-making character was often severely tested. A sect existed in those days which, while professing to remain within the pale of the Church of Scotland, at the same time separated itself from its communion and other public ordinances. The founder of this sect was Peter Stewart, who lived in Strathmore of Caithness, but who afterwards, in capacity of catechist, went to reside, first in the parish of Croy, and then in the vicinity of Inverness. Its tenets were: that divine influences were denied to ordinances administered by the ministers of the church on account of their secularity; and that the duty of all, who had in any measure felt the power of divine truth, was to separate themselves from the public ministry of word and ordinances, and to attach themselves to the leaders of the sect, who would read and expound Scripture to them. Those leaders were men of considerable talent; they made a very strict and imposing religious profession, and arrogated to themselves almost exclusively an experimental knowledge of the truth by divine teaching. Their influence among the people was therefore almost paramount, and even the truly pious were in great measure carried away by them. Their influence was promoted by various causes. The public ministry of the Word in that portion of the church was, it must be admitted, in a very declining state, and far from being either vital or efficient. Then, the leaders themselves were too much countenanced by old men of eminent piety and long-standing Christian character, such as John Grant of Strathy, whom I have already mentioned. With this sect William Calder could not fully agree. Their unscriptural and extravagant notion of a church without a stated ministry he decidedly opposed; yet with all of them, whether leaders or followers, who he could believe were walking according to the truth, he lived on terms of Christian amity. It was when he came into contact with such of them as were of a fierce and contentious character that the peaceful spirit of the gospel developed itself in him in all its strength, and, like a warm and plentiful summer shower, extinguished the kindling fire. One of those Separatists, at whose house he called on a certain occasion, fastened on him a keen and angry controversy for giving so much countenance to "graceless ministers" by his attendance at their public sacraments, and he went on with such a reckless strain of abuse as to work himself up into a violent passion. William Calder heard him patiently and answered him not a word, but, seizing a bible which lay on a table, he solemnly asked the divine blessing, sang, read, and prayed. His angry antagonist was subdued and melted even to tears. "Son of peace," said he, throwing himself on his neck and weeping, "while others with their idle tattle would only have supplied fuel to my too hot and angry spirit, you, in the spirit and service of your Master, have calmed and humbled it." Mr. Calder lived to an advanced age, and to almost the last day of his existence he was engaged in his calling. He died at Strathhalladale in 1829, after a very few days' illness. When death approached he addressed these words to his body and his soul: "Now," said he, "you have been long together, peacefully united in the mortal tie. That is now to be dissolved, and you must part. God bless you both, and may you have a happy and a blessed meeting at the resurrection." So saying. he yielded up his spirit.

With John Mackay, or MacIan, I was from childhood intimately acquainted. In personal appearance he was a tall, venerable-looking man. He resided at Scaill in Strathnaver, and was catechist of the Ach-na-h'uaighe district for nearly forty years. It is among my earliest remembrances to have seen him at Kildonan, busy in the little garret, making a pair of leathern gaiters for my father, to whom he was warmly attached. His mind was brought under saving impressions of the truth during the ministry of Mr. Skeldoch* of Farr, a very unpopular man when first settled there, but afterwards a useful and highly-honoured servant of God. John MacIan was warmly attached to an earnest Christian, William Mackay, or "Uilliam Shaoir," as he was usually called from his place of Saor, or Syre, in Strathnaver, whose praise was in all the churches as one of the burning lights of the five northern counties. With this eminent individual John MacIan lived on terms of the closest fellowship. As a catechist John stood at the head of all his contemporaries. He carefully instructed the people in the questions of the Shorter Catechism, taking care that they should repeat them accurately and that, by his judicious explanations, they should fully understand the doctrines stated in them. His favourite subject, however, was faith—the duty of man but the work of God, in its exercises, struggles, trials, triumphs, and fruits; and he had much tenderness and sympathy with those who, he knew, had "a root of true faith in them without being aware of it themselves."

* Mr. John Skeldoch was translated from Kilmonivaig, Inverness-shire, to Farr on 18th July, 1734; he died 26th June, 1753, in the 29th year of his ministry. His widow, who survived him 41 years, died at the age of 100.—ED.

The people of Achness received me as their pastor on John's recommendation. After the people were turned out of the Strath in 1819, John MacIan retired to a small and almost ruinous hovel on the heights of Kildonan at a place called Bad-an-t'sheobhaig. He, along with others, was offered a lot of land at the mouth of the Naver, but he preferred to end his days at this lonely spot, chiefly that he might be buried in the adjacent cemetery of Achanneccan, with which he had solemn associations. His wish was granted, and when he died in 1820, at the age of 84, his mortal remains were laid as he had desired.

William Mackay, commonly called Achoul, from the farm on the banks of Loch Naver, which he and his progenitors of the Clan Abrach had for many generations possessed, was another distinguished member of my congregation at Achness. If John MacIan was remarkable for the strength, William Achoul was none the less so for the childlike simplicity, of his faith. When a very young man he had deep convictions of sin, by which he lost all his peace of mind and even his sleep at night. But one evening, after humble prostration, Christ was revealed to him. "He promised to save me, I took Him at his word, and He has not allowed me once to doubt Him, not even for an hour, and that is sixty years ago." In recounting to me the incidents of his life, he said that he was about eighteen years of age during the rebellion of 1745. He had been sent on some errand to Dunrobin Castle, and, being permitted to look into the room where the Countess of Sutherland sat, entertaining two of her noble relatives who were of the prince's party, he noticed one of them (he was told it was Lord Elcho) with a stick in his hand attempting to demolish a print of the elector of Hanover which hung upon the wall. He also heard the firing of the musketry in the skirmish at the Little-ferry. He was turned out of his hereditary farm of Achoul when the whole district on the south side of Loch Naver was let to Marshall and Atkinson, from Northumberland, for a sheep-grazing by Campbell of Crombie, factor on the Sutherland estate from 1810 to 1812. William Achoul took a small farm afterwards on the north bank of the loch at Grumbeg. There his wife died, and he laid her lifeless remains in the churchyard at Achness. As he took his last look of the rapidly disappearing coffin, "Well Janet," said he, "the Countess of Sutherland can never flit you any more." Had he lived to hear of the dreadful doings at the reconstruction of Dornoch Cathedral, by the orders of this heartless woman, he might not have been so sure that even in her narrow house his Janet was altogether beyond another summons of removal from the same ruthless hand. His eldest daughter was married to a young man from Aberdeenshire, who had come to Achness as a teacher for the Christian Knowledge Society. He had boarded at Achoul in William Mackay's house, and, though he knew not a word of Gaelic, he noticed and was deeply impressed with the warm and unsophisticated piety of his host. He applied himself to the task of acquiring the Gaelic tongue with the whole energies of a highly-gifted mind. He also made daily progress in the Christian life, and engaged in prayer alternately with his father-in-law in the family and at fellowship-meetings. The teacher studied under the excellent Alexander Urquhart of Rogart, who was then stationed at Achness, and rapidly acquired the knowledge of Latin and Greek, thus preparing himself for the University. He was well on in life when he entered King's College, passing through the curriculum there, and studying for three sessions at the Hall, when he was licensed by the Presbytery of Tongue to preach the gospel. The individual thus prepared by God in circumstances of comparative obscurity was none other than the late Mr. John Robertson, minister of Kingussie in Badenoch, a man who became a most distinguished ornament of the Scottish Church. Soon after he was licensed to preach he was appointed to the mission at Berriedale, afterwards to the Chapel of Ease in Rothesay, and ultimately, in 1810, was settled minister of Kingussie, where he closed his life 4th March, 1825, aged 68 years. Old William Achoul lived to a patriarchal age. When turned out again in 1819 he went with a daughter and her husband, with whom he had lived at Grumbeg, to reside near Wick, where he died at the age of 101.

Alexander Mackay, or Alastair Taillear, as he was usually called, and his brother Murdoch, were among my first acquaintances. On commencing my ministry at Achness Alastair lived at Trudarscaig, but when expelled from thence he lived at Farr. He was one of the first of those pious men to whom I freely communicated the doubts and perplexities of my mind in regard to my personal knowledge of divine truth, and to the office and calling of the ministry. He dealt both tenderly and faithfully with me. His brother Murdoch went to Caithness, where he was employed as a catechist in the parish of Latheron.

I may also record my reminiscences of the clergy and laity of my acquaintance while I ministered at Achness.

Mr. David Mackenzie, minister of Farr, was my immediate predecessor at Achness, previous to his settlement in that parish in 1815. He was the eldest son of Hugh Mackenzie, tacksman of Meikle-Creich, a native of Ross-shire, the elder brother of Mr. William Mackenzie, minister of Tongue. Hugh Mackenzie was a man of eminent piety. His repeated failures as a farmer, however, by which he injured the temporal interests and tried not a little the patience of his best friends, obscured what would otherwise have been a very brilliant Christian character. In his latter days he lived in poverty at the village of Spinningdale, where his son David wrought as a day-labourer in the factory, and in that capacity had arrived at the years of manhood before he thought of directing his views to the ministry. His younger brother Hugh had lived with his uncle at Tongue, and by him been educated and sent to college. David was persuaded by his uncle to prepare himself also for college. I recollect meeting him once at Lairg manse, when he communicated to me his uncle's intentions. He did not then appear to entertain very sanguine hopes of ultimate success, as he lacked early literary training. He, however, made the attempt, and passing through College and Hall, he was licensed to preach by the Presbytery of Tongue in 1812, and was soon after appointed to Achness. Of him and his brother I have already made mention. His marriage to his cousin, Barbara Gordon, took place a year after his settlement at Farr. As a preacher, he could express himself in Gaelic with much readiness and accuracy, while his views of Divine truth were sound and scriptural.*

Dr. Hugh Mackenzie, during my stay at Achness, resided constantly at Tongue manse. When the parish of Assyut became vacant, by the translation of Mr. MacGillivray to Lairg, he was presented by the patron to the living, and, on the demise of Mr. Walter Ross, he was presented to the parish of Clyne in 1825. I remember being present on that occasion. He was inducted into the charge by Mr. Angus Kennedy of Dornoch, who preached in English, while the Gaelic sermon was preached by my father's successor at Kildonan, Mr. James Campbell. Dr. Mackenzie married first his cousin Nelly, who died at Assynt, and afterwards Miss Mackenzie of Old Aberdeen. He had not been many years in Clyne when, by the recommendation of Mr. George Sinclair of Ulbster, he was, in 1828, on the death of Mr. Macdougall of Killin, in Perthshire, presented to that parish. Not long after, as he was returning home in his gig from Taymouth Castle, on the evening of a communion fast-day, the horse took fright, when not far from the manse, and ran off. He was thrown violently out, and expired soon after he had been brought home. Dr. Hugh Mackenzie was a man of gentlemanly and winning manners, he was well-educated and most accomplished in ancient and modern learning, and of a very amiable disposition. His pulpit ministrations were clear expositions of Scripture doctrine, and specimens of finished composition both in English and Gaelic.

Mr. Hugh Mackay Mackenzie, the only son of the minister of Tongue, was assistant to his father when I was at Achness. He laboured most assiduously in the pastoral office; but his health was at all times so very indifferent that his father, then near eighty years of age, seemed rather the assistant than his son. Mr. Hugh Mackenzie married his cousin Mrs. Russel, a widow of great sense and prudence, who had seen much good society, and was of a very amiable disposition. The only fruit of the marriage was a son, who was named after his venerable grandfather William.†

Mr. William Findlater, minister of Durness, son-in-law and immediate successor of Mr. Thomson, I knew very imperfectly. He was the eldest son of the eminent Robert Findlater of Drummond, Ross-shire. His younger brother Robert was then missionary-minister of Loch Tay-side. Mr. William Findlater married Mr. Thomson's youngest daughter, a very handsome woman. This was not a happy marriage; but he found it turn to his spiritual advantage in the decided progress which, through manifold afflictions, he was enabled to make in the Christian life.‡

---

* Died 24th Feb., 1868, aged 85 years.—ED.

† Mr. William Mackenzie was ordained colleague and successor to his father in the Free Church at Tongue. He died in 1845, within a month of the death of his father, who had been minister for forty-nine years. (See an affecting description of "the two Mackenzies of Tongue," by Dr. Thomas Guthrie in his *Memoirs.*)—ED.

‡ Mr. William Findlater retired from pastoral work in 1865, and died at Tain, 29th June, 1869, in the eighty-sixth year of his age and sixty-second of his ministry.

The only two of my early clerical acquaintances hitherto unnamed are Mr. Murdoch Cameron, minister of Criech, and Mr. Alexander MacPherson, minister of Golspie. Mr. Cameron was the immediate successor of worthy Mr. Renny, after having been for some years his assistant. I have a distinct recollection of his induction. The people, to a man, were opposed to him, and his settlement was one of those violent ones which so much disgraced the Established Church at that period. The parishioners rose *en masse*, and barred the church against the presbytery, so that the Sutherland Volunteers, under the command of Captain Kenneth Mackay of Torboll, were called out to keep the peace. In the riot which ensued, Captain Mackay got his sword, which he held naked in his hand, shivered to pieces by stones thrown at him by an old woman over seventy years of age. The people never afterwards attended Mr. Cameron's ministry, but assembled at the rock of Migdol, and on the banks of the lake, to hear old Hugh Mackenzie already mentioned. Mr. Cameron tried to make the best of it, by employing, on communion occasions, the most popular and eminent ministers of the church who could be found in the north. He still lives, very old, very useless, but very wealthy.*

Mr. Alexander MacPherson, minister of Golspie, was a native of Ross-shire, and was the immediate successor of Mr. William Keith. Previous to his settlement, he was for some years rector of Tain Academy. He there married Harriet, second daughter of Donald Matheson of Shiness. She died before his induction to Golspie. The people of that parish petitioned the patrons for me, but they met with a peremptory refusal; and MacPherson, on the application of his wife's uncle, John Mackay of Rockfield, was appointed to the charge. He had not been many years there, however, when, seized with a morbid melancholy, he resigned his charge, and retired to his native parish. Donald Ross, the present minister of Loth, was presented by the patrons; but, just as he was about to be inducted by the presbytery, Mr. MacPherson came back upon them, and entered a protest against the proceedings. The case was ultimately carried to the General Assembly, and he was restored to his pastoral office. In creed Mr. MacPherson was an Arminian, and as a preacher was cold and uninteresting.†

I may dismiss my acquaintances among the laity in a few words. Captain John Mackay, of an infantry regiment, then lived at Syre, in Strathnaver. He was the only son of the eminently pious William Mackay by his first marriage. He had seen much service in the army abroad during the first of the Spanish campaigns, and when he retired on half-pay he came to reside in his native parish. He was appointed factor for Strathnaver by the Marquis of Stafford, with a salary of

He was a man of cultivated literary taste, faithful and refined as a preacher of the gospel. He wrote a memoir of his brother Robert, one of the ministers of Inverness.—ED.

* Mr. Cameron died 13th December, 1853, in the fifty-fifth year of his ministry. —ED.

† He afterwards had D.D. conferred upon him by Aberdeen University, and died in 1861, aged eighty years.—ED.

£120, which, combined with his half-pay, afforded him in that sequestrated spot a comfortable income. His father's house was then occupied by his widow and her family—two sons and a daughter. When he got his appointment as factor he built a neat addition to the cottage in which his step-mother resided. His half-brothers he sent to the West Indies. His eldest sister was married, a year or two before I came to Achness, to John Mackintosh, a native of Durness, of the Reay Fencibles. He lived at Syre, and was catechist of one of the districts of Latheron in Caithness, and of the parish of Daviot in Inverness-shire. He was a fluent and elegant speaker in Gaelic, and the intimate associate of Peter Stewart, one of the most violent of the Separatists. Captain Mackay's sister was his second wife. Her brother procured for them a good small farm in his immediate neighbourhood, but it was at the expense of turning out an infirm old man, Alexander Mackay, married to a sister of Thomas Breacachadh. This was, however, the only harsh thing which I knew Captain Mackay to do whilst he held the office. He was a warm-hearted and most gentle-manly man, and, residing as I was in his immediate neighbourhood, I very much enjoyed his society. He often refreshed me with reminiscences of his eminent father.

After the people of Strathnaver were cleared out to make way for the sheep in 1819, Captain Mackay was appointed factor for Strathy, in the north-east of the parish of Farr towards the shore. He relinquished this office in favour of Lieutenant Mackenzie, who married his second sister, and he himself went to America. When in Aberdeen in 1820 I saw him so far on his way. His errand thither was to get married. Many years previously he was with his regiment near Halifax, Nova Scotia, and when there became acquainted with a young lady, daughter of a wealthy merchant. They conceived a mutual attachment, and were to be married; but her father forbade the union on the ground of the young man's comparative poverty. The lady, however, refused to marry any other, and in course of time her father died, leaving to his only child his whole fortune. Although at the time of his death she was no longer young, yet she did not forget her youthful attachment. She wrote accordingly to a friend of hers in Scotland, making enquiries about Captain Mackay, and adding that, if he were unmarried and remembered her, she was unmarried and had not forgotten him. Captain Mackay went to America, was married to the lady, lived in great affluence, and became a member of the Provincial Parliament; but his health suddenly gave way, and he died in 1823. His widow long survived him, and, with her cordial con-currence, considerable sums of money were, in accordance with his will, transmitted from time to time to his relatives in Strathnaver.

My next neighbour, and often my kind entertainer, was Robert Gordon, tacksman of Langdale. As already mentioned, this gentleman was married to the eldest daughter of Mr. William Mackenzie of Tongue, the fruit of their marriage being an only daughter, Barbara, who married Mr. David Mackenzie, minister of Farr. Mr. Gordon possessed the farm of Langdale not only from the proprietor of the soil, but also from his own ancestors, who were tacksmen or wadsetters thereof. His remote ancestor was one of the Gordons, who were placed there by the Earl of Sutherland when he purchased the lands of Strath-naver from Donald, first Lord Reay. The Robert Gordon of my time was the last of his race. He was a kind old man, intimately acquainted with the simple annals of the church in times past. In youth he had known Mr. George Munro of Farr and all the worthies of the Reay country. He had stored in his memory all their sayings and doings, their views of Divine truth, and their remarkable experiences. His house, a rustic cottage, stood on a fairy-like knowe, on the banks of the Naver, and was freely open to all comers of every rank. His farm was parcelled out among a number of sub-tenants, to whom he granted every indulgence. He had a brother and sister; the former had pre-deceased him, and the latter kept house for him while I was in the district. His wife died soon after the birth of their only child. She was as much distinguished for her personal attractions as for her piety. For some time before her death she was rather unhappy; unbelief had clouded her past experiences of grace and her hope of glory. William Mackay of Syre was her constant visitor during her illness, and as the end approached he wrestled earnestly in prayer on her behalf. At last the light broke in upon her soul, and she was enabled fully to rejoice in the hope of the glory of God. Triumphantly pointing upwards and looking her Christian friend steadfastly in the face, with a smile of joy she yielded up her spirit to Him who gave it. Mr. Gordon of Langdale died a widower. When with the rest of the people, he was turned out of his ancestral home, he went to reside at Farr manse, where, after a lingering illness, he died a few years after.

In the Kildonan district of my mission lived also some individuals worthy of special mention.

Adam Gordon was tacksman of Griamachdary, and a shrewd, worldly-wise man. He was of the same age as my father, and had a throng family of sons and daughters. His eldest son John rose to the rank of major in the army, was thrice married, was acquainted with the late Duke of Kent, and thus got commissions for his three brothers, William, Adam, and Thomas. Adam Gordon, during my residence at Achness, got a life-rent of his farm. He and his wife lived in the exercise of the most unbounded hospitality, and at the same time economised so as to realise a good deal of money. Their eldest daughter Anne was married to John Mackay from Strathhalladale, who had come to reside with his father-in-law at Griamachdary. John Mackay was one of my father's elders—a kind-hearted and excellent man. He also had a numerous family, and one of his daughters, afterwards mar-ried to Charles Gordon, merchant at Thurso, resided with my sister at Achness. John Mackay now holds the small farm of Clyne-Milton, parish of Clyne. Adam Gordon's second daughter May was married. upwards of thirty years ago, to Joseph Mackay, second son of Angus Mackay, tenant at Dyke, Strathhalladale. By his brother-in-law's interest with the Duke of Kent, he got a commission in the army, went on foreign service, and was present at the battle of Waterloo. He returned on half-pay to reside at Griamachdary with his family about the end of the year 1815. Possessed of considerable acuteness, and a

ready speaker in his native tongue, he joined the party of the Separatists, or Stewartites, and became one of their most violent members.
He now lives in the parish of Reay, in Caithness.

Adam Gordon's third daughter Margaret I married to Lieutenant
Alexander Grant during the last year of my ministry at Achness.
Adam Gordon survived my father for some years. He and his wife
are buried at Kildonan.*

David Ross, the miller at Claggan in Strathbeg, was the only son of
Mr. John Ross, minister of Kildonan,† the immediate predecessor of
Mr. William Keith. His mother was the widow of Gunn MacSheumais
who had resided at Badenloch, which he had rented, or held as wadset,
from the Earl of Sutherland. MacSheumais had a number of sons,
who all went into the army and died in action. Mr. John Ross married
the widow, and the whole family then came to reside at Kildonan
manse. They were all very extravagant, however, and nearly ruined
Mr. Ross in worldly circumstances. By the decease of all her sons by
MacSheumais, the direct line of the Clan Gunn MacSheumais became
extinct. Mr. John Ross had two children, David and Catherine. Kate
Ross married David Gunn, eldest son of Robert Gunn of Achaneccan,
who, after the death of his wife's half-brothers, by the Highland law,
succeeded to the chieftainship of the Clan Gunn. David Gunn, however, never laid claim to the honours. He was an eminently pious
man; and leaving the honours of this world to be usurped by Hector
Gunn at Thurso, he himself humbly but ardently aspired after the
honours which came from above. During my time at Achness, he
lived at Achaneccan, but afterwards went to reside in Caithness-shire,
where he died in 1827. David Ross in early youth entered the army as
a private soldier, and being a young man of great promise and of good
abilities, he soon rose from the ranks and had every prospect of success
in the military profession. After his father's death, however, those
who had charge of him bought him out of the army and brought him
home to settle on a small farm. He married the daughter of a substantial tenant, with whom he got wealth of farm stock, thus renouncing
all prospect of the honours and comforts of social position. His wife
could not speak a word of English, but was an amiable and kind
woman, and she had a large family of sons and daughters. Their eldest
son went to America as a teacher. He himself was an acute and intelligent man. I have frequently been his guest during my ministerial
perambulations. He had an abundant store of the original poetry and
traditions of his native soil. He read a good deal also, chiefly the old
Scottish divines and ecclesiastical historians, of which he had very old
folio copies, the remains of his father's library. After the clearance in
1819, he went with his family to the parish of Rogart, and became
ground-officer to the proprietor. He still lives at an advanced age.
A near neighbour of his, Thomas Gordon, then resided at the place of

* The late Lord Gordon was also a descendant.—Ed.

† Mr. John Ross was ordained missionary at Farr 26th September, 1759, and
admitted minister of Kildonan 18th November, 1761; he died 28th March, 1775, in
the forty-second year of his age and sixteenth of his ministry. He succeeded in
Kildonan Mr. Hugh Ross, who died in 1761 after a ministry of six years.—Ed.

Torghordston. He was a decided Christian of great simplicity, far advanced in life. He had a grown-up family, who persuaded him to accompany them to America.

Samuel Matheson lived at Badenloch. He was second son of Donald Matheson at Kinbrace, catechist of the upper part of the parish of Kildonan during the ministry of Mr Hugh Ross, predecessor of Mr. John Ross. Donald Matheson was a very distinguished Christian in his day. He was also a poet, and composed a number of spiritual songs, which his son Samuel printed and circulated. Donald Matheson was the contemporary of Rob Donn; and the character of Donald's poetry may best be understood by Rob Donn's remark upon it. They met, it is said, at a friend's house, and each sang one of his own songs. When they had concluded, Donald submitted his song to the judgment of the Reay Country bard. "Donald," answered Rob, "there is more of poetry in my song, and more of piety in yours." Matheson lived to an advanced age. He was a man of much piety, but was also diligent in his calling of cattle-dealing. He had two sons, Hugh and Samuel. The former lived at Badenloch, and was a deeply-exercised Christian. Samuel was also a man of reputed piety, but he associated with the Separatists. His wife was the daughter of a pious widow who first resided at Rhimisdale in Kildonan, and afterwards at Ceann-na-coille in Strathnaver. Samuel Matheson was also a self-taught mediciner and surgeon, and in many cases was most miraculously successful. He died at Griamachdary in 1829.

Charles Gordon and his wife, of whom mention has already been made, then resided at Ach-na-moine. Mrs. Gordon was universally esteemed; so, however, was not he altogether. He had some feud or other on his hands every day of the year. His two brothers, Hugh and Adam, resided with him, as well as two of his sisters. Hugh was an ensign in the army, retired on half-pay. After staying here some time on his return, he took the farm of Bad'chlamhain, and first married his cousin, a daughter of Gordon of Innis-verry, parish of Tongue. He married a second time, and took a farm in Strathhalladale, where he died of paralysis in 1824. Adam, the other brother, went to America. The second sister married a man from the parish of Clyne. After I had performed the ceremony, my sister and I were guests at their wedding, where the feasting was kept up for two days.

One Lieutenant Gunn lived at Ach-na-h'uaighe. He held the place in lease from the proprietor for nineteen years, which commenced four or five years before I came to Achness. He married a Miss Bruce of Thurso, a woman of colour, daughter of Mr. Harry Bruce, a West Indian planter, by whom he got some money, which was soon dissipated. They had a large family. After the dispersion of the tenantry in 1819, Gunn, for a compensation, resigned his lease and went to reside, first at Thurso, and afterwards at Balfruch, parish of Croy, which he held from Davidson of Cantray. He died at Inverness in 1844.

There were a few individuals of whom I have most pleasing recollections, but who resided beyond the limits of my mission. The most distinguished as a Christian was Mrs. Mackay of Sheggira, or of Cape

Wrath, as she was usually designated, the place of Sheggira being in the immediate vicinity of that far-famed northern headland. Her maiden name was MacDiarmid, and she was a native of Argyleshire. Her husband was a respectable man, a native of the Reay Country, but much her inferior in many ways. She was naturally a superior woman, quick in apprehension and particularly ready in repartee, especially so when provoked by ungodly taunts and sneers. She was above all things, however, distinguished for the vitality of her Christian character. She was usually designated "the woman of the great faith" (bean a chreidimh mhòir), a character which, as she once said to me, she did not wish to take from others, nor even to realise for herself. I observed that a great God was justly entitled to great faith on our part on account of the greatness of His own truth and of His promises. "True," said she, "but my desire is only to be enabled ever to exercise a little faith on a great God." "How so?" said I. She answered, "Because I need to behold that greatness not in my faith, but in Himself." She was a constant attendant upon public ordinances. She had resolved towards the close of her life, when she felt her strength, from growing infirmity, unequal to long journeys on foot, to leave the Reay Country, and to take up her residence in the parish of Redcastle, to be, as she said, in her declining years under "the latter rain," meaning the ministry of Mr. John Kennedy, Killearnan. This was not God's appointment for her, however. The late Duchess of Sutherland ever regarded those really influenced by the truth with the deepest veneration. On one of her summer rambles in the Reay Country, Mrs. Mackay was introduced to her at Tongue, and the interview much impressed the Duchess in favour of her new acquaintance. As a mark of her esteem, she granted to Mrs. Mackay and to her husband a free liferent of the house and lot of land which they occupied in Melness, parish of Tongue. For some years before her death, the health of this excellent woman became feeble, till, at last, she was constantly confined to her bed-room. The heavy tidings of Mr. Kennedy's sudden and unexpected death proved a great shock to her, and in the course of a month or two thereafter she was numbered among the "blessed dead who die in the Lord."

Another acquaintance of this period was the late worthy Charles Gordon of Ribigill, Strathnaver. Although he did not belong to the mission district of the Strath, yet he was not unfrequently a hearer on Sabbath, and a welcome and much-esteemed associate of our fellowship meetings. I have often met him on communion occasions throughout the county. His personal appearance commanded respect, and his views of divine truth were sound and experimental, expressed on all occasions with great perspicuity and force. He was a near relative of the Gordons of Clerkhill, and had himself a numerous family of sons and daughters by each of his wives, for he was thrice married. Most of his family, however, as well as his last wife, preceded him to the grave. He died in 1824.

Mrs. Mackay of Skerray was one of my earliest acquaintances. I have already mentioned her and her husband as guests at Kildonan during the days of my childhood. She lost her husband many years before I went to college. My father and she being related, through the Kirtomy family of the Mackays, a friendly intercourse was always kept up between us, and I have been a guest at her house both before I went to Achness and very frequently afterwards. She had three sons and two daughters. Her eldest son Hugh attended college at Aberdeen. About the time I was licensed, and during his second session at college, he was seized with a pulmonary complaint, which made such rapid and alarming progress that he hastened home in the hope of recovering in his native air. He arrived by sea, accompanied by his tutor, but on the very evening that he landed at Brora he expired. His remains were conveyed to the family burying-place at Torrisdale. Mrs. Mackay's second son took charge of the farm of Skerray after his brother's death. When, in course of time, the estate of Reay was purchased by the Stafford family, the place of Skerray was divided into a number of small lots for the accommodation of fishermen. James Mackay, along with a friend, came in 1825 on a visit to Ross-shire in quest of a farm, and they both spent a night in my house in Resolis. Poor James, about a year afterwards, was attacked by the same complaint which had proved fatal to his brother, and died after a lingering illness. His younger sister had also died of consumption some years before. The eldest daughter married a Lieutenant Mackenzie, and they reside at Borgie on the river of Torrisdale. The youngest son, who was quite a youth when I came to Achness, went at an early age to America. Mrs. Mackay's tutor I was intimately acquainted with. His name was Hugh MacLeod. His father, Robert MacLeod, was a native of Assyut, but then was resident in the parish of Durness, an eminently pious man and one of the quaintest and most original of speakers at a fellowship meeting, whether in prayer or in conference. The son Hugh was a very different man, and though he afterwards entered the ministry at Rosehall, he fell into habits of intemperance, which necessitated his going first to Canada and then to the West Indies, where he died. Mrs. Mackay of Skerray was a pious woman, and lived in habits of strictest Christian intimacy with those who were most distinguished for their spiritual attainments. She, perhaps, overmuch imbued her conversation with religious sentimentalism, and often mistook the marvellous or the romantic for the higher walks of spirituality. Whilst she sincerely wished to be the companion of those only who feared God, she was not a little ambitious also of being the fine lady among them. Mrs. Mackay is still alive at Skerray, having attained to very advanced age.·

It was while my sister Elizabeth and I were residing at Achness that we first became acquainted with Mr. Finlay Cook, minister of Reay. I had met him at Grimachdary a few months before, and frequently afterwards on parochial communion occasions at Farr. He came to Achness on a visit to see my sister, who, in little more than a year after, became his wife. He was a native of Arran, and when a young man was brought to the knowledge of the truth under the ministry of Mr. MacBride of Kilmory, a minister of great eminence and usefulness in that part of the country. Mr. Cook had been one of the most thoughtless, light-headed young men in the island; indeed, he was in the act of jibing and mocking the venerable servant of God, in his pew in the church, when the arrows of Divine truth smote him. From that momentous hour he ceased to mock and began to pray. He afterwards attended college, but his progress in literature was meagre, owing to the want of early training. Not so, however, his growth in grace. It was steady and prosperous, and it advanced and consolidated under the preaching of Dr. John Love, whom he heard during his attendance at the Glasgow University. When licensed to preach Mr. Cook was appointed lecturer to the Highlanders at the Lanark Mills by that strange visionary Robert Owen. From thence he came to be missionary-minister of Dirlot in Caithness. I shall recur to him later on.

It was towards the close of 1816 that Dr. Bethune of Dornoch died. I had frequently met with him since my ordination during sacramental occasions and at his daughter's house at Drummuigh, parish of Golspie. His last illness was very short. At his burial the parishioners held a meeting in order to adopt measures for procuring a successor, but the patrons at that time never encouraged nor countenanced such measures on the part of the people. A petition in my favour was drawn up and cordially signed, but in answer they were haughtily informed that the patrons had already elected a minister for the parish; as to the object of the popular choice, Lady Stafford conceived that he had so many patrons among the people as not to stand in need of any provision which she had in her power to extend to him. I knew nothing of this at the time, not having been invited to the funeral, The patrons' nominee for Dornoch was my near relative, Mr. Angus Kennedy, then of Lairg. He was the son of my father's second sister Mary, whom, with her husband Mr. Donald Kennedy of Kishorn, I have already named.

Mr. Angus Kennedy was born in 1769, and when a mere lad he came to visit my father at Kildonan. By dint of hard study and unwearied application he fitted himself for college, became schoolmaster at Lochalsh, and was licensed to preach in 1801 by the Presbytery of Lochcarron. His first charge as a minister was the assistantship at Lairg. Mr. Thomas Mackay had, for some years before, been entirely confined to his room, and from the time he was first laid aside had employed several assistants in succession. On the death of Mr. Mackay in 1803 Mr. Kennedy was appointed in 1804 as his successor, and he laboured with such efficiency and zeal as very much to attach the parishioners to his person and ministry. He had received his first religious impressions under the eminent Mr. Lachlan Mackenzie of Lochcarron. As a preacher he was remarkable more for the strength of his judgment and shrewd common sense than for the gifts and graces of the ministerial office. The people of Dornoch did not at first relish his ministrations, although his venerable age, his genuine piety, and his spotless, consistent life, have almost entirely eradicated their prejudices. He still lives at Dornoch at the age of seventy-six.[*]

[*] Mr. Angus Kennedy died 22nd June, 1855, aged 86, in the 53 year of his ministry. His son, Mr. George Rainy Kennedy, was ordained as his assistant and successor, 23rd Nov., 1837, and has attained to the 50th year of a faithful and valued ministry.—ED.

CHAPTER XVI.

THE SUTHERLAND CLEARANCE OF 1819.

HE period of my ministry at Achness, however, was drawing fast to its close. The reckless lordly proprietors had resolved upon the expulsion of their long-standing and much-attached tenantry from their widely-extended estates, and the Sutherland Clearance of 1819 was not only the climax of their system of oppression for many years before, but the extinction of the last remnant of the ancient Highland peasantry in the north. As violent tempests send out before them many a deep and sullen roar, so did the advancing storm give notice of its approach by various single acts of oppression. I can yet recall to memory the deep and thrilling sensation which I experienced, as I sat at the fireside in my rude, little parlour at Achness, when the tidings of the meditated removal of my poor flock first reached me from head-quarters. It might be about the beginning of October, 1818. A tenant from the middle of the Strath had been to Rhives, the residence of Mr. Young, the commissioner, paying his rent. He was informed, and authorised to tell his neighbours, that the rent for the half-year, ending in May, 1819, would not be demanded, as it was determined to lay the districts of Strathnaver and Upper Kildonan under sheep. This intelligence when first announced was indignantly discredited by the people. Notwithstanding their knowledge of former clearances they clung to the hope that the "Ban-mhorair-Chatta" would not give her consent to the warning as issued by her subordinates, and thus deprive herself of her people, as truly a part of her noble inheritance as were her broad acres. But the course of a few weeks soon undeceived them. Summonses of ejectment were issued and despatched all over the district. These must have amounted to upwards of a thousand, as the population of the Mission alone was 1600 souls, and many more than those of the Mission were ejected. The summonses were distributed with the utmost preciseness. They were handed in at every house and hovel alike, be the occupiers of them who or what they might—minister, catechist, or elder, tenant, or sub-tenant, out-servant or cottar—all were made to feel the irresponsible power of the proprietor. The enormous amount of citations might also be accounted for by the fact that Mr. Peter Sellar had a threefold personal interest in the whole matter. He was, in the first place, factor on the Sutherland estate at the time; then, he was law agent for the proprietors; and, lastly, the lessee or tacksman of more than a third of the country to be cleared of its inhabitants. It may easily be conceived how such a three-plied cord of worldly interest would bind him over to greater rigour, and even atrocity, in executing the orders of his superiors on the wretched people among whom he was thus let loose

like a beast of prey. But the effects produced by these decided measures I now distinctly remember. Having myself, in common with
the rest of my people, received one of these notices, I resolved that, at
the ensuing term of Martinmas, I would remove from Achness, and go
once more permanently to reside under my father's roof, although I
would at the same time continue the punctual discharge of my pastoral
duties among the people till they also should be removed. I could not
but regard the summoning of the minister as tantamount to the putting
down of the ministration of the word and ordinances of religion in that
part of the country. And, indeed, it is a fact that, although this desolate district is still occupied by shepherds, no provision has, since that
time, been made for their spiritual wants. I left Achness, therefore,
about the middle of November, 1818, sold my cow at the Ardgay market, and got my furniture conveyed to Kildonan by my father's horses
and my own. The people received the legal warning to leave for ever
the homes of their fathers with a sort of stupor—that apparent indifference which is often the external aspect of intense feeling. As they
began, however, to awaken from the stunning effects of this first intimation, their feelings found vent, and I was much struck with the
different ways in which they expressed their sentiments. The truly
pious acknowledged the mighty hand of God in the matter. In their
prayers and religious conferences not a solitary expression could be
heard indicative of anger or vindictiveness, but in the sight of God
they humbled themselves, and received the chastisement at His hand.
Those, however, who were strangers to such exalted and ennobling
impressions of the gospel breathed deep and muttered curses on the
heads of the persons who subjected them to such treatment. The more
reckless portion of them fully realised the character of the impenitent
in all ages, and indulged in the most culpable excesses, even while this
divine punishment was still suspended over them. These last, however,
were very few in number—not more than a dozen. To my poor and
defenceless flock the dark hour of trial came at last in right earnest.
It was in the month of April, and about the middle of it, that they
were all—man, woman, and child—from the heights of Farr to the
mouth of the Naver, on one day, to quit their tenements and go—many
of them knew not whither. For a few, some miserable patches of
ground along the shores were doled out as lots, without aught in the
shape of the poorest hut to shelter them. Upon these lots it was
intended that they should build houses at their own expense, and cultivate the ground, at the same time occupying themselves as fishermen,
although the great majority of them had never set foot on a boat in
their lives. Thither, therefore, they were driven at a week's warning.
As for the rest, most of them knew not whither to go, unless their
neighbours on the shore provided them with a temporary shelter; for,
on the day of their removal, they would not be allowed to remain, even
on the bleakest moor, and in the open air, for a distance of twenty miles
around.

On the Sabbath, a fortnight previous to the fated day, I preached
my valedictory sermon in Achness, and the Sabbath thereafter at Ach-
na-h'uiaghe. Both occasions were felt, by myself and by the people

from the oldest to the youngest, to be among the bitterest and most overwhelming experiences of our lives. In Strathnaver we assembled, for the last time, at the place of Langdale, where I had frequently preached before, on a beautiful green sward overhung by Robert Gordon's antique, romantic little cottage on an eminence close beside us. The still-flowing waters of the Naver swept past us a few yards to the eastward. The Sabbath morning was unusually fine, and mountain, hill, and dale, water and woodland, among which we had so long dwelt, and with which all our associations of "home" and "native land" were so fondly linked, appeared to unite their attractions to bid us farewell. My preparations for the pulpit had always cost me much anxiety, but in view of this sore scene of parting they caused me pain almost beyond endurance. I selected a text which had a pointed reference to the peculiarity of our circumstances, but my difficulty was how to restrain my feelings till I should illustrate and enforce the great truths which it involved with reference to eternity. The service began. The very aspect of the congregation was of itself a sermon, and a most impressive one. Old Achoul sat right opposite to me. As my eye fell upon his venerable countenance, bearing the impress of eighty-seven winters, I was deeply affected, and could scarcely articulate the psalm. I preached and the people listened, but every sentence uttered and heard was in opposition to the tide of our natural feelings, which, setting in against us, mounted at every step of our progress higher and higher. At last all restraints were compelled to give way. The preacher ceased to speak, the people to listen. All lifted up their voices and wept, mingling their tears together. It was indeed the place of parting, and the hour. The greater number parted never again to behold each other in the land of the living. My adieu to the people of Ach-na-h'uaighe was scarcely less affecting, although somewhat alleviated by the consideration that I had the prospect of ministering still to those among them who had leases of their farms, and whom Mr. Sellar, the factor and law-agent, had no power to remove.

The middle of the week brought on the day of the Strathnaver Clearance (1819). It was a Tuesday. At an early hour of that day Mr. Sellar, accompanied by the Fiscal, and escorted by a strong body of constables, sheriff-officers and others, commenced work at Grummore, the first inhabited township to the west of the Achness district. Their plan of operations was to clear the cottages of their inmates, giving them about half-an-hour to pack up and carry off their furniture, and then set the cottages on fire. To this plan they ruthlessly adhered, without the slightest regard to any obstacle that might arise while carrying it into execution.

At Grumbeg lived a soldier's widow, Henny Munro. She had followed her husband in all his campaigns, marches and battles, in Sicily and in Spain. Whether his death was on the field of battle, or the result of fever or fatigue, I forget; but his faithful helpmeet attended him to his last hour, and, when his spirit fled, closed his eyes, and followed his remains to their last resting-place. After his death she returned to Grumbeg, the place of her nativity, and, as she was utterly destitute of any means of support, she was affectionately received by her friends, who built her a small cottage and gave her a cow and grass for it. The din of arms, orders and counter-orders from head-quarters, marchings and counter-marchings and pitched battles, retreats and advances, were the leading and nearly unceasing subjects of her winter evening conversations. She was a joyous, cheery old creature; so inoffensive, moreover, and so contented, and brimful of good-will that all who got acquainted with old Henny Munro could only desire to do her a good turn, were it merely for the warm and hearty expressions of gratitude with which it was received. Surely the factor and his followers did personally not know old Henny, or they could not have treated her as they did. After the cottages at Grummore were emptied of their inmates, and roofs and rafters had been lighted up into one red blaze, Mr. Sellar and his iron-hearted attendants approached the residence of the soldier's widow. Henny stood up to plead for her furniture—the coarsest and most valueless that well could be, but still her earthly all. She first asked that, as her neighbours were so occupied with their own furniture, hers might be allowed to remain till they should be free to remove it for her. This request was curtly refused. She then besought them to allow a shepherd, who was present and offered his services for that purpose, to remove the furniture to his own residence on the opposite shore of the loch, to remain there till she could carry it away. This also was refused, and she was told, with an oath, that if she did not take her trumpery off within half-an-hour it would be burned. The poor widow had only to task the remains of her bodily strength, and address herself to the work of dragging her chests, beds, presses, and stools out at the door, and placing them at the gable of her cottage. No sooner was her task accomplished than the torch was applied, the widow's hut, built of very combustile material, speedily ignited, and there rose up rapidly, first a dense cloud of smoke, and soon thereafter a bright red flame. The wind unfortunately blew in the direction of the furniture, and the flame, lighting upon it, speedily reduced it to ashes.

In their progress down the Strath, Ccann-na-coille was the next township reached by the fire-raising evictors. An aged widow lived there who, by infirmity, had been reduced to such a state of bodily weakness that she could neither walk nor lie in bed. She could only, night and day, sit in her chair; and having been confined for many years in that posture, her limbs had become so stiff that any attempt to move her was attended with acute pain. She was the mother-in-law of Samuel Matheson, and had, with her family, been removed by Mr. Sellar from Rhimisdale some time before. His treatment of her and others on that occasion had brought Mr. Sellar into trouble as we have seen, but now, in the Providence of God, she was once more in his power, "Bean Raomasdail," or "the good wife of Rhimisdale," as she was called, was much revered. In her house I have held diets of catechising and meetings for prayer, and been signally refreshed by her Christian converse. When the evicting party commenced their operations in her township, the aged widow's house was among the very first that was to be consigned to the flames. Her family and neighbours represented the widow's strong claims on their compassion, and the imminent danger to her life of removing her to such a distance as the lower end of the Strath, at least ten miles off, without suitable means of conveyance. They implored that she might be allowed to remain for only two days till a conveyance could be provided for her. They were told that they should have thought on that before, and that she must immediately be removed by her friends, or the constables would be ordered to do it. The good wife of Rhimisdale was, therefore, raised by her weeping family from her chair and laid on a blanket, the corners of which were held up by four of the strongest youths in the place. All this she bore with meekness, and while the eyes of her attendants were streaming with tears, her pale and gentle countenance was suffused with a smile. The change of posture and the rapid motion of the bearers, however, awakened the most intense pain, and her cries never ceased till within a few miles of her destination, when she fell asleep. A burning fever supervened, of which she died a few months later.

During these proceedings, I was resident at my father's house; but I had occasion on the week immediately ensuing to visit the manse of Tongue. On my way thither, I passed through the scene of the campaign of burning. The spectacle presented was hideous and ghastly! The banks of the lake and the river, formerly studded with cottages, now met the eye as a scene of desolation. Of all the houses, the thatched roofs were gone; but the walls, built of alternate layers of turf and stone, remained. The flames of the preceding week still slumbered in their ruins, and sent up into the air spiral columns of smoke; whilst here a gable and there a long side-wall, undermined by the fire burning within them, might be seen tumbling to the ground, from which a cloud of smoke, and then a dusky flame, slowly sprang up. The sooty rafters of the cottages, as they were being consumed, filled the air with a heavy and most offensive odour. In short, nothing could more vividly represent the horrors of grinding oppression, and the extent to which one man, dressed up in a "little brief authority," will exercise that power, without feeling or restraint, to the injury of his fellow-creatures.

The Strathnaver Clearance of 1819 dissolved my connection with my first congregation, and extinguished a ministerial charge in that part of the Highlands. The Assembly's committee for the Royal Bounty, on being certified of the removal not only of their missionary but of his whole congregation along with him, withdrew the stipend and dissolved the mission.*

The space of time intervening between the demission of my charge at Achness and my appointment to the Gaelic Chapel at Aberdeen might have been about three months. The various events which took place during the interval I may briefly record.

During the last year of my ministry at Achness I assisted, along with Mr. David Mackenzie of Farr, at a communion at Thurso. Mr. William Mackintosh, afterwards my father-in-law, was minister of that

---

* The Free Church of Scotland sanctioned a regular charge, with an ordained minister, at Altnaharra in Strathnaver, in 1871. The congregation consists of a few shepherds, gamekeepers, and summer visitors.—ED.

parish. I preached on the Thursday, and intended to engage in the services of Sabbath and Monday as well. But, late on Saturday evening, an express arrived from Mr. Phin, minister of Wick, who administered the sacrament on the same day, very earnestly craving assistance, as those whom he had engaged to officiate had taken ill. I rode to Wick on Sabbath morning and arrived there to breakfast. After Mr. Phin had, very ably indeed, preached the action sermon I served the tables alternately with him, when he concluded with an exhortation. I preached also on Monday both in the forenoon and afternoon. The services of the Sabbath and week days on that occasion at Wick were conducted in the open air, as the parish church was then in a ruinous state, the foundation having some years before given way, and rents having appeared in several parts of the back wall. The church itself was comparatively new, having been erected, after a long litigation with the heritors, during the incumbency of Mr. Phin's immediate predecessor, Mr. Sutherland.* The foundation, however, was unsound, and the building soon gave way. The consequence of which was, that the heritors were under the necessity, very soon there-after, of erecting a new church at an enormous expense. Mr. Phin was then married and had two of a family, a son and a daughter.† His wife was a daughter of Bailie Macleay of Wick, a native of Invergordon, and in his younger years ferryman there. From this humble sphere he rose rapidly to wealth and distinction, after having emigrated to Caithness. Mr. Phin, his son-in-law, was a popular preacher, and popularity he very much affected. His sermons were very excellent, but the best of them were said to be borrowed; the people of Wick said, "He's a guid man, oor minister, an' a' the things we hear frae him on the Sawbath we can read in godly authors when we come hame."

Some months before my departure from Achness, a young man, Robert Sutherland, a native of Loth, but then employed in Aberdeen, came north to be married to Evan MacPherson's eldest daughter Christian, an amiable and handsome young woman. They were married by my father at Dalcharn, but as this young man was expressly deputed by the congregation at Aberdeen to make enquiries after me in the prospect of a vacancy occurring, by the appointment of their minister, Mr. Duncan Grant, to the parish of Alves, the young couple

---

* Mr. W. Sutherland, A.M. (whose father and grandfather were eminent ministers in Ross-shire), was ordained minister of Wick 1st May, 1765. He got the parish church rebuilt in 1799. He was a man of great tact and unbounded hospitality, but had considerable trouble with obdurate heritors. In public prayer he used to inter-cede "for the magistrates of Wick, *such as they are.*" He died 23rd June, 1816, in the 79th year of his age and 52nd of his ministry. His son, the Hon. Jas. Sutherland, became judge and member of Council, Bombay, where he lived in princely style. His daughter Elizabeth was married to James Miller, Esqre., merchant in Leith and St. Petersburg; their son was the late Sir William Miller, Bart. of Manderton; his daughter Christian was married to Mr. Mackintosh, minister of Thurso. His wife, Catherine Anderson, by whom he had a large family, died 3rd October, 1813.—ED.

† Mr. Robert Phin was ordained assistant and successor to Mr. Sutherland 13th March, 1813. He was a man of energy, and had a new parish church erected in 1830; he died 22nd March, 1840, aged 63 years. Dr. Kenneth Macleay Phin, minister of Galashiels, who became, latterly, a conspicuous ecclesiastic in the present Established Church of Scotland, was his son.—ED.

came on the Sabbath to hear sermon at Ach-na-h'uaighe. I knew nothing of this at the time, but Robert Sutherland's report was the first step towards my settlement in Aberdeen in the September following.

On the 8th day of June, 1819, Mr. Cook and my sister Elizabeth were married at Kildonan. I performed the marriage rite. It was in the nether bedroom, where my beloved stepmother lay. She was then very low, but at her special request the ceremony was performed in her presence. Mr. Cook arrived at Kildonan on the evening of the preceding day, accompanied by Robert Sutherland from Scoriclate, an eminently pious man, and extremely attached to Mr. Cook, his minister. Mr. Cook and my sister were married about 3 o'clock, P.M., my father and mother and the servants only being present. The married pair remained at Kildonan that night, and next day set off "through the hill" to their residence at Dirlot. The parting between my sister and her stepmother was deeply affecting. "God bless you, my dear Betty," said she, "I shall never see you more." I accompanied them till about two miles to the north of Cnoc-an-Eireanaich. In other circumstances I would certainly have gone all the way with them; but I had, about three weeks previously, received a call from the congregation at Aberdeen to preach as a candidate on the ensuing Sabbath, and I was under the necessity of setting out by the mail-coach from Inverness that same week. I had therefore only a day or two to remain at Kildonan before my departure for the south, and this very limited time I can never forget. My stepmother was sinking fast. She often called for me, and her distress seemed alleviated when she knew I was there. The bitter moment at last came when I was to part with her, never again to behold her. With my heart like lead within me I dragged myself to her bedside. Awaking out of a feverish slumber, she looked up at me. That look and the pallid countenance are at this moment, after the lapse of twenty-six years, before me. "Farewell, my dear mother, for the present," I said, "I hope very soon to see you again." "No, no," said she, "I shall never see you more, my dear Donald; this is the parting hour on the earth; farewell, may we meet in that place of rest where there is no separation!" I was completely overwhelmed; I bent over her, and bathed her pallid face with my tears, then tore myself away, and rushed out of the room.

I arrived in Aberdeen on Saturday morning. I found my friend Robert Sutherland waiting my arrival at the inn where the coach stopped in Union Street, together with a few other members of the Gaelic congregation. They conducted me to lodgings in Frederick Street. I called upon my predecessor, Mr. Grant, and found him engaged in packing up his furniture and arranging his secular matters previous to his departure for his new charge at Alves. He told me that he was to preach his valedictory sermon in Gaelic in the forenoon of the ensuing day, and, from the general conversation which we had respecting the congregation, it seemed to me that he and his flock had quarrelled, and were to part in something like a huff. The event justified my suspicions. On the Sabbath he preached as he had intended, and his sermon, particularly the practical part of it, was one of the most perfect scolds I ever heard. He was naturally a warm-hearted man, but very choleric; besides that, he was at the time afflicted with a stomach complaint which affected his nervous system, and fomented his irascibility.* I preached in Gaelic in the afternoon, and in English in the evening at six o'clock, to most attentive audiences. During the course of the week my election and call as minister were harmóniously entered into by the congregation. Returning to my lodgings one evening I found a letter on the table addressed in my father's handwriting. My heart bounded between hope and fear. I eagerly snatched it up and looked at the seal. It was large and black. I anticipated its contents. My poor mother was no more. My letter communicated the sad intelligence that, after a short but severe struggle, she had departed this life on the 25th of June, eight days after I had parted from her. These heavy tidings completely stunned me. The congregation entreated of me to remain for two Sabbaths more, but I could not, so, after preaching on the Sabbath following, I returned home by the coach on the Monday. The north mail-coach had not previously run further than Tain. But by an arrangement entered into between the Postmaster-General and the proprietors of Sutherland and Caithness, it had been agreed to continue it all the way to Thurso, round by Wick. On my return from Aberdeen I was one of the passengers with the first mail from Tain to Thurso. I took my seat only to Helmisdale. It was rather a dangerous mode of travelling, the danger arising, however, not from the state of the roads, but solely from the welcome given to the newly-started conveyance by all the proprietors, tacksmen, towns and villages on the line of road by which the coach passed. Every one of them must treat the passengers, guard and drivers, with glasses of whisky, with which the drivers in particular so regaled themselves as at length to be totally unfit to manage the horses. The coach at different times therefore made many hairbreadth escapes from being overturned.

I rode from Helmisdale to Kildonan, and instead of taking the short road through the township to the manse, I went round by the churchyard. There, behind the church wall to the north, a new-made grave smote upon my eye. It was my beloved stepmother's. I sat by it for a while overwhelmed by emotion. I then went up to the manse, where my widowed father met me at the threshold, and we mingled our tears together. Not feeling very well next day, I mentioned it to my father, when he replied, "She lies low who would have cured you." The words so penetrated my heart that I wept the whole night. My dear father, from the day of his wife's death to his own, lived the life of a hermit. All his family had left him, and the township, and indeed

---

* Mr. Grant usually preached in English on Sabbath evenings in the Gaelic Chapel, which, on some occasions, was crowded by Aberdeen people. At their request, he proposed that the afternoon service should be conducted in the same language. This the Highlanders strongly opposed. They appealed to the Presbytery, which gave them a constitution according to their wishes. This occurred in 1819. Mr. Grant, who knew Gaelic imperfectly, was a powerful and popular English preacher. He was translated from Alves to Forres 27th September, 1827, and in 1843 became minister of the Free Church congregation of that town. He died 17th March, 1866, in the 76th year of his age and 52nd of his ministry.—ED.

the whole parish of Kildonan, were depopulated, so that, except his own servants, male and female, the schoolmaster George MacLeod and his family, and Muckle Donald and his wife, he had not a human being to converse with for many miles around. My stepmother died in her 64th year, and he survived her about six years.

Before I returned to my charge at Aberdeen I paid a visit to my friends at Dirlot, accompanied by Muckle Donald. We set out early in the morning, and, after a tedious ride across the hills by Morven and Strathmore, we arrived at my brother-in-law's at seven in the evening.

I returned to Kildonan from Dirlot after a stay of two days, and on the succeeding Sabbath I attempted, but with much pain and anxiety, to preach the funeral sermon from the words, "Enter thou into thy chamber." I met with some individuals of my former congregation from the heights of the parish during the time I remained at Kildonan, among others poor old Breacachadh, who shed tears at parting with me.

Having gifted my furniture at Achness to my sister at Dirlot, and left my faithful dun pony to be sold to any one who would take care of him, and having taken an affectionate leave of my only surviving parent, I went to Aberdeen about the latter end of July to enter on the duties of my new charge.

CHAPTER XVII.

MINISTRY AND CONTEMPORARIES IN ABERDEEN.

1819-1822.

J ARRIVED in Aberdeen by the "Duke of Gordon" stage-coach at the end of July, 1819. My arrival was waited for and welcomed by a few of the leading men of the Gaelic chapel. They conducted me to lodgings at a Mrs. Hume's in Virginia Street, not indeed very conveniently situated, but where, notwithstanding, I was under the necessity of remaining, until in November I took up house for myself at Gilcomston.

Of my new charge the late Dr. Ronald Bayne, minister of Kiltarlity, was the founder. This excellent man was a native of Dingwall, and the lineal descendant of the Baynes, Knights of Tulloch, in Ross-shire. He was a man of great mental acuteness, and of an exuberant imagination. In youth he was so much under the power of an evil heart as to be far ahead of his compeers in recklessness and folly. His neighbours knew him then only by the name of "Raoghalt Molluichte," or cursed Ronald. But, at a comparatively early period of his life, he became a subject of Divine grace. All the energies of his active and powerful mind were at once turned into a new and contrary channel, so that he became fearless and faithful in the ways of God. His first ministerial charge was the chaplainship of the 42nd Regiment which, under the command of Lord MacLeod, had been ordered to India, whither he accompanied them in 1780. After remaining there for some time he was under the necessity of returning home for the benefit of his health, and came to Aberdeen to reside in the neighbourhood of his wife's relatives. It was while there that his attention was directed to the moral destitution of the Highlanders in the city and district. They were "as sheep without a shepherd." With the cordial concurrence of Mr. Abercrombie, one of the ministers in Aberdeen, Dr. Bayne succeeded in collecting the Aberdeen Highlanders together, formed them into a congregation, and statedly preached to them wherever a hall sufficiently large for the purpose could be found. The congregation was thus constituted by Dr. Bayne. In 1798 he received a call from the congregation of the Little Kirk at Elgin, which he accepted, and was succeeded in Aberdeen by his brother, Mr Kenneth Bayne, who was his equal and contemporary in the Christian life, but his inferior in natural abilities. Dr. Ronald Bayne, after an unsuccessful contest with the Presbytery of Elgin respecting the spiritual liberties, and even the existence within the Establishment, of the Little Kirk, left Elgin in 1800 for Inverness, where he officiated in the Chapel of Ease until he was appointed minister of Kiltarlity, in Inverness-shire, 5th May, 1808.

Mr. Kenneth Bayne continued for some years minister of the Gaelic congregation in Aberdeen. It was during his residence and ministry there that the chapel was erected. He afterwards accepted a call to the Gaelic chapel in Greenock. Many persons, natives of Greenock who did not understand Gaelic, went to reside in the Highlands for the express purpose of acquiring the language in order to profit by his preaching. He was succeeded in the Aberdeen Gaelic chapel by Mr. John Mackenzie, a pious man, who in 1798 was translated to Glasgow, as minister of the Duke Street Gaelic chapel. His immediate successor in Aberdeen was Mr James MacPhail, second son of the venerable Hector MacPhail, minister of Resolis. He remained only a year, after which he became minister of Daviot, Inverness-shire. Mr. MacPhail very much resembled his revered father in the simplicity of his Christian character. After him came Mr. William Forbes, whose ministry in Aberdeen was *brief* in point of time, but *eternal* in regard to its real effects, he having had " many seals " whilst there " of an accepted ministry." He became minister of the parish of Tarbat, Ross-shire, in 1800.

Mr. Forbes was a man of highly respectable talents, a profound and scriptural divine, a pious man, and a truly devoted servant of the Lord Jesus. His pastoral duties to his people he discharged with the strictest fidelity, and his pulpit exercises in both languages were accurate, able, and deeply impressive. His temperament was intensely nervous, and often threw him into moods of feeling the very reverse of each other—at one time in a high flow of spirits, laughing until his eyes ran over at his own anecdotes, told with no ordinary powers of humour and drollery—at another sunk in the deepest gloom, which his countenance, naturally dark and sallow, was peculiarly well fitted to express. His wife, my sister Jean, was in the most important sense a helpmeet for him. She was a truly pious woman, and, through the mists which so often overspread them, she was capable of discerning, and fully appreciating, the excellencies of his Christian character. My stepmother always entertained the profoundest esteem for Mr. Forbes, and he on his side cherished feelings of regard for her, so much so that he named his second daughter Jane* after her. His successor in Aberdeen was the late eminently pious Mr. Neil Kennedy, a man of prayer and of deep Christian experience. He was minister of the chapel during my first two sessions at college, and in 1813 was settled minister of Logie in Easter-Ross, where he died in 1836, aged 56 years. After Mr. Kennedy's departure the congregation recalled Mr. John Mackenzie, who, not feeling himself suited as pastor of the Duke Street chapel in Glasgow, readily returned to his former charge. Mr. Mackenzie very soon after returned to Glasgow, not indeed to his

---

* Afterwards Mrs. Mackay of Garrochty, now the only survivor of the family. Two sons died while attending their classes at college. Mr. Forbes married Miss Jane Sage on 26th Nov., 1813 ; he died 12th May, 1838, in the 72nd year of his age and 48th of his ministry. Mrs. Forbes died at Edinburgh, 29th Dec., 1852. For interesting particulars regarding the ministry of Mr. Forbes, see volume of his sermons, published by Gemmell, Edinburgh.—ED.

former charge, but to a newly-formed Gaelic congregation in the Gorbals. He was succeeded in Aberdeen by Mr. Duncan Grant, who, at the time he received the call, was a teacher in Fortrose Academy. When I first settled among them I found the Gaelic congregation to be a very respectable one. My annual income was £150, £10 of which were paid by the S.P.C.K. The stated services on every Lord's day were, a sermon forenoon and afternoon in the Gaelic language, and an optional English sermon or lecture in the evening. I was the first minister inducted by the Presbytery, for it had only been sanctioned as a charge by the General Assembly of 1819. During the winter I usually lectured in English at six o'clock on Sabbath evening, but in summer I devoted that portion of the Sabbath, as well as week days, to the duty of catechising. I commenced my catechetical exercises among them by family visitation, which I found to be at once satisfactory to myself, and edifying and acceptable to the people.

With one exception the ministers of Aberdeen were, I think, the same who had held office when I was at college thirteen years before. At that time Mr. Doig was minister of the Trinity Chapel, but since then, on the death of Mr. Gordon of East Church, he became the colleague of Dr. Ross. Aberdeen was not then, as it is now, divided into parishes, the ministers of which are independent of each other, and have each their respective kirk sessions. In 1819 there were only four ministers of the Church of Scotland for the whole population of the city of Aberdeen, amounting then to upwards of 40,000. The spiritual destitution of the extra population in connection with the church was supplied by those who were then styled Chapel of Ease ministers, *i.e.*, ministers who, though they were ordained to discharge all ministerial functions to their own congregations, were not members of the courts of the church, nor were they even moderators of kirk sessions for the due regulation of their congregation. Besides, the East and West Churches were collegiate charges, *i.e.*, two ministers preached to the same congregation, the one in the forenoon and the other in the afternoon of every Lord's day. These four, therefore, were the only strictly constitutional ministers of the city, the Chapel of Ease ministers being, Dr. Dewar of Greyfriar's. Dr. Thomson of Footdee, Dr. Kidd of Gilcomston, and Mr. Murray of Trinity Chapel, besides myself.

With the ministers of the West Church I, as a minister. hardly ever came in contact, but was more intimately acquainted with those of the East Church. Dr. Ross was a man of great modesty and unfeigned piety, but a dry, uninteresting preacher. He was much beloved by his own flock, and by all his friends and acquaintances. By the great body of the citizens of Aberdeen he was highly esteemed; indeed, all who knew him were, by the uniform sweetness of his disposition and the faultless purity of his life, inclined to make a great deal of him. He died in 1824, aged 64 years; and was succeeded by the most intimate friend of the latter part of his life, Dr. James Foote, minister of Logiepart, in Forfarshire. Dr. Ross's funeral was the most numerously attended in the memory of the oldest man then living.

Mr. Robert Doig was the colleague of Dr. Ross, and successor of Dr. Gordon. During my attendance at college he was minister of the

Trinity Chapel, but now of the East Church. Mr. Doig was a very respectable preacher. It was he who inducted me into my charge. He was professedly of the Evangelical party. He died at Edinburgh in 1824, shortly after having attended the General Assembly as a member. He was thrice married, but had only one son who, when I was in Aberdeen, was minister of the second charge in Arbroath. He was, some years thereafter, presented to the parish of Torryburn, in the Presbytery of Dunfermline, and has since been Free Church minister of that parish.

I have mentioned Dr. Glennie as a professor; let me now record my impressions of him as a minister. His sermons, like his lectures, were very prosing and dull, but what was specially noticeable was his cold and bitter Moderatism, the more so as, at first, he was strongly suspected to have cherished leanings towards principles and views of a very opposite character. He began his ministerial course as the minister of Greyfriar's, or College Church, and his services there were, at first, very faithful and acceptable. But when he was, like the scribe, "not far from the kingdom of heaven," the leading Moderates in Edinburgh made such a determined and simultaneous assault upon him for his evangelical tendencies, as not only to cure him effectually of these "morbid sensibilities," but to engender in his heart the most implacable hatred of all evangelicalism, or whatsoever tended thereunto. Some years after I left Aberdeen, Dr. Glennie resigned his charge of the West Church, and confined himself entirely to the duties of the Professorship, which he held till his death in 1845.

Mr. John Murray, of Trinity Chapel, was one of my earliest acquaintances of the clerical order after I became minister of the Gaelic chapel. He was a truly pious man, a sound divine, and a most respectable scholar, and when he began his ministerial labours in Aberdeen he was highly esteemed by the serious, and was evidently owned and honoured by God. His preaching, plain, faithful, and truly scriptural, was made effectual in bringing many to feel the power of the truth. Mr. Murray's faithfulness drew upon him the reproach and scorn of unbelievers. As an example of this, I was credibly informed that, shortly before I came to Aberdeen, the agent of an English commercial establishment, dealing chiefly in the article of sulphur or brimstone, came to Aberdeen for orders. Apparently he did not confine his applications to grocers and others dealing in that article, but visited individual families for the purpose of taking orders. Passing through the Shiprow, a street leading directly to Trinity manse, where Mr. Murray resided, the agent called on several individuals on his way. Some of them refused the article for their own use, but told him that there was a gentleman of the name of Murray, residing at the end of the street in a house enclosed with an iron railing, who dealt very largely in the article. Thither the unconscious agent wended his way, knocked at Mr. Murray's door, and being admitted, stated the reason of his coming, and assured him that the article in which he dealt so largely would be furnished by his firm on reasonable terms and of the best quality. Mr. Murray was naturally of a keen and rather combative disposition, but he at once saw from whose quiver the bolt had been selected, so, giving a grave explanation to the agent, he civilly dismissed him. Mr. Murray's irascibility of temper and indolence in the pastoral office tended to circumscribe his sphere of usefulness, and were obstacles in the way of his attaining to that place among his brethren in the ministry to which he was otherwise so justly entitled. He was ever zealous, however, in promot. ing the cause of God throughout the land, and of the numerous societies for such purposes in Aberdeen he was a most efficient member. During my residence in that city Mr. Murray entered into the married state with his present excellent wife. Miss Margaret Brown was the eldest daughter of Bailie, afterwards Provost, A. Brown, bookseller in Broad Street, Aberdeen. Mr. Murray was a native of the parish of Insch. His father had been a respectable farmer there, but was dead long before I knew his son. He had a brother residing with him, Mr. Andrew Murray, a young man of decided piety and a student of divinity. He was afterwards licensed to preach and ordained a minister in the Helvetic Church, where he is at present. In 1825, on the demise of Mr. Doig, Mr. Murray became the senior minister of St. Nicolas' church, the designation then of that church and parish. He was, when first settled there, the colleague of Dr. Ross, who survived Mr. Doig about a year or so, and after his death, Mr. Foote became Mr. Murray's colleague in the East Church. Some years thereafter the collegiate charges of the East and West Churches were dissolved, and the whole city was divided into parishes, each minister being a member of Presbytery, and holding his own session. In consequence of this arrangement Mr. Murray became the minister of the North Church and parish. The church itself is a fine building, in the Grecian style, with a tower and steeple, and is situated at the south-east end of North Street at its junction with King Street. In that church he continued to labour until the Disruption. He is at present one of the Fathers of the Free Church of Scotland.*

Dr. Daniel Dewar was then in the zenith of his popularity. He had succeeded Prof. Scott in the Moral Philosophy Chair at King's College, and Dr. Glennie in the Greyfriar's Church, some years before I came to Aberdeen. He resided at the College in the old town, and preached every Sabbath in Greyfriar's Church. His sermons were highly finished pieces of composition; they had, moreover, a sprinkling of evangelicalism, and these qualities combined recommended them to a certain class of hearers then very common in Aberdeen. They were those who desired to find in the sermon what would gratify their taste by its style, and soothe their feelings by its flavouring of pious sentiment, but to whom anything pointed or rousing would be most offensive. To such hearers Dr. Dewar was highly acceptable as a preacher. A slight personal account of him may not be uninteresting. He was a native of Argyllshire, and was born in the humblest circumstances. His father was a blind fiddler, who earned his bread by travelling through the country and playing at weddings, etc. He was attended by his son Daniel for the purpose of being the bearer of the

* Dr. Murray died 1st March, 1861, in the 77th year of his age and 46th of his ministry. His wife died 4th Feb. of the following year.—ED.

fiddle-case, and his father's guide. Some wealthy individual took notice of the musician's son, and thought he could discover, under the guise of his poverty, the germs of future greatness; and so, at his own private expense, sent him to a public school. From this circumstance Dr. Dewar could date his subsequent rise in the world. He joined the Independents, or perhaps was of this sect as a member of his father's family. After he left school he studied, with a view to become one of their preachers, at their Academy at Homerton in England, under the tutorship of Dr. Pye Smith, then at the head of that seminary. There his training seems to have consisted principally in studying English composition. Whether at his first outset in life he was engaged as an Independent preacher, I am not certain, but it is probable that he was, as it has been the custom of that sect from the time of Oliver Cromwell to suffer any one of their adherents, whatever their circumstances or education might be, to step into their pulpits, and edify a congregation by their pourings forth. But Mr. Dewar soon found out that the Independent connection, however numerous in England, presented but a very limited sphere of action in the north, and he therefore joined the Church of Scotland. Passing through all his preparatory studies at Edinburgh University and Hall, he was licensed to preach, and became pastor of a small congregation in Argyllshire. The first time I ever saw him was in the pulpit of the old Gaelic Chapel in Edinburgh, where he preached in Gaelic with considerable hesitation. He had come to Edinburgh for the purpose of preparing one of his first works for the press. On the decease of Mr. Kirkland of Trinity Chapel, he was a candidate for that charge. but was unsuccessful; he was appointed to the Moral Philosophy Chair subsequent to his becoming minister of Greyfriar's. I was, whilst he remained there, on a very friendly footing with him. He was at the time greatly ahead of us all in the zeal and ability with which he pleaded the cause of truth at the public meetings of every religious society with which the city of Aberdeen then so much abounded. For that was the very age of religious societies. No public meeting could be conducted without Dr. Dewar. No sermon could be preached for any religious or charitable object but by him only. Not any new scheme could be formed, nor recent society established, without his countenance. In consequence of the Plurality Act of Assembly he experienced so much annoyance from the majority of the Senatus of King's College for holding both livings, the charge of Greyfriar's and the Professorship, that he sought interest for. and procured his appointment to, the Tron Church in Glasgow. Thither he removed towards the close of the first half-year of my residence in Aberdeen, from whence he returned, on the death of Principal Brown, to succeed him in that office. But in all his changes of place and circumstances, and in his dealings with mankind, his principles and character preserved the same aspect. He sat in a vehicle drawn by two horses, Ambition being the name of the one and Avarice that of the other.

Dr. Thomson, minister of Footdee, was one of my intimate friends. He was a medical man as well as a minister. His stipend was very considerable, and he contrived to at least triple its amount by his medical practice. His church was a very small one, occupying the same site as that on which the present large and elegant structure is erected in the centre of the churchyard. Dr. Thomson was a well-meaning man, and maintained uniform consistency for ministerial character and great zeal in promoting the success of every religious society having the cause of truth or benevolence as its objects. But he was secular in spirit, and while his views of the things unseen were vague and superficial, his mental grasp of this world's wisdom was proportionately tenacious. He was very hospitable, and I was frequently and kindly entertained in his house. Although his charge at Footdee was a distinct and separate parish, yet, previous to the division of the city into parishes, it was only on the footing of a Chapel of Ease. He died in 1838. He was succeeded by Mr. Spence.

Among all my clerical friends, during my ministry at Aberdeen, none left such a vivid impression upon my mind as Dr. James Kidd, who was both professor of Oriental Languages at Marischal College and minister of Gilcomston Chapel of Ease. Dr. Kidd was a native of Ireland, and so also was his most amiable and pious wife. From his own lips, in my not unfrequent private conferences with him, I learned the following particulars respecting his early history. He was born of humble parents at Lough Brickland, county Down, on the 6th Nov., 1761. He was the youngest of three sons, and in consequence of the death of his father he and his family removed to county Antrim, to reside at Broughshane, the place of his mother's nativity. He spoke of his mother in the most affectionate terms, as he recalled the days of his childhood; and of her maternal care and early instructions, not only in secular knowledge, but also in religious instruction by the aid of the Shorter Catechism and prayer. "She made me then read to her a chapter of the New Testament daily," he said, "and verse by verse commit it to memory, in all which the grand and prominent object to whom she never failed to direct me from almost every verse I read was Christ—what he said or did, and what he suffered. Yes, Sir, the last pulse of my old heart will cease to beat when I cease to forget my mother." It was, he said, in the Presbyterian meeting-house of Broughshane that he first received and ever afterwards cherished the idea and subsequent hope of preaching the gospel. He proceeded: "I first learned the rudiments of Latin from a friend whom I loved as Jonathan did the son of Jesse. But death, Sir, robbed me of him, and in my poverty of money and of friends, I was again cast upon Providence, and put to my shifts. A kind friend sent me again to school, where I was an enthusiast for literature and science. I afterwards set up a school at Elginy at an age when, instead of being a master, I ought to have been a scholar. But, with the profits of my teaching and hard economy, I scraped together so much of pounds, shillings and pence as enabled me to put a finish to my rudimental education in Belfast, under a Mr. Mason, one of the most popular teachers of English in the north of Ireland. Then I went to Kildownie, where I laboured for four years as a teacher. It was there that I first became acquainted with my wife, then Miss Boyd. After our union, having made a little money by the most persevering industry, in April

1784, I embarked with my wife on board the 'Irish Volunteer' from Larne to Philadelphia. Without any acquaintance of influence, or a single letter of introduction, I was compelled to work my own way. By the recommendation of a friend, I first undertook the tuition of a family near Egg Harbour in the State of New Jersey. Next I became preceptor in the family of a Mr. Ewing of Pennsylvania, and went back again to Philadelphia as assistant teacher in the school of my friend Mr. Little. By his persuasion I afterwards opened a classical academy in Philadelphia, in which I was completely successful. Some of the leading characters in America were my pupils, and afterwards acknowledged that their future distinction took rise, first of all, from the instructions and bias which their minds had in youth received at my academy and under my guidance. I then became a student in the College of Pennsylvania."

Mr. Kidd purchased a Hebrew bible of a bookseller in Philadelphia with the money which he had with difficulty put together to purchase a suit of clothes, of which he stood not a little in need. He became then, and continued, an enthusiast for oriental literature; so much so, that he was on the eve of setting out to travel in the East, in order the more fully to perfect himself in oriental languages. But his whole soul was wrapt up in the desire to preach the gospel in Scotland, and, therefore, he embarked for that country, furnished by his friend Dr. Rush, with letters of introduction to the eminent literary persons in Edinburgh whose acquaintance he had made while studying medicine there. In Edinburgh Mr. Kidd studied philosophy and the languages, and afterwards attended the Divinity Hall. In the meantime, and under the auspices of Rabbi Robertson, he set up as a teacher of oriental languages; and was so successful that, when the chair of this department at Marischal College became vacant by the death of Dr. Donaldson, he was strongly recommended by several leading persons in the church and in the literary world to the patron, Sir Alexander Ramsay of Balmain, in consequence of which he was appointed in October 1793. After attending four years at the Divinity Halls of Old and New Aberdeen, under Doctors Campbell and Gerald, sen., he was licensed to preach by the Presbytery of Aberdeen. His first ministerial appointment was that of evening lecturer in Trinity Chapel, then lately erected. But in the year 1800, the Gilcomston Chapel of Ease becoming vacant, he was elected by an immense majority of those qualified to vote, and in that charge he continued to labour till the day of his death.

Dr. Kidd preached to overflowing audiences three times every Sabbath. When circumstances permitted I was often, on Sabbath evenings, a much edified and not seldom a much amused auditor. His preaching was eloquent, powerful and scriptural. His mind appeared to be deeply imbued with the truth, and exercised in it. His sermons were evidently prepared; the fluency and eloquence with which he delivered them were quite natural to him, and his views of the subject he discussed were calculated to lead his hearers to serious reflection. Not only in private, but even in the pulpit, Dr Kidd indulged in those eccentricities which have been generally associated with his name. I have seen him act a part in the pulpit as would have disqualified any man, holding the office of a minister, from ever entering it afterwards, himself only excepted. For example, lecturing on the book of Daniel, when he came to describe the sudden and appalling appearance of the "handwriting on the wall," as well as its paralysing effects upon the guilty Belshazzar, Dr. Kidd was not content with merely describing the scene in so many words, but, to impress the minds of his congregation still more with all the strong points of the case, he considered it necessary to act the scene before their eyes. Accordingly, after giving a very natural and powerful picture of Belshazzar's terror, to the utter amazement of his auditors, he became the identical Belshazzar himself. He began to tremble from head to foot, he raised his hands and his eyes in parallel lines to the roof of the church, knocked his knees vigorously together, and ultimately dropped down, gradually and gracefully, on the pulpit floor. After remaining there just long enough to allow his astounded hearers to recover their breath, the doctor got up again and concluded his lecture. Now, I will not allow myself to think that all this was mere affectation or love of effect. I can only account for it by ascribing it entirely to his eccentricity, which was essentially that of an Irishman who, feeling his eccentricities once on the move, cannot calculate himself, nor can any one else for him, to what extent they may carry him away before they subside. The worthy doctor was much annoyed by drowsy hearers. There was one man, clothed with a red waistcoat among other of his vestments, who had got seated directly under his eye. The man began first to nod, his head giving thereby clear enough indications that, if not fairly asleep, he was on the verge of being so. "Waken that man," exclaimed the preacher. The man was pinched, and wakened accordingly by his neighbour. But he awoke only to fall asleep again. "I say, waken that red-breasted sinner there," shouted the doctor, and a second time the sleeper was roused from his slumbers by his neighbouring and more wakeful fellow-worshippers. But it would not do. In a twinkling, he was fast asleep a third time, and the worthy pastor's patience being therewith fairly exhausted, he grasped a small pocket-bible lying at his hand on the pulpit cushion, and sending it at the sleeper, with unerring aim, he hit him on the side of the head. "Now, sir," said he, "if you will not *hear* the Word of God, you shall *feel* it." There certainly was not another man or minister in the kingdom who might have ventured on so *striking* a reproof.

For the Highlanders Dr. Kidd entertained a strong attachment. During sacramental occasions in the Gaelic Chapel he and his people always attended the lectures on the evenings of Thursday and Sabbath. One Sabbath evening during my time the doctor and his people, with many others, had come to the chapel doors a little before six, and found them shut. The crowd was immense, and the crush to get in was likely to be serious, as the numbers outside were increasing. Dr Kidd, in an authoritative voice, demanded why the doors were not opened and, receiving no answer, called out, "If they are not opened instantly, break them open." This utterance, unseemly on any occasion but much more so on the peaceful evening of a communion Sabbath, was in very bad taste, and savoured, indeed, not a little of the atmosphere of an Irish row. The Highland elders felt most indignant at the doctor's conduct, and a deputation of their number waited upon him to remonstrate with him on the subject. He apologised by saying that, being a native of Ireland, he was suddenly seized with an "Irish fit," but that he had no sooner uttered the words in question than he had repented of his rashness, and felt that he had spoken unadvisedly. The peace was thus soon made up between him and the "Highland host," but he told me afterwards that their appearance in a body at his house, and their stern pertinacious faces, made him feel rather uneasy. "Of two of them," he added, "I had an instinctive terror. I was afraid of Alexander Murray's prayers, and equally so of Alexander MacDonald's fists." The allusion evidently was to a pugilistic encounter of MacDonald's with a drunken nephew. "Poor Saunders," he used to say, "was sorely tried; it was really too much for flesh and blood. There was a pitched battle between Saunder's Highland blood and Saunder's godliness, and the Highland blood won the day. A stalwart Highlander may be as godly and praying a man as you could wish, but plant your fist on his face, and he can't for the life of him choose but give as good a blow in return."

The two great branches of the Secession, after various conferences and consultations, had united under the name of the "Associate Synod." Dr. Kidd rejoiced at the union, and said that he believed that it was entered into by both parties under divine guidance. "For," he added, "had such a proposal been made many years ago, and had the very angels of heaven come among them to recommend it, the Seceders would have driven them away with pitchforks." There was nothing, however, which I more admired than Dr. Kidd's method in conducting divine service whenever he preached. After giving out a psalm, and uttering a beautiful prayer, he read a chapter. But, before doing so. he directed the attention of his hearers to the lessons found in it. This done, he read the chapter without note or comment from first to last. The simple reading of the chapter exactly corresponding with the previous running commentary brought the lessons prominently into view, and let his hearers at once into the scope and substance of the whole taken in connection. I never more fully entered into, nor highly relished, the reading of a chapter of the Bible than when I was listening to Dr. Kidd.

But the most interesting conversation I had with Dr. Kidd was on the almost unsurmountable difficulties which he met with in preaching the gospel soon after he was licensed. One evening, which he spent with me in my own house at the Braehead of Gilcomston, has left a vivid and most endearing recollection of him by the frankness and Christian sincerity with which he stated the following particulars of his first outset in the ministry. "The great question with me then," said he, "was not what the gospel was in itself, for that, I thought, I not only understood, but in some measure felt in its power. But my difficulty was—How was I to preach the gospel as a trust committed to my charge? I was altogether dissatisfied with myself. I felt that I had taken too much upon me, that I had run unsent, and therefore, to satisfy my mind on the subject. I visited and consulted those who were considered pillars in the church." He then mentioned several eminent ministers with whom he had conversed on the subject. None of them, however, found for him a solid bottom in the deep waters through which he was passing, and in which he was frequently very nearly sinking altogether. He had nothing for it at last but to cast himself simply and entirely on the Head of the church, and on His promise, "Go ye and preach, and, lo, I am with you always, even unto the end of the world." "O, Sir," he added with much fervency and with tear-moistened eyes, "men have failed me. and I have more than once fainted and failed myself, but He has failed me never, and I bless His holy name that He ever put me in trust with the gospel." He died of apoplexy on Wednesday, the 24th Dec., 1834, at his own house in Aberdeen, in great peace and in the exercise of a good hope through grace. He was in the 74th year of his age and 34th of his ministry.

With Dr. Cruden of Nigg, near Aberdeen, I became intimate, and I cherish the most pleasing and kindly remembrances of him. He was then an old man, and his personal appearance was truly venerable. His face was long, very thin and minutely marked with the wrinkles of old age. When he preached or addressed a public audience, it would be exceedingly difficult, indeed, for those who only saw or heard him for the first time, to keep their gravity, as, not being a very fluent speaker, and not at all eloquent, he did not find it easy to express himself, and the difficulty which he felt in doing so was embodied in the most ludicrous contortions of countenance ever witnessed. To overset one's gravity and to excite an irresistible sense of the ludicrous, therefore, was the impression made at first on the mind of a stranger. But a more intimate acquaintance with this venerable man, and anything like a right estimate of his moral worth, speedily wore it off, so that, screw his features as he choose, he would never excite one solitary smile on the face of any audience who knew and valued him as he deserved. He was a man of simple but fervent piety, of unshaken and unwearied zeal, and was ever labouring in the service of Christ among the people committed to his care. He assisted at every sacramental occasion and preached, at an average, four or five sermons per week. One minister, indeed, characterised him as a "preaching machine." This was not, however, at all an epithet descriptive of Dr. Cruden. It was true that the worthy doctor's sermons did not cost him much previous study, nor did they exhibit much reach of thought, or depth of theological knowledge. They were the artless and unaffected effusions of a deeply serious mind, full of faith and love, and breathing a Christian and philanthropic spirit. Dr. Cruden was a most zealous supporter of the many religious societies then established at Aberdeen. He not only contributed very liberally to them all, but at public meetings advocated the cause most earnestly. When Dr. Cruden intimated his intention to the Town Council of Aberdeen (who, as the patrons, had the living of Nigg in their gift), of having an assistant and successor, on account of his increasing infirmities, Mr. Alexander Thom, Rector of Gordon's Hospital, was by them nominated to the office. His settlement accordingly took place soon afterwards

On the evening of that day Dr. Cruden, after attending the services in church and inviting his relatives to meet him, retired to his manse. After partaking of a slight repast, he said with much cheerfulness that he had now got his heart's wish in regard to his beloved flock fully gratified, in having such a man as Mr. Thom settled among them, and that he now felt that his course was finished and his work ended. He told them that he had on his mind the irresistible impression that the first peep of dawn on the coming day would be the hour of his departure, and he begged his friends to watch with him, just to accompany him, as he said, to the borders of the heavenly Canaan. His friends agreed to the proposal, but fancied that the old man had got into his dotage. He asked them all to seat themselves beside him on the sofa, and then began to speak with an earnestness and fervour which they had never, till then, witnessed. He continued thus to address them for several hours, till at last his voice faltered and then failed altogether, when, gently reclining his head on the back of the sofa, he breathed his last. The dawn of day was observed at that moment to break upon the sky.*

With the other members of the Presbytery or Synod of Aberdeen I had no sort of intercourse or acquaintance whatever, with the exception of some of those of their number already mentioned. There was hardly one of them who could be said in truth either to preach the gospel or even to understand it. While such was their general character as a body, many of them individually were so openly profane that they were known to be the most ungodly men in their respective congregations. Ross-shire they denounced as "the hot-bed of fanaticism," but Aberdeenshire, with far more truth, might justly have been denominated the icy region of stern, unmitigated Moderatism. Two of their number especially were the faithful representatives of the genuine Moderates of that day. They stuck at nothing, Sabbath desecration, profane swearing, drunkenness, or the most open contempt of God's truth and ordinances. Men guilty of such palpable recklessness, while daring publicly to hold the ministerial office, thus became prominent examples for evil in their parishes.

My acquaintance among the dissenting ministers was not very intimate nor extensive. The Secession body, consisting as they did of the two great divisions, burgher and anti-burgher, underwent about this time two great changes. The first was their union into one body as the united associate Synod. To this union, however, many ministers of both sections would not agree. The Original Seceders, or Cameronians, did not join them at all. Another and far more vital change to which this united body subjected itself, and in which it made common cause with other dissenting churches, was its adoption of the voluntary principle. This nostrum effected a complete revolution in the Secession Church. It consisted simply in this: that a Christian church must necessarily be contaminated by being connected with the State in the matter of receiving temporal support from it; and that it ought to be upheld by its members, who in this religious capacity only are under

* Dr. David Cruden died 8th Nov., 1826, in the 81st year of his age and 58th of his ministry.—ED.

obligations to do so, while in a civil capacity no one is under any such obligation. This notion when first started spread like wild-fire among the Seceders, particularly after the union of these two septs, and by its adoption they renounced one of the leading principles held by the eminent founders of the Secession when they left the National Church.

To some of the professors of Marischal and of King's Colleges I may now briefly allude. I renewed my intercourse with my kind old friend Professor Stewart, of Marischal College, and his amiable family. I have frequently been at his house as one of a numerous tea-and-supper party, where the old man was full of fun and anecdote. It was towards the close of my residence in Aberdeen that he lost his excellent wife. I attended her funeral. She was buried close by the west wall of the churchyard of St. Nicolas. Her maiden name was Mowat, and she was the very last descendant of the Mowats of Ardo, in Aberdeenshire, a family who could, until half a century ago, by almost an unbroken descent, trace up their ancestral pedigree considerably beyond the age of King Robert the Bruce. The professor himself was of a good family in Kincardineshire. He was the proprietor of a small estate in that county, called Inchbrake, which he inherited from his ancestors through many generations. He died in 1827.

Dr. Hamilton was then living, but he had retired from the public duties of his professorship, and one John Cruickshanks, a contemporary of mine in Marischal College, had been appointed his assistant and successor. He had left his house at the college, and resided, after he had retired from his public duties, in a country house at the west side of the town. Mr. Cruickshanks was appointed to the chair in 1817, and the doctor died in 1829.

The professors of King's College were, since my attendance at the Divinity Hall, almost all removed by death, and their places filled by their successors. Principal MacLeod, brother of the Laird of Harris, was in 1816 succeeded in the principalship by Dr. Jack, the sub-principal and professor of mathematics, a native of Shetland.

Dr. Gilbert Gerard, professor of divinity, was in 1815 succeeded by Mr. Duncan Mearns, the minister of Tarvas. The appointment to the theological chair in King's College was vested in the Synod of Aberdeen, and when a vacancy occurred candidates were invited to compete for the office. Trial exercises were prescribed, and a decision thereafter given in favour of one of the competitors. Dr. Mearns' competitor was the late eminent Dr. Love of Glasgow. Though much inferior to Dr. Love, Dr. Mearns was by no means unworthy of the office to which he was thus elected. He was a man of superior ability, extensive and accurate information, and whose views of Divine truth, if not profound, were strictly according to Scripture and the Standards of the Church. He was besides one of the ablest lecturers I ever heard, while his criticisms on the pieces of trial delivered before him were judicious, candid, and instructive. He was both a Christian and a divine, in knowledge and in form; but the animating principle was wanting, and he more resembled the highly-finished, but cold and lifeless, marble bust, than he did the living reality which it is intended to represent. When at Tarvas he had no heart for the work of a parish minister. But his

discharge of the duties of the professorial office, which were more
congenial to the habits of his literary mind, was most able, while his
conduct was uniformly consistent and irreproachable.* His father,
Alexander Mearns, was minister of the parish of Cluny, in the Presbytery of Kincardine o' Neil, and during my time at Aberdeen died at a
very advanced age.

William Ogilvie, the renowned professor of Humanity and Natural
History at King's College, died about the year 1816. His successor
was Patrick Forbes, minister of Boharm, afterwards of Old Machar.
Professor Ogilvie was fresh in the memory of all my contemporaries at
Aberdeen College. They never wearied talking of him, and of his
unrivalled translation of Virgil's Eclogues. It is much to be regretted
that these were not published. He devoted nearly every third hour of
his literary life to the study of these magnificent specimens of ancient
pastoral poetry.

Mr. Eden Scott was, during my college years, professor of Moral
Philosophy at King's College. He was unquestionably at the head of
his contemporaries in point of mental capacity and knowledge of the
particular science which he taught. He died about 1815, and was
succeeded by Mr. Andrew Alexander, who, in 1819, was appointed to
the Greek professorship at St. Andrew's College. When Dr. Daniel
Dewar, who next filled the chair, resigned it after a year, it was
conferred on Dr. John Lee, professor of Church History at St.
Andrew's, who contemplated holding both offices by employing a
deputy to read his lectures at Aberdeen. In the May following, he
resigned both charges on being installed minister of Lady Yester's
Church, Edinburgh. Dr. Lee is now Principal of the Edinburgh
University. He had held more offices than any other Scottish church-
man, and that restless spirit which induced his many changes has
procured him the sobriquet of the "Solicitor General."†

Prof. John Tulloch was appointed to the Mathematical Chair of
King's College in 1811, and became the successor of Dr. Jack, when he
was promoted to the office of Principal of the University. Prof.
Tulloch had previously been, for some years, one of the teachers of the
Inverness Academy, where his diligence and success as a teacher, and
his high character as a man, procured him universal esteem. He was
a native of the parish of Reay, and a contemporary at school and at
college of the venerable Dr. MacDonald of Ferintosh. One of my
earliest recollections is seeing them one evening at my father's house at
Kildonan on their way to or from Aberdeen. Prof. Tulloch was my
most intimate friend during my residence in that city. We walked

* Dr. Duncan Mearns of Tarvas was admitted Professor of Theology at King's
College in 1817 ; he died 2nd March, 1852, in the 73rd year of his age and 53rd of his
ministry.—ED.

† Principal John Lee, D.D., LL.D., was a man of varied culture, but delicate
health impaired his energy. He had been Professor of Divinity and Church History
at St. Andrew's. In 1825 he was translated from Canongate parish to Lady Yester's,
and from thence in 1835 to the Old or High Church in Edinburgh. In 1837 he was
appointed Principal of St. Andrew's United Colleges ; on 12th March, 1840, he became
Principal of Edinburgh University. He died 2nd May, 1859, in the 80th year of his
age and 52nd of his ministry.—ED.

together in every direction to and from both Old and New Aberdeen, then we dined together alternately at his house and mine. Our converse with each other in the house and by the way brought me into the knowledge of his private history and of many things else which constituted the domestic and historical occurrences of that period. He had a rare capacity for drollery, and was a determined punster. It happened that a theft had been committed both in his house and Principal Jack's in the course of the same week. Dr. Jack's silver plate was stolen, while the professor lost a fat Caithness goose. Dr. Jack, who loved a joke, rallied the professor on the particular commodity which had taken the fancy of the nightly depredators in his house. "Aye," said Tulloch, "but pray notice the distinction, in my house the thieves took the goose and left the plate, but in yours they took the plate and left the goose."

I have already mentioned Mr. William Brown, oldest son of the Provost of Aberdeen. He had three brothers, Alexander, David, and Charles John. Alexander was a very thoughtless youth. He had been abroad. When his brother and sister came under serious impressions of the truth, which were cherished by their mother, he and his father ridiculed them mercilessly. Returning on one occasion, however, on a steamer from Leith to Aberdeen, Alexander had, as a fellow-passenger, the late eminent Cæsar Malan, a French Protestant minister, who was then rejoicing in the days of his spiritual youth. Mr. Malan asked of him some close and pointed questions regarding his spiritual state. This conversation, under God, led to his conversion. David and Charles were, during my residence at Aberdeen, very young men, students at college, and very intimate with Mr. Black of Tarvas, a most learned man, who, on the death of Principal Brown, became his successor in the Theological Chair at Marischal College. David Brown, some years later was licensed to preach, but his views of the truth became distorted and visionary, and he sank into the errors and delusions of Edward Irving. He continued for some time as Irving's missionary in London, but reason at last returned to him, and, disgusted with the errors and ravings of that sect, he renounced them, and re-entered the church which he had forsaken.* Since then he has been engaged as a minister in Glasgow, and he has written long articles on the Millennium in modern periodicals. His brother Charles, from youth upwards, seemed to be one of God's chosen vessels to honour. The Bible and the Confession of Faith were his most

* "At length Mr. Irving called me, and after being seated, and a long pause—each appearing to expect the other to break silence—he rose up and said, 'Well, Mr. Brown, you have left us.' 'Yes, Mr. Irving, I have; but not, as you know, while there was in my mind any shadow of ground to think that this work was Divine. But when that was gone, I had no option.' After a momentary pause, he said, with a good deal of suppressed feeling, 'Your intellect, sir, has destroyed you.' 'Yes, sir, I confess it; my intellect *has* done the deed, whatever that may mean; I am responsible for the use of my intellect, and I have used it.' With his hand held to mine and mine warmly grasping his, he left me—my feelings very acute, and his I am sure the same. And thus ended my connection with this grand man, whose name can never be uttered in my hearing without a feeling of mingled reverence and love arising within me." (Principal David Brown, D.D., of Aberdeen, in "The Expositor" of Oct., 1887.)—ED.

familiar acquaintances. He was licensed to preach in due course, and became, first the successor of the eminent Dr. Love of Glasgow, and afterwards minister of the New North Church in Edinburgh. He is now an honoured minister of the Free Church of Scotland, is married, and has a family.*

Provost Brown, the father of this interesting family, is still alive, and upwards of eighty years of age. He long retired from business, but when I was in Aberdeen he was active and prosperous in it. His old shop was in Broad Street, at the sign of Homer's head—a huge gaunt-looking effigy of that patriarchal poet painted on a board, with the name in Greek characters beneath. When his business extended, and Union Street became the great commercial thoroughfare, his shop was removed thither. Mrs. Brown still lives also, and is, as she then was, the punctual, scrupulous, and truly pious member of Mr. Aitkin's congregation. They had two daughters; the one was married to the devoted Mr. Joseph Thorburn, minister of Union Chapel, Aberdeen, afterwards of Forglen, in Banffshire.† The youngest daughter married Mr. William Barclay, minister of Auldearn. She died some years ago, quite young, but decidedly pious.

* Dr. Charles Brown was ordained minister of Anderston Church, Glasgow, in 1831 ; was translated to New North Church, Edinburgh, in 1837 ; at the Disruption his whole congregation adhered along with him to the Free Church of Scotland. He died 3rd July, 1884, aged 78 years. He was an eminent leader in all the great movements which agitated the church in his time, and he excelled as a preacher and a pastor. During the seven years he was laid aside from work, he continued by letters to comfort the bereaved among his flock : and to the last he kept a list of the members of his congregation that he might remember them in prayer. (*Minutes of Assembly.*)—Ed.

† Mr. Thorburn finally became minister of the Free High Church congregation at Inverness, where he died in 1853 of typhus fever caught by visiting patients in the Infirmary of that town. He was one of the most devoted and beloved of pastors—a true servant and follower of the Lord Jesus. The present handsome church edifice at Inverness was erected during his incumbency.—Ed.

CHAPTER XVIII.

THE GENERAL ASSEMBLY OF 1820.

J MUST now advert to the state of opinion in the Church of Scotland during the years 1820-21. Perhaps at no former period of its history did the two opposing church-parties pit themselves with greater energy or more uncompromising hostility against each other. These were the "Moderates" and the "Evangelicals." The contest between them appeared to be equally well-sustained, particularly on the battlefield of the General Assembly, where each side was led on by men of influence and ability. Dr. John Inglis of Edinburgh was at the head of the Moderate party. His known principles led him to adopt a carnal, worldly policy, and his mind, stern and unbending, was altogether free from what he regarded as the mere trammels of pietism or fanatical precision. Every minister of a parish who looked to stipend, manse and glebe more than he looked to Christ, ranged himself at once under the guidance of Dr. Inglis. He was the pole-star of ministerial duty! he was the oracle of the Church of Scotland! But Dr. Inglis thought for himself, and was quite capable of so doing; in all matters of policy or duty he acted sturdily, and with home-spun honesty and straightforwardness, up to his light. He took up his own position with dogged determination. If others followed him good and well, if not, he was somewhat displeased, perhaps not a little rude, may be even ferocious, but still he let them have their way, he could not help them, and would not undertake to furnish them with the understanding which God had evidently denied them. Such was Dr. Inglis, the helmsman of the Moderate party of that day.*

In his wake followed Dr. Nicol, Principal of the United Colleges of St. Andrews, and the wealthy proprietor of a goodly estate in Moray-shire. His intellect, nevertheless, was but third-rate, and in any undertaking he was at his wits' end if some one of more acuteness and resolution than himself, did not go before him to break the ice, and mark out a path or track for him which he could distinctly see and manfully follow. He was always watchful, therefore, to avail himself of such golden opportunities. He was annually elected a member of the Assembly, and his great ambition was to be one of its leaders. His social position and literary qualifications contributed not a little to

---

* Dr. John Inglis was minister of Old Greyfriars', Edinburgh ; he died 2nd Jan., 1834, in the 72nd year of his age and 48th of his ministry. In 1824 he was appointed convener of the General Assembly's first committee for sending the gospel to India, the duties of which he very ably discharged   The Rt. Hon. John Inglis (Lord Glencorse),'the present distinguished Lord Justice-General and President of the Court of Session, is his son.—ED.

gratify the wish of his heart, all the more that he had a rare capacity for "wording" himself *into* a subject when he took it in hand, and *out of* a scrape when he happened to get into one.

Side by side with Dr. Inglis as a leader, although of course in a subordinate capacity, seeing he was a much younger man, was Dr. Duncan Mearns, Professor of Theology in King's College. As a ruler of the church, Dr. Mearns exceeded all his compeers in the characteristic of consistency. His course in all the outgoings and incomings of church policy was even, undeviating and pertinacious, and the older men, in prospect of soon passing from the stage, looked upon him as one of the main props of their party for the coming years.

But perhaps the most active and efficient, and I fear I must add unscrupulous, of the Junta of Moderate rulers was the well-known Dr. George Cook, then minister of Laurencekirk, but afterwards Professor of Moral Philosophy in the University of St. Andrews. He was nephew of the celebrated Principal Hill, a leader who more than filled any place which he attained in the ecclesiastical courts. Dr. Cook strove to reach the same public eminence and notoriety. He failed, however, to do so, in spite of the sacrifices which he made of the principles cherished by his party in order to further his ambitious projects.*

In connection with these personages there was also a sort of nondescript named James Bryce, whom I scarcely know how to describe. Of his father I had heard much when in Aberdeen, and towards the close of my residence there I was in some measure acquainted with him. He was minister of a Relief Chapel in Belmont Street, the back part of which looked into Gaelic Lane, right opposite the Gaelic Chapel. Mr. Bryce was admitted, with his whole congregation at their request, into the pale of the Established Church of Scotland on the Chapel of Ease footing. His son James had, some years before, joined the Establishment, and was first presented to the parish of Strachan, Presbytery of Kincardine o' Neil, but afterwards went to India as minister of the Scotch Church, Calcutta, while at the same time he was connected by membership with the Edinburgh Presbytery. This man was shallow, flippant, and loquacious, and full of bitter hate against all who exhibited the spirit of Christ. He became the scavenger of the party; if any dirty work was to be done, which if proposed to any of their leading men would be received with a frown and regarded as an insult, Dr. Bryce of Calcutta was ready at a wink to come from the uttermost parts of the earth to do it.†

Another worthy on the same side was Dr. Macfarlane of Drymen,

* Dr. George Cook was the son of Prof. John Cook of St. Andrews. He was unanimously elected Moderator of the Assembly of 1829, for which position he had been an unsuccessful candidate in 1821 and again in 1822. He resigned his charge on being appointed Professor of Moral Philosophy at St. Andrews, and died 13th May, 1845, in the 73rd year of his age and 50th of his ministry.—ED.

† By Act of Assembly (1814) it was decided that "the three churches endowed in India were acknowledged as branches of the Church of Scotland, and allowed to send one minister and one elder to the General Assemblies." Dr. Bryce had been appointed to the church in Calcutta in 1814; he died 11th March, 1866, in the 56th year of his ministry.—ED.

afterwards Principal of Glasgow College and one of the ministers of that city. His abilities and attainments were of the same use to his party as ballast is to an empty ship at sea, chiefly valuable for its inertness and dead weight, and at the same time giving the vessel a tendency to sink rather than to swim.

But I must now glance at the leaders of the opposite party. And, first, I will mention Sir Henry Moncreiff Wellwood, senior minister of St. Cuthbert's, Edinburgh. My earliest conceptions of the high responsibility of the Christian ministry stood connected with this able man. As a leader of the Evangelical section of the church, Sir Henry did more for the interests of truth by his great moral weight as a minister of Christ, and his unswerving adherence to the vital doctrines of the gospel and to the great fundamental principles of the constitution of our Church, than by any of his polemical discussions on the platform of the Church court.

To Dr. Andrew Thomson of St. George's I have already referred. As a preacher he was clear, consecutive, and scriptural. His great mind at once understood the beauty and harmony of the whole system of gospel truth as held by the fathers of the Church, and so explicitly laid down in its standards. He was a born controversialist; in this direction the vigour and power of his mind scarcely knew any limit. It was remarked by Lord Brougham, who had been his school-fellow, that there was not a man living whom he feared to meet in debate but one, and he was Andrew Thomson. Dr. Thomson's speeches in the General Assembly not only shook the listeners, but penetrated with a thrilling influence into the heart of every member of the whole Church. His ministry was eminently distinguished for its faithfulness. To his hearers' progress in knowledge and soundness in the truth; to the spiritual and secular instruction of the youth of his flock, and to the consolation and right exercise of the sick and the dying, Andrew Thomson devoted his days and his nights. The schools which he established in his own congregation, the school-books which he compiled for their use, and the method of teaching which he brought into practice, might with truth be said to stand at the head of all educational efforts and institutions of the day in which he lived. He was the editor of a periodical work, entitled "The Christian Instructor," in which he "defended the rights and privileges of the Scottish Church against all invasion."*

Till I came to Aberdeen I had heard little or nothing about these parties and their leaders. My father, in all his life, only attended one

* Dr. Andrew Thomson, the most illustrious divine of his time, died from an affection of the heart instantaneously, within a few feet of his own door, when returning from a meeting of Presbytery at which he had been actively engaged. His death occurred 9th Feb., 1831, in the 53rd year of his age and 29th of his ministry. His zeal, energy, and eloquence were without parallel in his day. He was translated from New Greyfriars to St. George's, Edinburgh, 16th June, 1814. He devoted himself to the circulation of the Bible in its purity, and to the abolition of slavery in the British colonies. "The Christian Instructor," which he edited, numbers 50 volumes. About 200,000 copies of his "Catechism on the Lord's Supper" were printed and sold. He also published several theological works and essays, and contributed to the "Edinburgh Encyclopedia."—Ed.

Assembly. My first Assembly was that of 1824, and from that time forth I began to take an interest in ecclesiastical proceedings.

On the 18th of May, 1820, the General Assembly met at Edinburgh in the New Church aisle. Dr. Macfarlane of Drymen was succeeded, as Moderator, by Dr. MacKnight, son of Dr. MacKnight, the author of a critical work on the New Testament. The King's Commissioner was the Earl of Morton, a man of open profanity and loose character, but, being also poor, the appointment was given him in charity. The most notable members on the Evangelical side present that year were, besides Dr., then Mr., Andrew Thomson; Dr. A. Stewart of Dingwall; Mr. J. Robertson of Kingussie; Mr. Forbes of Tarbat; Dr. MacGill, professor of Divinity in Glasgow; and Mr. Doig of the East Church in Aberdeen, ministers. The ruling elders on this side were Mr. James Moncreiff, advocate, eldest son of Sir Henry Moncreiff Wellwood, Bart., D.D., and afterwards a Lord of Session; and Mr. George Ross, brother of the late Sir Charles Ross of Balnagown. On the Moderate side were Dr. Cook of Laurencekirk; Dr. Lee of St. Andrews; Dr. Irvine of Little Dunkeld; Principal Nicol; Mr. Mylne of Dollar; Mr. Donald Mackenzie of Fodderty; Mr. Wightman of Kirkmahoe, ministers; while among the Moderate elders were the Lord Justice-Clerk Boyle; the Lord Hermand; Lord Succoth; Mr. John Hope, Solicitor-General (afterwards Lord Justice-Clerk); Mr. Walter Cook, W.S., brother of Dr. Cook; Sir John Sinclair of Ulbster, Bart.; and Dr. Bryce of Calcutta.

It is unnecessary to notice particularly the ordinary business which came before this Assembly. One case, however, brought matters between the Moderate and Evangelical parties to a decided issue, and as it was in fact the seed which, then sown, broke through the soil at the Disruption of 1843. I shall record it with some minuteness.

After the report of the Committee on Bills was read, Mr. Thomson gave notice of a motion " for the production of the Order in Council intended to regulate the form of prayer for the several branches of the Royal Family." This very plain and ordinary request fell upon the Assembly, or at least upon the Moderate section of the House, with all the effect of a thunderbolt. Speaker after speaker rose up, one class contending that they could not conceive the object of the motion, that it was informal, that it ought to be withdrawn, and so forth. Those on the side of the mover, on the contrary, maintained that the Order in Council ought to have been produced independently of any motion to that effect. It was at last agreed that the motion should be discussed on Wednesday, the 24th of May, when the report of the Commission would be presented. But the motion, or what it implied, or the real causes of the excitement which it produced, cannot be fully understood unless I refer to some events in the national history. George III. died on 29th of January, 1820. George, Prince of Wales, had long previous to his father's death, and in consequence of his protracted illness, acted as Prince-Regent. Between him and his consort, the Princess Caroline of Brunswick, ever since their marriage in 1795, nothing at all approximating to connubial happiness had ever subsisted, and their indifference to each other had gradually ripened, particularly on the part of the Prince, into absolute loathing. In 1814 the Prince attempted to divorce her by setting on foot "the delicate investigation" into some charges whispered against her moral character, but of which she was fully acquitted. Immediately on the demise of George III., the Regent was proclaimed King as George the Fourth. In the month of February following, the Privy Council met at Carlton House, and there issued "An Order intended to regulate the form of prayer for the several branches of the Royal Family." The Order proceeded thus :—

> "At the Court at Carlton House, the 12th February, 1820.— Present the King's most Excellent Majesty; Archbishop of Canterbury; Lord Chancellor; Lord Privy Seal; Duke of Wellington; Lord Stewart; Marquis of Winchester; Earl of Liverpool; Earl of Mulgrave; Viscount Castlereagh; Viscount Melville; Viscount Sidmouth; Lord Charles Bentinck; Mr. Wellesley Pole; Mr. Canning; Mr. Chancellor of the Exchequer; Mr. Bathurst; Mr. Robinson.
>
> "In pursuance of an Act passed in the 10th year of her late Majesty Queen Anne, and of another Act passed in the 32nd year of his late Majesty King George III., wherein provision is made for praying for the Royal Family, in that part of Great Britain called Scotland, it is ordered by his Majesty in Council that henceforth every minister and preacher shall, in his respective church, congregation, or Assembly, pray in express words, 'For his most sacred Majesty King George, and all the Royal Family;' of which all persons concerned are hereby required to take notice, and govern themselves accordingly.
>
> (Signed)   "JAS. BULLER."

Now, two things are evident in this document; first, the King's persevering hatred of his unfortunate Queen—even all mention of her is studiously avoided; next, that prescribing prayers for the Royal Family, "in express words," to the Church of Scotland was unconstitutional and Erastian. Yet the Privy Council not only so framed their minute, but transmitted it to Dr. Macfarlane, Moderator of the General Assembly in the following terms :—

> "COUNCIL OFFICE, WHITEHALL, 12th *Feb.*, 1820.
>
> "SIR,—You will herewith receive an Order of his Majesty in Council, directing the necessary alterations to be made in the prayers for the Royal Family, so far as relates to Scotland, which you will be pleased to communicate in such manner that due obedience may be paid thereto. I have the honour to be, Sir, your most obedient, humble servant,
>
> (Signed)   "JAMES BULLER.
>
> "The Rev. Duncan Macfarlane,
> "Moderator of the General Assembly of
> "The Church of Scotland."

The Order in Council, prescribing prayers for the Royal Family to the Church of Scotland, was the point which Mr. Andrew Thomson took up. To the slur cast upon the Queen he did not make the most distant allusion. Every British subject who knew aught about the quarrel was full of it; so much so indeed that, when Mr Thomson first mooted the Orders in Council in the Assembly, the officers of State had it that to set up a defence for the Queen, and make a direct attack upon the reigning sovereign was the object which the speaker had in view. Of these surmises he was fully aware, and therefore on the Wednesday thereafter, and after the Order was produced. Mr. Thomson, in submitting his motion, stated "that he believed a great deal had gone abroad respecting it that was erroneous, and that topics had been mentioned, as those which he should have occasion to introduce, which had not the most distant relation to the subject, nor had indeed ever entered his mind to entertain." His motion clearly brought out both the principle which he advocated and the object he had in view. He moved:—

"That it be declared by the General Assembly that no civil authority can constitutionally prescribe either forms or heads of prayer to the ministers or preachers of this Church, and that the Orders in Council which have been issued from time to time respecting prayers for the Royal Family are inconsistent with the rights and privileges secured by law to our ecclesiastical Establishment; but that as these Orders appear to have originated in mistake or inadvertency, and not in any intention to interfere with our modes of worship, the General Assembly do not consider it to be necessary to proceed farther in this matter at present. And the General Assembly embrace this opportunity of declaring the cordial and steady attachment of the Church of Scotland to their most gracious Sovereign, and to all the Royal Family, and of further expressing their unqualified confidence that, actuated by the same principles of loyalty and religion which have hitherto guided them, her ministers and preachers will never cease to offer up, along with their people, their fervent supplications to Almighty God in behalf of a Family to whom, under Providence, we are indebted for so many distinguished blessings, both sacred and civil."

The motion was thus framed with what we may call a beautiful propriety, but this does not express its intrinsic value. It, in fact, embodies in few but most comprehensive terms that great scriptural principle of the Church of Scotland, her Spiritual Independence, for which, at the moment I now write, the present Establishment has ceased to contend, whilst all who adhere to that principle are discarded by the State, driven from their homes and maintenance, and branded, like their apostolic predecessors of old, as "the movers of sedition" against the "law of the land." It was evident that the motion was understood in the sense thus indicated, for no sooner was it announced than it stirred up a determined opposition. The Procurator stated that it was a motion to which they could not agree. Mr. Thomson was, therefore, under the necessity of entering more particularly into the merits of the question. He stated that it was an incontrovertible principle of the Church of Scotland that IT HAD NO SPIRITUAL HEAD ON EARTH, and that consequently the King in Council had no right to interfere in its worship. He proceeded to show that it was a vital privilege of our ecclesiastical constitution, essential to the safety of the Church, and for which our fathers had vigorously struggled in the covenanting times, while the order in Council trenched upon this privilege by prescribing prayers to its ministers and preachers. He then considered the Acts of Parliament referred to, on which the Order in Council professed to be founded. The Act X. of Queen Anne, in which ministers of the Scottish Church are enjoined to pray in express words for the Royal Family, the Church did not oppose. But of that Act he would say in general, that it proceeded on Erastian principles and ought not to have passed. But at that time there were peculiar circumstances in which it had been allowed to become law. These were, that then the interests both of civil and religious liberty were in great jeopardy, from the schemes of the Pretender abroad, and from the machinations of his clerical abettors. not only among the non-jurant Episcopalians, but even among the Presbyterian ministers of the Established Church, who prayed for the Royal Family without mentioning in express words who they were, and who thus left their audience to fill in mentally any name, just as their political bias might direct them. The Assembly, participating in the alarm, did not oppose the passing of the Act, but at the same time did all in their power to counteract its consequences to the Church by passing an Act of their own to the same effect. Besides that, the Act X. of Queen Anne was inapplicable to this or any other case succeeding the period of her reign, seeing it required all ministers to pray exclusively for her most sacred Majesty Queen Anne, and the most Excellent Princess Sophia, "so that," said Mr. Thomson, "if we were to pray according to that Act, we should not pray for his Majesty King George, but for these other royal personages now passed away." He then took up the Act of George III., so prominently referred to in the Order of Council, and showed that it had still less to do with the subject in question, inasmuch as it had respect exclusively to the Episcopal Communion in Scotland, seeing that it conferred upon them certain immunities on condition that they should pray for the Royal Family in the form prescribed by the liturgy of the Church of England. He concluded a long and able speech by meeting anticipated objections to his motion, and by most forcibly insisting on its necessity and moral force.

Mr. Thomson's motion was seconded by Mr. James W. Moncreiff, advocate, but before he addressed the Assembly, he was preceded by three speakers of the opposite side, the Solicitor-General, Dr. Cook, and Principal Nicol of St. Andrews. The speech of the Solicitor-General abounded in unhappy personalities. He began by saying that, though he differed entirely from the rev. gentleman, he must do him the justice to say that he had treated a very delicate subject with a degree of temper, decorum, and propriety which he could not but commend; but in the sequel of his speech the learned gentleman entirely failed in just these qualities, and first misrepresented Mr. Thomson's views and sentiments, and then made a furious onset on his own interpretation of them. He must disapprove, he said, of Mr. Thomson's sentiment that the civil authority had been inattentive to the interests of the National Church. Where, he would ask, was this inattention to be found? Was it in the appointment by his Majesty as his representative in that Assembly of a distinguished nobleman of our own nation, whose character and conduct adorned his lofty station? Was it in the gracious extension of the amount of the donation granted to the Church to advance its own form of worship at home, or in the Royal Aid to propagate abroad, particularly in India, its own principles and doctrines? It was impossible, he continued, in viewing all these circumstances, to justify the observation of the rev. gentleman. Then, to damage Mr. Thomson's case, he ran out into personalities. "The rev. gentleman," he said, was by his own showing the only person, for a century back, who thought it necessary to become the Church's champion by bringing forward the present complaint, and he could not help thinking that in this he assumed a lofty presumption." The rest of his speech was devoted to showing the special and invincible objections which he did most seriously entertain to Mr. Thomson's motion. These were, first, that the motion was one which " could not be received," and as this looked very like arguing in a circle, he proceeded to say that, if he had but time, he could easily show that it was a motion which affected, in a declaratory form, the very constitution of the Church, and he added, " that any man must have been but for a short time a member of Assembly, or have employed his time to very little advantage, who was not able to take precisely the same view." Dr. Cook then addressed the house, and the substance of what he said may be briefly summed up in three things. First, that he coincided with the general proposition laid down in the motion, that no civil authority could constitutionally prescribe forms or heads of prayer to our Church, and that this principle, so strenuously entertained by Mr. Thomson, he would also maintain. But, next, he qualified all these sentiments by saying that, *in the present instance*, he did not see that this great and important principle was infringed. And, lastly, he therefore agreed with the right honourable gentleman that the motion ought to be submitted to a committee, according to the uniform practice of the Church.

Principal Nicol began by proclaiming aloud his strong attachment to the Church of Scotland. To no living man would he yield on this point, but then he had a fear upon him that the present discussion, going forth to the public, would appear to them to be something very like a split between Church and State, and this, it appeared to him, would be the greatest of all evils. Besides, "this was not the time for any such misunderstandings, when both throne and altar are alike threatened by misguided men." As to Queen Anne's Act, "he did not know what it was that had excited the rev. gentleman's alarm, as he had already confessed that what he now complained of was practised in the days of Queen Anne." The poor Principal was galloping on, full tilt, on this broomstick sort of argument, when he was at once brought up by an emphatic " No, no," from Mr. Thomson. Dr. Nicol tumbled down at once, and quickly dropping the reins, said, " I mean that the Church in Queen Anne's days was quite as pure as it is at present," and so forth. He concluded by moving that the house do now adjourn; but not with the view of evading the discussion, for there would still be room for that on the question of adjournment. This was fairly beating a retreat, giving both his opponent and the discussion what is usually called *leg-bail.* But the Solicitor-General came to the rescue of the floundering Principal. He moved, as an amendment to the last motion that the question be dismissed, that it may be hereafter referred to a committee on overtures, upon which the Principal recovered from his panic, obediently got up, and said, " I withdraw my motion."

Mr. Thomson's motion was seconded and supported by Mr. Moncreiff, who, in an able speech, stated with great clearness and force his reasons for giving the motion his support—following the mover consecutively on every point, and thereby giving additional weight to his statement of the case.

This motion of Mr. Thomson called up many speakers on both sides; but as the whole force of his reply at the close of the debate fell on the defence of the Orders in Council set up by the Justice-Clerk, I shall only notice his leading arguments. This vigorous adherent of the Moderate party, Lord Justice-Clerk Boyle, was one of the presiding judges of the Court of Session, and a member of the Privy Council, so that his political influence was very considerable in Scotland both in Church and State. With his learned friend the Solicitor-General, his Lordship agreed as to the propriety with which the motion was introduced. As, however, he considered the subject of great importance, he could not agree with those who were inclined to dismiss it on a point of form. He boldly and openly deprecated the idea that the Assembly wished to evade the motion, but then, he would not say whether the proposition before the house was declaratory or not. He would, however, call upon every member present to say how its conclusions were arrived at. Mr. Thomson's motion, he continued, carried on the face of it a most unfair mode of procedure by, first, denying the power of the civil authority to prescribe prayers, then, alleging an encroachment on the rights of the Church in this respect, while lastly, professing loyalty. This was but a trap and a snare for their feet, but he would throw such a flood of light on the authority and the substance of this questioned Order, that the way would be made plain before their feet. As to the Privy Council's authority, his Lordship could not see why the Order should not be referred to the two Acts to which they allude. He had carefully looked into the X. of Queen Anne, and could not find that it was repealed, and it mentioned particularly the members of the Royal Family that were to be prayed for. He deprecated also the unfair construction put upon the term " Sacred Majesty " in the Order, which an honourable gentleman seemed to think was meant to intimate that the sovereign was Head of the Church. He would affirm that it meant no such thing. It was borrowed from the Act of Queen Anne, and was the language of addresses from church courts at all times. But who could suspect either King or Government of any wish or intent to encroach upon the rights of the Church of Scotland. Did, or could, this Assembly forget the gracious manner in which their deputation was lately received by the King—how they were admitted to a closet audience of His Majesty, when he expressed his resolution to support the constitution of the Church of Scotland. And were they, in the face of such things, to declare, by assenting to this motion, that almost the first Act of His Majesty's reign was an encroachment on the privileges of the Church. The learned Lord then threw himself into the substance of the Orders in Council. He would undertake to put it in the very light of a meridian sunbeam, and that, too, by an illustration the simplest and most obvious. The Order did not prescribe a form of prayer; it was absurd to suppose so. It merely prescribed the individuals that were to be prayed for. This he could prove by a most clear and convincing illustration. It often happens, when a clergyman is requested to remember in his prayers a sick person, that a paper is handed up to him mentioning the name and case of the individual; but is the minister on that account to pray for the individual by using the very terms written on the paper? Is it expected that he will adhere to the express phraseology of the paper any more than that he will think of praying for an individual of the family who is not named at all? Certainly not. He may use any terms he pleases, and so in the case of this order. In conclusion he said that, since it had been the fashion in the course of the debate, to make professions, he would also state that he yielded to no reverend or learned gentleman in attachment to the rights and privileges of the Church, for this most potent reason that he was lineally descended from a character who had occupied a conspicuous post in those struggles in defence of the Church which had been vaunted with so much pride by gentlemen on the other side of the House. He possessed therefore a sort of hereditary attachment to a cause which had been signalised by so much glory and by so much sacrifice. He therefore moved that, "whereas the independence of the Church of Scotland in all matters of faith, worship, and discipline is fully established by law, the General Assembly finds it unnecessary and inexpedient to adopt any declaration with regard to the late, or any former, Order in Council relative to prayers for His Majesty and the Royal Family."

The Justice-Clerk's pointed allusions to Mr. Moncreiff's speech called up that gentleman to offer an explanation. He expressed his distinct disavowal of the statement imputed to him by the learned judge, that it was the intention of His Majesty's Government, in framing the Order in question, to violate the rights of the Church of Scotland. He confessed himself much mortified that he should have been so unfortunate in expressing his opinion as to leave such an impression on the mind of any member of the Assembly, more especially of the Lord Justice-Clerk. He thought he had repeatedly stated that the Order had originated in mistake, and not in any injurious design. He did indeed use an argument drawn from the words "Sacred Majesty," in the terms of prayer prescribed, as indicating that the Order referred to the Church of which the King was supposed to be head. Therefore that the words were intended as a precise form of prayer, but he added that there was surely a great difference between the supposition of an intention to prescribe a form of prayer and that of a deliberate intention to invade the rights of the Scottish Church.

Mr. Walter Cook, W.S., younger brother of Dr. Cook, now rose and said that, on looking into the records of the Assembly of 1760, which he now held in his hand, he found that on that occasion, similar to the present, an Order in Council had been issued respecting prayers for the Royal Family, and what, he proceeded, did the Assembly do? They minuted the Moderator's report, transmitted it to presbyteries, and approved of the conduct both of the Moderator and of the Commission. This, he added, was what had been done in 1760, and were they now going to find fault, as it were, with the course of that Assembly's proceedings without sufficient cause shown? What was more, were they, by a side wind, going to censure the Throne for taking a step which a former Assembly did not challenge but approve?

Mr. Andrew Thomson then rose to reply. Mr. Walter Cook, he said, laid stress upon the circumstance that his motion was contrary to the sentiment of former Assemblies; but this argument really went the length of implying that the sentiments and doings of all succeeding Assemblies should be those of all Assemblies preceding—a doctrine with which he could not agree. The attention of the Assembly of 1760 was not called to the subject by any motion or overture. They had given their favourable opinion, he was entitled to say, *per incuriam.* Judging of the question on its merits—supposing that the Assembly consisted of 200 members, and that 199 believed the Order in Council to be a violation of our ecclesiastical privileges, would it be sufficient for the 200th member to rise up and say, "You must not find it so, because the Assembly of 1760 thought it otherwise." Besides, if the Privy Council had authority to issue any such order, why did the Assembly think it necessary to add on the back of it an order of their own? His motion, it was said, was, by a side wind, pronouncing a censure upon the Privy Council; but if these orders of the Privy Council possessed perfect authority over the Church, was not this Assembly, by a side wind, throwing contempt on that body by pretending to give a strength to this Act which yet, we are told, it did not require? He disclaimed going to work by side winds; he went straight forward to his object, he would do his duty boldly without being intimidated or discouraged by the opposition of any one. Referring next to a speech of Dr. Lee, Mr. Thomson said that the reverend professor's acquaintance with church history he owned to be extensive and accurate, but that in this case he was unfortunate in his facts. He first referred to the submission of the clergy to the orders of the sovereign in what were the most rigid and primitive times. But he forgot to tell the Assembly that the clergy at that period were beginning to conform, which was no good example for us to follow—a conformity which excited the alarm of the people, and finally riveted their opposition to Episcopacy. Next, he referred to the Acts of the Assembly appointing prayers in terms of the Order in Council, but he should have recollected what he (Mr. Thomson) believed he had urged before, that this was a proof of their regarding the power in this case as lodged, not in the Crown, but in themselves. Then the rev. doctor had adverted to the power of the Crown, acknowledged by the Church, to appoint fasts and thanksgivings. But here also he was mistaken. The instructions of the Assembly to their Commission would prove the very reverse of what he had alleged. Those instructions were, that the Commission, year after year, should consult with the State respecting the fasts and thanksgivings to be appointed. He next adverted to the speech of his much-respected friend on the other side of the table (Dr. Cook). He had acknowledged that no power on earth had a right to prescribe forms of prayer to us. Here was a well-spring of sound and constitutional doctrine, which Mr. Thomson declared to be quite refreshing to his soul amidst all that he had that day heard. But unluckily we did not enjoy it long; for it soon found a hidden channel for itself, and was no more heard of. The learned doctor objected strongly to his motion being voted upon before it had been submitted to a committee on overtures. But what was his conduct when that of the learned Lord was proposed? Why! he thought fit not to repeat his objection, although it was just as reasonable and valid in the one case as in the other. Now he expected his learned friend to be consistent; and, at all events, if he did not give his vote for his motion, neither would he give it for that of the learned Lord, though he rather hoped that he would come back and vote for *principle*, since *form* seemed to be matter of indifference. With regard to what fell from the Lord Justice-Clerk, his Lordship had complained that the motion was artfully put together. To this he must reply that no art was employed in contriving it. It was plain and simple; it hung well together, and was abundantly intelligible. The learned Lord had said a great deal about the Act of Queen Anne being still in force. He did not pretend to vie with his Lordship in interpreting Acts of Parliament, but he thought himself possessed of as much common sense and judgment as to dispute his Lordship's authority on this point. He maintained that the Act of Queen Anne alluded to was not binding, and he put it to the learned judge, if any person were brought to his bar for disobeying the Order in Council, could he venture to try or to punish on that statute? The learned Lord would not say so. It was impossible he should. But then the learned Lord maintained that the Act of Queen Anne did not authorise the phrase " express words " to be considered as dictating a form of prayer. He had sufficiently explained himself on that head; he had never dwelt on that Act alone; he had referred to several circumstances totally overlooked by the learned Lord, and particularly his Lordship had found it convenient to blink altogether the Act of George III., quoted in this Order, and for this good reason, he supposed, that the argument from that source was irresistible. With regard to the statute of Queen Anne, he had chiefly alluded to it to show that the Order of Council derived no authority from its enactments, and to this the learned Lord had given no satisfactory answer. And then as to the Act of Geo. III., while he (Mr. T.) had demonstrated that it did not apply to the subject at all, yet the reference to it by the Council was a proof that they meant the express words to be used, because it regulated the devotions of a church having a liturgy—the liturgy of the Church of England—in which no liberty was given to deviate from the *ipsissima verba* of the Order. His Lordship found fault with the sentiments of a certain pamphlet written on the subject now before the Assembly, and it had been noticed and condemned on a former day by Mr. Solicitor-General. Now he would say this much, that he believed it would require all the combined efforts of the learned Lord and the learned Solicitor-General to give a proper answer to the substance of that pamphlet. He had read it; and were he to write on the subject, he would certainly adopt its leading statements and reasonings, although there were some things he would omit. But the learned judge was not entitled to identify the whole of the anonymous pamphlet with the argument urged by him and his friends who had spoken on the same side. They must be allowed to think and speak for themselves, and be judged of by the sentiments which they expressed and avowed. The learned Lord had brought forward an argument to prove that the Order in Council was not imperative as to the express words, of which argument he must say that it was curious and amusing. It was introduced by his Lordship with all the solemnity that became such a serious subject, but really, in its progress and result, it became utterly ludicrous. "Suppose," says the learned Lord, "a case where a clergyman is requested to remember in prayer a sick person, and a paper is handed up to him to that effect, the clergyman will never think it necessary to use in his prayer the exact words used in that paper," and from this, said Mr. Thomson, we are to conclude that clergymen need not, in praying for the Royal Family, make use of the *ipsissima verba* of the Order in Council! Why, the two cases were as different from one another as could possibly be conceived. Did it never strike the mind of the learned Lord that Janet Meiklejohn, who happens to be sick, has a great deal less authority to dictate a prayer for the clergyman than the Privy Council are said to have in prescribing prayers for the Church. Poor Janet, in the simplicity of her heart, humbly requests her pastor to pray for her; and her pastor complies with her request in the way which he thinks most suitable to her circumstances and most for the edification of his people. But the Order in Council makes no request, it enjoins, it speaks of express words, it puts the prayer in inverted commas, it requires due obedience, it comes from the Sovereign of Great Britain, and has all the form of a peremptory command. And yet the two things are compared and the comparison is brought forward by the learned Lord with wonderful gravity as a very capital illustration and a most conclusive argument! His Lordship's case was not applicable; but he (Mr. T.) would take the liberty of putting a case which was exactly parallel, and he would be glad to know how the learned Lord could get the better of it. Supposing his Lordship was to send a letter to his steward, and order him to write to A.B., in *express words*, that such a thing was to be done, putting these in inverted commas, and supposing the steward to use the freedom of obeying the order in substance, and not literally— employing his own language and not the language set down for him by his Lordship—and supposing, farther, that some hurtful mistake were to be the consequence of this, what would his Lordship say? Would he deem it a sufficient apology if the steward pleaded that he did not think himself restricted? Or, would he not rather condemn his steward, and refer to his *express words* and to the *inverted commas* as quite decisive with regard to his meaning? So much then for the *remember in prayer* argument. A great deal had been urged by the learned judge and the Solicitor-General as to the proofs of the King's attachment to the ministers of the Church of Scotland collectively and individually; that they had got this thing and that thing and a thousand good things; and that the deputation was graciously received; and that some of the individuals who composed it had received many personal favours. Now, he did not understand this sort of argument as applied to ministers of our Church. He did not consider it fair and decorous, and would not admit it. For, what did it amount to? To this, that, because the Crown had shown us attention and kindness, therefore we should be ready to give up our independence. But he was just as ready to acknowledge the benefits received by the Church from the Crown as the most strenuous on the other side. This was fully and strongly expressed in his motion, from which he believed, after all, their sentiments on that point were actually borrowed. For his own part he had never asked and never received any personal favour, and yet he was as much attached to his Sovereign as any one of them. He was of no political party; never was a member of any political club; never attended a political meeting; never sat down to a political dinner; and yet he felt grateful and attached to his Sovereign for the blessings and privileges enjoyed under his government. He was grateful and attached to the Royal Family on grounds which sunk all the paltry and selfish considerations urged by the Solicitor-General into utter annihilation. He was grateful and attached, because he shared along with all his fellow-subjects in those benefits which that Family had been the means of conferring on the country. He had been unfairly dealt with, he thought, by the learned gentleman, the Solicitor-General.- That gentleman observed, indeed, that he (Mr. T.) had behaved himself with propriety, and he felt himself obliged to him for his favourable testimony. But he certainly must remark that the observations of the learned gentleman had no great tendency to make him persevere in that propriety. He had said that he (Mr. T.) had set himself up as the champion of the Church. He was not at all aware that he deserved the appellation, especially as applied by the learned Solicitor; but, if to defend the rights and privileges of the Church against all invasion was meant by that language, then he gloried in being the champion of the Church. But besides this, or on account of this, it seemed that in the opinion of the learned gentleman, he was a presumptuous man. The Solicitor-General here rose and denied that he called the reverend gentleman a presumptuous man; he only said he assumed to himself a presumptuous character. Resuming his address, Mr. Thomson said, as to that charge of presumption which it seemed by some very nice logical distinction, which he for his part did not understand, was attached to his *character* and not to *himself*, he thought, if there was any presumption in the case, it lay with the learned gentleman who was so extremely bold as to give a direct and unqualified denial to his assertions. The Solicitor again interrupted Mr. Thomson by affirming that he said no such thing. "Very well," said Mr. Thomson, "I have now done with the hon. gentleman's speech, and I conclude by saying that it was nothing but my warm and inviolable attachment to the Church that has urged me to make my stand against this encroachment; that, according to the direction of the learned lord, I can lay my hand upon my heart and say, I regard this Order of Council as a manifest encroachment on its independence; and I trust that the breath of official authority will never be allowed to wither one leaf of that Plant of Renown which our fathers watered with their blood, and of which we have been permitted by a kind Providence to eat the pleasant fruits."

The Assembly then divided, when the Justice-Clerk's motion was carried by a majority of votes amounting to 73, there being for Mr. Thomson's 53, but for the Justice-Clerk's 126. On the following day fifteen of those who voted for Mr. Thomson's motion, along with himself, recorded their dissent.*

* See Report in *Christian Instructor.* " The result was really a triumph for Mr. Thomson and his supporters, who did not, after what had been said, think it reasonable to depart from the construction which they had put upon the terms of the document, while frankly conceding the plea of mistake or oversight on the part of His Majesty's advisers." (Rev. Sir Henry Moncreiff's lectures on *The Free Church Principle.*)—ED.

CHAPTER XIX.

MINISTERIAL PROSPECTS.—MARRIAGE.

1820–21.

J WAS invited when in Aberdeen on several occasions to assist Mr. MacLeod, of the Gaelic chapel in Dundee, at the communion. His church was nothing else than an ordinary-sized dwelling-house converted into a place of worship by being fitted up with seats and galleries. The congregation consisted of Highlanders from the mountainous districts of Perthshire—plain, unsophisticated men. It was during my visits to Dundee that I first became acquainted with Dr. Peters, who was married to a sister of the wife of Professor Stuart of Marischal College. Mr. MacLeod and I were invited to sup with him, where we found before us Mr. W. Thomson of Perth, brother of Dr. Andrew Thomson of Edinburgh. Mr. Thomson of Dundee was, I think, there also. Mr. MacLeod sang a few of the old Gaelic psalm tunes.* These tunes, producing the most solemn impression when sung by a congregation in the open air, laboured under every possible disadvantage when set forth by Mr. MacLeod, whose voice, naturally husky and coming exclusively through his nose, made the effect so perfectly ridiculous that his guests had the greatest difficulty in reducing their countenances within the limits of decorum. Another of the acquaintances I formed at Dundee was a Mr. Kirkaldy. He was then a wealthy merchant in town, and had been married to a daughter of Dr. MacLauchlan, one of the town's ministers; but she had died, and the trial, a very sore one, for they lived most happily together, was eminently sanctified to her widowed husband.

In the year 1821 I received a unanimous call from the congregation of the Gaelic chapel at Rothesay. The offer was a most advantageous one in every way, and in looking back upon the circumstances, I can only wonder that I did not see my way to accept it. But Providence had designed for me another sphere.

About this time a great breach was made among the veteran watchmen on the walls of our Sion by the death of Dr. Ronald Bayne, minister of Kirtarlity, Inverness-shire, of whom mention has already been made. He died in February, 1821, aged 66 years. His second son, Charles John, was at the time a preacher. He was a candidate for his father's

---

* "In 1626 Lord Reay, Munro of Fowlis, etc., with thousands of their retainers, were influenced by their Protestant zeal to embark for Germany and fight for the ascendancy of their religion in that part of the continent Many of them fell there, others returned, and afterwards upheld the covenanting cause in Scotland under General Leslie. The old Gaelic tunes are only to be found in those parts of the Highlands whence those soldiers came, and it is supposed that they learned them in Germany, and brought them to this country." *(Gustavus Aird, D.D.)*—ED.

charge and living, but the patron disappointed him. He became minister of Fodderty in 1826, and died in 1832, at the age of 35 years.

Mr. Kenneth Bayne, minister of the Gaelic chapel in Greenock, died in 1821. This truly eminent minister was brother of Dr. Bayne of Kiltarlity. who preceded him to his everlasting rest only a few months before. Mr. Bayne's ministerial labours at Greenock were very specially owned and blessed. His wife, an eminently pious woman, died some years before then, and Mr. Bayne, tenderly attached to her, never fully rallied from the shock which that heart-rending event had inflicted upon him.

From the president of the Greenock Gaelic chapel committee I received a letter asking me to preach as a candidate. I did not precisely understand the general regulations by which Chapels of Ease were guided, particularly during vacancies, and the letter of the committee to me was framed in a way to darken, rather than to enlighten, my views upon the subject. The purport of it was that, having heard of me as a minister of the gospel, and that I was, in my public teaching, at one in views and sentiments with their departed pastor, the wish of the congregation was that I should preach at Greenock on a certain Sabbath shortly thereafter, which was particularly mentioned. What occurred to me at once, on receiving this intimation, was that, as the congregation is situated in the very heart of a large district of the south-west of Scotland where the Gaelic was not understood, the request of the managers to me was neither more nor less than to favour them with a supply during the vacancy, Gaelic preachers being few in that part of the country. On this understanding solely, and not with any, the most distant, desire of preaching there as a candidate, I agreed to go. I went by the stage-coach from Aberdeen, first to Perth, and next day to Stirling and Glasgow. After remaining there for a night at the "Black-bull" hotel, I went next day by one of the small Clyde steamers to Greenock. I arrived on Saturday, and met on the pier my worthy friend Mr. Bannatyne, under whose hospitable roof I lodged during the whole time I remained there. I preached in the chapel on the Sabbath. What the effect on the audience, a very large and crowded one, really was I could not well say, but I felt very much straitened. Being quite unconscious of any intention on the part of the congregation to think of me at all, as their future pastor, even youthful vanity did not urge me to keep up appearances. My residence with Mr. Bannatyne, under his own roof, served to raise him high in my esteem. On the Monday he had planned an expedition, along with his brother James, to Rothesay, or "Rosay" as he called it. We went thither by a steamer, and the wind almost blew a hurricane. The smell of the steamboat, together with the violence of the waves, made me both squeamish and frightened. Mr. Bannatyne, to keep up my spirits, although I was not much disposed to listen to it, told me an anecdote of Mr. Kenneth Bayne, their late excellent minister. He and his truly Christian brother, Mr. Mackenzie of Glasgow, had resolved, immediately after a communion occasion at Greenock, to go on a *gospel expedition* to Rothesay. They came to the boat; but, before stepping on board, Mr. Mackenzie who was but a "timid sailor," took out his handkerchief, held it up to the wind, and, finding that it very considerably "flickered" in the breeze, expressed his doubts as to the safety of going in "an open boat." Mr. Bayne laughed at his fears. "O, man." said Mr. Kenneth, "where is your faith?" "Oh," said Mr. Mackenzie, "there are many who have no faith to be afraid." We arrived at Rothesay in safety, and were kindly received by our friends. I found Mr. D. Fraser, the minister they had chosen when I declined, there before me. We landed at a house situated close by the ruins of Rothesay Castle, and although the conversation between us was altogether on a very different subject, and far more profitable, yet I could not entirely keep my mind's recollections away from the majestic ruin so distinctly seen from the windows. I said nothing of it to my friends, and it was just as well. Our time was limited; the boat, after a rest and delay of half-an-hour, was just on the tiptoe of departure; we rose up. bade our friends a hasty adieu, and sailed back to Greenock. I left Greenock for Aberdeen next day, under the impression, on my part, that I was no candidate for the chapel at all, but on their part that I was. I had not, therefore, been but about a month at home, when, by a letter I received from Dr. Dewar, I was at once made aware of the precise circumstances in which my agreement to preach at Greenock had placed me. I wrote off at once to the president of the managers of the chapel there requesting of him to withdraw my name from the roll of candidates, assuring him that it had been owing purely to mistake on my part that it was ever attached to it.

On the day of my arrival at Aberdeen by the coach from Greenock, I found a letter on the table before me from my then most intimate friend and acquaintance, Nathaniel Morren. It made a very plain and pointed reference, though not a little in the bantering style, to one of the most important events of my life—my first entrance into the marriage relation. The preliminaries had been begun some time previous to my visit to Greenock. I had, since my first arrival in Aberdeen, been intimate with and almost a weekly visitor in the family of Mrs. Robertson at Tanfield, near Aberdeen. The eldest daughter I ever regarded, since my first acquaintance with her, as a thorough and devoted Christian. Her piety was vital and ardent. Maria, the youngest of the three sisters, was also a subject of divine grace, but her piety was more concealed. She deferred much to her eldest sister Frances. Harriet, however, was different from them all. She naturally possessed all that amiability and native power of mind which attach us to things spiritual and temporal at one and the same time. There was, therefore, in her, even from the very moment of our acquaintance, a tie and an attraction which I could not attempt to define; and this before either the one or the other of us ever thought of the relation in which we might stand connected with each other.

Some time in the month of February or March, of 1821, going out from Aberdeen towards the Printfield, with the view of visiting some of my congregation residing there, I met Mrs. Robertson and her two daughters, Frances and Harriet, near the Old Town. After a cordial greeting, Frances said that she and her mother had, on special business, to go to Aberdeen, but that Harriet was to return home.

Harriet I offered to escort on her homeward journey. We entered the house, walked into the parlour, and sat down each of us on the sofa. I stammered out my attachment to her, long felt but concealed until now. At last she said, with a frankness peculiarly her own, that our attachment was reciprocal, but that, before we could take any important step, both our surviving parents ought to be consulted, for their approbation and blessing. Our conference, so interesting to us both, had just come to this point, when the entry-door opened, and her mother and two sisters entered the room. We had time to compose ourselves, rise from the sofa, and to stand, with all possible calmness, to receive them.

The house of Tanfield stood at the foot of a rather steep hill. The top of the hill was crowned with the ancient and, at that period, rather dilapidated and much decayed house and policies of the ancient family of the Johnstones, Baronets of Hiltoun. The place of Hiltoun stood at the top of the eminence above, and to the north of Tanfield. Thither Harriet and I, often afterwards, strayed together. We passed the house, and entered a clump of trees behind the garden wall, where there were several green glades opening up here and there between them. There we sat down, and conversed upon various topics, but always concluded with the renewal of our warm attachment to each other, and thus the intervening time between our engagement and our nuptials passed away.

I happened one day to be passing down slowly from my own house, through Woolmanhill Street, and had entered School-hill Street on my way to the discharge of some congregational duty. I had not very far passed the gate of Gordon's Hospital when I noticed two respectable and clerical-looking persons talking very cordially and anxiously with each other. As I drew nearer I recognised one of them, and discovered him to be none other than my old teacher of Moral Philosophy, namely, Dr. George Glennie, and I overheard him say, " I am exceedingly sorry to learn that our truly excellent brother, Mr. Arthur of Resolis, is no more." Some weeks thereafter I had occasion to pass up Gallowgate Street, and had just reached the end of it, when a Highlander, a member of my own congregation, met me fully in the face. After the usual salutation I was about to pass on, when he said, " Stop, sir, if you please, I have something to tell you ; you will have heard, perhaps, that Mr. Arthur of Resolis is dead." I replied that I had. " Then," said he, " I am a native of the Black Isle, and have just returned from visiting my relations in that country. I had occasion to know, when in the north, that the people of Resolis have held several meetings in expectation that the patron, the laird of Newhall, will give them their choice. So far as I could ascertain, they are likely to choose you. I replied, in general terms, that such a thing might be probable enough, but that I had never heard of it till now, nor even thought of it. I left him, but the intelligence, however undecisive, took a stronger hold of my mind than I had anticipated. Could it be true? If it were not, would it not be strange that, when two parishes (Dornoch and Golspie) had not the power of choosing, I should have been their selected candidate, and if now, when a parish had the power, I should not be

R

the object of their choice? Soon afterwards, however, I got a letter from a Mr. Young, a writer in Fortrose, and married to one of the Gordons of Swiney, cousins of my own, intimating that the people of Resolis, having got their choice of a minister from the patron, had held several congregational meetings; that they were divided into two parties; that they had three candidates in view, viz., Mr. William MacPhail, then in Holland, Mr. John Munro of the Gaelic Chapel in Edinburgh, and that I was the third. He suggested that, as he was on an intimate footing in the way of business with many of the Resolis people, I should privately authorise him to canvass the parishioners to secure a majority in my favour. I wrote back that such a measure I utterly repudiated, seeing that one of the questions expressly to be put to me, if I were settled there, would be, "Did I use any means to procure the living?" and that I would rather be without the living than so burden my conscience.

My marriage took place, according to appointment, on the 21st of July, 1821. My brother-in-law, Mr. Forbes, officiated, and Prof. Tulloch of King's College acted as "best man." After the ceremony, we all partook of a glass of wine and the marriage cake. Our marriage-jaunt had been planned to be a visit to the north, to my dear and venerable father. Into the same post-chaise which had carried me from Gilcomston to Tanfield we stepped immediately, accompanied by Mr. Forbes and Harriet's elder sister, Frances. We arrived that evening at the inn of Pitmachie, about twenty miles north of Aberdeen, where we remained that night. How often have my recollections hovered around that country inn! It was my usual resting-place on my way to and from college, but its only association in my mind is with that wedding journey. With all our joy and mirth, we never once thought of joining "trembling." Nay, the very anticipation of sorrow or bereavement in the future, I should have regarded as mere morbid apprehension.

Next day we rose early in expectation of the coach, and had full time to take a stroll before breakfast. Mr. Forbes, in the course of his walk, had fallen in with a Ross-shire Highlander employed as a day labourer on a farm near the inn. He greatly shocked us by repeating the man's description of what he had seen in the parish church on the preceding Sabbath at the communion table. He had seen old and young, male and female, rushing forward to the table, jostling each other rudely in order to get a seat, and boys, not much above fourteen years of age, tittering and laughing, and throwing the bread in each other's faces. No wonder that the man said he would not presume to be a communicant in such a manner.

The coach-hour arrived, so, dismissing the chaise, we took seats for Alves on the outside, as those inside were occupied. We dined at Elgin, and met there Captain Mackay, old Araidh-chlinni's son, who then lived at Inverness. We now set out for the manse of Alves, alighting right opposite to it at a small village. Mr. Duncan Grant, my predecessor in Aberdeen, was then minister there. We found him waiting for us, and got a most hearty reception from himself and his sister. The next day we resolved to proceed to Burghead, about six miles to the north, and thence to hire a boat and crew to take us to Tarbatness, or to land us as near the manse of Tarbat as possible. Mr. Grant, accordingly, conveyed us thither in a cart, and no sooner had we arrived than we sought out, found, and arranged with the boat's crew; so we proceeded on our journey. The weather was sufficiently mild, and we experienced neither difficulty nor danger in crossing, in an open boat, that wide arm of the sea. At the Tarbat shore we landed in a small creek called Wilkhaven, two or three miles to the east of the manse, where conveyances awaited us. We received a cordial welcome from my sister and her family, who all, then in the bloom of youth, still clustered around her.

We remained at Tarbat over Sabbath, and on Monday we all three, Harriet, Frances, and myself, left by a fisherman's boat for the Sutherland coast, which stretched out, right opposite, about twenty miles across. We landed at about six o'clock below the manse of Loth. After dismissing the boatmen, we went to Kilmote, then tenanted by Mr. Robert Mackay, one of the sons of Robert of Achoul, parish of Farr, and nephew of old and venerable William of Achoul. We left Kilmote that evening for Wester-Garty, the abode of Mr. James Duncan, where we remained during the night. Mr. Duncan was kind enough to furnish us with a conveyance to the manse of Kildonan next day. We left his house after breakfast, and arrived at Kildonan, coming by Helmisdale and the Strath, about three o'clock in the afternoon. My father met us at the door. His gigantic figure and his large countenance, beaming with love and kindness, were calculated to make a deep impression upon us all. He stood before us with all the affection of a venerated father, and with the native dignity of a gentleman of the old school. I presented to him my young and dearly-beloved wife. He opened up his large and massy arms, into which dear Harriet, in the gushing warmth of her natural affection, threw herself at once. He clasped her in his embrace, and imprinted a paternal kiss upon her forehead. We spent many happy days at Kildonan, every one of which we enjoyed.

But the time arrived when we must depart. We left Kildonan for Aberdeen, but many things intervening prevented us from getting there so soon as we had intended. We went first to the manse of Dornoch, where we remained for some time. While here, my father wrote asking me to return and assist him, as he proposed administering the sacrament. Leaving my wife and her sister, therefore, in Dornoch, I returned to Kildonan. There I found my sister Elizabeth, though her husband, Mr. Cook, being similarly engaged in Caithness, could not be present. On Sabbath I preached the action sermon in English. My sister was my hearer, but she was dissatisfied. She expressed this feeling to me at the close of the communion season. Her objections were well-founded, but I did not receive them as I ought to have done, and it was no wonder. Her mind and mine were, at the time, in two very different, and even contrary, frames. She was in sorrow, I was in joy; she mourned the loss of a beloved babe, whilst I rejoiced in my recent union to the wife of my youth; her sorrows turned her to Christ's death and atonement, my joys, alas! of a far less spiritual character, turned me to the opposite side, even to the world, which whispered insidiously into my mind's ear that to-morrow would be as to-day, and every day thereafter accordingly. How egregiously was I mistaken! I was then like a foolish boy spending his time in pursuing the butterfly which, as he caught it, was crushed in his grasp. This I afterwards bitterly realised. I spoke to my sister of her recent bereavement, but she was silent, and could not find utterance for the swelling of her heart; she turned from me and walked away.

I forgot to mention that, while we were at the manse of Tarbat, I received a letter from Mr. Macdonald of Ferintosh in which, after congratulating us on our marriage, he proceeds to say:—"The presentation in your favour to the parish of Resolis is drawn out, and no time, in that case, is to be lost in proceeding to the other steps requisite to be gone through. On this account you would require to be at hand, say at Kirkhill or at my house." My letter of acceptance of the presentation to the church and parish of Resolis, or rather Kirkmichael and Cullicudden, was drawn out by Mr. Fraser of Kirkhill, and signed by me. It was dated at Killearnan on the 14th day of August, 1821. We went to Kirkhill for some days. Harriet and Lilias Fraser, Mr. Fraser's eldest daughter, a very lively and affectionate girl, got enthusiastically fond of each other. They were kindred spirits; whilst they both knew and revered the truth, which evidently was the undercurrent of their souls, the playfulness of youthful minds and their natural vivacity during these halcyon days, like a gentle summer breeze, swept over their more serious thoughts. To entertain us, Mr. Fraser proposed a trip to the Fall of Foyers, in which Lily was to accompany us, a proposal which we readily accepted. We set out for Inverness on the preceding evening, and were most kindly received by my aunt, Mrs. Fraser, widow of Dr. Alex. Fraser of Kirkhill. Thence, next morning, we set out for the canal to proceed up Loch Ness by the steamer as far as Foyers. We landed at Foyers by the steamer's yawl, and proceeded through a few glades and thickets, until we came to the banks of the river at the foot of the mountain, down which the fall in its course runs headlong. We then began to ascend, and about midway, within a few hundred yards of a cottage built in 1737 by Gen. Wade, and commonly called the "General's hut," a narrow, scrambling pathway brought us to the lower fall which, hidden as it was by the rocks and trees rising on each side of it, burst upon us all at once, and overpowered us with a sense of its rugged grandeur. We stood upon a protruding ledge of rock which brought us within 20 feet of the cataract, and from which we had a perfect view of the whole sheet of the lower fall both upwards and downwards. Looking upwards, we could see that the river was compressed between two rocks not apparently more than 15 feet apart. Thence it began its downward foaming course of at least 90 feet. It passed us on our stance enveloped in a cloud of spray and with a deafening noise. Looking downwards, we could see its termination. It threw itself into a deep chasm considerably dark, but not so obscured that we could not discern its boiling rage lose itself in a still-flowing current. On the opposite side of the river, and situated on a fairy knowe, we saw far beneath the manor-house of the proprietor of this beautiful Highland domain, Mr. Fraser of Foyers. The "General's hut" was very justly so designated. It was a low, old-looking building; its walls, gables, and chimney tops evidently the rude, clumsy rubble-work of the masons of 1733, when set to execute, no matter how, in that hyperborean clime, a Government contract, responsible only to the final approval of General Wade, who knew nothing about the matter. The roof was of heather thatch, not of course so old as the walls, but pretty well stricken in years notwithstanding, as its appearance very plainly showed. The internal arrangement and whole aspect of the hut were still more in unison with its name. There was a huge chimney in the principal room which did not vent, for the obvious reason that it never was intended for any such purpose, and the walls which, when originally built, had been plastered with lime, and, of course, quite white, were jet black, bearing upon them the annual incrustations of smoke and soot from the chimney of nearly a century. We left the "General's hut," and proceeded towards the shore of Loch Ness, where, after waiting about an hour, the steamer made its appearance. Next day we returned to Kirkhill, and soon after went home to Gilcomston, where we arrived about the end of August.

On our arrival, our domestic establishment underwent a complete revolution. Mrs. Robertson and her two daughters could not possibly separate themselves from Harriet. Frances they all looked up to as a faithful and conscientious monitor, but Harriet was the very soul and life-spring of the whole family circle. If I remember well, Mrs. Robertson kept her house at Tanfield until we finally left Aberdeen for the north, but she and her daughters resided principally with us at Gilcomston.

My reception by my congregation was not altogether what I could have expected. They had all heard to a man that I had been presented, at the request of the people, by the patron to the parish of Resolis. I naturally thought that when I returned to them again, they would have been, if not angry at me, at least disappointed or sorry. Not so, however, they were rather gratified that a parish in Ross-shire had chosen their minister above others; though they would have been far better pleased had I elected rather to remain with them than to accept, as I had done, the offer made to me. I was just three years minister of the Gaelic Chapel, and the people were attached to me. But the call to Resolis just came in time both to foster their attachment to me, and to raise me in their estimation. Many of them told me so.

From December, 1821, till the following May, when I was inducted minister of Resolis, most of our time was occupied in preparation for our departure, and it was resolved by us all, both at Gilcomston and Tanfield, that we should live together at Resolis under the same roof.

My intercourse with my congregation, in the meantime, was nothing less cordial and confidential than it was before. I had abundant proof of their attachment to me, especially from such of them who truly feared God. There were but few of these comparatively; in going to

Ross-shire, certainly, true Christian intercourse would be very much increased. The eminent and decided piety of Ross-shire was well known all over Scotland, both to the friends and to the enemies of the truth. The Moderate party in the church was wont to point the finger of scorn at that county, and say, "Behold the hot-bed of fanaticism," meaning, by that expression, the vital influence of divine truth on the heart. How true it is that "the natural man receiveth not the things of God; they are foolishness to him!" Those, however, in the north or the south, who had experienced that influence on themselves, regarded it as the mother-county of true Christianity in Scotland. The peculiarity connected with it was, however, that while, in other parts of the country, true religion was to be found among the middle classes, in Ross-shire it was almost entirely confined to the peasantry.

At this particular period of my life the country had scarcely yet settled into a calm after the political excitements of 1815. The battle of Waterloo terminated a long and sanguinary struggle, during which the balance of power in Europe, after being often nearly lost, and as often nearly won, was at last settled by the triumph of the allied armies and the downfall of Bonaparte. The great military leaders who had survived that bloody contest, at the head of whom was the Duke of Wellington, were loaded with emoluments and honours. But a great many more, natives both of England and Scotland, had fallen during the Spanish and other wars, and no reward could be conferred on them but the honours usually accorded to the mighty dead. The fallen heroes of England had already a Westminster Abbey in which their deeds and their prowess could by suitable memorials be perpetuated. But Scotland had nothing of the kind, and therefore the idea of a National Monument was started. It was proposed that an ornate edifice should be erected on the Calton Hill of Edinburgh, and that, within this building niches or stalls should be prepared for the monuments of those Scottish heroes who fell fighting the battles of their country, and further, that, like its Westminster prototype, the building should be a place of worship in connection with the National Church. Such was the scheme itself, and the question then came to be discussed, how the funds were to be collected? For this purpose was named a committee, described as "The Committee of the National Monument." This committee consisted of many of the nobility and gentry, and of the principal subscribers, and, by means of their exertions, a very considerable sum was realised. But as this fell far short of that required for the purpose, and as it was moreover to be, in the strictest sense, a national monument in which the whole body of the Scottish people was to have a personal interest, the committee made application, in 1819, to the General Assembly for sanction to apply to all the ministers of the church for subscriptions. These efforts failed, yet the redoubtable secretary, Mr. Michael Linning, was able to collect as much money as cleared the expenses of the erection of a few pillars on the Calton Hill, which remain a picturesque object, but, at the same time, a monument of the great power of design with which Scotsmen are endowed, and of the limited power they have of executing those designs.

On the 28th of April, 1821, the foundation stone of Lord Melville's monument was laid in the centre of St. Andrew's Square, Edinburgh. The monument is a huge stone pillar, hollow in the centre, containing a spiral staircase, and surmounted by a full length statue of the political hero whose fame it is intended to transmit to posterity. I can well recollect the enclosed centre of the Square previous to the erection of the memorial, and I also remember to have seen it when half up.

On Thursday the 17th of May, 1821, the General Assembly met. Its proceedings were not very interesting, the only thing worthy of notice being the contest between Dr. Cook of Laurencekirk and Dr. Mearns of King's College for the moderatorship. Both were of the Moderate party in the Church, but, from the animosity of this party against Dr. Cook, and of the Evangelicals against Dr. Mearns, it so turned out that, while Dr. Mearns was supported by his own party, Dr. Cook had for his supporters the whole of the Evangelical party with Dr. Andrew Thomson at their head. Dr. Thomson was not a member of the Assembly, so he could not vote, but he did what was far more effectual. He, in the "Christian Instructor," of which he was editor, gave on the question of the moderatorship, his strong support in favour of Dr. Cook.

CHAPTER XX.

"THE VALLEY OF THE SHADOW."

1822-24.

WE left Aberdeen in the month of May, 1822, by coach for the north. We were accompanied by my wife's sister, Frances, her mother, and other sister, Maria, choosing to go before us by sea. We came that evening to Nairn. Our fellow-passenger was Capt. Robert Mackay, Araichlinni's son, who left us at Nairn on his way home, after dining with us at Forres. Next morning we hired a coach at Nairn to Resolis, crossed the Fort-George ferry, and arrived there in good time next day. We found Mrs. Robertson and Maria before us. The meeting was a joyful one, but it was mingled up not a little with a gloom which hung over us, we could not tell how.

Shortly thereafter, my induction took place within the church at Resolis. All the members of the Presbytery of Chanonry were present. These were, Messrs James Smith of Avoch, Roderick Mackenzie of Kilmuir-Wester and Suddy, Robert Smith of Cromarty, John Kennedy of Killearnan, and Alexander Wood of Rosemarkie. My father was also present, and Dr. John MacDonald of Urquhart or Ferintosh. Mr. Roderick Morrison, factor for Newhall, was there also, and remained to a late hour in the evening. The services of the day were conducted by Mr. Kennedy of Killearnan, and throughout the whole service, from first to last, he "approved himself to the consciences of all" as the servant of the Lord. The service ended, the Presbytery dined, at my expense, at the inn at Balblair, where we passed the time agreeably enough, the men of every age associating and closely drawing up with each other. I cannot dismiss without a short notice the venerable minister who officiated on this day. Mr. Kennedy of Killearnan had long been an eminent father in the Church of Christ, and throughout his ministry his work had been acknowledged by his Heavenly Master. His settlement had been a most harmonious one in so far as the parishioners were concerned, but a very violent one as regards the Presbytery. The gloom of Moderatism rested upon the Church in that part of the country, and Mr. Kennedy's settlement was dreaded as the breaking in upon it of a new day. He was not an orator in any sense of the term, nor was he a scholar, for his early education had been neglected. But he was thoroughly imbued with the spirit of the

Puritan divines, and of some of our own old Scottish preachers. The leading features of his ministerial and personal character were piety and prayer, the one the necessary off-shoot of the other. His closest preparations for the pulpit, and for the week-day discharge of the duties of the ministry, chiefly consisted in prayer. As the close of his life drew near, his cries for divine help became more urgent, and more frequent and importunate, so that prayer became, at last, the great and leading business of every day. After a ministry of 43 years, he died in 1841, aged about 70 years.

Mr. Robert Arthur was my immediate predecessor in the charge of Resolis, where he laboured for forty-seven years, and if his life and ministry were anything but what they should have been, it was not for the want of a bright example clearly set before him of one who, as a Christian man and a gospel minister, had adorned the doctrine of God his Saviour. This was Mr. Hector MacPhail whom he succeeded.

Mr. MacPhail was truly a man of God, for whom "to live was Christ." He was perhaps one of the most deeply-exercised Christians of his time, equally and minutely conversant with the depths of Satan on the one hand, and the " unsearchable riches of Christ" on the other. His faith, to himself scarcely perceptible, was great in the sight of the Searcher of Hearts—winging its flight upwards, like the eagle's towards the Sun, whose ineffable light, instead of obscuring its gaze, served only to strengthen and enlarge its capacity of spiritual apprehension. But this faith took its rise from a sense of utter hopelessness of help in man to save, and it made its way to "that which is within the veil," through the darkness of unbelief, and in the face of Satan's deepest devices to ensnare and deceive.

His first introduction to his future charge was by means of an "elect lady" then residing in the parish, Lady Ardoch, otherwise Mrs. Gordon of Ardoch, now called Poyntzfield. He was settled over the united parishes of Kirkmichael and Cullicudden, 22nd September, 1748, and continued to labour fervently, zealously, and successfully in word and in doctrine for twenty-six years thereafter. His residence, for the first seven years, was in the manse of Cullicudden, and he preached alternately in the church there and in that of Kirkmichael at the other end of that parish. The manse and both churches, however, became ruinous, and were besides inconveniently situated. The heritors and Presbytery resolved therefore to select a more central situation, and accordingly made choice of a small farm situated at the western extremity of the old parish of Kirkmichael, called *Ré-sholuis*, or the ridge of light. Here they erected a manse and a church, each about double the size of the old ones, and the united parishes, though individually retaining their ancient names, have ever since been known, *quoad sacra*, under the name of Resolis.

During the earlier part of his ministry Mr. MacPhail was much tried with strong temptations to atheism. But, soon after he came to reside at Resolis, and after a longer than ordinary period of depression of mind, he was, through the Word and the Spirit and the Works of God, for ever delivered from its grasp. He was of the happy number who, "in the day of power," had their minds humbled to the simplicity of children, and who, receiving the truth as such, gave God full and implicit credit for truth in the whole of his testimony, without any reservation, and who were thus happily freed from those painful struggles which others of a more highly intellectual and abstract turn of mind so sorely felt. These features of Mr. MacPhail's mental and Christian character rendered his ministry eminently successful among his own flock, and all over the North, while his private dealings with those under serious impressions were signally blessed for removing their doubts and establishing their minds in the faith of the gospel.

Mr. MacPhail's life was not a long one, for his health soon began to decline. As long as he had any strength remaining, however, he continued faithfully to discharge the duties of his office. He died 23rd Jan., 1774, in the 58th year of his age.

Mr. Robert Arthur, his successor, was inducted into the charge in 1774. He assumed at first an evangelical strain of preaching, and associated with the most highly-esteemed ministers, such as Mr. Calder of Urquhart, and Mr. A. Fraser of Kirkhill. His knowledge of Gaelic, however, was very imperfect, and this rendered his preaching in that language utterly inadequate to convey the simplest truths to his Highland hearers. Another circumstance led to an estrangement between him and the pious among his people, and ultimately put an end to his usefulness among them. Mr. Gordon of Ardoch dying, and the family becoming extinct, the estate was sold to a stranger of the name of Munro, who, in honour of his wife, changed the name of the place and called it Poyntzfield. He was succeeded by his nephews, first George, and then Innes Gunn Munro, the latter a Colonel in the army. The Munros of Poyntzfield have, in all their generations, been the votaries of gaity and pleasure rather than of the more staid and money-making pursuits of the world. Mr. Arthur, then a young, unmarried man, became only too intimately acquainted in his new heritor's family. This intimacy let to his marriage with the laird's sister, and his consequent residence almost entirely at Poyntzfield, to the utter neglect of the week-day duties of his office. This course of action alienated from him the more serious among his parishioners, while he himself became a bitter and implacable enemy of all the Evangelical ministers with whom he came in contact. His acquired fluency in after years in the Gaelic language, and a certain knowledge of medicine, by which he made himself useful to many, retained the majority of his parishioners as his hearers; but all the seriously disposed regularly attended the ministrations of the eminent Mr. Charles Calder of Ferintosh. Mr. Arthur was thrice married. His eldest daughter, an excellent and amiable woman, was the wife of the late Mr. Alexander Gunn, minister of Watten in Caithness. When the close of his life approached, and he was confined to bed, he was glad to receive supplies for his pulpit from all the ministers who were willing to give them. Mr. Calder had long before " gone into heaven," but his successor, Mr. MacDonald, sometimes preached in the open air close to the manse, Mr. Arthur sitting at the window and listening. He was a sound theologian, and admired Mr. MacDonald as a preacher, but, alas, he gave no sign of any change of heart. He was the same in the immediate prospect of death as he had been through life. He died in 1821, in his 78th year and the 47th of his ministry. .

The day after my settlement my wife was confined to bed. The pains of labour had set in, and, alas, with more than ordinary symptoms of a fatal termination. That night I had a few hours of hasty sleep. I awoke from my troubled slumber, with a deep sinking of the heart, to the realities which my dreams had been presenting to me. During the course of her illness I was frequently at the side of her dying bed. Our first alarm was excited by the peculiarity of her case ; it was that of difficult and protracted labour. Mrs. Smith of Cromarty, the wife of my much-esteemed co-presbyter, being informed of the affecting circumstances, volunteered her services in ministering to our comfort and encouragement under the burden of anxious fears. My poor Harriet was delivered of a dead child. And, alas, when the pains of labour were over those of dissolution followed. Death came in his wonted manner—slowly, irrevocably, without giving way. Harriet uttered a few incoherent sentences, she fell into a swoon, and breathed out heavily for a few moments her last sighs. It was the 7th of May, 1822, at six o'clock of the evening.

The funeral was numerously attended. I was so completely prostrated as to be quite unable to accompany her beloved remains to their last resting-place. My venerable and sympathising father, however, supplied my place as chief mourner. Tne body was deposited in Cullicudden churchyard, a beautifully sequestered spot, lying on the southern shore of the Cromarty Firth.

Mr. MacDonald of Ferintosh often visited me, and preached to my people. Shortly after the death of my beloved wife, he passed on his way to preach at Cromarty, and I accompanied him on horseback. The ride thither and back on the same day completely exhausted me, and I lay down on my return wishing that I might die. Such a desire came upon me so strongly that I hailed with delight every unsuccessful effort of nature to regain its former position under the pressure of present weakness, as so many sure precursors of death would unite me to her from whom I had been so recently and sorely separated. I gradually recovered, however, but still the notion haunted my mind. Then conscience began to ask, "Why did I wish to die?" My sorrows at once responded to the inquiry—"just to be with Harriet." "But, was I sure of that? If Harriet was in heaven, as I could not but hope that she was, was nothing else to be the consequence of death to me but to go to heaven merely to be with her?" l was struck dumb; I was confounded with my own folly. So then, the only enjoyment I looked for after death was, not to be with Christ, but to be with Harriet! as if Harriet without Christ could make heaven a place of real happiness to me! This discovery of my own miserable sources of comfort threw me into a dreadful state of despondency. I was perambulating the garden of the manse at the time; I left it, and betook myself to my bedroom, and felt all my props suddenly crumbling down under me. I was in a state of indescribable alarm. I had a bitter feeling of insecurity and of discontent. I threw myself on my knees to pray, but could not. My spirit was angry, proud, and unsubdued, and all these unhallowed feelings took direction even against God Himself. He it was who had deprived me of the object of my warmest affections. Not only so, but He had withdrawn from me the only source of consolation out of which I could draw strength to bear me up under so great a bereavement. Oh, what a God had I, then, to deal with—how like Himself—how unlike me! "But who is a God like unto Him, who pardoneth iniquity, and who passeth by the transgressions of the remnant of His inheritance." I was somewhat humbled, and I made another attempt to pray. But now I felt that I was entirely in His power. All my sins stood out before me. I attempted to come to a settlement with God about them, on the terms of a covenant of works. But I soon found that I was sadly out in my reckoning; like a schoolboy, in a long and tedious arithmetical question, who has come to an erroneous conclusion, and who has blundered more in searching out the cause of his error than when at first he erred, so it was with me. God brought to my remembrance the sin of my nature, the sins of my youth, and the sins of my daily omission and commission. I had no chance with him; He was too holy and too just a God for me. I attempted to justify myself; I betook me to the oft-repeated, but just as often foolish and unsuccessful, plan of "washing myself with snow-water to make myself never so clean." But the result was the same as in the case of Job, "He plunged me into the ditch, so that my own clothes abhorred me." This conclusion threw me into despair; I flung myself on the floor, not to pray, for I deemed that, in existing circumstances, quite needless, but just to wait like a condemned criminal for the coming forth of an irrevocable sentence of condemnation. I felt that I deserved it, and I felt equally hardened to abide the result. But, "who is a God like unto Him" in dealing with transgressions? In my then present state, and in the sovereignty of the Spirit's influences, that passage came to me with much power, "I am the door." It glided into my mind without any previous attempt to get at it. But, like a light, dim at first, it gradually and rapidly brightened. My bonds were forthwith unloosed, my darkness was dispelled. Like the lepers in Israel of old I had only the alternative of life or death in any case. But God was gracious. I laid hold of the hope set before me. I thought, believed, and felt that I had actually entered the "Door." I found it was wide enough for a sinner, and high enough as a door set open by *God* and not *man*, by which to enter. If I may dare to say it, I did enter that door, even then, and at that solemn moment, notwithstanding the pressure of my outward bereavement and of my inward conflicts; having entered, I did experience "all joy and peace in believing." In the world I had only "trouble," in Christ I had "peace;" and in that peace I was enabled to resign, without a murmur, my beloved Harriet, soul and body, to His holy care and keeping. I resumed prayer, and felt much liberty, comfort, and enlargement. It was in the evening of one of the days in the week immediately after her death. I had, about an hour or two before then, gone from the garden to the parlour, and risen from the table in an uncontrollable agony of sorrow, rushed out at the door, and hurried up to my room. But after the mental conflict above described, and the most gracious deliverance afforded me, I returned to the parlour, to the society of my beloved friends, in that peace of mind which Christ describes as "peace in Him," in the very midst of those "troubles" which we must, and shall "have in the world," but as the result of His "victory" over it. My present tranquillity, compared with my former "fight of afflictions," and so immediately succeeding it, astonished my friends, and they could not but ask the reason why. I could only say that, "the Lord had given, and the Lord had taken away, blessed be the name of the Lord." For many days, and even weeks and months afterwards I passed my time in prayer, in faith, and in sorrow as to the things present, but rejoicing not a little in the God of my salvation. Alas! this sunny season was succeeded afterwards by a long dreary day of coldness, clouds, and darkness, but it has never been forgotten, nor have its salutary effects been dissipated or lost.

My revered father, having been present at the death and burial of my beloved wife, soon afterwards returned home. He went by Tarbat manse across the firth to Golspie, and from thence he immediately proceeded to Kildonan.

As my mind became more composed, and the soreness of my sorrows, by the healing hand of time, was gradually wearing off, I engaged in the Sabbath and week-day duties of my office. I commenced a course of ministerial visits to the families of the parishioners. The whole parish I divided into districts, each comprehending as many families as I could conveniently visit during the course of a day. Intimation was also given from the pulpit, and the whole was finished in a period of ten months from the time I began until it was concluded. It was true indeed that the time was prolonged farther than it would otherwise have been, owing to various other duties interposing in the meantime. The line of work which I prescribed to myself was, to visit each family separately, from which all not belonging to it were excluded. With the heads of the family I held a confidential conference alone, the children or servants not being present. These were then called in, and, after asking each of them a question in the Shorter Catechism, beginning with the heads of the family, concluding with the servants, and addressing to all a few admonitions, the visitorial duty terminated. I took up, at the same time, a census of the whole population, one column being devoted to the names of individuals, divided into families and numbered as such; another, setting forth their designation and places of residence; and a third, containing what might strictly be called the moral and religious statistics of the parish, or remarks illustrative of the state, character, and knowledge of each individual. My kirk-officer, John Holm, accompanied me in all my peregrinations through the parish on this occasion from first to last.

During my incumbency in Aberdeen, one of my most esteemed acquaintances was Mr. Nathaniel Morren, then a student of divinity. Soon after the death of the venerable Kenneth Bayne of Greenock, I was, as already stated, invited to preach as a candidate for that vacant charge. I was succeeded by another, Mr. Angus Macbean, some time before then assistant preacher at Croy within the presbytery of Nairn.

In the choice of a minister which followed, Mr. Macbean was chosen. But there was a minority for myself, and these were so dissatisfied with the choice of the majority that they resolved to withdraw and to build a church for themselves. At the head of them was Duncan Darroch, an eminently pious man of the old school, with whom afterwards I became acquainted intimately. I was now minister of Resòlis, and to ask me to become their minister was, in the circumstances of the case, out of the question. But my recommendation had weight, and I warmly recommended my friend Mr. Morren, who, accordingly, became their minister. Soon after his induction to his new charge at Greenock, he married Miss Mary Shand, with whom, and her excellent mother and sisters residing at King's Street, Aberdeen, I was most intimately acquainted. He and his wife, some years afterwards, visited me on their way to Strathpeffer. He then preached for me a most able sermon. But my recollection of that is not so distinct as of a lecture at family worship on the Sabbath evening. by which, in its soundness of doctrine, depth of thought, and even of soul-exercise in the truth of God, I felt my soul refreshed as it seldom had been before. Previous to the Disruption of the Church of Scotland in 1843, Mr. Morren's conduct was not what had been expected of him. He was not content with joining the Moderate party, to whom, from professed principle, he had been conscientiously opposed, but, besides, he became their champion in a series of pamphlets at once the ablest and most malignant that were written on the whole subject. Having fought in the battle, he at once rose in the esteem and confidence of those with whom he had identified himself. Lord Panmure presented him to the church and living of Brechin, vacant by the resignation of Mr. MacCosh,* whose successor he became. He died there very suddenly.

My father died at the Manse of Kildonan, at half-past seven in the evening of the 14th day of April, 1824. I had no sooner received the tidings of his death than I immediately set out for Kildonan. The preparations for his funeral occupied our time and consideration. To all those of the most respectable classes, in a worldly point of view, funeral letters were duly issued by a bearer sent for that purpose through the immediate vicinity in the parishes of Loth and Clyne. The length, depth, and breadth of the coffin, elegantly mounted, exceeded anything of the kind I have ever seen. The procession, after leaving the manse, proceeded in a westerly direction; and in order to give each of his parishioners the opportunity of paying the last tribute of respect to their beloved and venerable pastor, the body was carried shoulder-high by six men, relieving each other at intervals, all round the Dalmore, and by the banks of the river, to the churchyard, and deposited in a tomb which he had erected soon after my step-mother's death, and close beside her remains and my mother's in their last resting-place. To their memories he had erected a monument, with a suitable inscription; and, in remembrance of him also, I inserted in

---

* Afterwards Dr. MacCosh, the eminent President of Princeton Theological Seminary, New Jersey.—ED,

the back of the wall of the church a monumental slab bearing the following inscription :—

In Memoriam
Reverendi Viri
A L E X A N D R I S A G E,
Hujus Ecclesiæ Pastoris,
Qui obiit,
14mo Aprilis,
M D C C C X X I V.
Anno Ætatis 71o, Laboris suæ in hac Eccles. 37o.*

---

* It should be recorded that Mr. Alexander Sage wrote an historical sketch of the " Clan Gunn," which still exists in manuscript. As regards the merits of this work, Mr. A. Gunn, minister of Watten, writes as follows :—" Some years ago, when investigating the history of Clan Gunn, I saw Mr. Sage's notes on the clan, and consider him to be the chief authority on the genealogy and traditions of the Kildonan branch, which included the family of the chieftains. As minister of Kildonan he had the best means of knowing these, and his notes did not go much beyond Kildonan."—ED.

CHAPTER XXI.

PAROCHIAL DUTIES AND EXPERIENCES.

1822-24.

WHEN admitted by the Presbytery minister of Resolis in 1822, I found the ecclesiastical state of that parish in utter confusion. There was no kirk-session, no ordained elder, and scarcely even an assessor, no roll of communicants, no list of poor. So many ordained elders therefore were required as would constitute a session. Those selected to be ordained by the Presbytery to this office were James Thomson, miller at Kinbaikie, and Robert Murray, tenant at Cullicudden. At a meeting of presbytery held at the manse in July, 1822, these were examined as to their religious knowledge, prudence, piety, and Christian conduct, a committee being appointed to publicly ordain them to the sacred office. Tuesday of the ensuing week was the day appointed for the ordination. Mr. John Kennedy of Killearnan, accompanied by Messrs Smith of Cromarty, and Wood of Rosemarkie, preached in Gaelic and performed the duty most appropriately.

The session thus constituted added five to their number, namely, Donald Maclean, tenant of Kirktown; David Murray, tenant at Cullicudden; James Forbes, tenant at Tobarchourn, catechist of the parish; Thomas Munro, tenant, St. Martins; and Barrington Ferguson, tenant at Brae. The character and standing of all the elders were according to godliness, each and all being men possessed of weight, and to whose judgment the people readily submitted. Robert Murray, though not a little opiniative, was notwithstanding a man of unfeigned piety, and possessed a sound and solid judgment, and was, without exception, the most judicious member of the session. His influence among the people was great, not only as an elder, but from his skill in certain bodily ailments, many of which he treated very successfully. Robert Murray is dead some years ago, and his death was the first breach in our session. I recall him to remembrance with feelings of affection.

James Thomson was not only an intelligent and deeply-exercised Christian, but a man of considerable native talent, and the ablest speaker at our fellowship meetings. He was much looked up to by his fellow-Christians not only in the parish, but also in the Black Isle and over Ross-shire. Previous to his conversion by grace, which did not take place until he was considerably advanced in years, he manifested his corrupt nature in bold and overt acts of sin. He had been possessed of more than ordinary bodily strength. It was in the act of uttering a tremendous oath to one of his horses that the "arrows of the Almighty" pierced his conscience, and, after a fiery struggle between hope and despair, he became another and a "new man." His after life exhibited the most decided evidences of a saving change. But being naturally a man of keen passions and of a proud and fiery spirit, these offshoots of his nature but too often broke loose to dim the lustre of his graces.

David Murray, the elder brother of Robert, was remarkable for the simplicity of his faith. In early life his conscience was awakened by the hearing of the Word, so much so as to prostrate him entirely in soul-despair. He then cast himself on the mercy of God in Christ, and appealed from the tribunal of a "just God" to that of the same God as "a Saviour." In answer to prayer, he received the assurance that his appeal was affirmed, and that "the handwriting of ordinances which but an hour ago was against him" had, through the atoning blood of the Redeemer, been "blotted out" for ever. To this assurance his faith so closely clung that, during the whole course of a long life, he never, for a single hour, allowed himself to call it in question. He was, uniformly and habitually, a trustful and Christ-loving Christian. At our fellowship meetings he heard, patiently and devoutly what others might say. and, when he rose to speak, he quoted, without note or comment, a number of Scripture passages exquisitely appropriate to the point in discussion. He could associate with the most thoughtless, and enter into conversation with them on those subjects which they could understand. But they were very soon made to feel that, even in worldly affairs, he acted as in the sight of an ever-present God, and in view of eternity. He entered his rest many years ago.

James Forbes, previous to his ordination to the eldership, had been appointed catechist. He was a man of deep and fervent piety, somewhat fretful in his natural disposition, but of great Christian meekness, and of unwearied watchfulness. It is not indeed too much to say that, though many of his contemporaries were his superiors in gifts, few, if any of them, equalled him in the spotless purity of his life. As a catechist he was conscientious and laborious, but his method was not happy. Like many catechists of his own time, instead of instructing the people in the questions of "the Shorter Catechism," his way was to lecture on these questions and answers at the particular meeting, or "diet of catechising," which he held. His expositions were obscure, and the obscurity was increased by the rapidity of his utterance, and the low nasal tones of his voice. He died after a short illness, and was, in his office, succeeded by James Thomson.

Donald MacLean had made money in London as a slater, and took a farm, first. in the parish of Roskeen, and afterwards in the parish of Resolis. His habits were penurious, and, while his piety was a reality, yet it was not a little derived from his close intimacy with many of the most eminent of the Ross-shire Christians who lived in his immediate vicinity. After his lease of Kirktown had expired, he took the farm of Alkaig in Ferintosh. He died of dropsy at Alkaig in 1846.

Barrington Ferguson was his superior in spirituality. But his understanding was very clouded, and in prayer or in speaking to the question he was long and tedious. He had been, at one time, a substantial farmer at Brae, but afterwards became reduced in his circumstances. His death took place in 1850. Thomas Munro, St.

s

Martins, was a man of very venerable aspect, and highly consistent in his conduct.

Such were the members of the first duly constituted session ever existing, perhaps, since the times of the venerable Hector MacPhail, in the united parishes of Kirkmichael and Cullicudden. The first case which came before us was the state of the Cullicudden churchyard. As the old ash trees, with which it was surrounded, were, by the directions of the late incumbent, Mr Robert Arthur, cut down and sold for behoof of the poor, I, with the concurrence of the session, employed James Elphiston, gardener, Braelangwell, to re-plant it with young trees, consisting of ash and elm, the expenses of which, amounting to £2, were defrayed by the session.

Previous to the administration of the sacrament in 1823, for the first time since my settlement in May of the preceding year, the session took steps to make up the communicants' roll. This was a matter which I had been enabled, in some measure, to ascertain for myself, as one result, among others, of my course of visitation. But other measures became necessary. I had marked in my visitation list all who affirmed they were communicants. But I had no conversation with themselves on the subject. It was further required therefore that these individuals should be examined, not only on their knowledge of the gospel, but on their experience of divine truth in their hearts, and with reference also to the regularity of their admission to the Lord's table. The state of the parish previous to my admission rendered such preparatory steps necessary. My predecessor, indeed, annually administered the sacrament, but very few of the parishioners attended; and as Mr. Arthur had no session or communicants' roll, it was not known who did, or who did not, communicate. I was informed by the late catechist that, during a sacramental occasion at Resolis, towards the close of Mr. Arthur s life, the Gaelic service on each day was in the church, and the English in his barn, a ricketty old fabric thatched with straw. We accordingly gave public intimation to the communicants to attend on certain days to be privately examined. Some of them were found to be grossly ignorant, not only of the nature and design of the sacred ordinance, but of the whole system of gospel truth; others were less so, but knew nothing of the nature and necessity of divine teaching. The majority, however, seemed to me satisfactory as regards knowledge and attainments. I laid the result before the session, and it was resolved that all be faithfully warned of their danger in unworthily communicating; but as nothing tangible could be laid to the charge of the greater number of them, the session left the matter between God and their own consciences, and therefore when they did apply at the ensuing solemnity, tokens of admission were simply placed before them. The roll of communicants for 1823 amounted to only 47; it received no further additions until the year 1826, when eight more were associated.

On looking over a scroll of our session minutes, extending from 4th August, 1822, to 6th December, 1824, the annual, and also the half-yearly, business which came before us was the distribution of the poor's money. At that period, assessments for the poor were entirely unknown in the rural districts of Scotland, particularly in the northern part of the kingdom. The funds divided among the more necessitous consisted—first, of collections raised every Sabbath at the church doors, or, according to a practice in the Highlands, by wooden "ladles" handed over the church by the elders; next, of sums obtained during the year for the use of the *mort-cloth*, or pall, at funerals; then of small donations given by some of the resident heritors, and donations handed to every kirk-session in the county by the successful candidate at a Parliamentary election; and, lastly, by fines imposed upon special delinquents on account of immorality. All these sums put together did not in any year exceed £40. After deducting from this several disbursements for certain necessary articles, such as coffins for the poor, communion tables for the out-door congregation, etc., the balance to be divided on every poor person on the roll, which amounted to 56, never exceeded or even amounted to £20. These were divided into four classes according to their circumstances, and the money was divided accordingly.

The cases of church discipline which came before the session were the usual social offences. Other cases, however, were taken up, such as "defamation of character," which, by the old laws of Scotland, were to be judged by the Commissary Court of the county. The session at first took cognizance of these cases with the view of preventing litigation, and in the hope that parties applying to them for decision would more readily acquiesce than in a legal court. I cannot help thinking, however, that the session, in taking up such cases indiscriminately, exceeded their powers; and that, with the best intentions, they did not sufficiently consider whether their decisions might not be productive of much greater strife than if malignant talk were allowed to die out without notice. But the case of communicants, whose characters were defamed, was another thing; because, if the charges brought up against them were true, they ought to be deprived of their privileges; but if false, their character should be publicly vindicated. In course of time therefore the session came to the resolution to take up, as in duty bound, the case of communicants whose characters were defamed, but to refuse the applications of those not in full communion.

But there was another case, or rather class of cases, submitted to our decision as a church judicatory, which was really not of our own choosing, nor besides a strictly ecclesiastical one. It was simply this: two or more individuals disputed about some civil matter, and carried their dispute before the subordinate law courts. If the matter did not end there, or if the losing party considered himself aggrieved and found himself constrained to appeal to the Court of Session, but was unable notwithstanding to defray the expenses on account of his poverty, he was authorised by an Act of Sederunt to get himself put upon the roll of pauper litigants. But one thing necessary for this purpose was, that he should get a certificate from the kirk-session of the parish in which he resided, distinctly testifying three things—first, that he was poor and unable to defray law expenses; next, that his moral character was irreproachable; and, lastly, that he was not known to be a litigious person. Two cases of this kind came before us, the one in the case of two private individuals, the other a dispute between landlord and tenant. Our decisions were unfavourable to the applicants.

The session felt it to be their duty to furnish the people with the means of education, both secular and religious. At the place of Drumcudden, in the west-end of the parish of Resolis, a school had existed many years previous to my settlement. The teacher was Donald Murray, an old man, and the school, like himself, was for years verging into decrepitude. The people, dissatisfied with his mode of teaching, withdrew their children one after another from his school, until the attendance was at last a nullity. The people of the district asked Murray to resign. This he refused to do without some show of reason ; for, whilst the people insisted that he should give up the school-buildings, they made no proposals as to where the poor man should go to shelter himself. After discussion, it was ultimately resolved that the school-buildings should be left in Murray's possession, and that new buildings should be erected for the accommodation of a new teacher and the scholars. This arrangement was unanimously agreed to at a meeting held for the purpose ; a new site was given and measured out, 200 feet in length and 70 in breadth, sufficient in point of extent, not only for the site of the buildings, but also for a small garden for the schoolmaster. The session undertook to forward the buildings without delay, as well as to collect funds to defray the expenses, all of which was done in the course of three years afterwards. The expenses amounted in all to £48 13s. 1½d., wholly cleared off.

The next and more important part of the undertaking was to get a teacher. The Inverness Education Society, in the year 1826, was just at its first outset. Application had been made to the Directors of that Society in favour of a young man named Andrew Mackenzie, residing at Evantown. He afterwards became an eminent Christian, and one of our elders, but he was neither a scholar nor a qualified teacher. Having examined him, the Directors were under the necessity of rejecting him, but his friends made strong and earnest intercession in his behalf on the score of his character, and so effectually that, recalling their former decision, they appointed him teacher of the school. His piety and his diligence increased at once the respect of the people and the number of his pupils.

During part of autumn and the whole of the winter of 1825, Miss Robertson resided with me at Resolis. Her mother spent that time at the manse of Latheron with her other daughter, Maria Serena, who, in February, 1823, had been married to Mr. Davidson, minister of Latheron. Mr. Davidson, who is still living, is a man of strict principle and consistency of character as a minister, but one of the most unpopular perhaps in the Church. This may have arisen from a want of originality of mind, and a certain amount of secularity of spirit, but chiefly from his ignorance of the Gaelic language, which most of his parishioners only understood.* On returning from the Assembly on

---

* Mr. George Davidson, A.M., was ordained to the mission at Berriedale in 1819, and inducted to the parish of Latheron 15th June, 1820. He was twice married, his second wife having been Miss Angelica C. Murray, of Pitculzean, near Tain. He became Free Church minister of Latheron in 1843 and died in 1873.—ED.

one occasion, he came by Ferintosh to pay a visit to Mr. MacDonald who, by his first marriage, was the husband of Mr. Davidson's maternal aunt. He had not been long at the manse of Ferintosh when Mr. MacDonald rode down with him to Resolis to renew old acquaintance-ship with me, and to introduce him to my family circle. Maria and he had no sooner met than a mutual attachment was formed, and their marriage day was appointed, Mr. MacDonald of Ferintosh to perform the ceremony. Frances, even before we left Aberdeen, had come under a matrimonial engagement with Mr. Alexander MacDonald, a native of the parish of Halkirk, in Caithness. He was then a student of divinity in Aberdeen, and for some years before, tutor in the family of Mr. MacDonald of Ferintosh. He had under his charge Mr. MacDonald's two sons, John and Simon. During his attendance at the Hall he became acquainted with Mrs. Robertson, who then resided at Tanfield. When we removed from Aberdeen to Resolis, Mr. A. MacDonald was a frequent visitor to the manse, and the private engagement between him and Miss Robertson was understood by us all. Mrs. Robertson came afterwards to stay with us, having made a long visit to her daughter at Latheron, and they both continued to reside with me until shortly before my second marriage in 1826. In the meantime, Mr. A. MacDonald, after being licensed by the Presbytery of Dingwall, was appointed, in 1824, missionary at Strathconon, but his marriage was delayed.*

During the sittings in May, 1824, I was a member of Assembly for the first time. The Assembly hall at the time, and perhaps for nearly two centuries before then, was an ill-lighted, irregular, and awkward-looking apartment under the roof of St. Giles' Cathedral. The throne was placed at the east side of it, consisting of a carved, oaken, old-fashioned chair of state, surmounted with a canopy on which sat the Lord High Commissioner in his robes. On each side of him were also seated persons of distinction, such as the Scottish State officials. Behind him stood his pages in rich liveries, one or two of them the youngest sons of some of the oldest families in Scotland. Right below the throne was the moderator's chair, and before it a table, railed in and seated all around, at which sat the two Clerks of Assembly, the Procurator, and all the notables and leading men of the Church, both lay and clerical, each of whom had a liferent, from the respective Presbyteries or burghs by which they were chosen, of their annual membership. The seats of the members were placed lower down, occupying the floor of the hall on every side. The bar stood at its western extremity, right opposite to the throne and to the moderator's chair. Galleries for the spectators and the public were placed close to the walls of the apartment, more or less elevated to suit their

---

* Mr. Alex. MacDonald was translated from Strathconon to Plockton 28th Sept., 1827. His marriage with Frances Juliana Robertson occurred shortly thereafter. She died 17th May, 1831, aged 33 years. In 1844 Mr. MacDonald was translated to the Free Church at Glen Urquhart. He married a second time; died 15th August, 1864, in the 72nd year of his age and 40th of his ministry. He was a powerful, faithful preacher, equally at home in Gaelic and English. It was his custom, immediately after divine service, to greet many of his people with cordial hand-shakings as they retired from Church.—ED.

convenience. The whole taken together, however, was not only unsuitable for the purpose for which it was intended, but became utterly useless in course of time. The Assembly, therefore, came to hold its meetings in some one or other of the city churches, the better to accommodate its members, until the Cathedral of St. Giles should undergo a thorough repair. But after that had been done, the new hall was found, from its great height, to be more unfit for the purpose than ever, and the Assembly was again compelled to hold its meetings in one of the city churches as formerly. The opening of the high ecclesiastical judicatory, too, was very imposing. The Lord High Commissioner, as the representative of Royalty, held his court at Holyrood Palace. On the first day of the Assembly, a sermon was preached by the retiring moderator, and the Commissioner, in a close carriage, escorted by a troop of horse and a train of high civil dignitaries, proceeded in state from the palace, along the Canongate and High Street, to the High Church, and then to the hall where, after the Assembly had been by the moderator constituted by prayer, he addressed its members under the designation of "Right Reverend and Right Honourable." The moderator replied in suitable terms to the Commissioner, and then addressed the Assembly, after which the business of "the House," as it was usually called, proceeded according to its customary forms. I mention these things, not for the purpose of giving any information about them, for they are familiar to every Scotchman who, even by mere accident, has happened to be in the Scottish metropolis on these occasions. But I notice them as proceedings of which, for the first time in my life, I was myself an eye-witness, and which, consequently, left vivid impressions on my mind.

The proceedings of the Assembly of 1824 are distinctly present to my recollection. There stood before me Dr. Inglis, a tall, hard-featured personage considerably in the decline of life, with a voice in every respect the reverse of melodious. It not a little resembled in its tones the harsh and creaking sounds of a huge prison door when turning on its rusty, oilless hinges. With this harsh voice Dr. Inglis, notwithstanding, never failed to give expression to the conceptions of a vigorous mind. He was not eloquent, and his speeches, therefore, were devoid of elegance, but they were closely and shrewdly argumentative. On the side of his party, and indeed in support of any line of argument which he thought fit to adopt, he took up his position doggedly, and so confronted his opponents.

Dr. Cook of Laurencekirk almost equalled Dr. Inglis in ability, and greatly exceeded him in the powers of eloquence. But his eloquence was sadly marred by his delivery and the tone of his voice. He usually spoke with a sardonic sneer on his countenance, and with a sort of whine or howl peculiar to the natives of the south of Scotland.

Dr. Nicol was Principal of the United Colleges of St. Salvator and St. Leonard's, in the city of St. Andrews. His mental powers were most ordinary. A plodding, well-fed, active farmer, whose intellect could never reach a hair's-breadth beyond the management of the farm, could at any time stand a comparison with **Dr. Francis Nicol.**

He was at the head of a literary institution, it is true, but, for his elevation to the Principalship, as well as to the high place of a leader in the Church, his wealth, political influence, and landed property had everything to say. He was not, however, without qualifications. He had a readiness and fluency of speech, but he would not venture to say half a word more than he conceived was in accordance with the views of his party, or if, by accident, he said anything contrary to them, no sooner did he discover his blunder than he hastened to back out of it as best he could.

Principal George Husband Baird, in managing the Assembly's Education Scheme, was distinguished for his activity, prudence, and attention. He was the fittest man in Scotland for conducting this work with efficiency and success. Whilst the Principal of St. Andrews, therefore, spent his summers at county meetings and farming Associations, his brother dignitary of Edinburgh travelled the whole of the north of Scotland and the Orkneys in the cause of education during that season of the year. In the Church courts, Dr. Baird was more of the willing follower than of the ambitious leader.

Dr. Andrew Thomson, the famous champion of the Church's liberties and constitution—in himself a host—was in the House, but, not being a member, took no part in the discussion. He sat in one of the side galleries, taking notes of their proceedings, which, together with his own comments on such of them as were most notorious, he duly gave to the public in a monthly periodical, called the "Christian Instructor," of which he was the editor. He was the instinctive dread of the whole Moderate party. Even when the boldest of them put forth their creedless and Erastian dogmas, the corners of their eyes might be seen gliding unconsciously to the seat which he occupied, as if to read in his countenance their future castigation, their courage all the while quailing before the keenness of his hawk's eye.

While this Assembly was sitting, a printed document was handed to me privately, entitled a "Conference of Ministers, Elders, and other Members of the Church of Scotland," the subject matter of which was summed up in the words of Malachi iii., 16, "They that feared the Lord spake often one to another, and the Lord hearkened." It was issued by the Evangelical section of the Church, with whom I then and ever afterwards acted; and I trust I ever will act with them in so far as they shall be guided by Divine truth. Its object was to promote the interests of Christ's kingdom by prayer and mutual counsel, with a view to co-operation in the General Assembly. How far this proposal was approved of, and acted upon, I am not able to say. Some of the means to be employed, and the end to be kept in view, were good, but others of those means savoured more of men than of God, while perhaps through the whole of the document there was manifested too much of the spirit of party in things so holy, and too little of the expansive spirit of the gospel. This, indeed, was the fundamental error of the Evangelical party in the Church, in all their contendings against the aggressive power of Moderatism, from the days of Dr. Robertson, its first founder, down to the Disruption in 1843. Had the professed ministers of Christ turned their attention more than they did to the essentials and responsibilities of their high and holy office individually, and not spent so much of their precious time and strength in General Assembly debates and wranglings with the opposite party, matters might have been ordered otherwise, and the Evangelical party could have been placed on a different footing altogether from what it is at present. Moderatism, in all its generations and under all its phases, was evidently on the side of the "Prince of this world" and "the spirit that now worketh in the children of disobedience." None ever doubted this who knew its adherents; they themselves virtually admitted it. But on the other hand, the weapons which the Evangelical ministers wielded against them, instead of being "spiritual and not carnal," were, it is to be feared, more carnal than spiritual; and no battle, we believe, was ever yet won against Satan by "fighting him with his own weapons."

Among those with whom I became personally acquainted in Edinburgh was my future, though now, alas! my late, co-presbyter, Mr. Alexander Stewart. He was the eldest, and, by his first marriage, the only son of the late Dr. Stewart, minister of Moulin, in Perthshire, translated from thence to Dingwall, and, shortly before his death, to the Canongate Church in Edinburgh. His son Alexander, after passing a few years of his life in a counting-house in London, turned his views to the Christian ministry, and, soon after being licensed, was elected by the congregation of Rothesay Chapel as their pastor. The parish of Cromarty becoming vacant by the death of Mr. Smith, the great body of the parishioners set their affections on Mr. Stewart, whom they had never seen, for the sake of the father, "whose praise was in all the churches." The people then petitioned the Government in favour of Mr. Stewart. Sir Robert Peel attended to the request by presenting Mr. Stewart to the parish. The intelligence reached this county before I left for Edinburgh. It was when matters were in this state that I met with him, for the first time, in the Assembly, and congratulated both him and myself on the prospect of his becoming a member of our Presbytery. Soon after my return home, I received a letter from him, dated at Rothesay, 30th of June, which I transcribe:—

"MY DEAR SIR,—Although our personal acquaintance be but slight as yet, I am happy to think it may soon be much increased by our being near neighbours, co-presbyters, and, I trust, fellow-labourers in the service of the same Divine Master. The event to which this is owing has been ordered, I do hope, by Him who does all things well, and whose prerogative it is to appoint for us the bounds of our habitation, and choose for us the lot of our inheritance. Very limited as my experience no doubt is, I am by no means so sanguine as to imagine that trials and difficulties are now over. That they are but beginning is far more probable. But whether the way be rough, or thorny, or 'about,' if it be the way which God approves of, it is the right way, and the only sure one.

"Col. Ross has written to me saying that he expected to have the presentation to Cromarty in Cromarty last week, and asking me to forward to him a letter of acceptance, and a certificate of having qualified to Government. I have done so accordingly, so that it is probable the whole documents may be laid upon the Presbytery table next meeting. I understand from the Colonel likewise that it will be expected that I preach in Cromarty previous to the moderation of the call. Is this the custom? I rather think that it is not required by law of *ordained* men ; and, as it was on various accounts inconvenient, I once thought of asking the Presbytery not to require it of me. I am quite aware, however, that there may be an impropriety in throwing any obstacle in the way of the settlement that can possibly be avoided. It may be as well then to comply at once if they ask me. Our sacrament here is to be on August 1st. Until that is over I cannot go, but after that day I hope I may be able to go at any time. Do you not think this the best way of arranging the business ; maybe, that the Presbytery let me know through yourself, say, what their motions are, and then leave me,. as I am at such a distance, to take any day on which I may be able to go? I wished to let you know the circumstances in which I stand, so as to prevent any awkward arrangement being made. I shall take it kind that you write me at your convenience, and any information respecting the Presbytery or the parish which you may think may be of use to me I shall be happy to receive. We shall also be glad to know of any person whom you would recommend for Rothesay Chapel. I feel interested in this also, and it would be a matter of great satisfaction to me to see them in the way of being well provided. I can scarcely expect to hear from you until after the meeting of your Presbytery.

" I remain, with esteem, yours sincerely,

"ALEX. STEWART."

At our meeting the presentation and other documents were laid upon the table, and sustained. Having communicated Mr. Stewart's proposal, the Presbytery appointed him to preach at Cromarty on any day that best suited his convenience. Mr. Wood and I were appointed a committee of Presbytery to moderate in a call. A few weeks later we met in the church of Cromarty, and the call being read, a considerable number of the parishioners signed, while those who did not were either such as were away at the time, or, if at home, considered it unnecessary, having already given their cordial consent to the measure, all the more so after they had heard him preach. His settlement took place a few months afterwards. I presided on the occasion, and, associated with the Presbytery, were many of the leading members of the Synod, such as the late Dr. Angus Mackintosh of Tain, Mr. Forbes of Tarbat, Mr. MacDonald of Urquhart, and others.

Although the people of Cromarty, in the selection of a minister, did certainly at the outset, make it in the dark, yet their choice after all was a truly noble one. As a preacher, it is not too much to say, that Mr. Stewart rivalled at least, if he did not excel, the most eminently gifted ministers either in or out of the Establishment. His sermons were truly expressions of the character of his mind, and were powerfully intellectual. His comprehension of a subject never stopt halfway, but reached over the whole of it; and any subject which he, at the outset, felt difficult fully and clearly to understand he declined to enter upon. The language therefore which he employed was strictly appropriate. From the beginning to the close of his public addresses a single superfluous word could not be detected. His views of divine truth in general, but more especially of the deeper mysteries of redemption, were not only sound and scriptural, but vivid, striking, and impressive. He had also, in common with all great orators in

argument, the happy but rare art of concentrating the whole force of
his previous illustration of the subject into one short, comprehensive
sentence at the close.   In the fundamental doctrines of the gospel, or
on any of its practical precepts, I never heard a preacher so exquisitely
simple and impressive.   His temper was hard and rugged, and his
bearing supercilious and haughty.   In personal appearance he was short,
his legs almost unnaturally long, so that, when he stood upright, he
appeared a tall, stately looking man, considerably above the ordinary
size ; but no sooner did he sit down than the sudden diminution of his
stature was most striking.   The most marked, no less than the most
inexplicable, feature in Mr. Stewart's personal appearance was his
countenance.   It has often been affirmed that the countenance is the
index of the mind.   With Mr. Stewart* the case was exactly the
reverse.   While his mind was vigorous, active, and penetrating, his
eyes were small and lustreless, and his whole countenance betokened
obtuseness and lack of power.

When at the Assembly I had a note from Mr. William Macao, a
native of China, asking me concerning Miss Urquhart who resided at
Resolis.   Mr. Macao left his native country as the body servant of the
family of Braelangwell in the parish of Resolis, and had, under
Christian training, been reclaimed from heathenism to a saving
knowledge of the truth as it is in Jesus.   He held a situation in the
Excise Office in Edinburgh, and in his note he expressed his desire to
see me either at my lodgings or at No. 1 Dundas Street.   I called, and
had a short but very interesting conversation with him.   In his
becoming acquainted with divine truth, he had been indebted to Miss
Betty Urquhart, as to one among others who had been instrumental in
leading his mind to right views on that all-important subject.   He was
married and had a grown up son.

Miss Betty Urquhart was the daughter of Mr. Urquhart of
Braelangwell, and the sister of the late Dr. Urquhart, his son and
successor.   Dr. Urquhart studied for the medical profession, and went
abroad, whether to China or India I cannot say.   On his return to his
native country he resided on his paternal estate, and soon afterwards,
on the decease of Mr Lockhart who was married to the heiress of
Newhall, by whom he had a family of sons and daughters, Dr.
Urquhart became the second husband of Mrs. Lockhart, and had also a
family by her.   In the meantime, Miss Betty, as she was called, lived
at Inverness.   But long after her brother's death, and after the estates
of Newhall and Braelangwell had both been sold, she had an evident
wish to end her days in her native parish.   Her cottage was situated
in a beautifully romantic spot on the banks of the burn of Resolis, and
there she spent, in piety and peace, the few remaining years of her
earthly pilgrimage.   She had, however, some time before my
settlement in 1822, been entirely confined to bed by age and infirmity.

* Mr. Alex. Stewart of Cromarty died 5th Nov., 1847, in the 54th year of his age
and 24th of his ministry. (See Memoir, by Dr. Beith of Stirling, in "Tree of Promise.") His father, Dr. Stewart, had only been a year in Edinburgh when he died
17th May, 1821, aged 58 years.   He is the accomplished author of a Gaelic Grammar
—a work of great merit and original research.   He also revised the Gaelic translation
of the Bible published by the S.P.C.K.—Ed.

I frequently visited her, as did also both my sisters-in-law, and we certainly enjoyed the simplicity, humility, and heavenly-mindedness with which she recounted, in a retrospect of the past, "all that the Lord had done for her soul." It would also be about this time that her niece, Miss Harriet Urquhart, paid her a visit. She lived usually with her relative, Mrs. (Col.) Lewis Mackenzie of Scatwell, in England, or at Rouen in France. When Miss Urquhart visited her aunt at Burnside we had the pleasure of seeing her at the manse. She was an amiable young woman, and seriously disposed. To Miss Betty's comforts her niece was uniformly attentive. I have had several communications from her, containing remittances of money to be given to her aunt according as she stood in need.

Let me here record my reminiscences of Mr. David Carment, minister of Rosskeen. Previous to his settlement at Rosskeen he had been for many years minister of the Gaelic chapel, Duke Street, Glasgow. To that charge he was appointed at an early period of life, and he continued there till he was settled in Rosskeen, 14th March, 1822. He was a sound, scriptural preacher and a ready speaker. But he unhappily disturbed the gravity of his hearers by indulging no ordinary powers of humour and drollery in his public orations. His sermons and speeches teemed with anecdotes and quaint and ludicrous expressions, and whether he mounted the pulpit or stood on the platform, this was exactly what his audience expected. A broad grin settled down on the face of every one of them, plainly intimating that they had made up their minds, so long as Carment was speaking, to have some fun. The first outbreak between him and the more serious part of his congregation was about a chapel at Invergordon. During the lifetime of Mr. Ross, to whom he was assistant and successor, Mr. Carment agreed to take his turn with other ministers, preaching there on week evenings. Mr. MacDonald of Ferintosh was then at the very zenith of his usefulness, and he was chiefly employed to preach there by the unanimous desire of the people. On the death of Mr. John Ross, matters assumed a new aspect. Mr. Carment, as minister of Rosskeen, took the reigns into his own hands. Respecting the Invergordon chapel arose the tug of war, Mr. Carment insisting that this place of worship should be placed entirely at his disposal, and that no member either of the Presbytery or Synod should preach there, but such as he should invite. From that time, Mr. MacDonald, the favourite preacher of the day, notwithstanding many and repeated invitations from Mr. Carment, ceased to preach either at the chapel or on communion occasions at the parish church. To make up for the loss of Mr. MacDonald's monthly ministrations there, I asked him, and he agreed, to preach once a month at Resolis, an agreement to which he faithfully adhered until the Disruption, and from that period to within a few years of his death.*

* Mr. David Carment was born at Keiss, Caithness, where his parents resided; they originally came from the south of Scotland. "He was the grandson of John Carment, born in 1672, and baptised under cloud of night, in covenanting times, among the hills of Irongray in Kirkcudbright, by the well-known John Welsh." He died 26th May, 1856, in his 84th year and 47th of his ministry.—ED.

CHAPTER XXII.

CO-PRESBYTERS AND FELLOW-LABOURERS.

1825-1827.

THE members of the Presbytery of Chanonry in 1825 were—Messrs. Roderick Mackenzie, James Smith, Alexander Wood, John Kennedy, Alexander Stewart, and myself. The "Father of the Presbytery" was Mr. Rod. Mackenzie, minister of Knockbain. Previous to his settlement in that parish, he had been minister of Contin, in the Presbytery of Dingwall. His immediate predecessor there. was a weak, but well-meaning man — a Mr. MacLennan—and his successor was a Mr. Dallas, whom I recollect to have seen. Mr. Roderick succeeded, in the parish of Knockbain, a Mr. Robert Munro, noted for his loquacity and his pointed sarcasms. Some ludicrous anecdotes of him now rise to my recollection. On one occasion, for instance, he assisted in a neighbouring parish at the communion. One of his colleagues on the occasion was Mr. Joseph Munro, minister of Edderton, who loved to tease and play off his jokes on Mr. Robert. They slept in the same room, and Mr. Joseph, who, like Falstaff, delighted to take his "ease at his inn," and troubled himself little about the preparation of his sermons, got up early in the morning of the day on which he was to preach, and, laying hands on Mr. Robert's sermon which protruded out of his coat-pocket whilst he lay fast asleep, coolly took possession of it, and afterwards read it out to the congregation at the service in church, Mr. Robert, the real author and owner of the sermon, being seated in front of him as his hearer. The text Mr. Joseph duly read out; "That's my text," said Mr. Robert. The preacher proceeded to open the subject; "That's my introduction," said Mr. Robert. The preacher went on to divide the subject into its various consecutive heads; "That's my arrangement," reiterated Mr. Robert. Mr. Joseph read the whole sermon through without missing a word. "Ah," said Mr. Robert, "that fellow has ploughed with my heifer right well, but I'll be avenged upon him." Composing another sermon on the character of "Joseph," he pointed out the various excellencies which distinguished that patriarch, and then, looking his namesake of Edderton full in the face, exclaimed, "Oh, I wish every Joseph was like him." During Mr. Robert Munro's ministry, in 1762, the parish of Suddie and part of Killearnan were united to Kilmuir Wester, now called Knockbain. He died in 1790, in the 44th year of his ministry. Before his death he was fully aware that Mr. Roderick Mackenzie was to be his successor, not only from report, but by the frequent visits made by the latter both to himself during his declining years and to his heritors. On such occasions he used to say—"Poor Rory is in a great hurry to grasp the stipend of

Knockbain, but "—snapping with his mid-finger and thumb—" so long as I can do that. he daren't touch a plack of it."

After the most violent opposition on the part of the parishioners, Mr. Roderick Mackenzie was duly and legally settled minister of the parish. In regard to personal appearance, stature, and strength, few men in the five northern counties could compete with "Parson Rory," as he was usually called. He was upwards of six feet in height, with broad shoulders and massive, well-proportioned limbs. In his younger years he wore the Highland costume, and was universally allowed to have been one of the finest-looking Highlanders of his day. His features were bold and prominent, approaching to coarseness, and his eye had a twinkle in it strongly indicative of Highland cunning and sagacity. His character as a preacher and minister was much lowered by his leading spirit and habits as a man. The doctrines of the gospel he preached with Calvinistic purity, but in practice he coolly laid them all aside. As a faithful adherent to the Moderate party in the church, he hated the doctrines of divine influence, regeneration, and the exercise of spiritual life in the souls of believers. He seldom referred to these subjects, unless it were at communion seasons in order to make a sort of display before those who were considered "pious men." Owing to the universal influence of evangelical truth, and the high esteem in which faithful and evangelical ministers were held by both young and old in the north, neither Mr. Roderick nor any of his party had the courage openly to subvert the doctrines of the Confession of Faith which they had signed. But these doctrines were entirely blunted by the conduct and habits of their every-day life. In the courts of the church Mr. Roderick's aim was to foster the growth of Moderatism; he protected and patronised young candidates for the ministry whose characters were unsuitable or exceptionable; by shifts, evasions, and the most dishonourable modes of procedure, he defended ministers charged with gross delinquencies, and scrupled not to stop, if possible, all *bonâ fide* enquiries into the truth of the charges brought against them. The very worst measures too which the Moderate leaders in the General Assembly could devise, ever found in him an active and most unflinching advocate. Then his mind was wholly secularised. He was a first-rate shot and deer-stalker, the boon-companion and fellow-sportsman of all comers, English, Irish or Scotch. To do him justice, however, the only symptom of inebriety which he ever showed was to speak somewhat thick and to snivel through his nose. These were the days when drinking was more or less practised at every dinner-table. A notorious wine-bibber and glutton from England had on one occasion come on a shooting excursion to Belmaduthy House, the seat of Colin Mackenzie, Esqre. of Kilcoy, one of Mr. Roderick's heritors. This fellow never ceased taunting Kilcoy and the Scotch for their very slender capacity and attainments in what he called the manly science of drinking. Kilcoy, who himself indulged freely in his after-dinner potations, was quite scandalised at this, but attempting to compete with this redoubtable wine-bibber, had more than once to succumb under the table. At last he told the Englishman that although he acknowledged his own defeat, he would introduce a gentleman to him next day at dinner for a trial of skill. Kilcoy then drove down to the manse, and stated his grievances to Parson Rory. "Well," said the parson, "it would not do to make it public, but if you get us a good·dinner I think I'll try him." This was done accordingly. Mr. Roderick presented his huge corporation at the festive board, sitting right opposite the sportsman. After dinner, wine-glasses were placed before the sitters at the table. "Away with these trifles," said the Englishman, "and bring tumblers." The tumblers were brought. "Away with these silly tumblers," said the parson, "and place before this gentleman and me a cup and a bottle of port-wine for each of us." The order was obeyed. Parson Rory, decanting the bottle of port into the cup and raising it to his lips, said, "Sir, I pledge you," and then, at a single draught. emptied the contents into his stomach. The Englishman stared with astonishment, and declared himself fairly beaten. The parson felt none the worse for it.

Soon after his forced settlement at Knockbain, the majority of the people left his ministry. He never resented their conduct, however, but publicly prayed for them with much seeming earnestness- on the Sabbath. He was very benevolent, and particularly attentive to the poor and destitute. His character was accurately described by a shrewd old innkeeper at Contin, who lived during the successive incumbencies of Messrs. MacLennan, Mackenzie, and Dallas. On being asked by a stranger what sort of a minister they had at Contin, Boniface replied that he had both seen and heard three of them in succession; "The first we had, sir, was a minister, but he was not a man—a Mr. MacLennan; the second, Mr. Rory, was a man, but no minister; but he whom we now have is neither a man nor a minister." Mr. Roderick's mental powers were above par. He had also a rich vein of sarcasm. At a dinner given after the funeral of Sir Hector Mackenzie of Gairloch, which was numerously attended by the gentry and clergy of Easter and Wester Ross, Mr. Roderick displayed no ordinary powers of sarcasm. General Mackenzie of Belville, brother of the deceased, proposed the health of the Ross-shire clergy, "a highly-respectable body of men," he said, "who had ever been on the most friendly footing with the proprietors of Ross-shire." The late excellent Mr. Neil Kennedy, minister of Logie, was present, and sat opposite Mr. Hugh Rose of Glastullich, one of his heritors, who shortly before then had had a bitter quarrel with Mr. Kennedy for having appointed the communion to take place in autumn. Mr. Rose called out, "With some exceptions," looking Mr. Kennedy full in the face. Mr. Roderick, as the oldest minister proceeded to reply. "I beg," he said, "to return thanks in my own name, and that of my brethren, to General Mackenzie for the honourable mention he has made of the Ross-shire clergy. The clergy and the lairds of Ross-shire were ever on good terms, and my wish is that they will continue to be so. I was surprised to hear exceptions taken to the General's favourable testimony of them, and still more so at the gentleman here present who thought fit to make the exception. His father was a worthy minister of the Church. He was a very good man. But let his surviving sons beware that the old proverb be not fulfilled in their case, that 'where the Deil canna get the goose, he'll try an' get the goslins.'" This sally was followed by roars of laughter, and Rose felt himself so fairly beaten that he very soon afterwards rose and left. My father and Mr. Roderick had been school-fellows at Cromarty under the late eminent Mr. John Russel of Stirling, but they never met again until the day of my settlement at Resolis. Mr. Mackenzie was married to a sister of the late Mr. Charles Grant of Waternish, M.P., father of Lord Glenelg. The family consisted of several sons and daughters; the former all died abroad. One of his daughters married Mr. Edwards, a son of the first Sir George Munro's grieve, at Poyntzfield. He became Sheriff-Substitute of Inverness, and was afterwards promoted to a lucrative situation in one of the colonies. Mr. Mackenzie regularly attended our Presbytery meetings. I usually assisted him at his communions on Mondays in Gaelic. He died 4th July, 1835, in the 59th year of his ministry.

Mr. James Smith was ordained minister of Avoch in 1787. He married Miss Houston, daughter of the Provost of Fortrose, two years after his settlement. He preached the gospel, but more as a theory, or subject of history, than as the message of salvation. He read his sermons, and in composing them was most anxious about the construction of his sentences and the accuracy of his style. As a pastor he was diligent and painstaking. He was low in stature, had a short neck, a large head, shaggy eyebrows, and a fearful squint. He was temperate in drinking, but his ravenous appetite for savoury meat was the means of shortening his life. Money-making was the ruling passion of his soul. He claimed a right to the churchyard, not only to the grass, which legally belonged to the clergy, but even to the rights of sepulture. All the parishioners, if they opened a new grave, must pay him ten shillings sterling. This, however, was put a stop to in the following manner. A poor man had come to reside in the parish, who lost one of his family by death. A place in the churchyard was assigned him, and he proceeded to open the grave. Mr. Smith sallied out, and demanded ten shillings. The man replied that such a charge was neither according to law nor equity, and that never until then did he hear of such a demand. "It is the law here, however," replied the minister, "and you must submit to it before you open your grave." The poor fellow applied to the Fiscal, and stated all the particulars of the case, adding that the breach in his family had touched him sorely, but that such inhuman treatment was sorer than all. The Fiscal's indignation was roused. "Go," said he, "open your grave and bury your dead. If the parson attempts to prevent you, knock him down, and I will secure you against consequences." The man proceeded to obey; but he had no sooner entered upon his task than Mr. Smith endeavoured to resist. "Weel, sir," said the man, "before I pay your demand we must try and settle the account with our fists, so that either you knock me down or I you." Mr. Smith walked off, nor did he ever make a similar demand again. In money-making he was not a little helped and urged on, even contrary to his own better judgment, by his wife. The death of their only son James bore very hard upon both of them.

The people of Avoch under his ministry became, what the spiritu·

ally discerning would denominate, "strong believers," *i.e.*, persons who never encountered any difficulty in the exercise of faith in Christ. In former times there had been a minister in Avoch whom the people revered, and whose ministry had produced the most salutary effects. The General Assembly wished to translate him to Inverness, as being a larger sphere of usefulness. He refused to go, so the matter was left for determination to the people. They agreed to part with him. On leaving them he predicted that many years would elapse ere they would have a gospel ministry again. Poor Mr. Smith, during his incumbency, was invaded by the Dissenters. An Independent Chapel was set up close to his church. He did not like it, and it must be confessed, he had reason to dislike it; for, if matters were bad before, this made them much worse. This new sect made the mere fact of becoming Independents the head-corner-stone of hope for futurity, and Mr. Smith had little or no energy with which to correct the error. He died of paralysis, his death having been hastened by the operation of bleeding, performed upon him with all good intentions, by a neighbour. It took place 9th Dec., 1830, in the 44th year of his ministry. At his funeral, as his coffin lay upon two chairs, just outside the manse door, Mr. Stewart of Cromarty remarked to me that "nothing brought home to his own mind more forcibly the solemnity and responsibility of death than did the death of a minister."

Mr. Robert Smith, Mr. Stewart's predecessor at Cromarty, had, in his younger days been tutor in the family of Don. MacLeod, Esqre. of Geanies, Sheriff of the county. Through the influence of this gentleman he was presented to Cromarty, and ordained 21st May, 1789. He was a sound, scriptural preacher, and a laborious, conscientious minister. His mind, however, was very secular. During the latter years of his life he had to contend with considerable opposition from his parishioners, which he sorely felt. He died 20th March, 1824, in the 35th year of his ministry and 61st of his age.

Mr. Alex. Wood, of Rosemarkie, was the last representative of a clerical pedigree of three generations in direct lineal succession in the one parish. Reared up in ease and comparative affluence, experiencing no difficulties for this world from youth to hoar hairs but what might easily be removed, nor apprehending any evils, either temporally, spiritually or eternally, which might come upon him, he has continued to plod his easy way through life until, "fat and sleek and fair," he has reached the advanced age of threescore and ten. Not, indeed, that he had escaped the trials and grievances incident to "man of woman born" entirely; but he was naturally and largely endowed with that amount of stolidity and obtuseness of spirit as would almost bear with anything, however rousing and harassing to the ordinary feelings of humanity, and this always interposed to save him from that bitterness which, otherwise, he could not possibly but feel. He was rather nervous, moreover, arising solely from an excess of health and indolence, not to say over-indulgence in the luxuries of the table, so that his nervous fits, which otherwise might have passed off harmlessly enough, sometimes chose to associate themselves with some ugly symptoms of internal inflammation. Such symptoms usually manifested themselves on sacramental occasions, or when he had just commenced his annual visits for catechising. He, accordingly, made very dolorous statements to the Presbytery at their diets of "privy censure," just to save his head. Succeeding his father and grand-father, he entered upon his parochial duties very much in the same spirit as one would accept of the place and emoluments of some comfortable Government appointment, in virtue of which, however the duties might be performed, the income was secure. But it is needless to particularise any farther. Suffice it to say that he is now, at the age of 70, what I knew him to be at 37—the same in eating and drinking, in sleeping and waking, in stoutness of body and inertness of mind, and almost the same in ministerial energy and usefulness.

Of Mr. John Kennedy of Kilearnan I have already written in connection with my settlement in Resolis. His ministry was eminently acknowledged by his heavenly Master, and through grace he approved himself to be a faithful servant of the Lord Jesus. Mr. Alexander Stewart, who in 1824 succeeded Mr. Smith at Cromarty, I have also described.

The Church had since the days of Principal Robertson been divided into the two sections of Moderates and Evangelicals, and the majority of our body being of the former, Mr. Grant, who was himself a staunch supporter of the Moderate interest, had been annually elected an elder to the Assembly ever since my induction in 1822, as he had also been for many years before. This year, however, the Evangelical members combined to oust Mr. Grant from his protracted monopoly. On each side parties were equally balanced, but with this advantage to the Evangelicals, that one of their own number filled the moderator's chair. Mr. George Sinclair, eldest son and heir of Sir John Sinclair, Bart. of Ulbster, was the man upon whom their choice fell. This gentleman, born and brought up in the highest circles of society, had been a "lover of pleasure more than a lover of God." But "God's time of love" came. His heart was gained and given to the Lord, so that he became a vital, though not always a very consistent, Christian. As I had seen him in the days of his boyhood, though by no means intimately acquainted with him, I was deputed by my brethren to write to him, and to my communication he made the following reply :—

"EDINBURGH, 21*st Feb.*, 1825.

"MY DEAR SIR,—I had this day the honour to receive your kind intima-tion of the friendly sentiments and intentions cherished towards me by yourself and those esteemed members of your presbytery with whom you are of one accord and of one mind. I must candidly acknowledge that I should consider it a high privilege to be connected by so important a tie with Christian brethren whom I very highly respect, and I should endeavour to discharge the solemn duty entrusted to me in such a manner as becomes the doctrines of Christ. I could indeed only undertake such an office in humble dependence on divine aid, for I feel the deep responsibility which attaches to it ; and I should now accept it with much greater diffidence than I should have done a few years ago when, as I now see, I was totally unfit for it. I then imagined that every one might aspire to such an appointment as a matter of course. I now perceive how arduous and honourable it is to hold any office connected with the Church of Christ, and that His strength alone can make our weakness perfect. I should be very sorry at the same time to create any dissension between yourselves and any of your brethren, and I should venture to recommend a very earnest recommendation of the conduct and sentiments of your former representative, though certainly if you have reason to conclude that his views do not accord with yours, and that my services would be more acceptable, I shall feel highly honoured by the appointment.

"In regard to the certificates, I must request that you will have the kindness to write to my friend the Rev. William Mackintosh, minister of Thurso, on the subject, upon whose favourable testimony I have every reason to rely.

"I had the pleasure lately to forward to Mr. Peel (Sir Robert) an application from the principal heritors of the parish of Reay on behalf of Mr. Finlay Cook, who, I hope, will be appointed assistant and successor at Reay.

"I remain, my dear sir, with that regard which those who trust solely in Jesus feel towards brethren, though personally unknown, who cherish the same hope and rejoice in the same end.—Very truly yours,

"GEORGE SINCLAIR."

With the Christian sentiments which Mr. Sinclair's letter so simply and forcibly expresses Messrs. Kennedy, Stewart, and I were much satisfied. I was accordingly directed to write Mr. Mackintosh of Thurso* for his certificates, which I did on the 20th Feby., and to which, enclosing the certificates, he replied on March 4th. Mr. Mackintosh expresses the pleasure he "felt on hearing that we are likely to have Mr. Sinclair as our ruling elder; that he is a man of uncommon talent, piety, and benevolence; that during his residence at Thurso he visited the sick and the poor, to pour consolation into the heart of the former, and to supply the wants of the latter; that his beneficence was not confined to the parish, but that, in addition to all this, he has often been known to carry supplies in his carriage to other parishes in the county; that he now lives in Edinburgh, and though on a limited income, gives 36 bolls of meal to the poor of Thurso yearly, besides money and coals, and that thus, in all probability, the blessing of the widow, the orphan, and 'of him that is ready to perish' shall light on his head." The day on which our Commissioners for the General Assembly were to be elected arrived, when Mr. Sinclair was returned.†

* Mr. William Mackintosh, a native of Inverness-shire, was ordained to the mission at Bruan and Berriedale in 1795, and translated from thence to Thurso 29th Aug., 1805. He was much esteemed as an eloquent preacher, an able expounder of the Word of God, and a vivid but faithful delineator of the Christian's spiritual experiences. He died whilst on a visit to Strathpeffer mineral springs on the 18th July, 1830, in the 67th year of his age and 35th of his ministry. His body was interred at Cullicudden in Resolis.—ED.

† Sir George Sinclair, Bart. of Ulbster, was born at Edinburgh 28th Aug., 1790, and educated at Harrow and Gottingen. Travelling through Prussia when a student, he was taken prisoner as a spy by the French and examined by Napoleon the Great, but soon afterwards liberated. He became M.P. for Caithness in the 20th year of his age, and associated with the great and notable of his time. In 1816 he married Lady Camilla, daughter of Sir William Manners, and sister of the Earl

In the month of March of this year (1825) I received an intimation of the death of Hugh Houston of Creich. He died at an advanced age on the 19th of that month in his son-in-law's house at Kintradwell. His name was associated with my earliest years. Long before I was born he had been a prosperous merchant at Brora. From small beginnings he rose, and made steady progress towards being one of the richest men in the county. During his mercantile life he dealt in every sort of thing that could possibly be bought or sold—clothes of every texture, groceries of all descriptions, leather and hardware. But he had also a foreign trade. In those days contraband traders frequented the Sutherland coast. Foreign smuggling vessels landed their goods at every creek and harbour at which they knew they would find purchasers. Hugh Houston at Brora dealt largely, after the fashion of the times, in these contraband wares. The revenue officers, or "gaugers," as they were called, were ever on the watch to make seizures, and were warranted to search private dwellings and warehouses for that purpose. I recollect to have heard Mr. Houston himself, when dining at the table of the late Mr. Walter Ross of Clyne, his parish minister, give a minute account of a narrow escape he had made many years before from a party of revenue officers who were informed of his being in the receipt of a large quantity of smuggled spirits, and were on their way to seize it. The means of rescue, he said, came from Mr. Ross, who, on hearing of his perplexity, set himself to collect all the small carts and broad-shouldered men in the vicinity, appointing them to meet at the dead hour of night at his friend's shop door, to convey Mr. Houston's cargo of gin and brandy to the *church of Clyne*, and deposit them under the east gallery. This was done accordingly, and the revenue officers coming next day in full force found nothing to be seized. Winding up his business at Brora, Mr. Houston leased the farm of Clyneleish, in the neighbourhood of the manse of Clyne; it was occupied previously by Captain Sutherland. He then became major in the Sutherland militia, and afterwards purchased the property of Creich from W. Creich, bookseller in Edinburgh, which last purchased it from the family of Gray.

My excellent and affectionate friend, Mr. Barclay of Auldearn, wrote me a letter on the 25th of March to remind me of my promise to preach to the children of his parishioners on Wednesday se'nnight, the 6th of April ensuing. There was also more work cut out for me. His people, he said, would be expecting a lecture on the evening of that day, according to use when a stranger engaged in such a duty. He then earnestly enforces the duty prescribed, from the consideration that many of his stated hearers expressed the wish that I should do so, but above all that many of them are hungering after the bread of life,

of Dysart, who inherited the title from his grandmother. Endowed with extraordinary powers of memory, Sir George was an accomplished scholar, and, like his gifted father, a voluminous writer of books, pamphlets, and letters. In 1843, although an ecclesiastical non-intrusionist, he remained in the Establishment, but ultimately joined the Free Church of Scotland. He died in Edinburgh 23rd Oct., 1868, from whence his remains were conveyed to Thurso and laid beside those of Lady Camilla in Harrold's Tower.—ED.

and if their desire should not be complied with it would be a cause of regret. I complied with my dear friend's request, and did not repent of it.

I had received from Mr. Stewart of Cromarty a letter, dated the 30th of March, about Dr. Chalmer's "favourite" overture, as he calls it, ' regarding the course of study to be pursued by students of divinity." In the concluding paragraphs of his letter he mentions two things I was unable satisfactorily to explain. "It has just occurred to me also," he writes, "that it would be well you attended this rummaging committee of which you are a member. You might chance to obtain light on two or three things which might be of use as to *the order in which moderators were chosen.* You have only to notice who were chosen at each synod meeting in times by-gone. We must take care, or this moderatorship will be a complete declaration of war." What Mr. Stewart meant by a "rummaging committee" was a committee of enquiry appointed to ascertain the order in which the moderators of the Synod of Ross were chosen. He attached very considerable importance to the matter, remarking, "we must take care, or this moderatorship will be a complete declaration of war." Now I was moderator-elect of the Synod of 1825, my election having been unanimous and without discussion. In the concluding sentence of his letter he remarked that "some symptoms were appearing at Cromarty which he did not much like." "I should like," he added, "had we time, to have a serious confabulation with you."

He wrote me on the 4th of April asking me to meet with him on Wednesday, the 13th of that month, at Daviston, between 12 and 1 o'clock to examine Mr. Daniel Bremner's school there, as this was a necessary pre-requisite for the drawing of the teacher's salary. I went accordingly, and the scholars were examined in the usual way. The school was on the foundation of the Christian Knowledge Society, an educational Institute distinguished in accordance with its object, not so much for the literary attainments and qualifications of its teachers, as for their unostentatious, but decided, personal piety. Daniel Bremner was one of those godly, though comparatively illiterate men. He had, however, as much knowledge as fitted him for giving to the children of the peasantry a course of elementry instruction as efficient as they had any occasion for. Daniel Bremner brought the energies of a spiritually enlightened mind to bear on the religious instruction of his pupils. At the commencement of my ministry we held monthly meetings for Christian conference, which continue to be held still. At these meetings Mr. Bremner, though residing in the parish of Cromarty, was a regular attendant, and was accompanied always by a John Clark, a kindred spirit with himself; his twin brother, if I may so speak, in Christ. Though John excelled Daniel in the clearness of his views, yet he was inferior to him in solidity of judgment. When John Clark spoke to the question, we noticed many brilliancies and strikingly apposite remarks, but accompanied with many flights of fancy and applications of Scripture more specious than solid. But when Daniel Bremner spoke our attention was rivetted. To the deep exercises of his mind he added a logical and consecutive method of expressing them, and the language he employed was simple and natural. He was therefore, of all who spoke, listened to with the deepest attention, and such who spoke after him followed chiefly in the line of those views which he had so forcibly expounded.

On the 16th April I had a friendly letter from my cousin, Mrs. Matheson of Attadale, dated from Kildary, parish of Kilmuir, her mother's residence at the time. Mrs. Matheson was then a widow residing at Inverness with very limited means. In 1815 Mr. Matheson had got involved in many unfortunate speculations. His father left him an estate yielding a rental of a least £600 per annum, and a considerable sum of money besides. But entering into one losing adventure after another, the result was at last hopeless bankruptcy. The property, together with all his other effects, was sold to pay his debts and to defray law-expenses. He resided with his family at Inverness, and afterwards went to Canada, where he was employed in land-surveying, in which also he was unsuccessful. After his death his widow was supported by his friends. His eldest son joined a wealthy firm in Canton, at the head of which was his maternal uncle James, second son of Capt. Donald Matheson of Shiness, who, after nearly twenty years' sojourn there as an opium merchant, returned to his native country with half a million. He purchased first the property of Achany, then the island of Lewis, and afterwards the estates of Guids, Rosehall, and Ullapool, in the counties of Sutherland and Ross. He was returned member of Parliament, first for an English borough, and afterwards for Ross-shire. His nephew Alexander,* his chief partner whilst there, and head of the firm in Canton after his departure, soon followed his uncle to this country. Possessed of nearly a million sterling, he purchased large estates in Ross-shire, and he is, in point of extent of territory and valuation, the third proprietor in the county, his uncle (now Sir James Matheson, Bart. of the Lews, M.P.) being the first. Alexander Matheson's mother, and the sister of Sir James, in virtue of all these changes, was raised at once from poverty to affluence. Her son, on his arrival in Scotland, made his mother the object of his dutiful regards. Having purchased a villa in the neighbourhood of Inverness, he presented it to her, furnishing her at the same time with everything which wealth could procure to make her comfortable and independent.

I return to Mrs. Matheson's letter of the 16th of April. Having left Inverness by the coach, she came to Kildary with the intention of calling upon me by the way. But she came by the coach on the opposite side of the Cromarty firth, so could not accomplish her object. "But," she adds, "I was proposing to myself the pleasure of seeing you on Monday next (the 18th), and proceeding from your house to Inverness on the Tuesday following, until I learned on my coming here that you were to be at Tain on that day attending the Synod. Will you therefore have the goodness to say when you intend returning home, and when it may be convenient for you to send me across the hill? My mother desires me to say that, if convenient, she would be

---

* Sir Alexander Matheson, Bart. of Ardross, M.P.—ED.

most happy that you would breakfast with us on Tuesday on your way to Tain, in which event we can arrange when I am to leave." This arrangement, in all its friendly particulars, was carried into effect, and I distinctly recollect driving her over the hill to Kessock ferry.

The Synod of Ross met at Tain on Tuesday, the 19th of April, 1825. I was elected moderator, as one of the youngest members of the Court. The Synod sermon was preached by Mr. David Carment of Rosskeen, the retiring moderator. His discourse was highly characteristic of the man. It was made up of cursory and passing sketches of Scripture doctrine, of anecdotes, and of hard hits against all who did not fall in with his views and notions, and all this, accompanied with nods and emphatic movements of his head, to give force and point to his application.

On the 29th of April I was favoured with a letter from my truly Christian friend and brother-in-law Mr. Finlay Cook at Dirlot, in Caithness, where at this time he resided and acted with fidelity and vigour within the bounds of that wide and mountainous district which the Lord had appointed for him as the sphere of his labours. His son Alexander, who still lives, was then an infant, and shortly before had been "sick well nigh unto death." Mr. Mackay Gordon, who had attended my dear and venerable father during his last illness, was the physician in attendance there also. The fever from which the child suffered seemed to take a decided turn towards a fatal and immediate termination. The mother looked at the doctor, who could only reply by shaking his head and bursting into tears. It was then, however, that my excellent sister's Christian fortitude shone forth in its own dignity and strength. She had already been committing her now only-surviving child to that covenant God to whom, after many a hard struggle, she had been enabled readily to give up her other two babes whom, in His inscrutable wisdom, He had already been pleased to take to Himself. Instead of indulging therefore in useless wailings, she placed the child, until then lying on her knee, on the bed, sat down beside him, and without suffering a sigh to escape from her lips, or a tear to drop from her eyes, she waited in mute but humble submission for the final determination of the sovereign will of God. Mr. Cook himself was not present. He was in his closet at the time and on his knees, but soon entering the room he enquired for their sick son. "Hush," said his wife, "disturb not his last hour on earth." The devout but afflicted father said nothing, but acting on some grounds of encouragement he had got in prayer in reference to the use of means, he stepped softly to the table, took a tea-spoonful of sherry wine from a small glass, and gave it to his apparently dying infant. From that moment the child recovered. He has already attained to manhood, and has been working in the sphere of labour appointed for him in the Church of Christ.* In his letter Mr. Cook relates all this in his own

---

* Mr. Alexander Cook was a man of scholarly attainments, varied culture, and saintly disposition. He became minister of the Free Church congregation of Stratherrick, Inverness-shire, but was always in delicate health, and died at Inverness in 1862, aged 37 years.—ED.

simple way, and ascribes all the praise to Him who " bringeth *down* to the grave, and raiseth *up* again."

Mrs. Cook was my eldest sister. From that solemn moment of her life in which she was made to feel the first saving impressions of Divine truth upon her heart, even to her dying hour, she " grew in grace," and abounded in all the genuine fruits of it. Her husband was of a kindred spirit with herself; no two individuals, in the divinely-sanctioned relationship in which they stood to one another, could be helps more meet for each other than they were. In their low, thatched cottage and solitary abode at Dirlot I was frequently an eye-witness of their beautiful conjugal unity and harmony. They were constitution-ally hot-tempered, but not one hasty word was ever, by any accident, even once exchanged between them. In their views, tempers, and dispositions they seemed to tread the same path, " to walk by the same rule and to mind the same things." As the devoted followers of the Lamb, whithersoever He in His wisdom thought fit to lead them through the ever changing incidents of time, they were ever humbly tracing His footsteps as set before them in the Divine record—in the secret exercises of their souls—in their fellowship with God and with each other—in the unwearied and conscientious discharge of every Christian duty—in the exercise of brotherly love to all who bore the image and breathed the spirit of the Lord Jesus—and in all the ordinary occurrences of life.

As a preacher of the gospel Mr. Finlay Cook might truly be regarded as an "able minister of the New Testament." To native talent, or high grasp of intellect, or literary attainments, or powers of oratory, he had not even the slightest pretensions. He was obviously the simple, unadorned "earthen vessel" in which, for the fuller "manifestation of the excellency of the Divine power," the treasure was deposited. When he preached, the first thing exhibited to men was the earthen vessel in all its ungainly rudeness of form. In deliver-ing the first few introductory sentences of his discourse his auditors *felt for him.* It appeared to be little else than a bald, uninteresting statement of *gospel truisms,* every one of which not only exhausted itself, but presented an insurmountable obstacle to all further prosecu-tion of the subject. He went on, however, in that strength which was very soon to show that it was "made perfect in weakness," and, whilst thus groping his way, he seemed to be utterly indifferent to the disgust or the approbation of his audience. At last, however, he fully entered into and warmed on his subject, and then, indeed, "the tongue of the stammerer was unloosed"—his lips were opened, his words were uttered freely, fluently, and without hesitation or repetition. He was borne onward, not by anything in himself, but exclusively by his subject. His hearers at once participated in the heavenly influence. Their minds were both roused and arrested; every eye was directed to him, whilst the deep anxiety depicted on their countenances betokened the entrance of his words, as "words of fire" into their very inmost souls. Their former but ill-concealed apthy disappeared, and was followed by an almost breathless attention. It might truly be said that, "they who came to scoff remained to pray." Nor was it only during these more elevated frames of the preacher's mind that the "arrows of the Almighty" pierced the sinner's heart, or that the doctrine of God's holy word, proclaimed by his lips, descended like the "dew of Hermon" on the souls of humble and anxious enquirers. But as often did "the still small voice" penetrate the soul of the hearer, while he who ministered the truth felt himself sorely straitened, and was preaching with so much doubt and hesitation as to render it often questionable to himself, at least, whether the words he was uttering were intelligible to any one or not. I have had opportunities of knowing some individuals who ascribed the first impressions of Divine truth on their minds to sermons preached by Mr. Cook when in such lowly and self-mortifying moods of mind.

By the providence of God Mr. Cook was led to accept, in 1829, of a call to Cross, in the island of Lewis. In 1833 he became minister of the East Church, Inverness, and in 1835 of Reay,* as successor to Mr. David Mackay who, for a long time previous, had been aged and infirm. On the 12th of October of the year of his settlement in Lewis he addressed to me an interesting letter, describing the feelings of a faithful minister of Christ when suddenly removed from the society of a religious people, such as the majority of those were whom he had left, to the midst of a population rude in manners, filthy in habits, and lying under the thickest folds of moral and spiritual darkness. The people of the Hebrides were utterly unacquainted with the ordinary means of religious instruction. Their public teachers were both idle and inefficient. The ministers of Barvas and Stornoway were models of Moderatism in their day, but they were the "ruins grey" of what their system was in past ages. My friend Mr. Cook, however, found among the people generally a willingness to be taught the things of God, which they knew not before. One poor man had to testify that he never either witnessed or heard of a diet of catechetical instruction, and another that five of his children had been baptised, but that not one question was ever asked of him by the "reverend" incumbent concerning his own salvation or that of any of his children. The sacraments were administered, but in a stupified manner, and the usual services were curtailed or mutilated. Tents for the sale of intoxicating drinks were erected on the communion Mondays, and from them proceeded all the riot and drunkenness of a Highland country fair, commencing almost immediately after the benediction was pronounced at the thanksgiving-day service in the open air.†

Mr. Cook's firm but humble and unassuming services, though despised by the God-disowning multitude, and covertly opposed by his

* Mr. Finlay Cook died at Thurso 12th June, 1858, in his 80th year and the 41st of his ministry, "Unable latterly to go to church without crutches, and help from some one, it was delightful to see him sitting in the pulpit, and with the whole energy of his soul declaring 'the unsearchable riches of Christ' to his fellow-men." (*Fasti Ecclesiae Scoticanae.*)—ED.

† Such scenes were not unfrequent throughout Scotland in those earlier times. They have been described with realistic force by Robert Burns in "The Holy Fair." —ED.

faithless fellow-ministers, were to a large extent acknowledged from on High. Not only at Ness, but throughout the whole island of Lewis, a strong religious light broke out, while the savour of Divine things was, by the purity of gospel preaching, universally diffused throughout the moral wilderness of the Hebrides. Even until now the fruits remain. In that land God is well-known; the gospel is not only understood, but ardently sought after, and now, long after the venerable and faithful pastor, who first sowed the seed, has left the Lewis and the world, "this man and that man" there, as in Sion, may be seen whose names are written in the book of life. I may mention, in passing, though Mr. Cook was not permitted to see it, that about twelve years ago, a great and plenteous rain of spiritual blessing was showered down from on High, with which it pleased God to visit his heritage in these distant isles, so that it has become one of the most enlightened parts of Christian Scotland.

About this time I had an affectionate letter from Mr. Alexander MacLeod, minister of Uig, Island of Lewis, and formerly of the Gaelic Chapel, Cromarty. He states that both he and Mrs. Macleod were in the enjoyment of health and of all other comforts fully up to their expectations in that distant country. He misses much, however, the sweet converse of Christian friends; "nothing less," he says, "than special communion with the Head of all Divine influences, and the joy of seeing the work of the Lord prospering around us can possibly make it up to us." He affirms that "appearances throughout the island furnish very cheering evidences that there is plainly a revival, exhibiting itself under the preaching of the gospel in religious impressions, in a general thirst after instruction, and in a marked and almost incredible change in the morals of the people." He justly observes that there is a danger of underrating revivals on the one hand, and of exaggerating them on the other, and he feels considerable delicacy in saying anything with confidence, lest he should speak prematurely or inaccurately. He earnestly invites me to come over and witness for myself the heart-cheering prospects of that benighted land, now gladdened with the beams of the "Sun of Righteousness," and rendered fruitful unto God. Mr. Macleod concludes his letter by asking, "Who got the chapel at Cromarty?" The answer to this question could not be glad tidings to him. It was given to a death-dealing Moderate, while Mr. Finlay Cook, then of Dirlot, the choice of all the serious people there, was rejected.

Mr. David Campbell, minister of Glenlyon, Perthshire, became in 1836 Mr. Finlay Cook's immediate successor at Inverness. On the death of Mr. William Forbes, he was presented to the parish of Tarbat. Mr. Archibald Cook, missionary-minister at Berriedale and Bruan, was proposed as his brother's successor in the Chapel of Ease. But that congregation, so united and harmonious under the ministry of Mr. Finlay, divided on Mr. Archibald being nominated. The majority voted for Mr. David Campbell, and the minority, rather than be without the minister of their choice, formed themselves into a separate congregation, built the present North Church, and gave Mr. Archibald Cook a unanimous call, which he accepted. He had not been many years there, however, when he accepted a call to Daviot and Moy, where he still lives.*

Mr. Archibald Cook became in early life a subject of divine grace. He has continued ever since to be a growing and deeply-exercised Christian. When his views were first directed to the ministry he at once recognised that a decidedly Christian character was necessary for the proper discharge of the duties of that sacred office, and should be inseparably connected with it. He did not wish to be one of those who "run without being sent," and he laboured to realise in his own soul the influence and saving impressions of that gospel which he now felt himself called of God to preach to his fellow-sinners. In the discharge of this all-important function, his mind has ever been awake to the great end of the ministry, warning the careless and impenitent, unmasking the delusions of the hypocrite, entering minutely into all the perplexities of mind which so often harass the true but trembling believer in the Divine Word; and in addition to all this he earnestly and prayerfully watches the "lights and shadows" of the spiritual firmament. He diligently sows the seed of the word in the part of the great world-"field" given him to labour; and for the fulfilment of the promise that "the Spirit shall be poured upon us from on high," and "the wilderness shall become a fruitful field," none among a thousand in his day looks more earnestly, longs more ardently, or prays more frequently than does Archibald Cook. And yet, with all these brilliant features of Christian and ministerial character, no man was ever afflicted with a larger measure of human frailties and failings than is this otherwise truly excellent preacher. Though he is without doubt a devout and pious man, who has made great progress in the Christian life, yet, owing to the very limited range of his intellectual abilities, there has been gradually superinduced on his mind a large amount of spiritual pride, which greatly interferes with his usefulness. He deprives himself thereby of much spiritual enjoyment in intercourse with most of the really pious men and truly Christian ministers among his contemporaries. If any one departs a hair's-breadth from his own precise view of Scriptural doctrine or religious experience, he stands in doubt of him; nay, though he may never have held any intercourse with such a one, if he has but heard of him, he feels warranted to place him, without a moment's hesitation, in the category of those who "have a name to live, but are dead." His literary attainments are not high; his Gaelic is bad, his English worse. He rigidly adheres to the dialect of his native district, the Isle of Arran, one of the worst dialects in Scotland. His attempts to preach in the English language, both in regard to pronunciation and grammatical construction, are provocative of the ridicule of thoughtless men in the audience. He had of course attended school, and passed through the usual curriculum at college. Yet, in spite of these failings—merely human

* Mr. Archibald Cook was ordained to the Bruan mission 15th Jan., 1823; admitted minister of the North Church, Inverness, 31st Aug.. 1837; and translated to the Free Church, Daviot, in 1844; he died 6th May, 1865, in the 75th year of his age and 43rd of his ministry.—ED.

after all—I question if there be any of the age in which we live who, in pure disinterested zeal, in holy abstractedness from the world, in vital godliness, or in exclusive devotedness to the external interests of the kingdom of heaven, more nearly approximates to the divinely-trained disciples of Galilee than does Archibald Cook.

CHAPTER XXIII.

EVANGELISTIC JOURNEYS.

1822-1825.

A BOUT the 28th of May, 1822, I received a letter from Mr. MacDonald, of Ferintosh, in reply to an application I had made to him as to the dispensation of the sacrament in my parish on the 10th of June. He wrote me to say that I should not depend upon his assistance, as he had resolved to visit St. Kilda, an island of the west, situated nearly midway between the northern coast of Ireland and the Scottish mainland. He would, he said, hold himself in readiness from the 1st of June to proceed to St. Kilda, waiting only for a call to go thither when the Revenue cutter which, at the time, was employed in a cruise to the Western Isles, should be ready to sail.

I may here observe that Mr. MacDonald was distinguished above all his contemporaries by his missionary zeal. Living and labouring statedly in Ross-shire, Mr. MacDonald often cast an eye of pity towards those "dark places" of the north whose inhabitants, from one end of the year to the other, "heard not the voice of the Dove." Not satisfied, therefore, with engaging in the stated and ever-returning duties of the pastoral office at home, he made engagements for week-day preaching excursions. I accompanied him, not to assist—he had no occasion for that—bnt to witness the extent of his labours, and from Tuesday to Friday he preached thrice daily. But these daily engagements were not yet enough to satisfy his ardent desire to "spend and be spent" in the service of his Lord. It had, as he himself observed, become his *element* to preach the gospel, and, like our modern tourists in their own peculiar sphere making out new tours of pleasure through countries untravelled before, so he, in his heaven-bound course, cut out new work and sought earnestly after new fields of apostolic labour. St. Kilda was one of his recently discovered spheres. The inhabitants, on his arrival, he found sitting under that darkness which, for ages gone by had been gradually but steadily accumulating. The island formed a part of the parish of Harris, the ministers 'of which in succession no more troubled themselves about their parishioners there than they might be supposed to do about the inhabitants of Kamtschatka. Mr. MacDonald, however, came to them, "preaching peace by Jesus Christ." The subject was new to them, and they listened to the message with undivided attention and cordial welcome. An affecting illustration of this he personally communicated to me. He said that, after having set before them the plan of redemption and shown the necessity of faith in Christ for salvation, not only from its nature but from its fruits, he enforced the necessity of a holy life, which consisted in keeping Christ's commandments from love to Him. In his private intercourse with them he understood that, as fishermen on the sea and hunters on the land, they were in the habit of devoting to these pursuits the Sabbath no less than the week-days. Mr. MacDonald showed them that, to sanctify the first day of the week, in remembrance of Christ's glorious resurrection, was one of His commandments just as sure as any other precept of the moral law. "O yes, yes sir," said they, "did we but know that it was a sin we should not have done it." The gospel thus preached was not slow in producing its proper effects, and before Mr. MacDonald terminated his first visit the islanders were already united as a congregation of simple-minded lovers of the truth. They desired a stated ministry— a privilege of which for ages they had been deprived. This, therefore, became the next object of Mr. MacDonald's labours, and hence he annexed, as the indispensable condition of his compliance with the many requests made to him, either to assist at sacraments or for week-day preachings, that a collection be made for erecting a church in St. Kilda. His object was accomplished.

A gentleman, whose name I cannot recall, was tacksman of St. Kilda, and went twice a year to receive his rent, which the inhabitants paid in kind, namely, in fish and feathers. He proceeded in a Revenue cutter which cruised on the Western Archipelago during the summer months, and afforded the cheapest, if not the only way of going thither. With the captain of the cutter it was arranged that Mr. MacDonald should be conveyed back to the coast of Skye at any time he should elect. Having settled the preliminaries of his voyage, he next entered into a brotherly paction with Mr. Shaw, minister of Bracadale, a simple-minded and worthy man, who had agreed to accompany him.* The night before they went on board the cutter Mr. MacDonald lodged at the manse of Bracadale. Each lay in a separate bed but in the same room. The terrors of a long and, in all probability, boisterous passage on the Atlantic so wrought upon Mr. Shaw's fears that, during the night, he kept tossing on his pillow in anticipation of the voyage. "Oh, Mr. MacDonald," said the afflicted man, "are you awake?" "No," said the other, "I am not." "Is not the Bible a good book, Mr. MacDonald?" "O yes, yes," said the other, "but let us sleep at present," and seconding his advice by his example he set to it with such earnestness as to drown all farther queries. The summons to sail came with the peep of dawn. Mr. MacDonald speedily started out of bed, and dressed himself. Mr. Shaw did the same. They walked to the beach, and found the ship s yawl awaiting them, but as do the ocean's billows, restrained by an invisible and all-controlling power, so did Mr. Shaw under the dominancy of his fears, each so far came, but could no farther go. Mr. MacDonald sprang into the boat, took his seat, and beckoned to his friend to seat himself beside him. But Mr. Shaw's feet were rooted to

* Mr John Shaw, a native of Moulin, Perthshire, was translated from Duirinish to Bracadale, in 1813. He died 16th January, 1823, in the 39th year of his age and the 12th of his ministry.—ED.

the pebbles, his heart failed him, he waved his hands, bade him adieu, and returned to his home.

Mr. Shaw's timidity was ludicrous, but it proved portentous. The cutter, with Mr. MacDonald as sole passenger, was overtaken on the return journey by a furious storm, and was so far driven out of its course as to be many weeks behind the usual time of its arrival on the coast of Skye. In the meantime the report became current that the good ship, with Mr. MacDonald, the captain, and crew, had foundered at sea, which report continued to circulate some time after Mr. MacDonald's safe arrival at home. He himself indeed told me that, sitting at his own fireside, he read in the *Aberdeen Journal* a long account of his death and character. On another voyage Mr. MacDonald was accompanied to St. Kilda by his son Simon. Whilst the father was engaged in making himself acquainted with the moral state and conduct of the inhabitants, the son was occupied in ascertaining the extent, dimensions, and even the very *shape* of their sea-girt habitation. Having surveyed the island on every side by coasting it all around in a boat, and travelling over its rugged surface on foot, he contrived to block out a miniature model of it. The material consisted of a mass of blue clay, of more than ordinary tenacity, which he had so moulded and shaped as to exhibit all the heights and hollows and beetling precipices of the island more vividly and accurately than the best constructed map or the most finished drawing could have done. I have seen the model.*

My correspondence for 1825 reminds me of a society shortly before formed at Inverness under the imposing name of "The Northern Institution for the Promotion of Science and Literature," and having for its object the investigation of the antiquities of the country and its civil and natural history. The association was chiefly, if not wholly, got up by the Messrs. Anderson of that town, both men of considerable literary attainments. They had already published "The Tourists' Guide Book through the Highlands of Scotland," a work of much utility and interest. On the 21st of June, 1825, Mr. George Anderson, secretary to the institution, solicited my aid and co-operation in forwarding this object by furnishing replies to some queries on the antiquities and natural history of Resolis. My avocations were such as to afford me no time to spare for the purpose, and I was silent, while Mr. Anderson, as I had reason to know, was equally unsuccessful with the great majority of my brethren.

During the course of the same year, Mr. Kirkaldy, a wealthy merchant in Dundee, paid a visit to the north. I have already referred to him as a man of eminent piety, and, though he is now in great poverty and advanced in years, he was then a young man in easy

---

* Dr. John MacDonald was translated from the Gaelic Chapel, Edinburgh, to Urquhart or Ferintosh 1st Sept., 1813; he died 16th April, 1849, in the 70th year of his age and 43rd of his ministry. His eldest son John, whose memoir has been written by Dr. W. K. Tweedie, became one of the Church's most devoted missionaries in India. Dr. MacDonald visited St. Kilda in 1822, 1825, 1827, and 1830. His journals of evangelistic work among the people of that isolated island have been republished by his biographer, the late Dr. John Kennedy of Dingwall. —ED.

and even affluent circumstances. He came to reside for a few days among his friends in Ross-shire. One particular incident is recalled to my recollection. Mr. MacDonald was to preach a week-day sermon at Cromarty. For that town he and Mr. Kirkaldy and I set out from Resolis together. The day began to rain, but it was only a commencement. We got to Cromarty without being much inconvenienced. During the continuance of the service, however, and whilst we remained at Cromarty, the rain continued. In the evening we all three set out for the manse of Resolis, and arrived at the bridge of Newhall. But all farther progress homewards was here interdicted. The burn was swollen over " bank and brae." It had cut out a new channel on the north side of the bridge, so as to preclude all possibility of crossing. There was, however, still farther up, another way of access to the other side of this furious stream, a little to the north-east of the house and place of Braelangwell. This also we attempted, but it was equally impossible. The ford across lay in the bottom of a deep hollow, with high banks, upwards of ten feet, on each side. The water, however, rose to the very edge of the banks, and even overflowed them. The question then came to be—what next? Poyntzfield House stood on this side the burn, and was then occupied by Mr. Munro, the proprietor, and his truly excellent wife, both equally hospitable. I suggested that we should go thither, and ask quarters. We did so, and were most kindly received. Mr. MacDonald, *suo more* at family worship, gave a short but comprehensive exposition of the chapter which he read. Next morning, all intervening obstacles being removed, we breakfasted at the manse, and before we parted, among our other themes of conversation was the high ministerial character of Mr. Lachlan Mackenzie, late minister of Lochcarron, who had died about six years before. Mr. Kirkcaldy proposed to erect, at his own expense, a marble slab to the memory of so eminent a man, to be placed in the wall of the church of Lochcarron, and requested that Mr. MacDonald and I should undertake to draw out for it a suitable inscription. For this purpose I wrote to Mr. Roderick Forbes, a relative of my own, then a teacher at Plockton of Lochalsh, requesting him to favour me with information repecting the date of Mr. Lachlan's death, his age, and the number of the years of his ministry. On the 13th of June Mr. Forbes replied to say that he was furnished with answers to my enquiries by the late Mr. Lachlan Mackenzie's nephew, Mr. Donald Mackenzie, then residing at Lochalsh,* who stated that his uncle died on 20th April, 1819; that his age was 65 years, those of his ministry amounting to 37, two of which he had spent in the island of Lewis. Mr. MacDonald and I, soon after the receipt of this communication, met to draw out the inscription, embodying in it the above mentioned particulars, which I afterwards transmitted to Mr.

* Mr. Donald Mackenzie, on being licensed to preach the gospel, was appointed assistant to Mr. Mackenzie, minister of Comrie; he became minister of Ardeonaig in 1837. He acted as colleague to Mr William Burns (afterwards of China) during an evangelistic tour throughout the highlands of Perthshire in August, 1840, which was the occasion, under God, of a remarkable religious revival among the people of those parts. His character was simple and his manners primitive, but he was a very impressive and powerful Gaelic preacher. He died 10th October, 1873.—ED.

Kirkaldy. But the monetary affairs of that gentleman had, meanwhile, experienced a reverse, the house with which he was connected failed, and the monument to the memory of Mr. Lachlan was never executed. His memorial, however, is embalmed in the hearts of the many to whom his ministry was blessed, while, as one of "the righteous," his name "shall be had in everlasting remembrance."

My friend and relative, Mr. John Mackay of Rockfield, is recalled to my recollection by a letter which I received from him, dated at Kildary on the 18th of June, 1825. He usually resided, and especially during the winter, at his house, 122, Princes Street, Edinburgh. But, having purchased an estate in Ross-shire, he came north, where he spent the greater part of the summer months. His wife was niece of the late Mr. Donald MacLeod of Geanies, then Sheriff-Depute of Ross and Cromarty, the lineal representative of the ancient, but extinct, family of the MacLeods of Assynt, and the last of the lairds of Geanies; that property, after his death, having been purchased by a successful merchant of Tain, named Murray. With Mrs. Mackay I had got acquainted many years before, when on a visit to my fathers' house while I was but a mere youth. She was then Miss Bella Gordon, the third daughter of Mr. John Gordon, of Carrol, who lived at Kintradwell. My cousin and she had been married long before he wrote.

The General Assembly's Schools for the instruction of the children of the poor in the Highlands—having a similar object in view with the Inverness Education Society—were in full operation. The former, however, added to their supply of initiatory teachers for the children a class of instructors for the parents, called catechists, who, in the more remote parts of the Highlands and Islands, were ignorant of the first principles of Scripture truth. Catechists were a class or order of religious teachers not recognised by the founders of the Scottish Church. They were employed for the purpose of teaching the people —both old and young—to commit to memory and to repeat the Shorter Catechism, of which they also gave a short explanation. This was all the more necessary, as in many if not all parishes throughout the Highlands, with a population amounting perhaps to 2000 people, not a single individual of the working-classes could read. So far as I can ascertain, the General Assembly's School Committee, if we except the Christian Knowledge Society, was the first to recognise this order of instructors. As I had already received a school for the west end of the parish from the Inverness Society, I applied to the Assembly's committee for another school in the east end, at Jemimaville. My application to Principal Baird and the committee on the 6th July was immediately acknowledged. In the month of March, 1826, I received intimation that my claims were favourably entertained. The school was afterwards established and examined by Dr. Baird more than once.*

* Dr. George Husband Baird was born at Bo'ness in 1761. His diligence as a student attracted the notice of Principal Robertson, whom he succeeded in 1793 as Principal of the University of Edinburgh. In 1792 he was appointed minister of New Greyfriars, and professor of Oriental Languages in the University. He was afterwards translated to the New North parish, and finally succeeded Dr. Blair in the High Church. His wife was the eldest daughter of Lord Provost Thomas Elder. He died 14th January, 1840, in the 53rd year of his ministry.—Ed.

Since my settlement at Resolis I had continued to hold a close and brotherly intercourse with my highly-gifted and beloved relative the late Mr. Donald Fraser, minister of Kirkhill. Mr. (afterwards Dr.) MacDonald of Ferintosh, Mr. John Kennedy of Killearnan, and he, were my guides and friends, with whom I had delighted to hold sweet counsel on sacramental and other occasions at Kirkhill, Ferintosh, Resolis and elsewhere. Mr. Fraser was at the time secretary, as he was indeed the founder, of the Inverness Society for the education of the poor in the Highlands. With him was associated, in the same office, Mr. Alexander Clark, his co-presbyter and one of the ministers of Inverness, but on Mr. Fraser rested chiefly the labour and responsibility which attached to it. The Society established schools in every direction, but it was on the condition that, in every parish where one had been established, contributions should be made. This condition was but very partially fulfilled; and the Society began to be rather hampered for want of funds. To remedy this evil it appeared to Mr. Fraser that the proper course was to extend the sphere of the Society's operations. Adopting this proposal, he thought of the practicability of a mission, in favour of the Society, to Sutherland and Caithness, and he and I were, by the Directors, appointed for that purpose.

In the first instance Mr. Fraser begged that I should write Mr. Kennedy of Dornoch intimating all I knew of the subject, and asking in the most deferential terms if he would agree that our deputation should occupy his pulpit on a certain Sabbath, if so that he would have the goodness to intimate the same on the previous one. To my letter so written Mr. Kennedy replied, and, after some reference to Mr. Fraser's "very venal offence of being a young man," he agreed to the proposal. On informing Mr. Fraser of the success of my *negotiation* with Mr. Kennedy, he urged the necessity of our beginning operations as soon as possible. All preliminaries being determined, Mr. Fraser arrived at my house on the evening of the 23rd September, from which we on the next day went to Dornoch. On Sabbath, the 25th, Mr. Fraser preached at Dornoch, and I at the neighbouring parish of Rogart. I rode to Rogart on the morning of Sabbath, preached in Gaelic and English, and dined with the minister, Mr. John Mackenzie. He was the son of Donald Mackenzie, tacksman of Tagan, in Gairloch, Ross-shire, who had been my father's companion in youth. John had been my fellow-student at the Edinburgh Hall. After the Disruption in 1843 he became my successor in the Established Church of Resolis. He had some skill in medicine, not much, yet a great deal more than he had in "ministering to a soul diseased." He received me into his manse with polite kindness and civility.

I left Rogart the same evening for Dornoch, and on Monday, the 26th of September, Mr. Fraser and I went to Clyne, where Mr. Fraser preached, and a large collection for our society was made; and where both of us were hospitably entertained at the house of a Mr. Harper, the tacksman of Clynelish, and a distiller. This was during a vacancy in that parish—The Rev. Walter Ross having died shortly before. On Tuesday following we preached at Loth, Mr. Donald Ross being the minister of the parish. For some years Mr. Ross was minister of

U

Kilmuir in Skye. At the time that MacPherson, in a splenetic fit, resigned the pastoral charge of Golspie, resisted all the solicitations of the Presbytery of Dornoch, as well as of his own friends, to retract his resignation, and persisted in his intention, Mr. Ross was presented by the Marchioness of Stafford to the living. As he was about to be presented, however, MacPherson reappeared to claim the living, and, the case being carried by appeal to the Assembly, it was voted, on the motion of Dr. Cook of St. Andrews, that MacPherson should be restored, and Mr. Ross, although already inducted, set aside. The patrons resolved to make up the loss to the disappointed presentee. Rogart became vacant soon afterwards, by the death of my relative, Mr. George Urquhart, and Mr. Ross was presented, with the assurance that any vacant living in the gift of the patrons, preferable in point of emolument to Rogart, should be at his disposal. Accordingly when, by the death of Mr. G. Gordon, the larger living of Loth became vacant, Mr. Ross was presented to the living. He afterwards became involved in debt, and reduced in circumstances and in character.

We pushed on to Latheron. On our way we crossed the Ord of Caithness. The old road over this promontory—the same identically which William, Earl of Caithness, nearly four centuries ago, had passed with his gallant band, clad in green, to the fatal battle of Flodden— was really dangerous. It lay within a foot, and stretched along the very edge, without any protecting buttress, of a precipice 800 feet above the sea. We were, however, more fortunate. A new road had been made in 1804 from the Meikleferry to Wick, the expenses of which were paid partly by the proprietors and partly by the Exchequer. In passing the Ord this road, instead of edging on the brink of the precipice, as formerly, was carried by an easy sweep over the top of the hill. As we drove up the western side, a striking view of the German Ocean, just at its junction with the Moray Firth, suddenly presented itself. On Mr. Fraser the effect was solemnising; he remarked that a beautiful analogy subsisted between the material and invisible worlds; that he had often attempted to form purely ideal conceptions of Eternity without success, and that to him the most striking emblem of it—conveying a definite idea to the senses of that which of itself is altogether incomprehensible—was a view over the expanse of ocean from an eminence such as that on which we were stationed, knowing as we did, at the same time, that it extended invisible far beyond the line of the horizon.

We came to the manse of Latheron in the evening, where we were received with the utmost civility and welcome. My sister-in-law Maria (Mrs. Davidson), the very personification of meekness combined with unfeigned piety, was especially kind. Mr. Fraser preached, on the 28th Sept., in both languages. At Latheron we fell in and conversed with a goodly number of those from Kildonan who, when driven thence by territorial and aristocratic oppression, found an asylum in the parish of Latheron. Among others was the eminently pious and gifted George Mackay, the eldest son of Donald, my father's catechist. He received us with the ripe affability of an old believer. Though driven from Liriboll in his native Strath, he continued to.

minister in his vocation to the small remnant still residing in Kildonan.

The next day we went to Watten, where, on the 29th September, I preached. Mr. Fraser left us, intending to preach at Wick on Sabbath, October 2ud, and I remained with Mr. Gunn until the Saturday. During my residence in Caithness I had become slightly acquainted with him, but this was the first time that I had the opportunity fully to enter into and to estimate the excellency of his Christian and ministerial character. The simplicity of his faith, the soundness of his views, and the heaven-tending earnestness of his spirit made me feel that, while I was scarce a disciple, he was truly a master in Israel.* The intimates of his home at the time were his excellent helpmate, the daughter of Mr. Arthur, my immediate predecessor at Resolis, and a sweet-looking girl of about seventeen, his brother's daughter.

On Saturday, the 1st October, I went to the manse of Thurso, where Mr. Mackintosh received me with a hearty welcome. I had not seen him for several years, and I was not a little struck with his appearance. Stout and healthy before, he was now 'greatly reduced. Mrs. Mackintosh was almost the same as when I first saw her, twelve or thirteen years before. They had five of a family—four daughters and one son. The eldest, Catherine, a very handsome woman, whom I recollect to have seen as a mere girl twelve years before, was married to Captain Sutherland, who had in lease the farm of Ulbster. The second daughter, Elizabeth, had newly returned from Edinburgh, where she had been at a boarding-school. Christina, Camilla, and James were still at school. My first sight of Elizabeth was accompanied with an indescribable impression, for I took the fancy that her lot and mine were henceforth one and indivisible, or, as the English marriage service has it, "for better for worse." Next day I preached at Reay, and, in the evening returned to the manse of Thurso, and found Mr. Fraser there before me. On Monday Mr. Fraser preached at Thurso, and I at Dunnet. Among his hearers were, Sir John Sinclair, Bart., with his son Mr. George Sinclair of Ulbster, and wife. With Mr. Jolly, minister of Dunnet, I was acquainted ever since the year 1812, when I resided at Bower and Stemster. He was then, as formerly, vigorous and active in the discharge of his parochial duties, and as devoted as ever to the guidance of Arminius in Scripture interpretation. "Whitby on the New Testament" was his favourite commentary and *vade mecum* from his study to his pulpit. My sermon rudely crossed the path of some of his favourite points, but without any intention on my part.† After dining I left for Thurso and again

* Mr. Alexander Gunn, A.M., a native of Caithness, was ordained at Orphir, Orkney, in 1803, and admitted minister of Watten 26th Sept., 1805. He was a preacher of eminent ability and evangelical power. His church became a centre of attraction for the people of Caithness, and his ministry was fruitful in spiritual blessing to many. He died 28th August, 1836, in the 63rd year of his age and 33rd of his ministry. His son Alexander (who has completed the 50th year of his ministry) succeeded him on the 6th April, 1837.—ED.

† Mr. Thomas Jolly, A.M., a native of the Mearns, was ordained assistant and successor to Dr. Traill of Dunnet 10th August, 1784; he died 2nd December, 1844, in the 91st year of his age and 61st of his ministry. He was not appreciated as a

found my fellow-deputy before me at the manse. Next day we preached at Halkirk—I in Gaelic and he in English. On the morning of Tuesday, the 4th October, before we set out, we breakfasted at the castle of Thurso East. It was previously agreed that Sir John and Mr. G. Sinclair should accompany us to Halkirk, and the Lady Camilla had also agreed to go. Her husband Mr. Sinclair, however, had an appointment with Mr. Innes of Sandside for that day, and could not attend. Mr. Fraser and I, therefore, set out for Halkirk, Sir John and Lady Camilla almost immediately following. My sermon in Gaelic was preached in a cold and formal spirit to a cold and formal audience. Mr. Fraser's English discourse was different. It was a lucid and Scriptural exposition of that beautiful expression of holy desire, "O send forth thy light with thy truth." His application of the text, with reference to the godly upbringing of poor children in the Highlands and Islands, was appropriate, suitable and impressive. The sermon was greatly admired, and by none more than by Lady Camilla, and she thought fit to enter into a strict investigation with Mr. Fraser as to how, in so short a time, he could prepare so masterly a discourse. We dined with the worthy minister, Mr. John Munro, the cordial choice of the people of Halkirk, and, in accordance therewith, the presentee of the patron, Sir John Sinclair. In equally good taste, therefore, Sir John and the Lady were, along with us, invited as guests on the occasion. At dinner, as host, Mr. Munro did not feel himself exactly in his element. The carving he delegated to me, especially a well-roasted leg of mutton highly recommended to us for its excellent taste and flavour. Sir John, among his many other patriotic efforts to promote the improvement of the north of Scotland, had introduced the merino breed of sheep into Caithness. High compliments were paid Sir John during the repast, and after dinner the subject was renewed by our drinking the worthy baronet's health, to which he replied at great length. In the evening, Sir John returned home with his daughter-in-law, and Mr. Fraser and I remained over night, crossing the hill of Sordal next morning in order to preach at Bower.

The line of road was so rugged as, in many places, to put us within almost a hairbreadth of being overturned. We ascended the west side of the hill, until we reached the great road leading from Thurso to Wick; then, nearly at a right angle, striking off the road, we proceeded to the north-west, until we came within a few yards of the manor-house of Stempster, my old quarters in 1812, after which we drove in an easterly direction towards Bower manse by a road which had not been either improved, or even slightly repaired, for half a century at least. Mr. Fraser preached one of the clearest, most forcible and impressive sermons I ever heard. His concluding address in behalf of our society was in keeping with the sermon which preceded it. At

preacher, but as a dispenser of ordinary medicines to the sick of the parish he was much sought after. One of his sons, Thomas (who "came out" at the Disruption), was minister of Keiss, and afterwards of Bowden, while Peter was minister of Canisbay, and finally succeeded his father at Dunnet, the "living" of which has been in possession of the family for a period of 105 years.—Ed, the close of the services I met with my old patron Stempster. We greeted each other with cordiality. I was so full of my excellent and gifted friend's sermon that one of my first questions to him was, how he liked it? He said he did not know, but his object in coming from his home to-day was only to *gratify his curiosity* by hearing me preach and not the stranger, whom he neither knew nor cared anything about. I replied that "I regretted that very much," and so our conference broke off. The service in church being ended, we went to the manse. Mr. Smith, my early acquaintance, and his wife, whom as such I saw for the first time, received us with much kindness. Mr. Smith was not much changed from what he was about twelve years before, when, as parochial schoolmaster of Bower, I resided in his house. Mrs. Smith was a younger daughter of the late Mr. Sinclair of Barrock, one of his heritors. She was young enough to be Mr. Smith's daughter, since he himself had in her infancy baptised her. They had a numerous family, but none of them were with him at this time.

We drove to Olrig in the evening, distant from Bower about four miles. The plan agreed upon was, Mr. Fraser should preach at Olrig next day, and I at Canisbay, on Thursday the 6th of October. We arrived at Olrig manse, and found my early friend, Mr. William Mackenzie, waiting for us. I had frequently met with him when residing in Caithness about twelve years before. His father, the late Mr. George Mackenzie, was then living, and at his hospitable manse I was frequently a welcome guest. His eldest son was then, even as I was myself, a candidate for the ministry, neither of us very promising for the holy office to which we aspired. William succeeded his father as minister of Olrig, and when we visited him in 1825 he was unmarried, his sisters by his father's second marriage living with him.* Leaving my fellow-labourer to preach there, I set out early next morning for Canisbay.

Crossing the sands of Dunnet bay, and proceeding onward, close by the manse, I drove past the farmhouse of Rattar, and the old baronial castle of Mey, and arrived at the manse of Canisbay in time for breakfast. Mr. James Smith, the minister, met me at the door, and gave me a most gentlemanly reception. I had been at his house many years before on a sacramental occasion. He was brother of Mr. Smith of Bower, and both of them were the sons of Mr. Smith of Olrig, the immediate predecessor of Mr. George Mackenzie. The congregation, which I afterwards addressed, did not meet until 12 o'clock noon, and even then but a mere handful assembled. The majority of them, if they knew little of the value of education, knew far less of that of the gospel. Mr. Smith's sermons were fitter for the Chair of a Professor of Church History or Ethics than for the pulpit of a minister of "the pure Evangel." But at the hour appointed the bell rang, and Mr.

---

* Mr. William Mackenzie, who had been for five years minister of the Presbyterian Church, Monkwearmouth, succeeded his father as minister of Olrig in 1825; in the same year he married Miss Catherine S. Brodie, who long survived him. Through his exertions the Parish Church was built in 1840. In 1843 he became Free Church minister of the parish, and died in 1857, in the 67th year of his age and 38th of his ministry.—Ed.

Smith accompanied me down to the church, a ruinous Scandinavian building, intimating by its appearance, evidently, that it must have been erected as far back as the days of Paul II., Earl of Orkney, or of his successor, Rognvald Kalle. The inside of the fabric was, like all Caithness churches in those times, quite in keeping with the outside, that is, in utter confusion. The congregation was as small as it was unconcerned—they seemed as little impressed with the great truths of the gospel declared to them in their own, as if spoken to them in an unknown, tongue. Mr. Smith showed his hospitality both by precept and example. He was almost of gigantic proportions—considerably over six feet, and very stout. He indulged to an extent which I could not but think dangerous, in the luxuries of the table. My augury proved but too true, for he did not live much more than four months from that day. He died of inflammation of the bowels on the 31st of January, 1826, in the 51st year of his age.

I came to Olrig that evening, and from thence we proceeded to Thurso. Before leaving Thurso manse I took occasion, in a private interview with Mr. Mackintosh, to intimate the state of my feelings and affections towards his daughter Elizabeth, to which he lent a favourable ear, but said that she had gone to visit her sister, Mrs. Sutherland, at Ulbster, and was soon afterwards to accompany her younger sister Christina to Edinburgh to place her in a boarding-school. He would, he added, communicate my wishes to Elizabeth on her return from Ulbster, and she would write me personally.

On Friday, the 7th October, we left Thurso after breakfast, and taking, what is usually called the Causeymire road from Thurso to Berriedale Inn as the shortest, we stopped that evening at the manse of Latheron. From thence we came to Helmisdale, and there I remained to preach on the following Sabbath. Mr. Fraser preached at Golspie on the same day. At Helmisdale I had a great congregation, Mr. Campbell, my father's successor, deeming it unnecessary to preach at Kildonan at all, from the paucity of the inhabitants.

Our two remaining engagements in Sutherland were at Lairg and Creich. I met Mr. Fraser at Golspie on Monday the 10th of October; from thence we set out for Lairg. We were hospitably entertained in the evening at Rogart by Mr. Mackenzie, and lodged there at night. Next day we arrived at Lairg to breakfast, and, if my memory serves me aright, Mr. Fraser preached. Mr. D. MacGillivray, the minister, gave us a most brotherly reception, and next day, at an early hour, we left Lairg and arrived at the manse of Creich for breakfast. We after-wards engaged in the services of the day, when Mr. Fraser preached in Gaelic and I in English. And so terminated our engagements in behalf of the "Inverness Edinburgh Society," in the counties of Sutherland and Caithness. What the sums contributed by each of the congregations we visited were, or what the amount of the whole, I cannot now recall. But I do recollect that at the annual meeting at Inverness, some months after our return, where Mr. Fraser read a report of the Society's operations for the preceding year, the thanks of the meeting to Mr. Fraser and myself were moved by my old acquaintance, Captain Robert Sutherland, formerly of Drumoy in

Golspie, but then residing at Inverness. I may here observe that, the directors having appointed a committee to investigate the state of education in the Highlands and Islands and to report, that report was drawn up by Mr. Fraser* of Kirkhill, and read by him at the annual meeting held at Inverness on the 2ud Nov., 1825, and ordered to be printed. It was entitled "Moral Statistics," which indeed justly belonged to it, from the comprehensive view of the whole subject in all its bearings which it embraced. The report was so admirably constructed as to be favourably noticed by the "Edinburgh Review."

From this date I kept up a regular correspondence with Mr. Mackintosh and his daughter Elizabeth. On the 19th October he wrote me that he had spoken to Elizabeth, communicating my wishes, and that she herself would write me on the subject. His letter to me was so full of piety and good sense that I must refer to its more important passages. "Eliza," he wrote, "is just now at Ulbster, on a visit to her sister, where she may remain a week or two, for such is their mutual attachment as to find it not very easy to keep separate. I have not failed to deliver to her your friendly message, and I am happy to say that she expressed no objection to your person, profession, or plan—only regretted she had not more acquaintance with you, not so much as to have heard you preach, and that she felt shy to write. As far as I can learn, her affections are disengaged, and a little time and acquaintance may bring near what may now appear distant. Rest assured, my dear Sir, that my wife and I would always feel happy to see her with a highly-esteemed minister of the gospel, as well as to see you here. Yet your coming here immediately, so long a journey when the weather is broken, might put you to unnecessary trouble and expense; besides, your appearance would excite the curiosity of meddling neighbours, and expose you and Eliza to the tongues of the world, which the firmness of the philosopher can scarcely withstand." But, after giving such sound and philosophical advice, he adds that "if we be mutually spared until June next, when, *Deo libente et juvante,* I intend to dispense the Communion, and you come here to help at that solemnity, who knows, after the more sacred duties are over, but you might prevail to bring home with you a partner through life that, through grace, would prove a 'Mother in Israel.'"

. * Mr. Donald Fraser, A.M., succeeded his eminent father, Dr. Alex. Fraser, as minister of Kirkhill on 28th Sept., 1802; he died 12th July, 1836, in the 54th year of his age and 34th of his ministry. In 1834 he published a small volume of sermons entitled, "The Method of Salvation." His son Alexander was, at the time of his father's death, minister of Cawdor, and succeeded him at Kirkhill 20th Jan., 1837. Mr. Alex. Fraser accompanied the Highland Brigade, as chaplain, to the Crimea during the war. In connection with this appointment he frequently risked his life by ministering to the wounded, sick, and dying, both in hospital and on the field of battle. He died in 1885.—ED.

CHAPTER XXIV.

SECOND MARRIAGE; PERSONAL FRIENDSHIPS.

1826-1827.

THE time of my marriage was now close at hand, and I made preparations accordingly. The first was to *provide* supplies for the pulpit of Resolis during my absence, which could not be less than a fortnight. The Thurso sacrament was to be administered on the 11th of June, and my marriage to take place nine days afterwards. On my journey to Thurso I stopped at Kincardine manse, on Wednesday,. the 7th of June. Mr. and Mrs. Allan, my kind friends, received me with much cordiality. Mrs. Allan was sister of my co-presbyter, Mr. Stewart of Cromarty. Some years before then I had seen her when a young lady at the manse of Kirkhill. Her marriage with Mr. Allan took place very soon after mine with my departed and beloved Harriet; for on our way north we met Mr. Allan near Pitmachie going south for a similar purpose. Nothing could have conveyed to my mind at the time a more perfect idea of connubial bliss than that presented to my view by this most amiable couple during my stay under their most hospitable roof.* Next day I proceeded on my journey, and after crossing Bonar Bridge, struck across the hill, by Torboll and the Mound, to Golspie. I arrived at Thurso on the evening of Friday, the 9th.

I had resolved, in existing circumstances, to make as few public appearances on that occasion as I possibly could, and, notwithstanding Mr. Mackintosh's pressing solicitations, I declined preaching in English at all. I consented only to preach in Gaelic at the tent on Saturday, and exhort at a few tables in the same language on Sabbath. My venerable friend Mr. Cook of Dirlot preached in English on the Monday, and I engaged his services to solemnise our marriage.

On the 20th June, 1826, our marriage took place as appointed. Mr. Cook performed the nuptial rite. Those present were, Mr. and Mrs. Mackintosh and family, Capt. and Mrs. Sutherland. Mr. George Sinclair, yr. of Ulbster, and Mr. William Smith, minister of Bower. We all dined together at the manse, and my wife and I remained over night. Capt. Sutherland and his wife (who was Mr. Mackintosh's eldest daughter) and Miss Margaret Sutherland, from Dunfermline, the youngest daughter of Mr. William Sutherland, minister of Wick, accompanied us next day as far as Ulbster, Capt. Sutherland's place of residence. Whilst visiting at Wick, in her father's lifetime, I had seen Miss Margaret Sutherland, but had little or no acquaintance with her.

---

* Mr. Hector Allan was ordained missionary-minister of Fort-William in 1819, and translated on 12th April, 1821, to Kincardine in the Presbytery of Tain. He died 9th December, 1853, in the 63rd year of his age and 35th of his ministry.—ED.

She might then be about twenty years of age, and fifteen years had passed since, so that she was now considerably beyond her prime. She accompanied us from Caithness to Resolis, and resided with us for nearly twelve months. It was then that I was able to appreciate the excellence of her Christian character. In respect of meekness I never met with her equal. It was indomitable, and rose above every rude assault made upon it. Nor did this arise from any natural want of perception or sensibility. Her perceptions on all subjects were clear and scriptural, and she was largely endowed with all the finer sensibilities of our common nature. This great equanimity of mind, and temperance in all things, contributed to secure to her uninterrupted health; and, when at last attacked with a deadly disease, the patience with which she bore it helped to defer the final issue.

Arriving at Ulbster in the evening, Captain and Mrs. Sutherland received us with much cordiality. Next day I accompanied Captain Sutherland on an excursion over his farm. It was a sweet, south-lying, sunny, and sequestered spot, sheltered by the hills of Yarrows, and situated on the very edge of dizzy and beetling precipices. Some of them were huge, insular, and detached rocks, presenting to the eye the gigantic fragments of an antedeluvian world. To the far north-east might be seen the bold promontory of Noss Head, on which are situated the castles of Girnigoe and Sinclair, the baronial fortresses of the earls of Caithness when in the zenith of their power to do evil. South of Wick, but still to the north, and nearer Ulbster, were the dusky, weather-beaten walls of the "Auld Man of Wick" (or Auldwick), which had been the chief residence of Count Rognvald Cheyne; and nearer still was Castle Gunn, or the fortalice of the "Great Gunn of Ulbster," the old Norse lord of the district, situated on an almost entirely insulated rock jutting into the sea. I entered the burying-ground. My attention was first directed to the tomb—a square, low building covered over with a slated pavilion roof. The door was in the centre of its southern wall, the wood of which, once painted, was crumbling into rottenness, spray-pelted by the pitiless blasts of ocean. The Sinclairs came into the possession of the Ulbster estate immediately after the Gunns, and this tomb was their last resting-place. All the lairds were buried here down to, and except, Sir John Sinclair. As I was passing out of the cemetery, I came upon a large mossy slab which bore upon its surface some rude attempts at sculpture. I understood that this marked the grave of a Danish princess whom, as tradition of long standing affirms, one of the great Gunns of Ulbster married, but, after conveying her by sea to her future home, the boat in which she was passing from the ship to the shore was swamped, and the princess drowned.

Accompanied by Miss Margaret Sutherland we left Ulbster on Friday, the 23rd of June, 1826. On Saturday evening we arrived at the manse of Kincardine, where we received a cordial welcome. On the Sabbath I preached in Gaelic, and Mr. Allan in English. We left Kincardine on Monday after breakfast, but instead of crossing the Struhie, which was the shortest road, we came round by Tain to Invergordon, and arrived at Resolis late in the evening. There we

were received by our household servants with all honour and respect.＊
The Hon. James Sinclair was, with his amiable wife, a resident
proprietor in the parish of Resolis in 1826. According to the old
regime, Caithness and Bute returned members to the House of
Commons alternately. Bute had returned a member to the last
Parliament, which was dissolved sometime in the beginning of the
summer of this year. The electors' turn of Caithness next came to
send their representative. The family of Ulbster, though not the
highest in rank, was the most potent in point of territory in the
county. Sir John Sinclair, accordingly, for a long series of years, was,
alternatively with the representative for Bute, elected M.P. for
Caithness. His son Mr. George Sinclair succeeded him; but on the
present occasion an opposing candidate was started, supported by Mr.
James Horne of Langwell, who got a majority of the proprietors to
give him their votes. The opposing candidate was Mr. James Sinclair
of Braelangwell. The election took place on the 3rd July, and the
Honble. James carried his election by five votes. The vanquished
candidate, however, though rejected by the electors, was honoured by
the multitude. He was carried in procession in a chair of state, with
colours flying and a band of music, mingled up with the loudest
plaudits of the populace, whilst his successful opponent and his agent
Mr. Horne were saluted with every mark of scorn and contempt.

Mr. Sinclair of Braelangwell was the second son of James, Earl of
Caithness. He had been in the army, and had married in 1819 Miss
Triton, daughter of George Triton, a porter-brewer in London. I had
seen Mr. Sinclair many years before, when he was a mere youth, at the
manse of Canisbay. When he first came to Ross-shire he resided at
Allan Bank, in the parish of Knockbain. Having purchased the
estate of Braelangwell for £12,000 from the heirs of the late Mr.
Roderick Kilgour Mackenzie of Flowerburn, he came to reside there.
His wife, an amiable and accomplished woman, was in very delicate
health. Although intemperate and wasteful in his habits, he was
nevertheless, a most expert *financier*; he was always in need of money,
but never seemed at a loss to procure it to clear scores with pressing
creditors. At length, however, his estate fell to Mr. Duncan Davidson
of Tulloch, then a young man, who, having recently succeeded his
father—the head of the firm of Davidson, Barclay, & Co.—and being in
great affluence himself, had lent money to Captain Sinclair, and
entered upon Braelangwell as being the largest of the creditors.

On the 7th of July Mr. Mackintosh of Thurso wrote me a letter in
which he expresses the hope that " Miss Sutherland will see her sister,
Mrs. Milne, settled in Canisbay before she returns to Dunfermline."
He did not then anticipate any opposition to Mr. Milne's settlement.
" The presentation was received," he remarks, " from the patron's own
hands." Such a favour, however, whatever the intention might be,
could in no way enhance either the honour or the benefit it conferred

---

＊ Mrs. Elizabeth Mackintosh or Sage was born on the 13th Oct., 1807. In the
relationships of wife and mother she ever acquitted herself as a true and devoted
helper in the Lord. She departed this life on Friday, the 25th Jan., 1889, in the
82nd year of her age.—ED.

upon the presentee, when bestowed by such a man as Freswick, as he was supremely indifferent to what a minister's duty, or a congregation's benefit, really was. Freswick, who was an out-spoken, practical atheist, had no other object in view in giving Mr. Milne the presentation to Canisbay than to show forth his own "little brief authority" in the matter. He knew well enough that poor Milne, though naturally a mild, gentle creature, was neither a practical nor a popular preacher. It would therefore please him all the more if the parishioners should oppose his settlement, as an opportunity would be thereby afforded him for the sweeping exercise of his power as patron. But whilst all this was only what might be expected of such a man as William Sinclair of Freswick, it is also true that there were faults on all sides. My much-revered friend, the minister of Thurso, received the intelligence of his brother-in-law's promotion in too much of a secular spirit, and as a happy occurrence in Providence for providing a comfortable home for his wife's sister and family. The people of Canisbay were at first entirely passive in the matter. They knew so little of true religion that whatever their parish minister chose to preach from the pulpit on Sabbath, whether "orthodox, heterodox, or any dox," they supposed it must surely be what was called the gospel. But they had occasionally met with some who said they felt the power of it on their hearts. Such persons went among them at this time, and persuaded them to resist Mr. Milne's induction as that of one who could not edify the Church of Christ. Two pious men from Thurso were specially active this way, their only call thereto being the unerring accuracy and weight which they attached to their own private judgment. There was also one Alexander Campbell, a preacher, who had joined the separatists, and acted as a sort of missionary to the Highlanders in Dunnet, who busied himself to stir up the people of Canisbay against the presentee. The consequence was that, when the Presbytery met in their church to moderate in the call, the majority of the parishioners refused to sign it, and, instead, protested against Mr. Milne's induction. Several meetings of Presbytery followed, and in the discussions which ensued only the worthy Mr. Gunn of Watten took the part of the people of Canisbay, joining them in an appeal to the higher courts. Later, however, he too was led to alter his course. The appeal was fallen from, and Mr. Milne inducted.* Freswick was generally present at these meetings, and at one of them, when I was myself there, he indulged in one of his usual ebullitions of passion towards Mr. Gunn because of the opposition to his presentee.

The parish school of Resolis had at this time a very inefficient teacher, and, in great contrast to it, was a little subscription school at Balblair, in the easter end of the parish. This was taught by a young man named Henry Macleod, who kept it in a high state of efficiency and order. MacLeod's parents were from Sutherlandshire, and had been evicted with many others. I took a special interest in him, inviting him to come to the manse to learn Greek, and afterwards

* One objection made by the parishioners before the Presbytery was to the effect that Mr. Milne was "above the priests' age." He died in 1832, aged 64, after a ministry of 5 years.—Ed.

procuring for him the Assembly's school at Jamimaville. Mr. MacLeod of Cadboll helped him to get the parish school of Kincardine (Ross-shire), where he remained, highly respected by all, till he finished with the college and the hall, and was licensed to preach. He has now been for many years Free Church minister of Ardclach.

About mid-way between Inverness and Nairn, on the southern shores of the Moray Firth, is situated the parish of Croy, which, at the commencement of my ministry, from various associations in my mind connected with it, was to me at least a "Holy Land." In that part of the north I met with a goodly number of men, bearing the name of Christ, who were certainly among the most eminent Christians I ever had the privilege to meet during my life and ministry. Their names are engraved upon my most vivid and affectionate remembrances of the past. These were, Hugh MacDonald at Campbeltown; his senior in years and in grace, John Macnishie, and his son Donald, who lived at Connage of Petty; John MacIlvaine at Milton of Connage; John Munro at Croy; Angus Ross, catechist of Nairn; Hugh Cluness at Ardclach; William Sinclair at Auldearn; John Fraser, catechist, both of Ardersier and Petty, and many others. I was first introduced to this Christian circle in 1822, during the vacancy at Croy, caused by the death of Mr. Hugh Calder. John Munro had obtained permission from the Presbytery of Nairn to get supplies for all the vacant Sabbaths from the neighbouring presbyteries; and having made application to me, I at once agreed, and accompanied him thither. After crossing the Fort-George Ferry, we arrived at Campbeltown, and, in passing, dined at Hugh MacDonald's house. We afterwards proceeded to Culblair, the hospital mansion of Captain Eneas Shaw, who, conjointly with his brother George, leased the farm from the Earl of Moray. Thus then did I first become acquainted with Hugh MacDonald; and from that time until the day of his death, the more we knew of each other the more united we became in the bonds of Christian brotherhood, and the oftener we met the better we understood one another, as travellers to the same country and partakers of the same faith in the one common Lord. We journeyed together in the wilderness of this world for about 33 years. I look back, as on some of the most prosperous periods of my ministerial life, to the many passing hours, both by day and night, spent under his lowly and hospitable roof, on my way to and from the Moray side, when fulfilling my numerous engagements to preach either at sacraments or on special week-day services. When I entered the village, as his house stood close to the street, my eye was never satisfied until it lighted upon his tall, spare figure standing before his shop-door, clad with a linen apron, eagerly waiting for my arrival, of which he had got previous notice. Both his hand and his countenance bespoke at once how cordially he welcomed our meeting. We entered the house together, and, passing through his small shop or wareroom, ascended a narrow and somewhat steep stair, sat down in the neat little attic above, and eagerly engaged, so far as time permitted, in alternate question and answer on the business of a King and Kingdom which but few, alas! of the age in which we lived either knew or cared for. When we parted, if on my way going, he convoyed me to the top of the brac at the end of the village, or, if returning, he accompanied me from his house to the ferry-boat at Fort-George. He lived at that time in close Christian fellowship with John Macnishie, "an old disciple," then at the extreme limits of his earthly pilgrimage, who a few years afterwards entered into his "everlasting rest." But John Macnishie's son Donald, and John MacIlvaine, were Hugh's almost daily and inseparable companions and fellow-travellers to Sion. They were all three brought to the knowledge of Divine truth under the ministry of that eminent man of God, the late Mr. Charles Calder of Ferintosh, the immediate predecessor of Mr. MacDonald. They made me ashamed of myself, though it not a little "puffed up" self within me, by bringing my preaching into favourable comparison with that of so great a man and of so highly honoured a servant of Christ Jesus as Mr. Calder. From the similarity of our views of the truth, ever after they heard me at Croy on the occasion already alluded to, they continued to be my hearers at Resolis every Sabbath.*

But the oldest and most venerable of the many eminent Christians whom I found in Resolis was Hugh Ross, or Buidh, so called from the colour of his hair. He was a native of the parish of Alness, but resided afterwards in Rosskeen. At an early age he was led by the Spirit of God to feel deep anxiety about his soul's welfare in view of a world unseen and eternal, under the able and honoured ministry of Mr. James Fraser, minister of Alness, the author of one of the profoundest theological treatises ever written on "Sanctification." Under such ministerial training, Hugh became, in his time, an exceedingly bright example of "a sinner saved by grace." He finally came to reside in Resolis, where I frequently met with him, and he entertained me with many interesting passages in the life and teaching of his spiritual father in Christ. Though intimately conversant with the Scriptures, yet, strange to say, he could not read. It was justly said of him, however, that though he had not the Bible on his table or in his pocket, he had it in his heart. One anecdote which he told me of Mr. James Fraser is interesting. It was as follows :—Mr. Hector MacPhail, at the beginning of his ministry in Resolis, was very low-spirited. This arose, not from physical but from moral causes. Not having experienced the consolations of the gospel in his own soul, he was greatly straitened in preaching it to others. The impression on his mind, therefore, was that, in the circumstances, it was his duty to resign his office. He, accordingly, invited his beloved brother and neighbour, Mr. Fraser of Alness, to preach at Resolis on a day named, and to intimate his intention to the congregation. Mr. Fraser readily complied with the request to preach, but made no reference whatever to the intended resignation. Such was the fervour, the unction, and the enlargement with which he declared "the whole counsel of God," that the large audience present was deeply moved, and no one so agitated as was the venerable Hector MacPhail himself. The comforts of the gospel, to

* Groups of people also crossed the ferries of Invergordon and Alness from the north on Sabbath mornings, and took their places in the church of Resolis as regular hearers during the ministry there of Mr. Sage.—ED,

which he had been so long a stranger, returned with double their former energy and influence. He could no longer contain himself, but, starting up to his feet, his eyes streaming with tears, and his hands stretched out towards his honoured brother in the pulpit, he exclaimed —"My father! my father! the chariots of Israel and the horsemen thereof." This exclamation was instantly followed up by the sobbing of the people. Mr. Fraser paused for some minutes until the emotion had somewhat subsided. Then, addressing his weeping brother, he asked, "Do you still persist in your resolution to resign?" "O no, no, no," he replied, "I adopted that resolution hastily, but, so help me, my Father in Heaven! I resolve, in his name and strength, to devote myself to his service, in soul and body, mind and spirit." From that day Mr. MacPhail continued to be a living and eminently successful preacher of the gospel. "For the period of three years afterwards," said Hugh, "scarcely a Sabbath passed in Resolis without one or more being brought under saving impressions of divine truth." On a Sabbath afternoon, immediately after public worship, when partaking of some dinner with me in the manse, Hugh Buidh expired suddenly, and entered an eternal world as placidly as he had begun his former night's sleep.

The birth of our first child in the end of July brought me many congratulatory letters, but I shall only notice the writers of three of these. One was from Mr. John Sutherland of Dunfermline. This gentleman was the eldest son of Mr. William Sutherland, minister of Wick, and he was thus the brother of Mrs. Mackintosh of Thurso. His father was descended from a long line of ministers of the Episcopalian and Presbyterian Churches of Scotland, who had, besides John, a throng family of at least fifteen sons and daughters. Mr. John Sutherland had been for a time a linen manufacturer in Dunfermline, but at this period he had retired into private life. He was unmarried, and his sisters Mary and Margaret lived with him till his death some years after.

Mr. John Fraser, banker and merchant, Inverness, was another of our friends who, on this occasion, sent his hearty congratulations. This gentleman was the son of Mr. William Fraser, a wealthy burgess of Inverness, who, for reasons which I never could ascertain, was, by his fellow-townsmen, called Buchtie. His only son John succeeded his father in business. His mother was the daughter of a Mr. Munro, tenant of the farm of Delnies, on the estate of Cadboll. Mr. John Fraser had several sisters who were married respectively to Mr. Hugh MacBean, minister of Ardclach; Mr. James Russel, minister of Gairloch; and Mr. MacBean, a merchant in Florence, Italy. Some years before, Mr Fraser had married Miss Lilias Fraser, eldest daughter of my near and very dear relative, Mr. Donald Fraser, minister of Kirkhill.* In this same letter he intimates the birth of his third son William, which took place on 27th July, 1827.

A third letter was from my early acquaintance and next neighbour,

---

* Mr. William Fraser was proprietor of Buchtie, a small estate near Inverness. Mr. John Fraser finally removed to Canada, where he became a banker at London, Ontario. While there, he was the faithful friend and adviser of Highland Scotch emigrants, whom he directed to settlements in the surrounding forest-lands, which

Mr. MacDonald of Ferintosh. He always sympathised with us both in our joys and sorrows, and often visited us. He and I lived on terms of closest intimacy, interrupted only by his many engagements from home. These were entered into so much and so frequently that nothing but a more than ordinary, and perhaps more than human, zeal for the success of the gospel could justify. In the north or in the south, and especially in the Highlands of Perth, Argyll, and Inverness-shires he occupied himself in evangelistic work, almost uninterruptedly for at least two-thirds of the whole year. It is true that, at stated intervals, he returned and preached at home, but it as often happened that, on his way from the south to fulfil an engagement in the far north, he passed his own house, and remained within a mile of it until such time as a change of raiment could be sent to him. This was surely carrying matters to an extreme, the consequence of which was the neglect of his own people ; so much so, that even after the close of Mr. Calder's ministry, and during the whole of his own, piety and pious men rapidly declined, and finally almost died out among them.

At the time he wrote me this good man had set his heart upon entering on a mission to Ireland. The state of that country was such as would have awakened the sympathies of Paul the Apostle. It also arrested the attention of " the apostle of the North." He decided to go thither and preach the gospel, believing it to be the only moral, spiritual, and even political panacea for all the evils which lay so heavily on the poor Irish. He, therefore, made the necessary preparations, asking me, in common with other of his brethren, to supply his pulpit, and fulfil his other pastoral duties during his absence. On the 6th of · August, 1827, therefore, he set out for the Emerald Isle. He met with a most favourable reception from the Irish people, both Popish and Protestant. The strain of his preaching was calculated to gain him a hearing from all parties. It was purely and thoroughly scriptural, and all controverted points, so frequently and fiercely debated between ultra-Protestants and Papists, were carefully excluded. He preached the doctrines of the Cross in their divine and majestic simplicity, and this secured for them a reception into the hearts and consciences of men of every grade, class, age, and religious opinion. But as even in the apostolic age, so honoured by the presence of the Holy Ghost, was found an " Apollos, an eloquent man," so in his age was Mr. Macdonald. He had a natural eloquence not surpassed, or even equalled, by his ablest contemporaries. Like the gospel itself, it was powerfully and irresistibly persuasive. The impression it made on the minds of his audience was not altogether that conviction of sin which they might be led to feel by mere logical power of reasoning, so much as a sense of contrition and self-accusation for what they found and felt themselves to be under the rich manifestations of the superabounding grace of the gospel.

by industry they soon converted into fertile and fruitful fields. His third son William became minister of the Free Church of Scotland, first at Gourock, then in Edinburgh, and lastly in the Presbyterian Church, Brighton, where he died suddenly in 1887, when preaching a special sermon to soldiers. Dr. Donald Fraser, the distinguished and talented minister of Marylebone Church, London, is Mr. John Fraser's second son.—Ed.

To Mr. Macdonald, therefore, the Irish, without distinction of denomination, listened with profound attention. Addressing them as he did, if not in their own dialect of the Celtic, yet in a kindred one which they understood nearly as well, he was gladly heard, even by the Papists, for the sake of the language in which he spoke. They neither knew nor cared to enquire whether this extraordinary preacher was a Protestant or a Papist, an Episcopalian or a Presbyterian. These distinctions were swept aside by the flood of precious gospel truth poured so copiously from his lips upon their minds, and they received him as a preacher of righteousness, giving to the doctrines which he set forth a reception similar to that so readily accorded to those of his Divine Master by the mixed multitude when they acknowledged that " He taught as one having authority, and not as the scribes." Through the whole of his itinerancy in Ireland his fame always preceded him ; wherever he went he was never without a crowd and a welcome, and whether he travelled by day or by night he was equally safe. The wildest and most lawless of the Popish mob in Ireland, be they " White-boys " or " Peep-of-Day-boys," however much in use and wont to fight with others or among themselves, were under a law of amity and good behaviour towards the Irish-speaking, Scottish preacher. So far were they from injuring or annoying him that, if any difficulty arose to his onward progress from the state of the road, or any danger to his person were threatened by those who did not know him, they were ready to come to his rescue. Not so, however, did it fare with other preachers travelling through these same districts for similar purposes. Notwithstanding their good intentions, they unfortunately met with a very different reception. These zealous ministers (dissenters from the south of Scotland), fell unwittingly at the very outset into two blunders. In preaching to the native Irish, they used the language of the Saxon, the medium of all others the most abhorrent to the Irish people. This error, perhaps, they could not avoid, but they made a greater mistake when they decided to substitute, as the leading subject of their sermons, the Popish controversy for the gospel. This was the torch applied to light up a general conflagration. The preacher spoke and waxed hot on the abuses, delusions, and errors of Popery ; the Popish audience heard and waxed hotter still at the public insult thus thrown out against the religion of their country. The speaker was often obliged to stop, and even to flee for his life to find shelter from an enraged band of fanatical devotees.

It was in the end of this year that I received a letter from Mr. Hugh Davidson of Wick, conveying the melancholy intelligence of the death of his sister-in-law, Mrs. Davidson of Latheron. Maria Serena Robertson, wife of Mr. George Davidson, minister of Latheron, died most peacefully on the 1st of November, 1827, in the 25th year of her age. She was the younger sister of my dearly beloved Harriet, and was a meek, gentle, loving woman, on whose face was never seen a frown, and from whose lips was never heard a rude or angry word. I fully believe her to have been one of Christ's beloved disciples, and that when she gently glided from this earthly scene, it was to take her place in an infinitely better world.

CHAPTER XXV.

CHANGES IN THE NATIONAL CHURCH.

1826-1827.

I MAY here refer, by the way, to Mr. John Ross, who, in 1812, was expelled from the Divinity Hall in Edinburgh. Subsequently he went to London, and acted there as one of the reporters on the staff of *The Times* newspaper; he returned to Ross-shire in 1825, in the circumstances which I am about to relate.

It came out afterwards, though he took good care to conceal it at the time, that a certain Association in London, whether in connection with the then existing Government or not I am not prepared to say, entered into a speculation for conveying Highland labourers to Buenos Ayres, or some other part of Spanish America. To render their scheme all the more successful and efficient, it was resolved that this Highland colony should be placed under the superintendence, both on their passage thither and afterwards on their arrival, of an ordained clergyman of the Church of Scotland, to whom a stipend of £300 *per annum* should be secured by the Association. Ross, from his official avocations in connection with *The Times* newspaper, came in contact with the Association and its scheme, and the proposal being made to him, he at once closed with it. He was already a licentiate of the Scottish Church, and nothing stood between him and the object in view but *ordination*. Returning to the north, he collected, chiefly in Sutherland, upwards of fifty emigrants, who were all appointed to assemble at Cromarty on a certain day, and to go aboard the ship destined to convey them to their future settlement under *him* as their minister. He himself, in the meantime, was ordained by the Presbytery of Dingwall, and all things preparatory to their final departure being thus arranged, Ross wrote me a letter, asking my presence on board, as moderator of the Synod, to give them a word of exhortation, and afterwards to dine with him, along with Mr. Stewart of Cromarty and Mr. Finlayson, the minister of the Gaelic Chapel. I took no notice of his letter, but Mr. Stewart and Mr. Finlayson agreed to go. Whatever they did *officially* I know not, but they *dined* with Ross on board ship. After dinner, to indulge in a love of fun, he said that he really did not know which of them was the taller; would they both stand up, back to back, to let him ascertain the difference. They were simple enough to do so, and no sooner had he got the backs of both their heads into such close proximity with each other than, placing the palms of his hands on their foreheads, he rapped them both together with so much vigour as to make them *ring again*. Mr. Stewart felt justly indignant, and though Mr. Finlayson indulged a laugh, the end of the matter was that a boat was called for; on which both the reverend gentlemen left and went home. Ross, with his emigrant congregation, arrived in Spanish America, but he died not long afterwards.

On the 7th of June, 1826, I received a joint-communication from Messrs Matthew Norman MacDonald and James Bridges, as treasurer and secretary respectively of a Society recently formed for improving church patronage. The object of this Society was to collect funds all over Scotland for the purpose of buying up from its former owners, hereditary or otherwise, the patronage of the churches in the Establishment, to be settled in all time coming in terms of the Society's regulations, on the male heads of families in full communion with the church for a certain period preceding a vacancy; not hesitating to give a large price for any parish, if situated in the immediate neighbourhood of Edinburgh; and calling upon friends to come forward and assist, as many parishes are already and will continue to come into the market. The directors particularly refer to a recent purchase which they had made of the patronage of the parish of Colinton, the price of which was very large, and which the parishioners, however willing to re-imburse, were unable to do without public aid. Accompanying their letter was a form of reply, which was couched in the following terms:—"In consequence of the recent purchase of the parish of Colinton by the Society, I agree to subscribe . . . towards its funds." This was to be attested by the name of the subscriber, along with his address, and directed to M. Norman Macdonald, Esquire, W.S., Great King Street, Edinburgh, the treasurer of the Patronage Society. In existing circumstances the scheme was scarcely a feasible one; and its projectors did not seem to look at all either beyond the limits of their own time, or to future consequences, nor to foresee the Disruption of the Church, which took place only eighteen years afterwards. To buy up the patronage of one or two, or even more, of the parishes of Scotland, would have required more money than the Scottish people were either able or willing to give, while the scheme to purchase all the patronages in Scotland was Utopian. With the most distant reference to Disruption times such a scheme, the more it might inspire, the more mischief would it be instrumental in producing. It is but doing justice, however, to the directors of the Society that, in common with all of that period, without exception, they had not the most distant conception or anticipation of such an event. The patronage of the parish of Colinton was the first and last of their purchases, but whether that was afterwards secured to the people or sold to the highest bidder I know not. The only other attempt of a similar nature was to obtain the patronage of Dairsie in Fife; but the purchase was made not by the parishioners, or by the Society, but by Mr. William Innes of Sandside, a wealthy Caithness proprietor, who presented my friend Mr. Angus MacGillivray to the living, conformably to the wishes of the people.

The Moderate party in the church had at this time reached about the zenith of their power. Their ascendancy, however, was assiduously and successfully resisted by their Evangelical opponents, the consequences being that they were swamped and became the minority. The measures which the Evangelical section of the church adopted, for the increase of their own number and influence, were various; but that which most contributed to their success was a plan which about a year or two before they entered into—to promote and to consolidate union among themselves, and interchange of opinion with each other, with special reference to the points in dispute between them and their opponents. This union or combination was called the "Conference," and its object will be explained by stating the substance of a communication sent me by the secretary, Mr. Bridges, dated the 29th June, 1826, purporting to be a private circular addressed to each of its members on "some matters deserving of their attention." They are first earnestly reminded that this is a *spiritual* and not a *party union;* that its fundamental object is, by mutual counsel, to promote the good of the church; and that each of the members is expected to appropriate one hour of the week to prayer for the welfare of the church. The increase of faithful members of the Conference, by the proposal, from time to time, of those who in their quarter uniting in general views, are likely to act cordially with us, and the endeavour to procure the return to the Assembly of members of congenial sentiments, were other important matters to the consideration of which members were invited. The circular then refers to the leading matters in dispute, such as the plurality question, or the union of offices held by professors of divinity, and the debates on the subject of baptism, as in the case of Bracadale in Skye, and the case of Dunkeld. Such was the substance of the circular, which was issued immediately after the rising of the Assembly. It contributed largely to unite brethren to each other so as to present an unbroken front to their opponents. The stated meetings of the Conference were to be held on the last Tuesday of November, January, and March, on the second Tuesday of May, and on several days of the Assembly.

The only public event of any importance to us in this remote corner of the kingdom, during the year 1827, was the opening of additional places of worship in connection with our National Church in Scotland. These new charges were directly endowed by the State under an Act of Parliament which had been brought in by Sir Robert Peel (then Mr. Peel), the Home Secretary. They were therefore commonly called Parliamentary or Government churches, and were seven in number, viz., Duror, in the Presbytery of Lorn; Tomintoul, in the Presbytery of Abernethy; Kinlochluichart, in the Presbytery of Dingwall; Shieldaig and Plockton, in the Presbytery of Lochcarron; Keiss and Berriedale, in the Presbytery of Caithness. Both churches and manses were built on sites freely given to the Government for that purpose by the proprietors of land in the different localities. The stipends to the ministers amounted to £120, and the patronage was vested in the Crown. The whole scheme was completed in the autumn of this year. The ministers appointed respectively to the new charges were:—Mr. Donald MacNaughton to Duror; Mr. Charles MacPherson to Tomintoul; Mr. David Tulloch to Kinlochluichart; Mr. Roderick MacRae to Shieldaig; Mr. Alex. MacDonald to Plockton; Mr. Thomas Jolly to Keiss; and Mr. D. MacLauchlan to Berriedale. The ministers

of these peculiar charges, though fully ordained to preach and to
dispense the sacraments, were notwithstanding excluded from the
Presbyteries within whose jurisdiction they officiated. This, in regard
to the original constitution of the Scottish Church, was irregular and
inconsistent. But the arrangement originated entirely in the jealousy
of the dominant Moderate party, who wished the parochial ministers
(although not bishops either in name or *de jure)*, to be regarded as
having Episcopal powers in their respective parishes.

There were, however, in connection with the Church, other three
classes of ministers placed in exactly similar circumstances. These
were, first, the ministers of the "Chapels of Ease," of whom there were
at that time, distributed among the Presbyteries, fifty-five. A second
class consisted of the missionaries engaged by the General Assembly's
Committee for managing the Royal Bounty. Of these there were, in
1827, thirty-six, chiefly among the Highland Presbyteries. Previous
to the year 1819 one of these missions was stationed at Achness and
Ach-na-h'uaighe, within the bounds of the Presbyteries of Tongue and
Dornoch. This station was suppressed, as before described, by the late
Marchioness of Stafford who, in her eager and unhallowed haste to
establish the Moloch-system of sheep-farming, expelled the inhabitants,
burned their houses, and in the course of a comparatively short time
levelled with the ground no less than three places of worship.

A third class of ministers, ordained to the functions of the pastoral
office in connection with the Church of Scotland, but excluded from
her ecclesiastical courts, were those employed by the "Society for
Propagating Christian Knowledge," instituted in 1701. In 1827 Mr.
Patrick Butter had been stationed at Fort-William, and Mr. Archibald
Cook at Berriedale and Bruan. After Berriedale had been, that same
year, made a Parliamentary Church, Mr. Cook's labours were
transferred by the Society to the district of Bruan. The people of
Berriedale, however, continued to attend his ministry as long as he
remained in connection with the mission. Mr. Colin Hunter was
stationed at Lochtayside, and Mr. John MacAlister at Glenlyon. The
latter gentleman was afterwards minister of the Gaelic Chapel in
Edinburgh, then of the parish of Nigg in Ross-shire; after the
Disruption he went to Arran, where he died. The remaining ministers
of this class were, Mr. Alexander MacDougall, stationed at Strathfillan;
Mr. Alexander Ross, at Ullapool; Mr. Gilbert Brown of New Blyth;
while the two remaining stations, Eriboll and St. Kilda, were that
year vacant.

Of these four classes of ministers, those of the Government churches
were presented by the Crown, and paid by the State, as already
mentioned; those of the Chapels of Ease were elected and paid by their
respective congregations; the missionary-ministers were, with the
concurrence of the people, appointed and paid by the Committee for
managing the Royal Bounty; while the last class were appointed and
paid, also with the consent of the inhabitants of the respective districts,
by the Christian Knowledge Society. It was made a condition,
however, with reference to the two last classes of missionaries that,
while their Committees paid them a stipend of £50, their congregations

should by annual contributions, aim at doubling that sum. These were not the times, however, in which contributions for religious purposes, or for the support of ministers, were, within the Established Church, except in very rare cases, ever attempted. This was specially the case in the Highlands, and missionary-ministers in many of the out-lying districts were put upon very short commons. Nay, in some parts, the people felt much more disposed to *take* than to *give*, and, so far from contributing to *increase* the small money stipend, they did their best to *diminish* it by borrowing from him any little ready money he might have about him. Should he comply with their request, they could only assure him that they "*would be in his debt forever.*" This was the only re-payment which they were either able or willing to make.

The parish ministers were usually subjected to many delays and annoyances by their heritors. I received a letter, dated 12th March, 1830, from Mr. Mackintosh of Thurso, in which he refers to his projected new church. The only obstacle to its erection forthwith was, that the heritors could not unhappily agree about the plan—a most elegant one—which they, with the exception of Sir John Sinclair, thought too expensive. They would, indeed, have avoided the outlay altogether, if it had been possible. But the dilapidated state of the old church pressed it upon them as a matter of necessity. It was, indeed, one of the oldest relics of ancient, and probably of popish, times then existing in the county, and was dedicated to St. Peter. It was of limited capacity in proportion to the population, and was besides a tottering, dangerous ruin. The proposed plan had been for some time on the books of the Presbytery, and the heritors, at their last meeting, had promised to get all things ready for commencing the work, but still it was delayed. He justly adds that, even should he take legal steps, he could not compel them to hasten. It is remarkable that, although Mr. Mackintosh took such an active part in the first stages of these proceedings, and even participated in the ceremony of laying the foundation-stone, he did not live to see the building finished—he never preached in it. In the wise providence of God that honour was reserved for his immediate successor, Mr. W. R. Taylor.[*]

About this time I had considerable correspondence with the heritors of the parish of Resolis regarding the payment of my stipend and the repairs of the manse. In regard to the latter, one of them, Mr. Urquhart of Kinbeachie, wrote to me on 31st May, 1830, from the Isle of Wight, to say that he presumed that I did not demand more than what was absolutely necessary, and that the Presbytery granted no more than what was correct to give; so far, therefore, he could have no objection to do the needful towards these repairs. "But," he adds, "if

[*] Dr. W. R. Taylor was licensed by the Presbytery of Chanonry 14th Oct., 1828, ordained to the Scotch Church, Chadwell Street, London, 23rd Oct., 1829, and admitted to Thurso 14th April, 1831. He entered the new Parish Church in Jan., 1833. The stately Free Church edifice in which he has latterly ministered was opened by him in 1870. The old Parish Church of St. Peters is now become a venerable ruin; it is said to have been built by Bishop Gilbert Murray, in the 13th century.—Ed.

otherwise, the sum granted is always open to animadversion on my part, although I consider myself bound to pay my share of the expenses. I presume that, upon reflection, you will own with myself-that this is not the time for the Church to incur *extra* expenses, from the general feelings that are now fast arising in the minds of men in these king- doms to promote reformation and economy both in Church and State."

That both Church and State needed reformation then and now is undeniable. But the particular kind of reform desiderated by Mr. Urquhart and the Scottish landholders was of a peculiar complexion. These most patriotic men held in trust the property of the Church, which was set apart by the laws and constitution of these kingdoms for its use, and was doled out by the Court of Session as the Church from time to time required it. The economy they demanded was really such as would enable them to lay out these funds in improving their own estates. They wanted no such moral and spiritual reformation as was realised years afterwards at the Disruption. For how did the Scottish heritors act at that time? Why, in this way—that not in Great Britain had that reformation of the Church keener opponents, or more violent persecutors, than they. Nay, so far did they carry their rage against Christ and His kingdom that some of them refused to give a few feet of God's earth, even of the most worthless part of their property, as land on which to build a house for the worship of God. This line of action will yet tell against them, even in the course of time, but more especially when they shall come to settle their accounts with Him who, on "the Great Day," shall sit in judgment, with saints and angels as his assessors, on both the judges and the judged of this present world.

In looking back on that period of my life, when I was a minister of the Establishment, I have good cause to congratulate myself on the the exchange which, even from a worldly point of view, I have since made. For the twenty years consecutively in which I was a minister of the Established Church, I did not receive a farthing of my stipend without a *grudge*, or even without the *curse* of my heritors along with it. The delays they ever made in paying at the term, the insolent and ill-grounded excuses they advanced for such delays, and the vexatious, litigious disputes into which they led me to enforce payment, were calculated, not merely to prevent me from laying anything by for the education of my family, and for the necessities of old age, but even to deprive me of the means of paying my lawful debts, or of procuring the most ordinary necessaries of life. Nay, they thought that, in giving what justly belonged to me, they were only granting me a favour, for which I was to show my gratitude to them in any way in which they were pleased to call for or to expect it. How different was all this from, and how contrary to, the treatment which I have unformly received since I joined our beloved and truly noble-minded Free Church of Scotland! Its managers, instead of opposing me or adding to my expenses, more than half-way met my wants, and even anticipate them. After shaking myself free of the Establishment and its annoying, unhallowed appendages, in joining the Free Church, I may truly say that I exchanged debt and poverty for peace of mind and a competency, enabling me to supply my every-day wants and to pay all debts.

But I hasten to conclude these reminiscences of the past years of my life by expressing my thankfulness to God, for having so guided me in His providence as, at the Disruption of the Church in 1843, to set me free of the Establishment, with all its base appendages of lawyers, ministers, and patrons, so that I might join myself to a Church whose profession is—even if it be nothing more—that of being under the exclusive government of Him Whom men crucified, but Whom His heavenly Father hath made both Lord and Christ.

THE END.

INDEX.

University of California
SOUTHERN REGIONAL LIBRARY FACILITY
405 Hilgard Avenue, Los Angeles, CA 90024-1388
Return this material to the library
from which it was borrowed.

NON-RENEWABLE

ILL / CCH

APR 26 1995

DUE 2 WKS FROM DATE RECEIVED

NON-RENEWABLE

ILL / ORK

NOV 0 3 1999

DUE 2 WKS FROM DATE RECEIVED

UCLA URLILL

Lightning Source UK Ltd.
Milton Keynes UK
UKOW01f1605130917
309112UK00006B/986/P